HELP!

ARTISTIC INTELLIGENCE

A book by

freeters

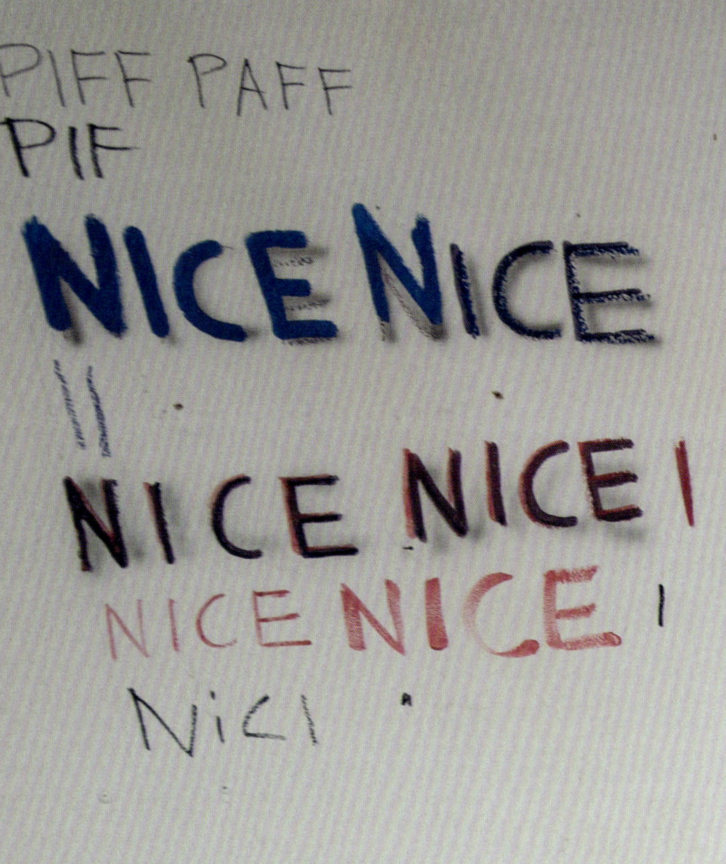

Wall drawing by freeters,
song lyrics “DieDie” by Unterkomplex,
it’s about stereotype thinking.
Before you get conveniently pigeonholed
rather do it yourself.

DIEDIE

NICENICE
VIELLEICHT BRAUCH ICH AUCH SIEBEN PSEUDONYME
TEIL MEINE SEELE FÜR DIE KUNST PACK SIE IN SCHUBLADEN AUF DIE BÜHNE
DOCH AUCH SIEBEN SCHUBLADEN UND AUCH SIEBEN LEBEN
SIND ZU KLEIN UND ZU KURZ UM ALLE GEISTESBLITZE AUFZUHEBEN

BEI LORD VOLDEMORT, PUFF DADDY, DIDDY, PUFFY, SWAG
LOVE AND BROTHER LOVE AVADA KEDAVRA PLÖTZLICH ALLES WEG
BAD BOY FOR LIFE OR TOY BOY FOR WIFE
SCHUBLADE AUF SCHUBLADE ZU BAD TOY IN LIFE
PP DIEDIE WIEDIE
P-DIEDIES GANZES HERZ OH MEIN HERZSCHMERZ
ICH BRAUCH MEIN GANZES HERZ

PIFF PAFF
IMMER WIEDER HÖR ICH "DIE", DAS SIND DOCH DIE DIE ALLES HABEN UND DIE DIE ARMEN SCHLUCKER ~~DIE~~
ALLE, DIE DIE MÄCHTIG SIND, ALLE, DIE DIE WINNER DIDDY, ALLE DIE DIE SCHWÄCHLICH SIND, DIE ALLE TRINKEN PIPI
ALLE WIE DIE ECHSENMENSCHE, ALLE WIE DIE CHEMTRAIL-ZOMBIES, DIEDIE TRAGEN ALUHÜTCHEN, DIEDIE SIND NO HIPPIES
ICH WILL MICH NICHT SPLITTEN, ICH FÜHLE MICH ZERSCHNITTEN ICH BRAUCH MEIN GANZES HERZ OH MEIN HERZSCHMERZ

DIEDIE ARMEN SCHLUCKER DIEDIE SCHWÄCHLICH SIND
DIEDIE MÄCHTIG SIND DIEDIE WINNER DIDDY
STARTDOWN DIEDIES, DIEDIE ISSO DIEDIES
ND LOST, DIEDIE FOR REAL
R DIEDIES, DIE DIE FAKER DIEDIES
E, DIEDIE HATER DIEDIE
HEN, DIEDIE CHEMTRAIL-ZOMBIES
RINKEN BLUT und PIPI

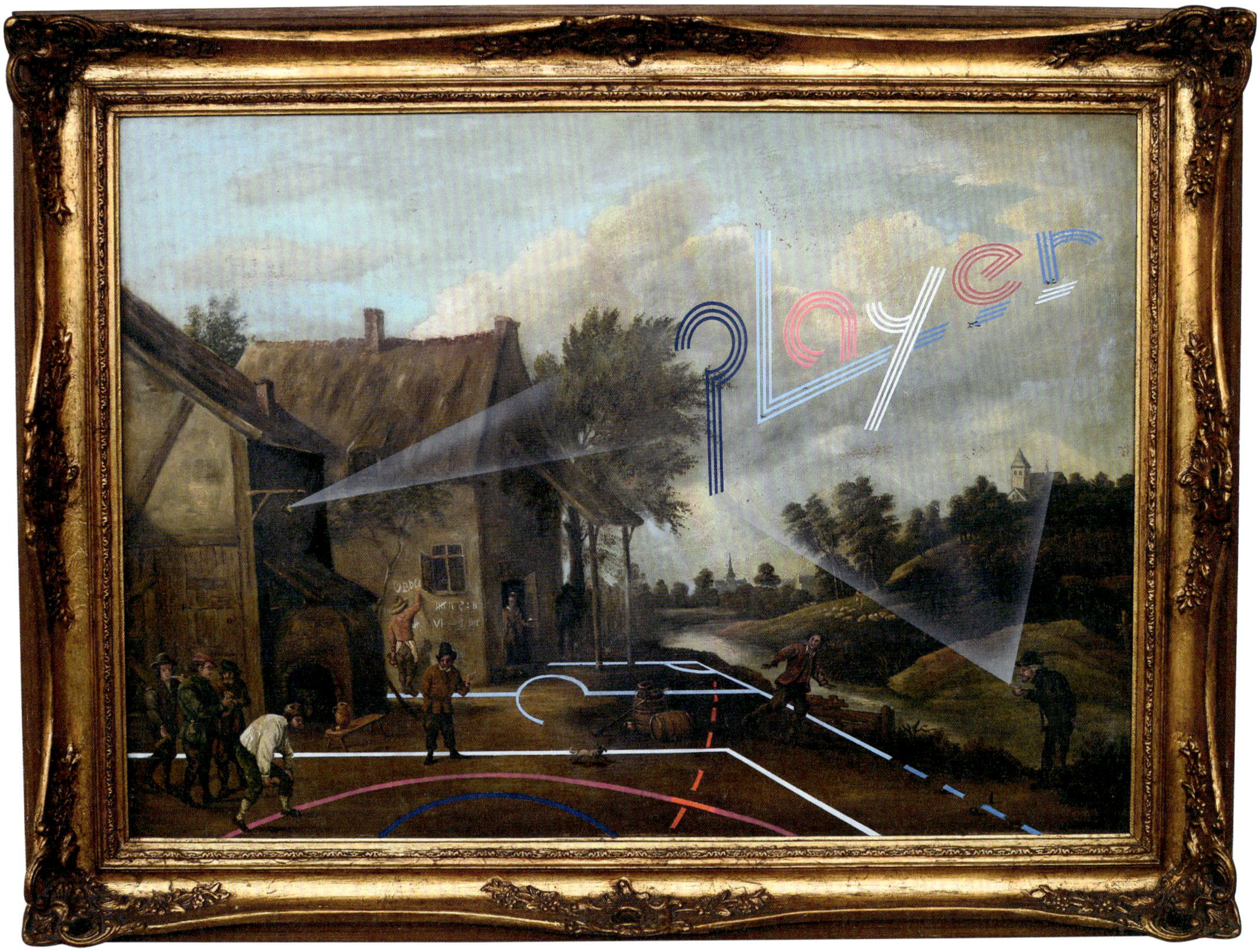

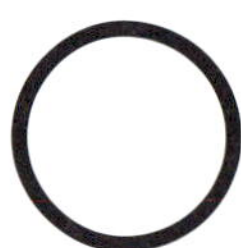

CHOOSE YOUR ROLE

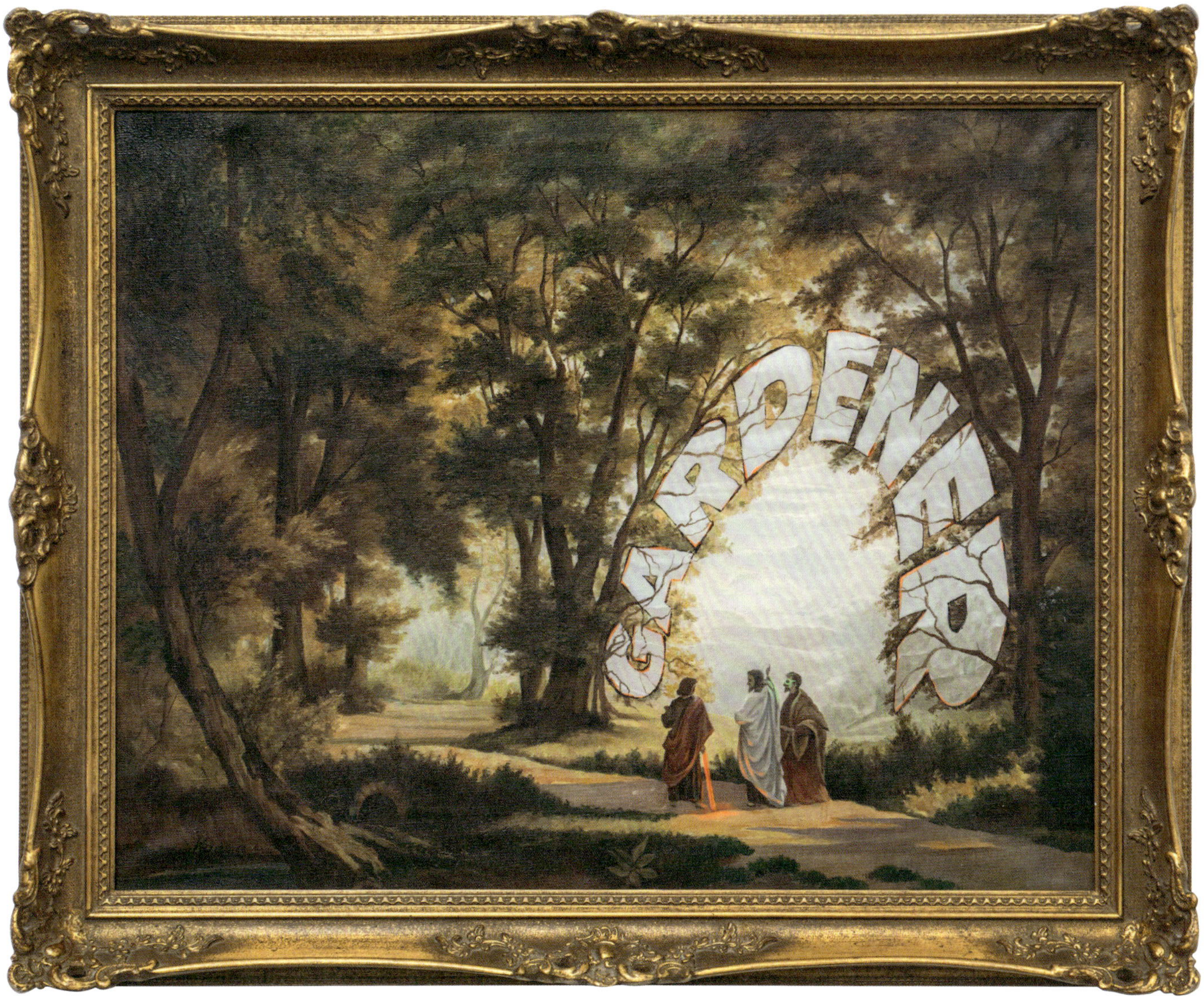

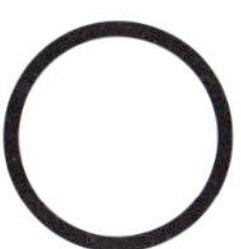

IN OUR COLLECTIVE WORLD

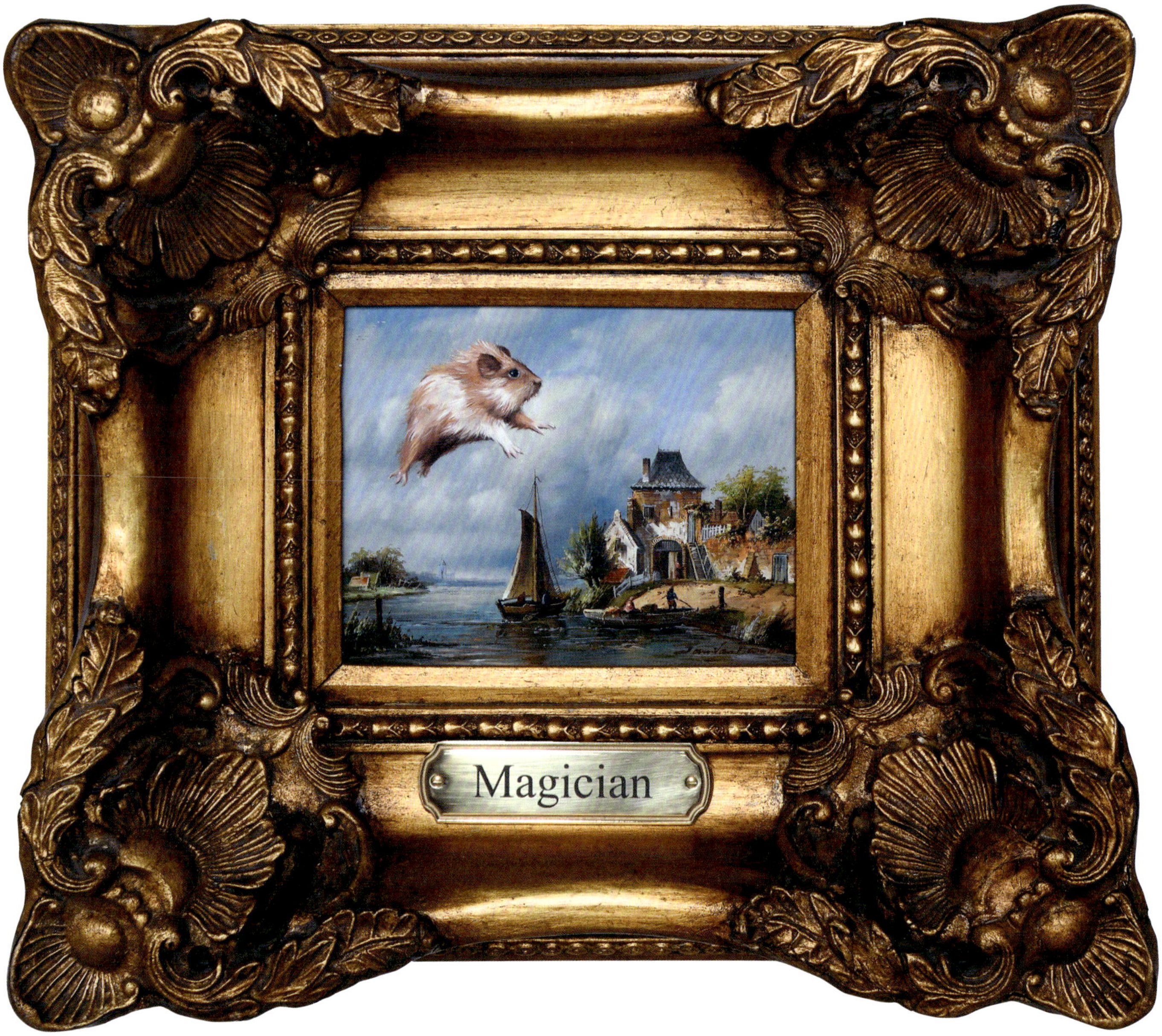

Magician

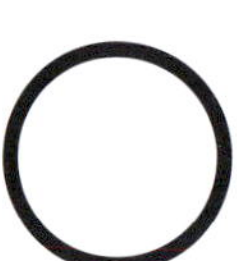

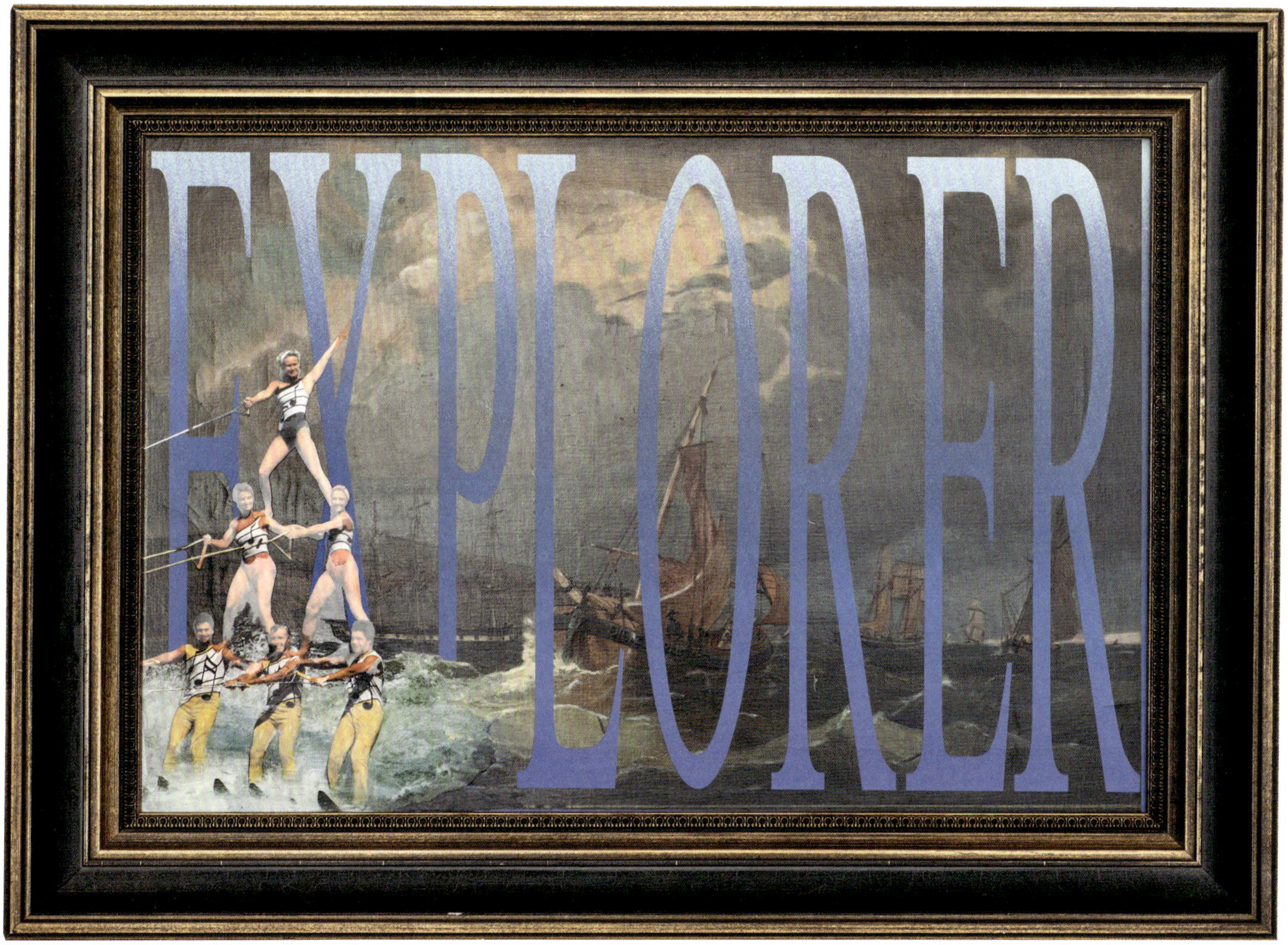

EXPLORER

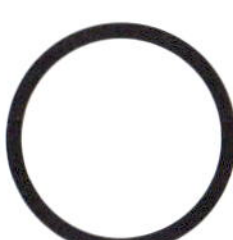

ARTISTIC INTELLIGENCE
OR SALVATION AS A GALLOPING LIQUID

Sandra Freygarten

"It is not to promote a new magical instrument, a new 'quick fix' for business. It is an attempt to show the great potential of 'artful creation' and at the same time point out that the birth of a new paradigm offers promising prospects for the future of business and society".[1]

The artist collective Freeters makes things. At the end of a complex process there is a result, an artifact. A chair with an umbrella canopy. A sofa made from a former telephone booth. A perspective-distorting uncertainty as a workspace. A renaissance painting with Superman. A series of poetic stagings from cloud cuckoo land. A workplace series: rude, fairy-tale-like, strange, calamitous, touching, serious, thought-provoking, prompting tears and laughter, inviting people to work, but differently.

Such a list of artifacts, even if it would fill pages, is always insufficient. This has to do with the sheer number of unique projects, with the abundance of inventions and tailor-made arrangements developed by Freeters.

But what literally gets left behind in concentrating on the diverse products is the track itself; namely, the trail that must first be uncovered in an undeveloped area in order to turn an immaterial subject into a tangible thing. Every path is different, which has to do with changes of pace and direction. The path from the starting point to the finished product is never known in advance, it always has to be found first. It holds surprises, runs into the wall, or gets lost in the unspecific or the arbitrary, only to take promising turnoffs at unexpected points.

Actors of contemporary art create works in which individual and social questions are condensed and thus enable viewers to take a new look at relevant themes. The paths that lead to such new perspective-expanding artifacts are themselves characterized by factors such as uncertainty, experimentation, and ignorance.

In addition, the artistic results of Freeters develop through a collective process in multistage phases of thinking and acting, perceiving and exposing, dreaming and manifesting, playing and planning, showing and analyzing, dissolving and specifying.

Some artistic strategies can readily be seen in the works. The combination of seemingly unrelated things: lampshade and garment, roof and hammock, rubber ball and seat. Materials are examined not for their usual function, but for a potential that lies outside the usual. Things are de-normalized: gondolas are used as a cozy retreat on wheels instead of for transport, height differences, small things are enormously enlarged and huge things shrunk tiny. Materials are torn out of context and relocated, like the crafty fusible beads of childhood exploding their 15 x 15 centimeter pegboards and completely covering a furnished room, a millionfold pixelation in 3D.

These works are not created in a vacuum. The collective must negotiate them together within a framework shaped by certain self-determined temporal and spatial conditions, including rules of play related to theme, material, and action. The emphasis is on acting. Experiments are made with material, context, and theme, the experiments are reflected on, and the results of these reflections are fed into new experiments.

And because the artists build these experimental arrangements from the outset in such a way that surprising results are challenged, it creates a field of action defined by uncertainty, which must be con-

1 **Darsø, L. (2004):** Artful Creation: Learning-Tales of Arts-in-Business, Copenhagen, Samfundslitteratur.

2 **Reck, Hans Ulrich:** Dissonante Perspektiven – Unruhe, in: KUNSTFORUM international, vol. 263, Köln 2019.

3 **Freygarten, S./Strunk,M. (2017):** Transformation – Complementary Artistic Strategies. A handbook for women artists, consultants and multipliers in change and educational processes. Hamburg, Potsdam, Berlin: HPB University.

stantly rearranged, reevaluated, rearranged, and reevaluated. This form of artistic work has less to do with erraticism or unpredictability and more to do with the systematic provocation of chance and the unknown for the sole purpose of learning something new about the specific question of the project.

If we take a closer look at the art processes, procedures such as experimenting, improvising, calibrating, playing, and fumbling are elementary strategies that spring from the principle of restlessness.[2] Restlessness here is an artistic movement that is to be seen against the background of the experimental arts of the 20th and 21st centuries and which deliberately brings chance and the unintended into play. It means an opening of the senses, a scattered attention, a holding out for possibilities at the edges of perception, a deliberate shifting of tendencies into a prolonged dissonance between chaos and order.

It is precisely in the initial stages of a project's development that artists engage in such restless, searching activities. They provoke coincidences and "mistakes" in order to consciously keep this space of possibility open. Their "strategies of action are composed of general modes of action, which can be broken down once again into a multitude of subactivities, such as trying things out, improvising, or irritating, as well as specific modes of procedure, such as fragmenting or copying".[3] These procedures are not only strategies that represent outwardly active activities, but also fragments of inner perceptual activities that are, however, essential to the art process.

A viewer trained in reflection does not miss the fact that the works are the result of extraordinary procedures that are non-standardized, non-receptive, non-repeatable.

The artistic practice of Freeters is characterized by strategies of thought and action that are needed in a society with constantly changing conditions, in a working world that overturns itself in its dynamics, and in social interactions that must be readjusted again and again. The need to shape the present through artistic action is no longer limited to the context of art alone. Through experiences with such processes, skills are developed that are suitable for overcoming the challenges of everyday life. The ability to experiment, to stretch one's thinking, to see the fundamental in the seemingly unrelated, to have a thirst for experience, the desire to create, the burning energy. Increasingly, nonartistic contexts also have the urgency for change, which could be organized and modeled by artistic professionalism, provided one does not locate art practice only within an isolated, self-contained organism apart from all systemic relevance.

Freeters' approach works just like their products. Contradictory, exacting, absurd, refined, fitting, risky, provocative, playful. Freeters' processes of creation are galloping liquids that sound like electro swing, are sung by Heidi in Gelsenkirchen or Metallica in Mallorca, depending on the order, and alternately shimmer in gold, pink, or neon yellow. The containers with the labels economy, education, and politics urgently need some of this substance, because their solutions are stuck dried to the bottom or have long since expired.

CONTENT

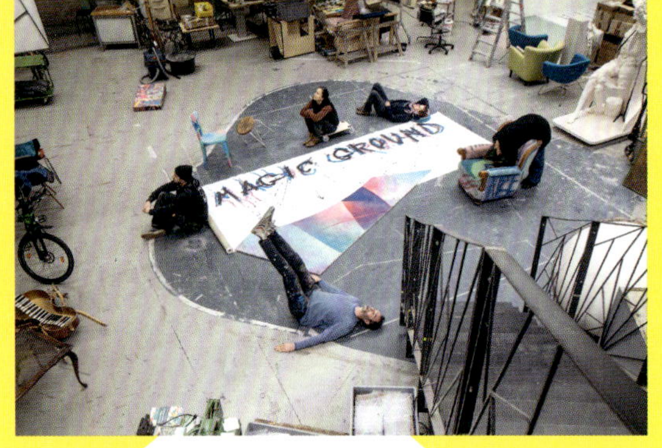

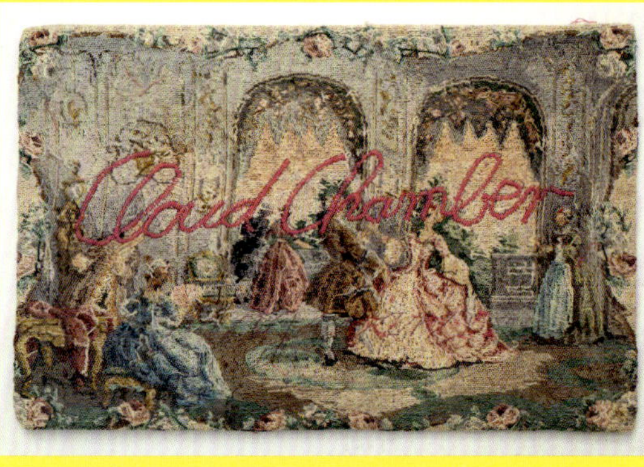

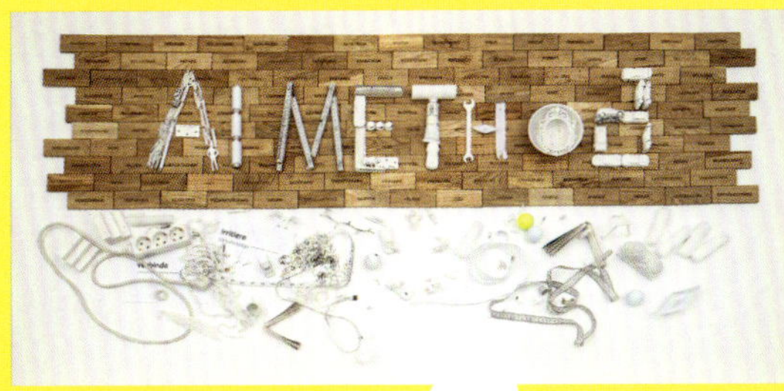
AI METHod

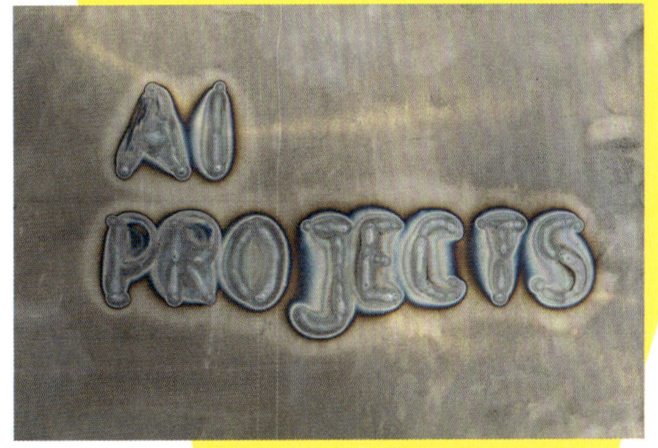
AI
PROJECTS

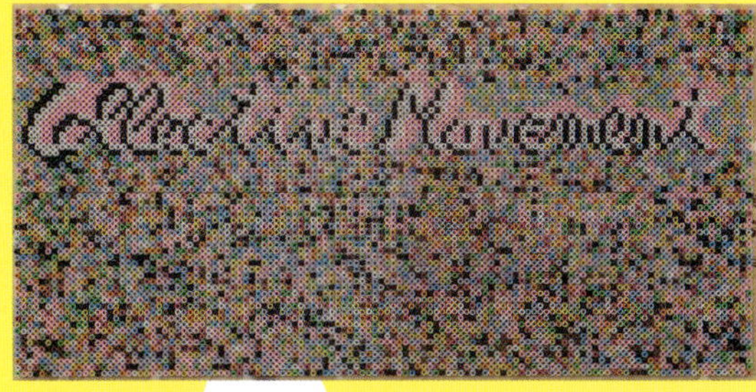

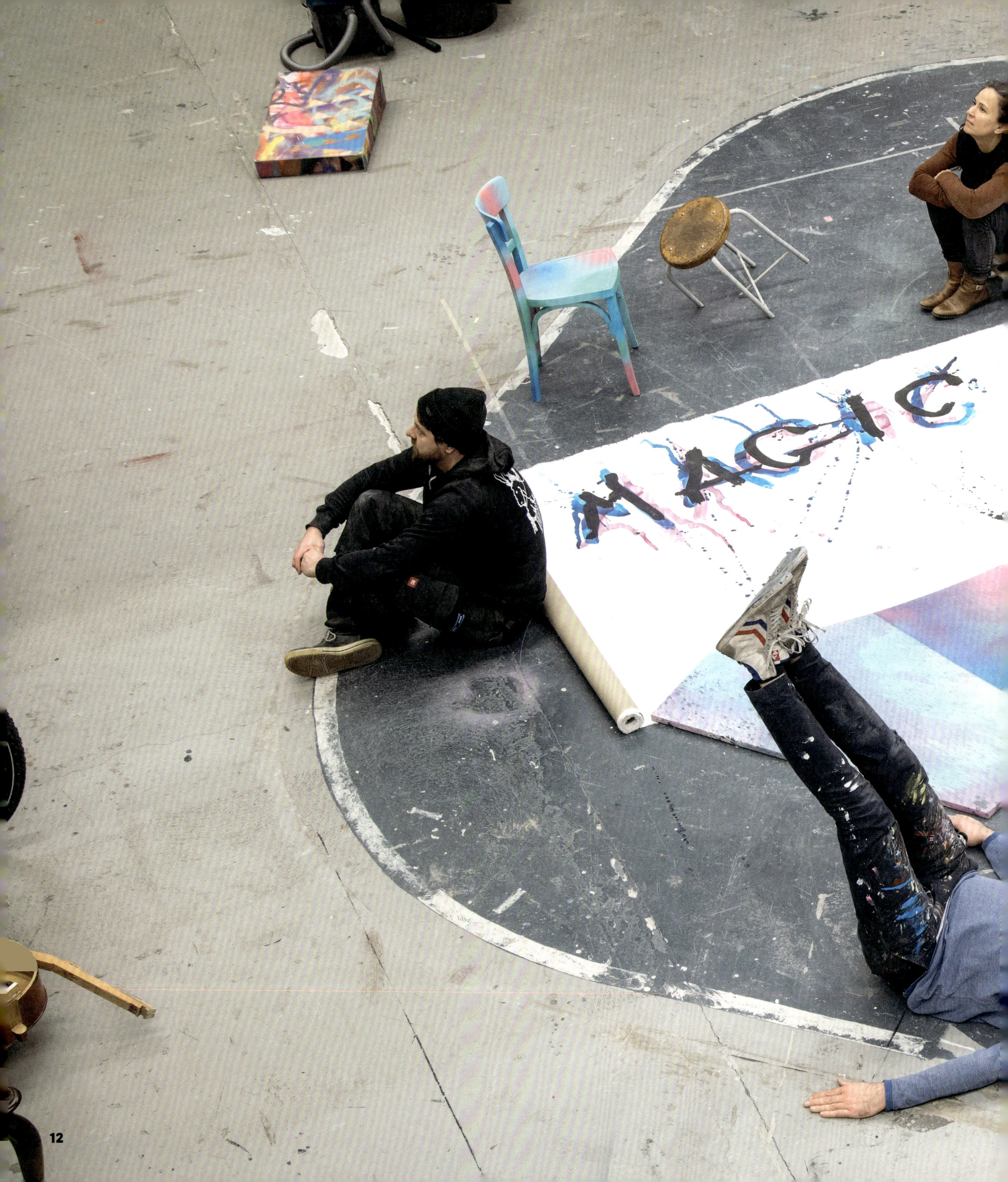
MAGIC

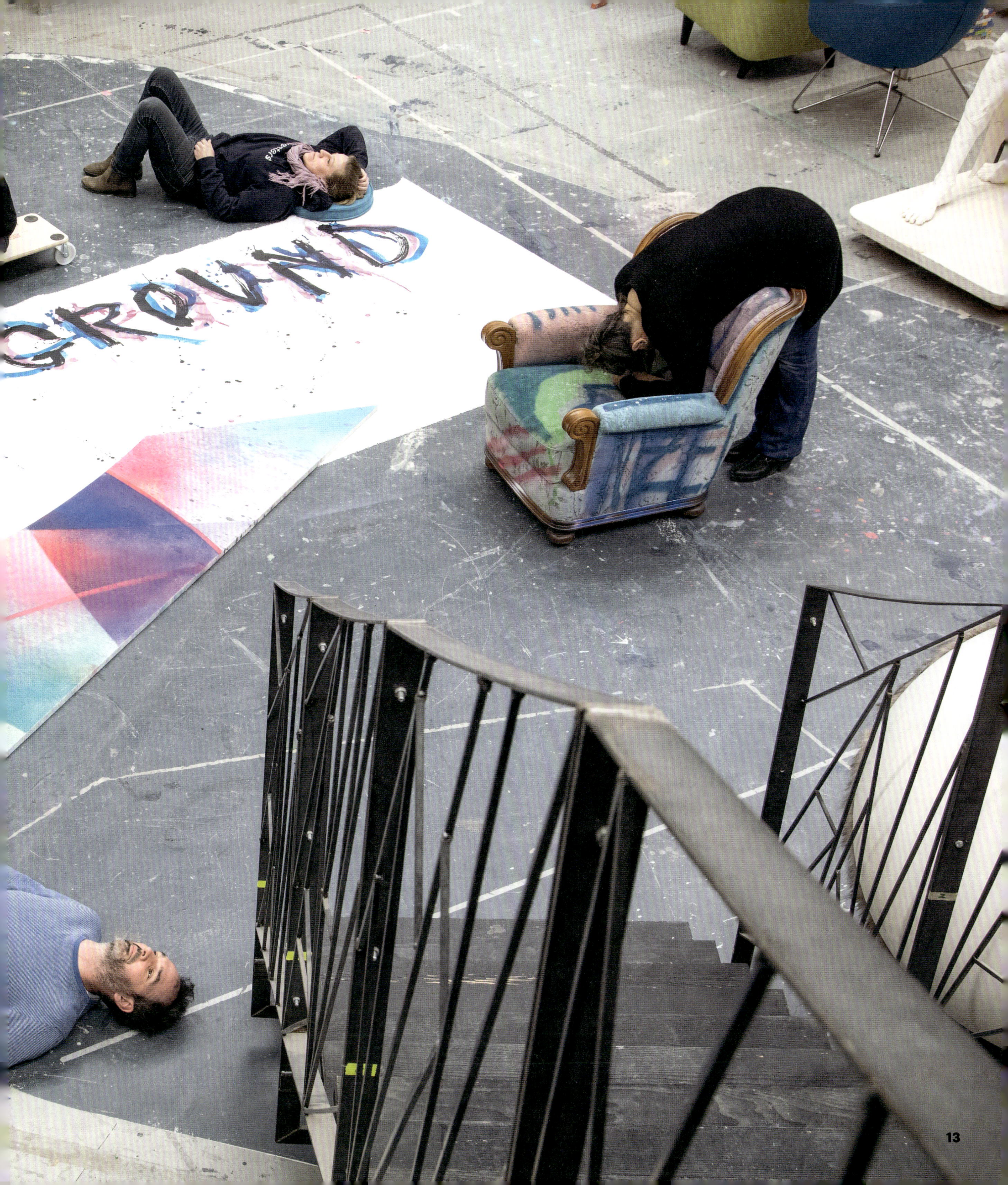
GROUND

MAGIC GROUND

The artist collective Freeters deals with the effect, form, and nature of the most diverse spaces. Spaces are transformed into tools that influence perception, feelings, and consciousness, providing impulses for identity and inspiration. Artistic freedom and functional design are not at odds with each other in transformative interior design, they enter into a fruitful symbiosis.

The need for workspaces that create points of contact between business and art and establish a new form of cultural location is great, and so was the response to the initial pilot projects with Freeters. Further projects with different companies followed, always with the aim of visually and structurally anchoring artistic impulses, modes of action, and processes in the everyday working world. In addition to projects with companies, other focal points have been established over the years, such as socio-cultural projects and workshops in the field of management consultancy. In contrast to outside work or the laws of everyday life beyond

art, an inner niche has formed with the Cloud Chamber platform, where the collective goes beyond the boundaries of workday structures and refuels with fresh color and playfulness for projects at the intersections.

Through renting a permanent work and studio space and founding a cooperative in 2018, the artist collective has also been structurally consolidated. Joint research projects and bringing culture into contexts beyond established areas have led to international cooperation partners and friendships, such as with the art laboratory ESMoA.

With this publication, all these facets come together and are captured in their entirety. The bundled experience of artistic strategies and processes of action at the intersection of culture and art are illustrated with image-rich documentation. And like an organism that is more than the sum of its parts, the collective idea works like a rhizome linking the projects, ideas, companies, and artists.

THE PLACE
LIEVELINGSWEG 82

With the studio and workshop on Lievelingsweg, a place has developed over the years that functions as the heart and the engine of the Freeters project and which has charisma beyond its spatial boundaries. Spanning 1,000 square meters, the complex in Bonn's Nordstadt encompasses a broad concept of home. The premises offer a home base for workshops, color laboratories, material storage, studio space, and desk space. And ideas gather in the niches – in other words, the boundaries between artistic freedom, professional production processes, and idea workshops are sometimes fluid and create added value in a magical way through multiple, synergetic use in the sense of the collective idea.

Beyond its spatial organization, the space embraces a social dimension of home with various programs and regular events, such as the artist in residence program, the weekly pub night with band rehearsal, the annual exhibition, and the quarterly salon. Meeting rooms, seating areas, outdoor exhibition spaces, and the large pizza oven provide space for different ways of being together. Spontaneous guests and friends, clients and other interested parties are equally welcome to come to the Magic Ground at any time for inspiration and coffee.

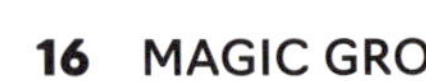

In this way, the collective idea finds a natural home in an atmosphere of colorful spots, Monday colloquia, shared lunchtime cuisine, music, urban gardening, the familiar sounds of the workshop, and fruitful niche conversations.

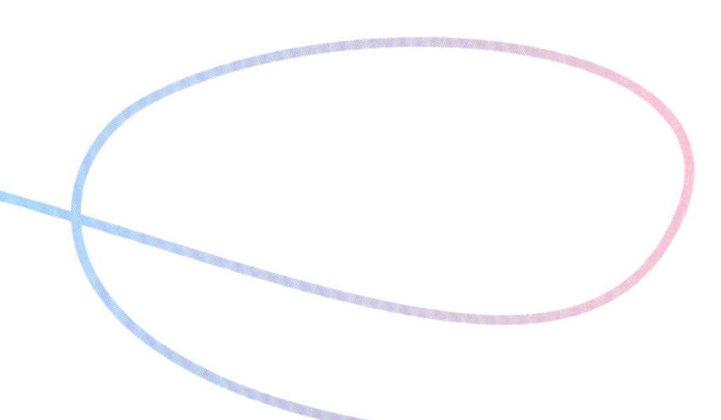

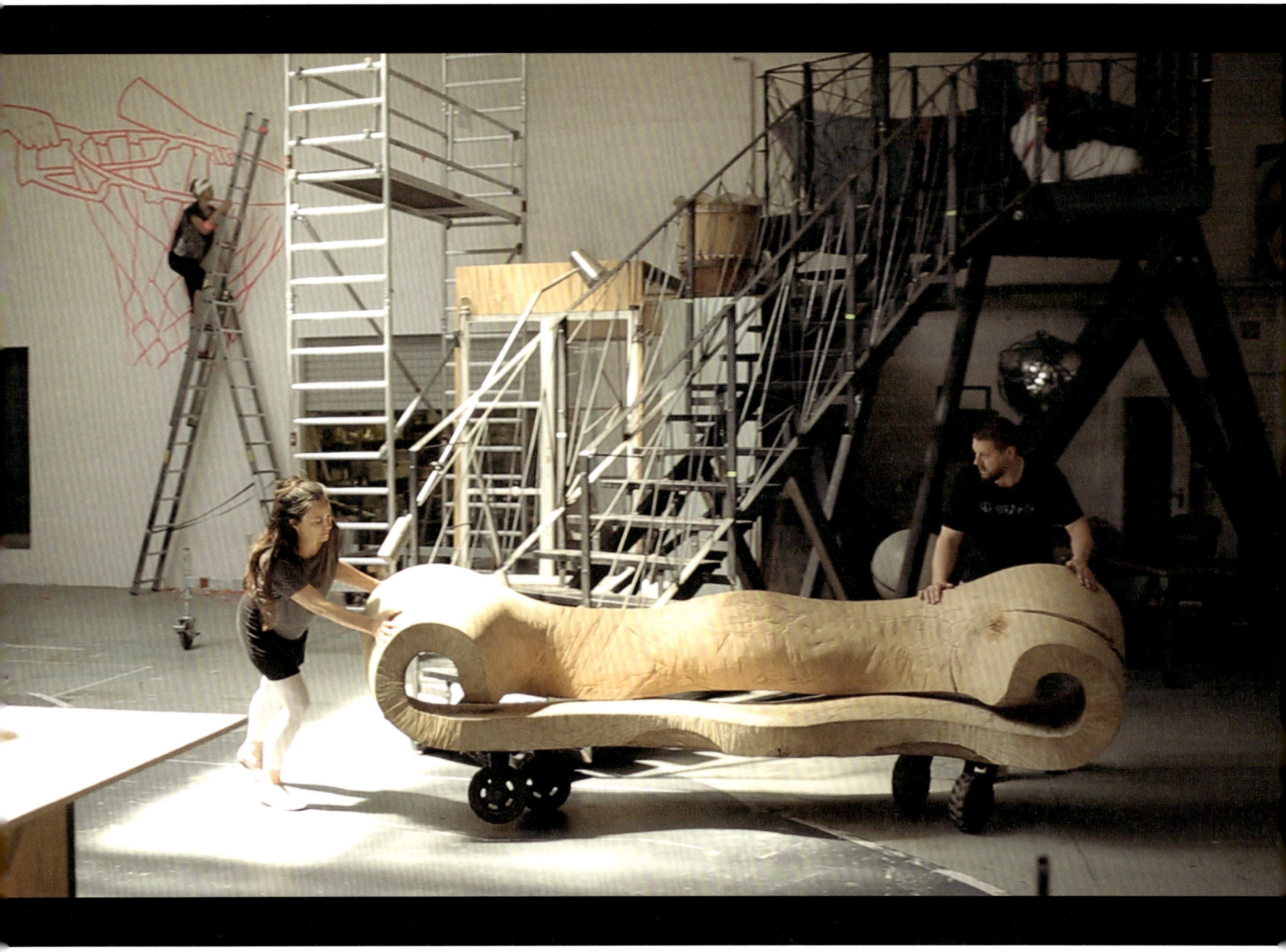

ART IS A STATE OF MIND
DOCUMENTARY

by Aljoscha Pause

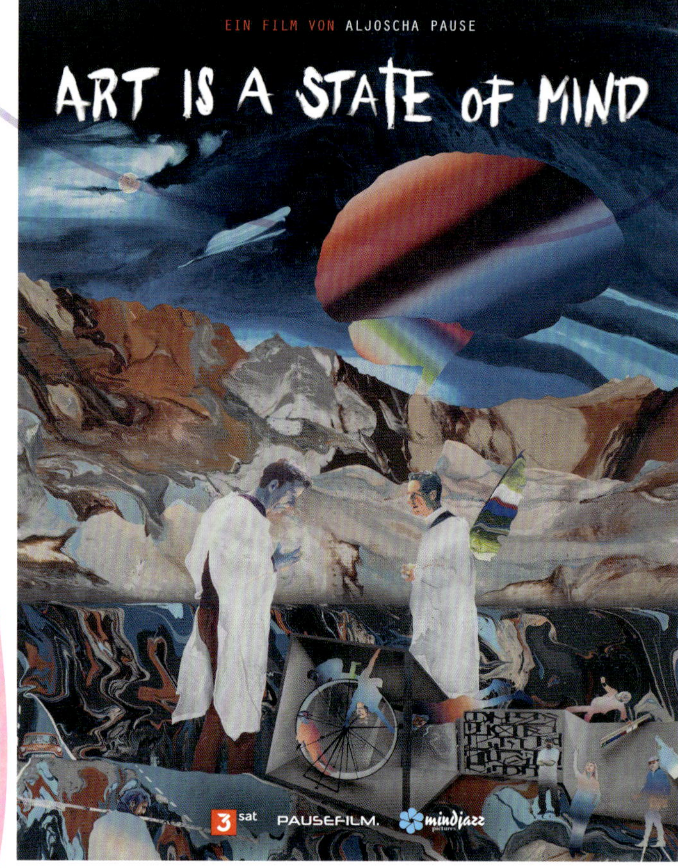

For nine years, documentary filmmaker Aljoscha Pause accompanied former attorney Bernhard Zünkeler around the world documenting his departure from his old life in business law (a life in which he had to conduct dismissal interviews for the largest bank in the world), his uncompromising devotion to art, and a concept of a successful life that is all his own. Along the way he attempts to change the world with art and struggles against the art market establishment and outdated thought patterns.

Cover of the film "ART IS A STATE OF MIND", Cover-Artwork painting by Michael Sistig

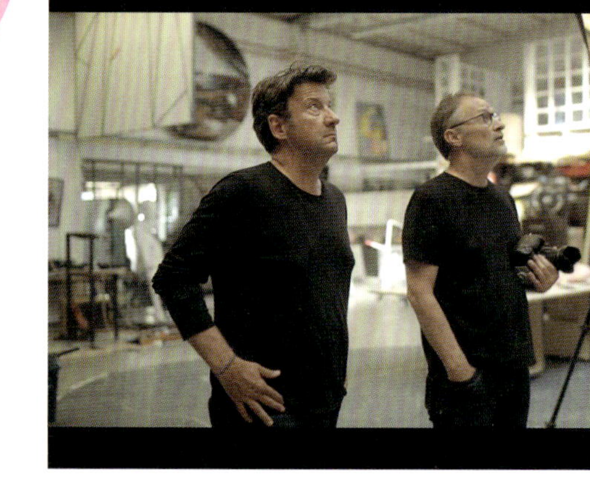

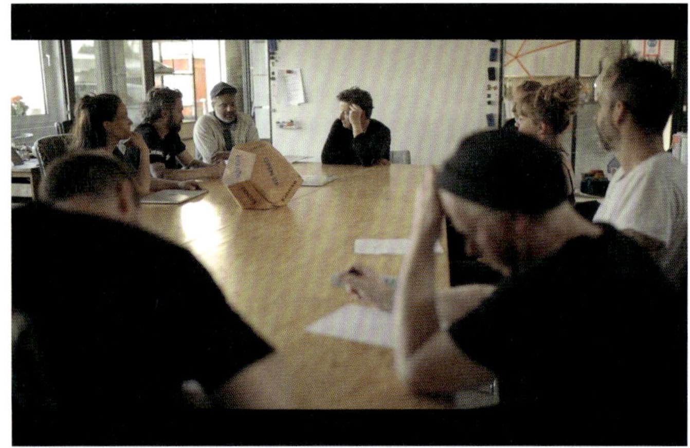

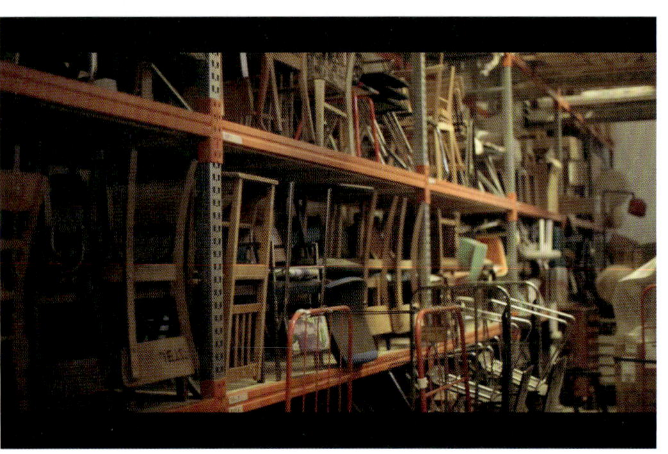

The documentary series follows Bernhard Zünkeler as he builds his own art labs and artist collectives and establishes a global network of like-minded people, ranging from Cuban dissidents to gang members in South Central Los Angeles. The research around his thesis of art as a state of consciousness is also explored.

Art Is a State of Mind is an inspiring road trip with a conceptual artist and jack-of-all-trades in search of his very subjective definition of success; an encounter with extraordinary international artists and art projects in Germany, Cuba, and the United States; and a consistent discourse on what art can and must be today. It approaches the question of how much radicalism and consciousness are necessary to sustain the happiness of an individual and to cope with the collective challenges of our time.

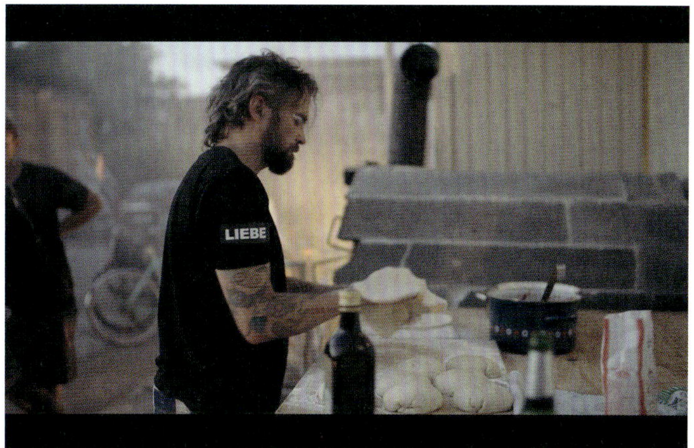

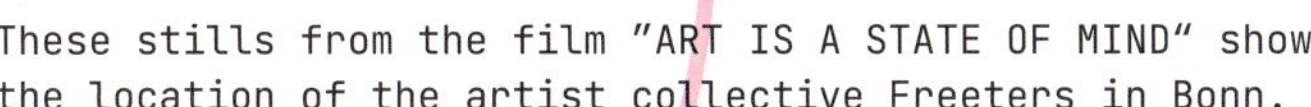
These stills from the film "ART IS A STATE OF MIND" show the location of the artist collective Freeters in Bonn.

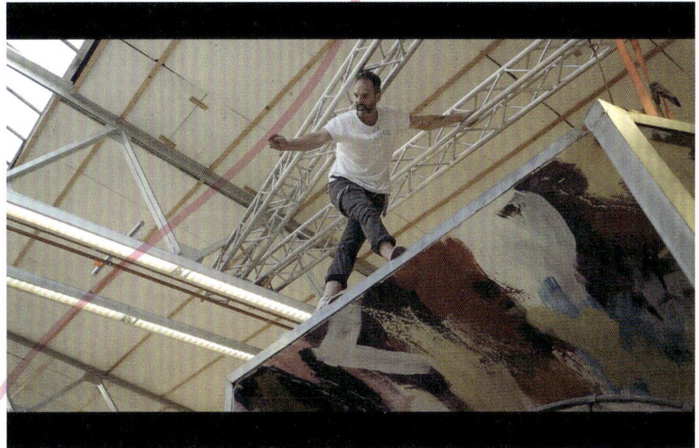

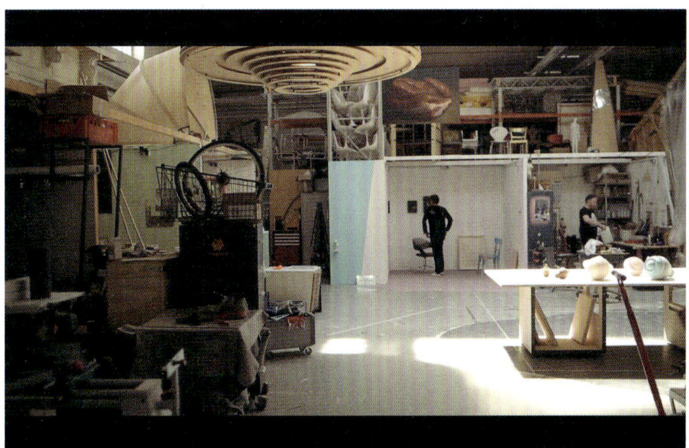

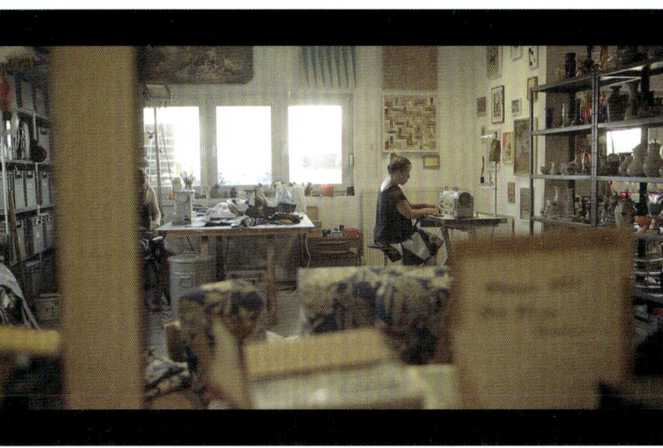

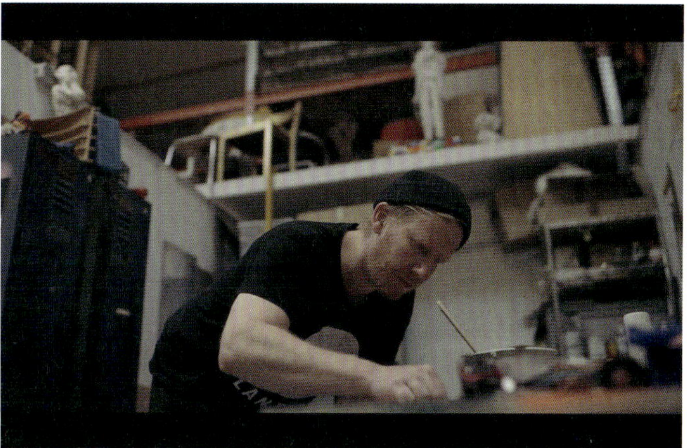

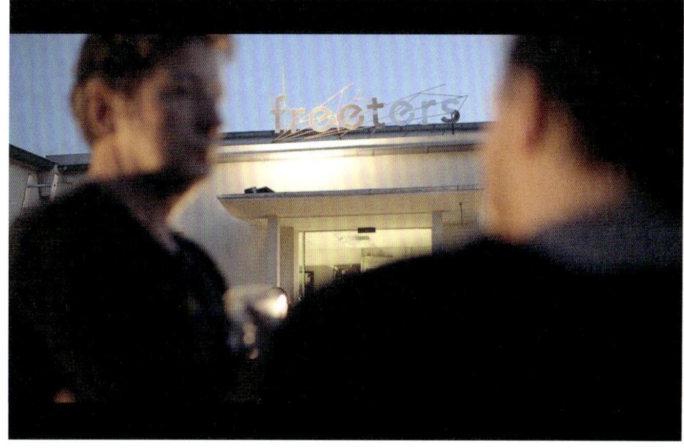

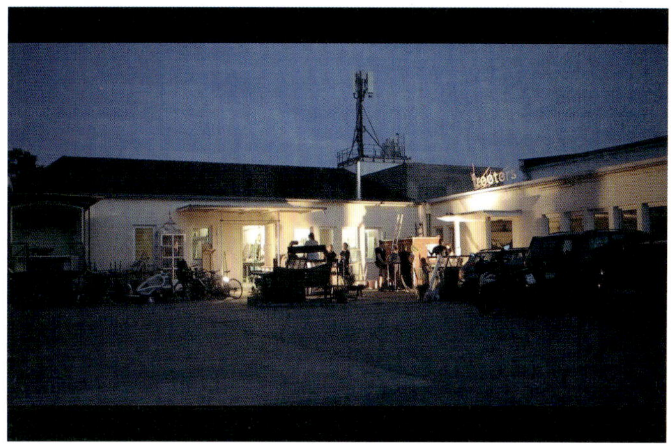

PROF. FREETERS
MULTIPLE PERSONALITY, MULTIPLIED PERSONAL

Originally, in addition to an application as a collective to the Kunstakademie Düsseldorf, an application was also submitted for the position of director of the Bonner Kunstverein, also as a collective or "multiple personality."

To ignore the stated hiring guidelines of a job advertisement in order to apply for it as a collective is something of a prank, but one that can be taken seriously. The qualifications are, for a multiplied personality like Freeters, generally easy to fulfill. One can confidently assume that several individual biographies have at their disposal a "higher" horizon of consciousness and life experience, privately as well as professionally. The resulting strategies that develop through the joint work lead to intuitive decision-making, flexible processes, and sound results.

ES, OR COLLECTIVE CONSCIOUSNESS?

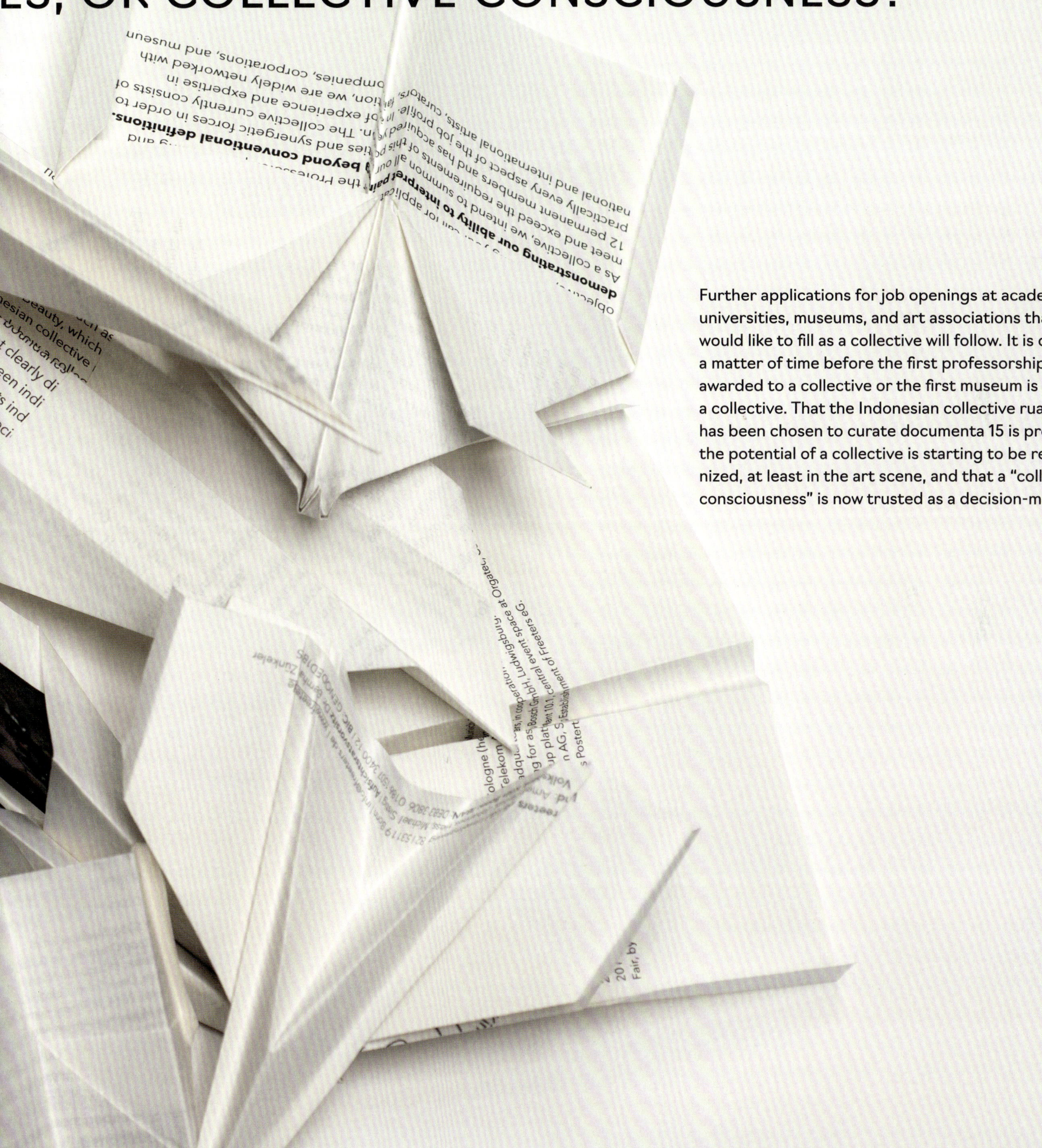

Further applications for job openings at academies, universities, museums, and art associations that we would like to fill as a collective will follow. It is only a matter of time before the first professorship is awarded to a collective or the first museum is run by a collective. That the Indonesian collective ruangrupa has been chosen to curate documenta 15 is proof that the potential of a collective is starting to be recognized, at least in the art scene, and that a "collective consciousness" is now trusted as a decision-maker.

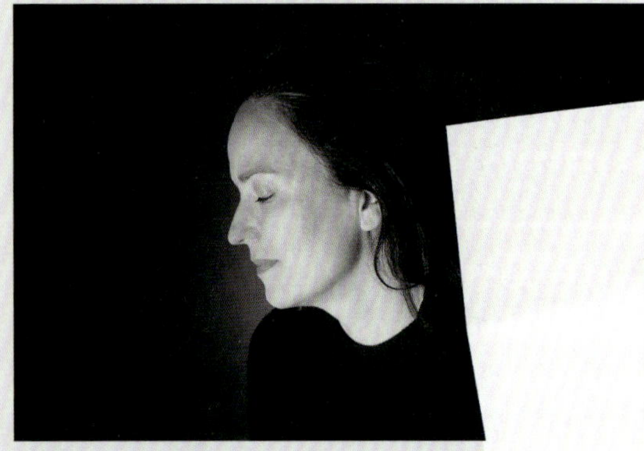
Amely Spötzl

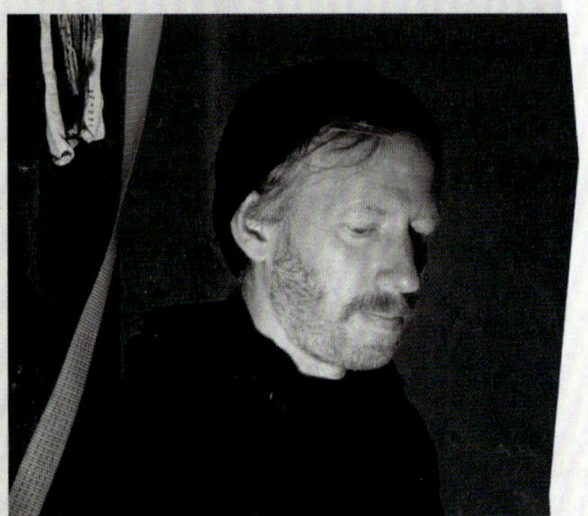
Ben Beyer

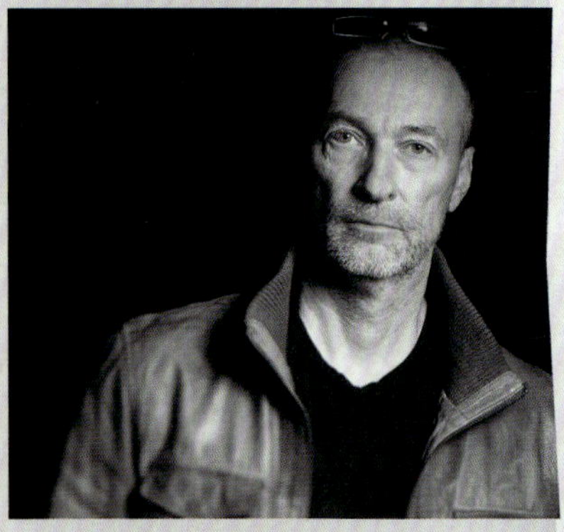
Bernd Zöllner

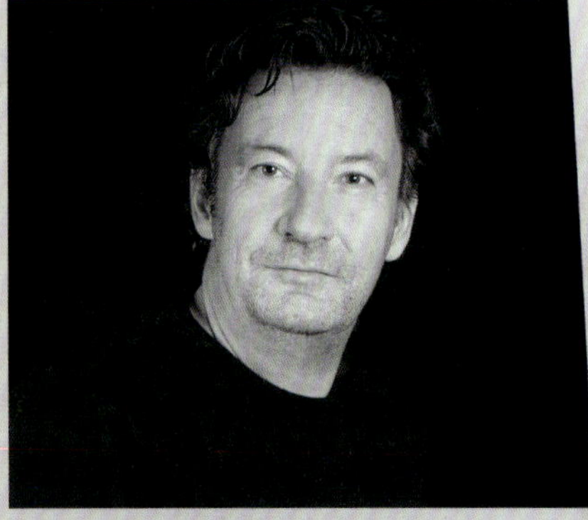
Bernhard Zünkeler

freeters

Freeters eG i.G. | Lievelingsweg 82 | 53119 Bonn
Freeters Showroom | Maxstraße 55 | 53111 Bonn

//Application professorship for painting//

Datum: **19.6.2019**

Dear colleagues of the hiring panel,
Dear Director Prof. Petzinka,

with this letter, we, the artist collective Freeters eG, apply for the Professorship of Painting position at the Kunstakademie Düsseldorf. **We would like to take on as a collective the pedagogical and artistic responsibility of guiding a class of artists.** We intend to shape and coexist with groundbreaking currents in contemporary art as an international collective movement. Our students will profit from a multifunctional and interdisciplinary approach, preparing them well to take on the even more global future of art to come.

We are confident the following pages of our application will meet your criteria for the advertised Professorship of Painting position at the Kunstakademie Düsseldorf. We are fully aware that our proposal for a **poly-identity structure for a professorship** may have legal implications, since it appears to be ahead of its time and certainly a challenge to the spirit of German civil service code. But considering the open spirit Düsseldorf has had in the past and the LGBTQ+ currents in society, where ONE person can identify as MANY, we feel that MANY can equally act as ONE. Especially in the context of art development, with our approach we hope to vitalize the values of synergy and sustainability, bringing fresh perspectives into art education. With these ideas in mind, we respectfully ask you to consider our application as more than just a thought experiment.

As the Kunstakademie Düsseldorf has always been at the forefront of new currents in art we hope to convince you of a spectacular new way of interpreting what a professorship in the 21st century can mean. In the following pages we give you a brief overview of who we are and what opportunities we bring to a holistic teaching experience.

Freeters originated a decade ago from a loose group of artists starting to artistically advance various projects as a collective. Freeters is a legal entity; it is registered as a Genossenschaft, or cooperative society. Our explorations went from being an artistic cooperation partner in industrial or administrative contexts, to being a freelance artist collective. What was initially smirked at as "beautification" through art on walls has increasingly inspired, transformed, and polarized ways of thinking, especially in the working world. These impactful new ways are now being discussed with passion as Future Work or New Work. We call this artistic work **Artistic Intelligence Method and Projects**. In short, we discovered a critical way in which art creates an important portal into our society.

To give some examples of our work, Freeters has influenced the redesign of the Deutsche Telekom AG headquarters in Bonn, as well as the main offices of its consulting affiliate Detecon in Cologne, Frankfurt, Dresden, Berlin, Munich, and San Francisco. Another major industrial project has been the reinterpretation of space for the Bosch start-up platform grow in Ludwigsburg. Based on our positive public reception, Freeters was invited by ORGATEC, the world's largest office environment trade fair, which takes place at the Cologne Trade Fair, **to inspire new concepts and artistic thinking** across 600 square meters of open floor space. Interventional and conflict-reducing artworks have also been developed in social contexts, such as the shared accommodation refugee housing in Kiel.

Nonetheless we consider our key resource to be our core artistic work, where all individual ideas are melted into an everlasting chamber of ideas. Our collaborations with other collectives and institutions also fall into this category. Among other things, we want to mention our projects with ESMoA, an LA-based art laboratory exploring new collaborations ranging from neighborhood projects like Mychal's Learning Center to big art institutions like LACMA or the Getty Center. We have helped to launch the Elsegundissimo Experience, which will eventually lead to an urban transformation of one of the most interesting industrial parts of LA.

The Freeters collective includes academically trained artists as well as artists from various other professional backgrounds, yet all of them look back on many years of experience as curators or cultural workers. Which brings us back to our original objective, answering your call for applications for the Professorship of Painting and **demonstrating our ability to interpret painting beyond conventional definitions.** As a collective, we intend to summon all our abilities and synergetic forces in order to meet and exceed the requirements of this position. The collective currently consists of 12 permanent members and has acquired years of experience and expertise in practically every aspect of the job profile. In addition, we are widely networked with national and international artists, curators, fairs, companies, corporations, and museums.

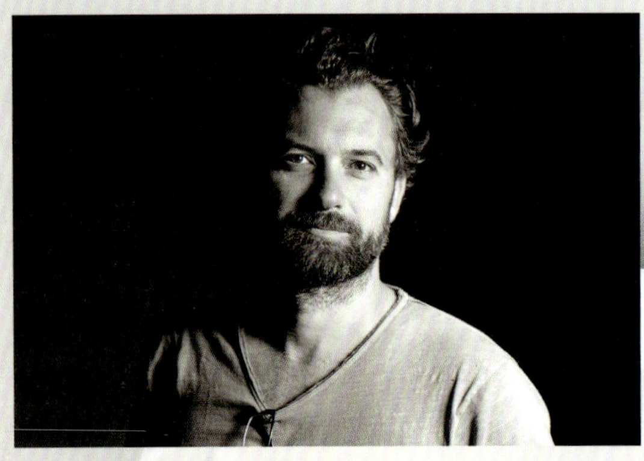
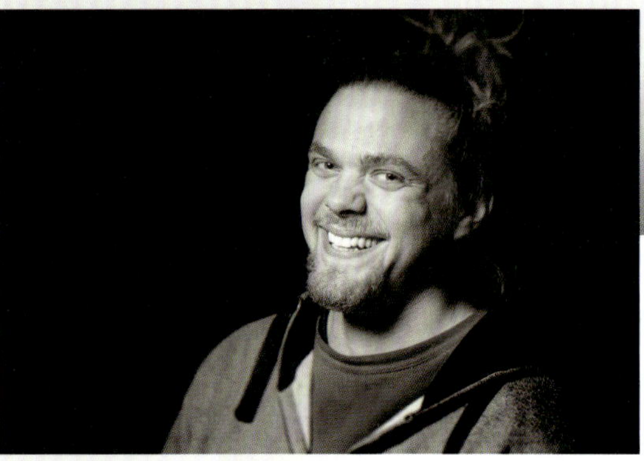
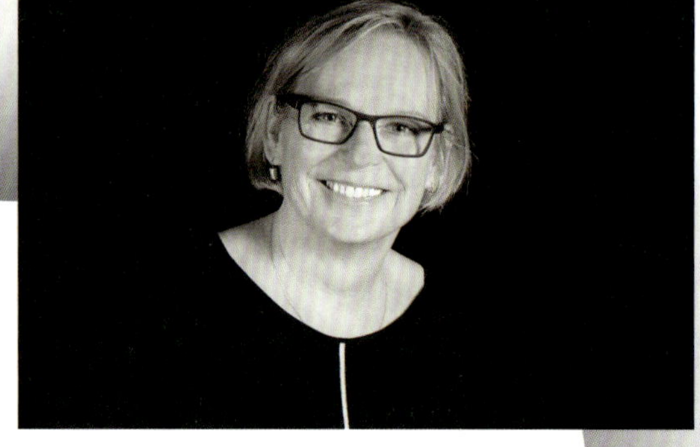

Florian Benet-Riedel

Frowin Schweer

Ingrid Blessing

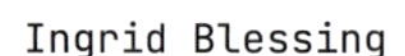

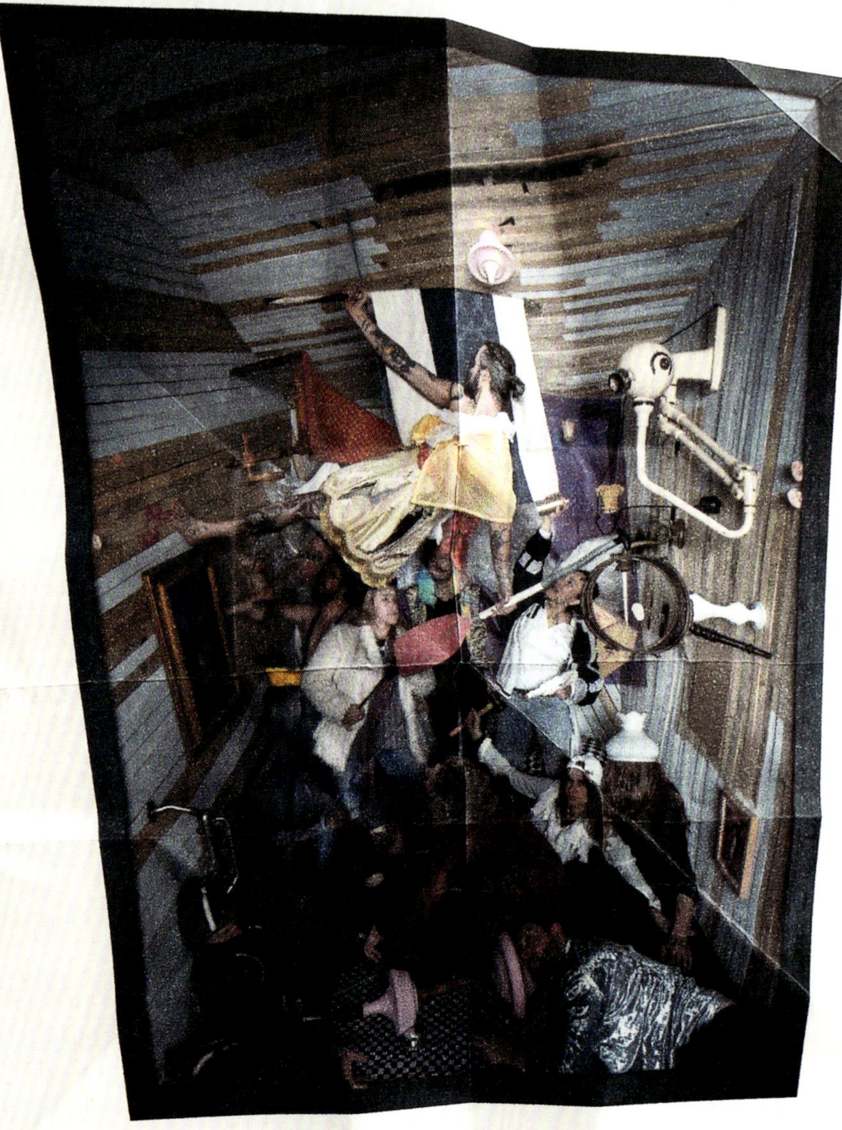

2012: Founding of Freeters.
2012–14: Refresh/redesign, Detecon Cologne (head office), Munich, Berlin, Frankfurt, Dresden, San Francisco.
2014–17: Refresh campaign, Deutsche Telekom AG Headquarters, Bonn, three construction phases.
2016–18: Renovation redesign, IGLO Headquarters, Hamburg.
2016: Shared accommodation and housing for asylum seekers, in cooperation with AWO / City of Kiel.
2017–18: Concept and design of the start-up platform grow, Bosch GmbH, Ludwigsburg.
2018: Refresh campaign, Deutsche Telekom AG, Stuttgart; Plant 10.1, central event space at Orgatec, Cologne Trade Fair, by special request of director Thomas Postert, Cologne; Establishment of Freeters eG.

SHORT BIOGRAPHIES OF THE BOARD MEMBERS

Amely Spötzl, board of directors, Freeters eG. 1997–2001: Studies in sculpture and liberal arts, Alanus University of Arts and Social Sciences, Alfter/Bonn. 2003: Diploma in Sculpture. Liberal arts teaching assignments at various universities for drawing and mixed media; workshops and seminars in adult education; international scholarships; exhibitions in nationally and internationally renowned galleries and museums. www.amelyspoetzl.de

Michael Sistig, board of directors and artistic direction, Freeters eG. 2003–2009: Studies in painting with Prof. Albert Oehlen and Prof. Peter Doig, Kunstakademie Düsseldorf. 2008: Studies at the Royal Academy of Arts, London. 2009: Academy brief at the Kunstakademie Düsseldorf; master's student with Prof. Peter Doig. Numerous exhibitions and scholarships in national and international galleries and museums. www.michaelsistig.com

Johannes Hess, Member of the board, Freeters eG. 2004–2010: Studies in sculpture and liberal arts, Alanus University of Arts and Social Sciences, Alfter/Bonn. 2008: Diploma in Sculpture, Liberal Arts. 2010: Master of Fine Arts with distinction. 2011–2015: Teaching in the Department of Sculpture and Architecture, Alanus University of Arts and Social Sciences, Alfter/Bonn. www.johannes-hess.com.

Bernhard Zünkeler, Chairman of the supervisory board, Freeters eG. Studied law and received his doctorate with a thesis on the free movement of workers in Europe. For more than ten years worked as a lawyer and focused on restructuring processes in international companies. In 2009 co-founded the research institute artlab21, from whose work the art laboratory ESMoA in Los Angeles emerged in 2012. ESMoA is an urban intervention project in which the various dimensions of art's are investigated. As a founding partner of E105 GmbH, primarily concerned with the integration of art thinking into operational processes and the implementation of participative methods in urban development. www.esmoa.org

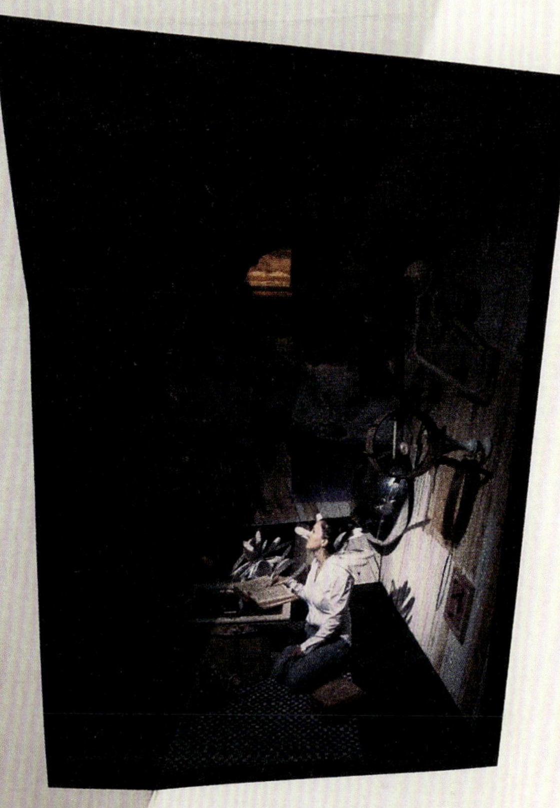

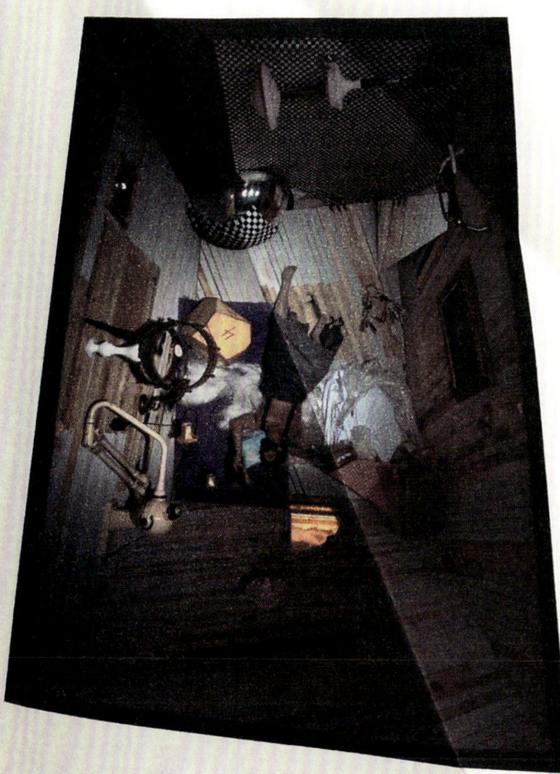

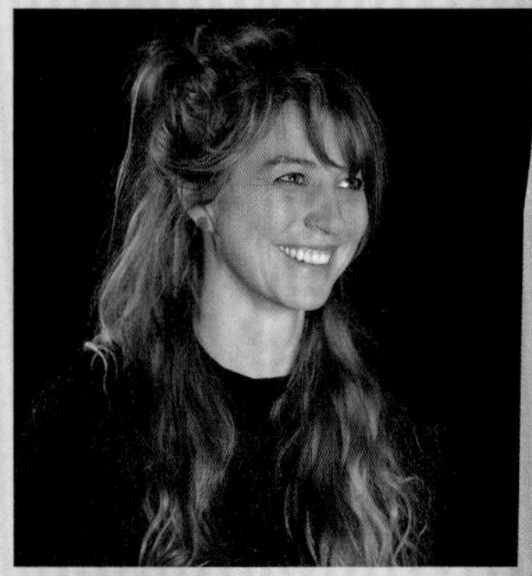

Johanna Hendel

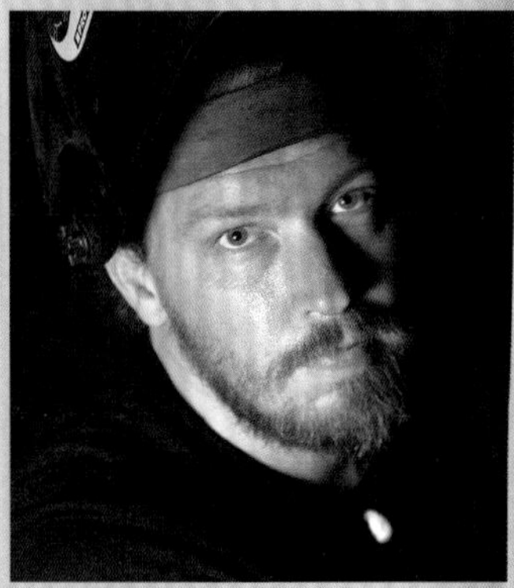

Johannes Hess

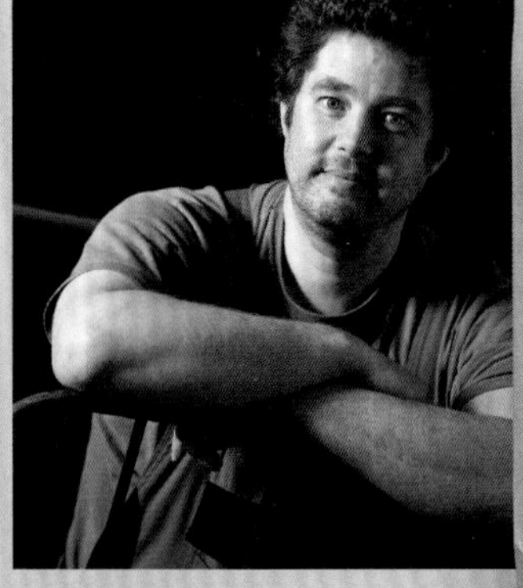

Ludgar Molitor

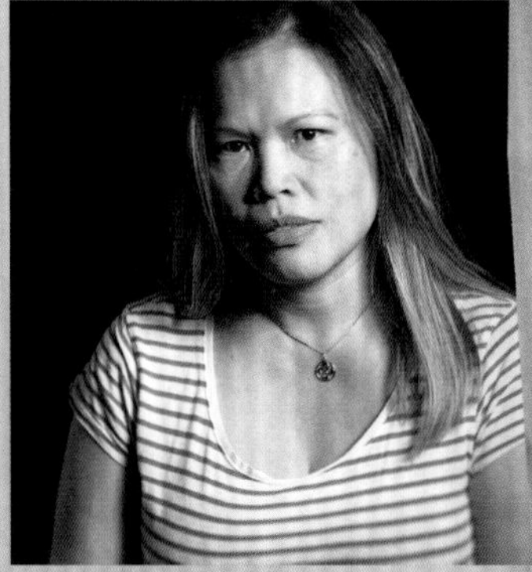

Maya Moll

It should be mentioned that all members of the collective have at least a degree in the arts and/or art therapy. In addition, most of the members have experience in art education, adult and youth education, as well as academic teaching assignments and artistic collaboration at various art colleges. A wild mix of work experience in various sectors ensures a well-integrated knowledge of artistic fields of exploration. This is also supported by experiences made in leading positions in the gastronomic sector or managing positions in the performing arts, decades of experience in body art, collective interventions in public and museum spaces. Our expertise includes knowledge of Anthroposophy, Christianity, Buddhism, Islam, and nature religions. This is not an accumulation of random experiences, but authentic characteristics of our poly-identity. We feel justified in saying that we are living diversity and that we are experts in diverse fields. As a collective, we not only have a command of the German language, but also English, Spanish, French, and Italian. To make it even more authentic, we love to speak Swiss German, as well as various dialects such as Rhenish, Bavarian, Ruhr German, Catalan, and Roman.

EXHIBITIONS

Due to our collective's very large number of different exhibition projects we take the liberty, for the sake of an overview, of using four of our members as examples, listing their artistic and curatorial activities to date.

Michael Sistig, freelance artist
2018: Cloud Chamber, Aki Gallery, Taipei (solo). 2017: The Grand Design, Kunstverein Sundern-Sauerland (solo). 2016: Matter, El Segundo Museum of Art, Los Angeles (solo). 2015: Mimacrocosmic, Aki Gallery, Taipei (solo); Matter-Antimatter, Daab Salon, Cologne (solo); Songs of the God Particles, Richard Haizmann Museum of Modern Art, North Frisia (solo). 2014: M-Theory, Kunstverein Fuhrwerkswaage and Kunstverein; Cherry Pickers, Cologne (solo); Silence, El Segundo Museum of Art, Los Angeles (group). 2013: Anti-Ark Installation, El Segundo Beach, Los Angeles (solo); Desire, El Segundo Museum of Art, Los Angeles (group); Young German Art, Aki Gallery, Taipei (group). 2012: Von Sinnen, Kunsthalle zu Kiel (group); Michael Sistig / Roland Persson, E105, Berlin (solo); Pentaton, Hansa Coking Plant, Dortmund (group). 2011: Michael Sistig, Firestation El Segundo, Artlab21, Los Angeles (solo); Young German Art, Aki Gallery, Taipei (group). 2010: Worship, Artlab21, Los Angeles (group); One on One, Hansa Coking Plant, Dortmund (solo); Young German Art, Aki Gallery, Taipei (group); Veranda at the House to Hades, E105, Berlin (solo). 2009: Beyond the surface, Artlab21, Los Angeles (group); Balloon Man / Head Walker, E105, Bonn (solo). 2008: Klasse Doig, Zollverein Coal Mine Industrial Complex, Essen (group); Light and Irrlicht, Oechsner Gallery, Nuremberg. 2007: Sturm und Drang, Gallery E105, Bonn (group); Archaeologies, Oechsner Gallery, Nuremberg (solo). 2006: Man's End?, Space for Art and Music, Cologne (solo). 2005: Kunstverein Malkasten, Düsseldorf (group).

Amely Spötzl, freelance artist
Grants and fellowships 2014: Artist in Residence Fellowship, ESMoA, El Segundo / Los Angeles. 2011: Visual Arts Fellowship, Lucas Artists Residency Program, Montalvo Art Center Saratoga, CA. 2010: 1st Alanus Prize for Visual Arts. 2009: Project grant, Just a Moment, artlab21, Berlin, Los Angeles. 2007–2012: Studio Grant of the City of Bonn / Kunstverein Bonn. 2003: Representative of the Art Liaison, Kunstmuseum Bonn / Musée d'Art Contemporain Lyon; Exhibition grant, FICF Germany/Italy, Lo Spirito del Tempo, Rapallo, Italy. 2002–2007: Support Studio Frauenmuseum, Bonn. *Art in public space (selection)* 2014: Phytomagnetics Post Office, El Segundo / Los Angeles; Phyto-Organic Systems, Gallery Valentien, Stuttgart. 2011: Just a Moment, Berlin, Main Station; Just a Moment, Brussels; Phytomagnetics, Gallery E105, Berlin (catalogue); First Alanus Prize for Visual Arts, Stadtmuseum Siegburg (catalogue); Amely Spötzl, Art Association Linz. 2010: Plantas Part, Stadtmuseum Siegburg; Blattwerk Foundation,

Industrial Monument Coking Plant Hansa, Ruhr 2010, Dortmund. 2009: Just a Moment, Taipei / Berlin / San Francisco / Los Angeles; Just a Moment, Gallery E105, Bonn. 2006: Rosa Canina, Christuskirche Cologne. 2004: Museé d'Art Contemporain, Lyon; Played from the page, Goethe Institut Lyon. *Exhibitions (selection)* 2014: Silence, ESMoA, El Segundo / Los Angeles; Signs + Wonders, Gallery E105, Bonn. 2013: Desire ESMoA, El Segundo / Los Angeles; Art Works, Gallery E105, Berlin; Detecon, Frankfurt. 2012: Extraschicht Foundation, Industrial Monument Coking Plant Hansa, Dortmund; Insight Cologne, Detecon, Cologne. 2011: Interface Patterns – Biology and Art Society for Art and Design, Bonn (catalogue); FORTUNA, Gallery E105, Berlin. 2010: GET CLOSER, Aki Gallery, Taipei / Art Stage Singapore; ONE ON ONE, High-rise Hansa, Dortmund; RUND, Society for Art and Design, Bonn, After Nature, Science Centre, Bonn; WORSHIP, Celebrity Vault, Hollywood (catalogue); Urban Intervention, Art Association, Los Angeles (catalogue). 2009: Open Your Mind – New German Art, AKI Gallery, Taipei (catalogue); Beyond the Surface, artlab21, Contemporary Fine Art, Los Angeles (catalogue); Members Choice, Kunstverein Heidelberg; Kunstverein Bonn (annual gifts 2009). 2008: GOOD VIBRATIONS, Geometry and Art, University Collections for Art and Technology, TU Dresden (catalogue); Thorns and Devilish Beasts, Frauenmuseum Bonn (catalogue); Blind Date, Gallery E105, Bonn (catalogue); Art Fair 21 Cologne. 2007: Gallery E105, Art Fair Cologne; Kunstsalon Berlin. 2006: Transformation, Gallery E105, Bonn (catalogue). 2005: Gallery Arsenal, Festival Inner Spaces, IF-Museum Poznan (catalogue).

Dr. Bernhard Zünkeler, gallery and museum director
2013: Museum director, founder of El Segundo Museum of Art – curated and organized 41 exhibition projects inside and outside the museum, some of them in cooperation with the Getty Center and the Los Angeles County Museum of Art. 2005–2012: Gallery E105, Bonn, Berlin, Los Angeles, Taipei – Numerous exhibitions and projects, catalogue productions; Revitalization projects with the Stiftung Industriedenkmal NRW, artlab21, Bonn, El Segundo; Co-founder of the research institute from which ESMoA emerged after four years of activity, Los Angeles.

Pasquale Demeco, founding member and organizer
2019: since May temporary showroom of Freeters www.kunst-bedarf-kunst.de). 2017: Provision of the premises for Videonale.PARCOURS. 2014–18: Participation in the Bonn season launch. 2012: S.Y.L.A.NTENHEIM / Art Supply Quarter (Art Project/Offspace), Bonn, initiator and administrator. Probably the only exhibition space that guarantees all artists an exhibition. It is financially and conceptually independent, self-managed, self-financed, radical and consistent. Since its inception over 100 exhibitions, concerts, performances, readings have been organized on our own initiative. Parallel development of a collection currently consisting of over 90 pieces. 2006–2009: SUPPORT YOUR LOCAL ARTIST, Bonn, the association has opened at least one exhibition every month, making it possible to implement international exchange projects and print exhibition catalogues. The LVR supported the project in the exhibition year 2007/08. The association has mainly financed itself through membership fees, as well as the exhibition rooms and studios (200 square meters).

PUBLICATIONS (selection)

2017: ICU, Distanz Verlag, Berlin. 2014: M-Theorie, Kunstraum Fuhrwerkswaage, Kunstverein Kirschenpflücker, Cologne. 2012: Michael Sistig, Elementarbrechung, Kerber Verlag, Berlin; Von Sinnen – Perception in Contemporary Art, Kerber Verlag, Berlin; Pentaton, Artlab 21 Press, Berlin. 2011: Rising – Young Artists to Keep an Eye On!, Daab Verlag, Cologne; Interface Pattern – Biology and Art Society for Art and Design, Bonn. 2010: Urban Intervention, Art Association, Los Angeles; WORSHIP Celebrity Vault, Hollywood. 2009: Open Your Mind – New German Art, AKI Gallery, Taipei; Beyond the Surface, artlab21 Contemporary Fine Art, Los Angeles. 2008: GOOD VIBRATIONS / Geometry and Art, University Collections for Art and Technology, TU Dresden; Thorns and Devilish Beasts, Frauenmuseum, Bonn; Blind Date, Gallery E105, Bonn. 2006: Transformation, Gallery E105, Bonn. 2005: Arsenal Gallery, Festival Inner Spaces, IF Museum Poznan, Poland.

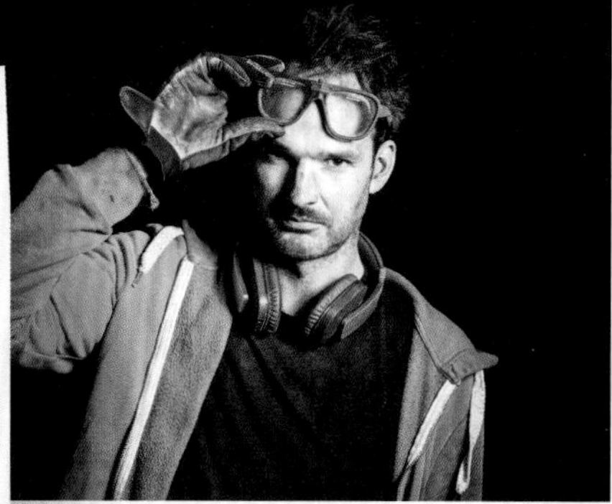

Michael Sistig

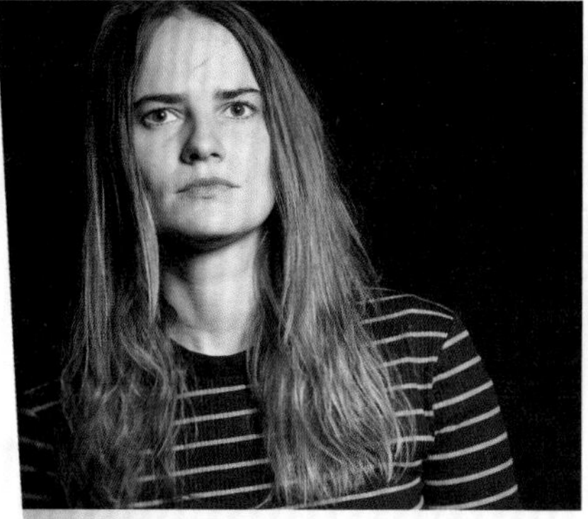

Miriam Nolte

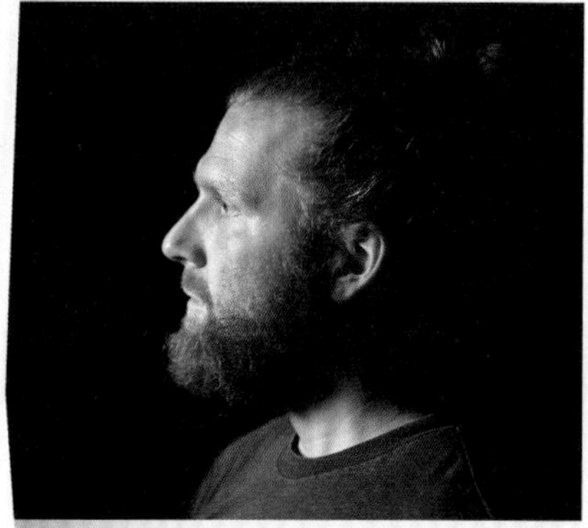

Nils Machel

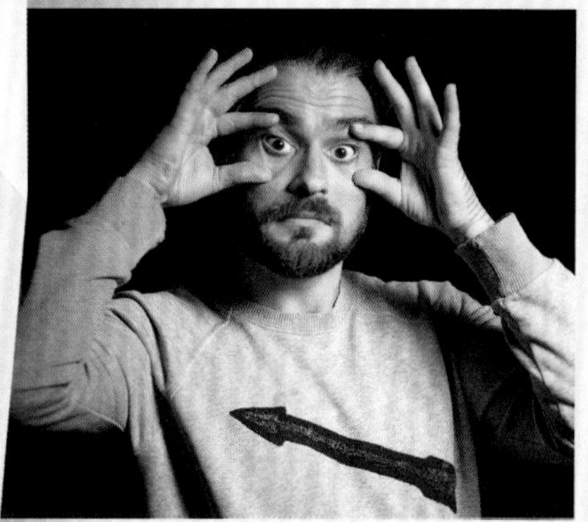

Pasquale Demeco

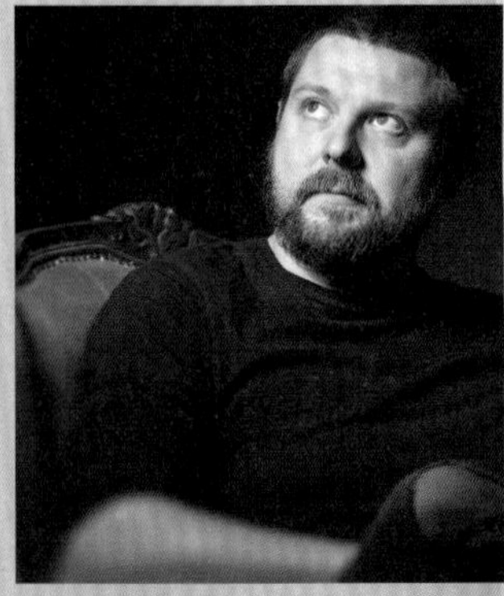

Rafael-Maria Hildebrandt

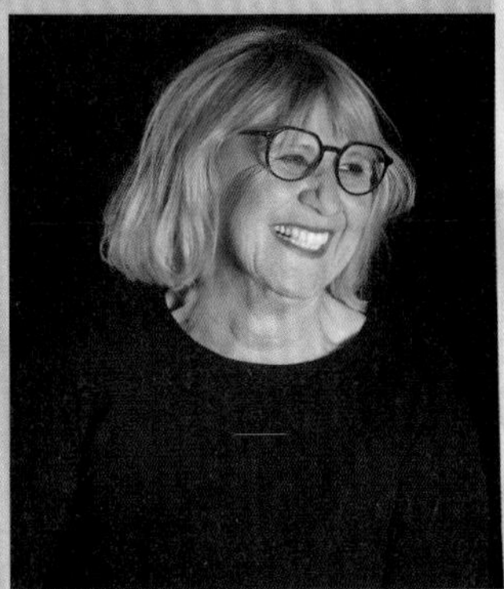

Rita Baus

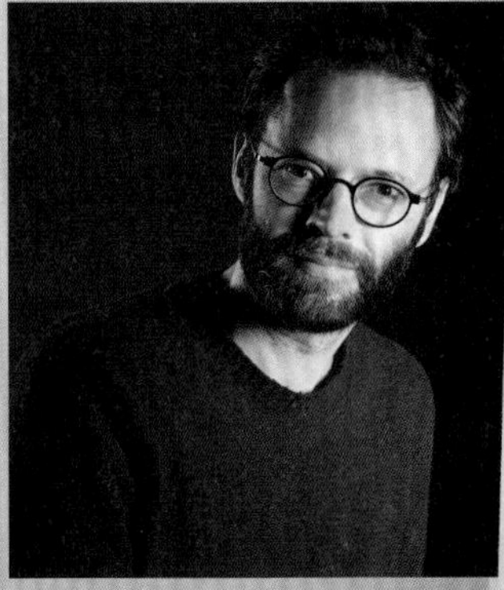

Roman Thomas

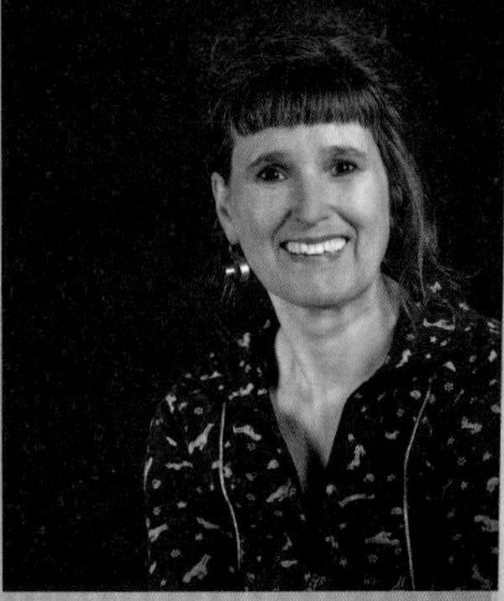

Sandra Freygarten

ALTERNATIVE SCIENTIFIC RESEARCH

We focus our artistic research on the phenomenon of creative collectivity. We explore origins and developments of collective ideas including all aspects of collective consciousness and awareness. In recent societal developments, it has become more and more apparent that monocausal, egocentric, and fragmented approaches are a major cause for conflict and monopolistic worldviews that are pushed even harder by self-centered social media algorithms. In contrast to these developments, various collectives have become increasingly present in public perception. In art in general, collective creativity is not new. Throughout history, artist collectives have always played a major role in driving art development: from the architectural workshops that built the European cathedrals to the painters' workshops of the Renaissance, from the smallest collective consisting of just two people, such as the Yes Men, to postwar painters' collaborations, such as Warhol, Clemente, and Basquiat, or more recently, the Center for Political Beauty, which has attracted attention through its consistent actions, or the Indonesian collective ruangrupa curating documenta 15. We would like to explore with our work how a collective as a swarm can be more flexible, more agile, and quicker to react to social and aesthetic questions. We would like to see how uniqueness and individuality can merge and survive in a holistic and synergy-driven collective. We believe we are a collective because art makes us one. We seek to explore the boundaries. Since future artistic and socio-political paths can only emerge through exploration and transgressing boundaries, we see it as our task to point out these aspects of our research and carry them forward both pedagogically and artistically. There are boundaries between art and design, applied art and industrial production. They are not clearly distinguishable, very rarely discernible. The role of art in this struggle between individualism and collectivism is a great field of discovery to us, and hopefully benefits individual freedom and social solidarism. The individual is generally in a struggle with society, today possibly more than ever, and at the same time a struggle for the self has also broken out. The self seems to separate itself from family, nation, religion, and politics and willingly merges with them as well. Self-optimization is cultivated, new traditions discovered, old visions abandoned. The permanent fathoming and oscillation between boundaries are often connected with suffering, but inevitably lead to the future. Art may be at the center of it. **Maybe art is the borderlands, keeping doors open to contradiction, transgression, and oscillation**. Art seems to form the perpendicular to the future we would like to explore even more.

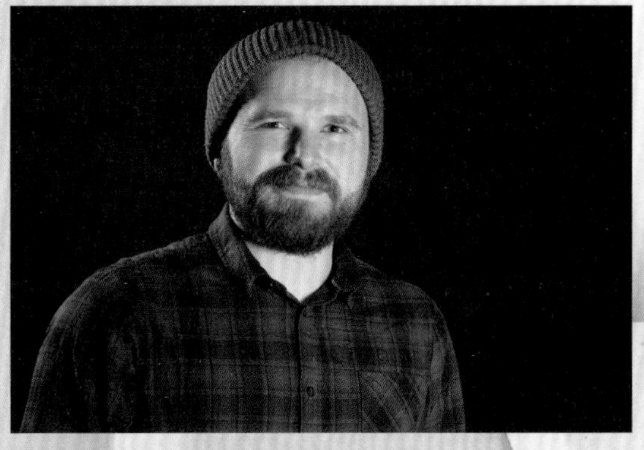
Sebastian Chorus

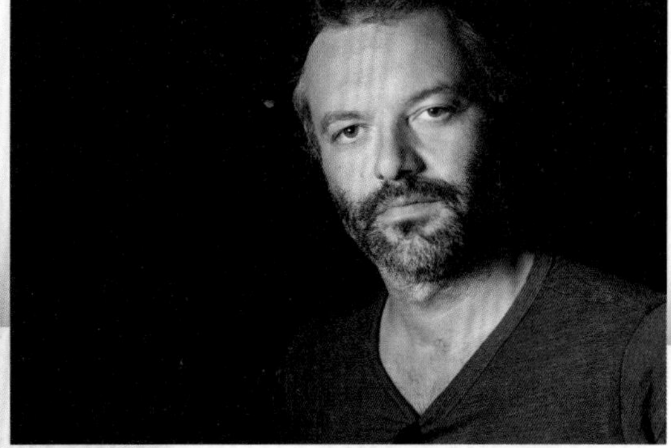
Sebastian Keller

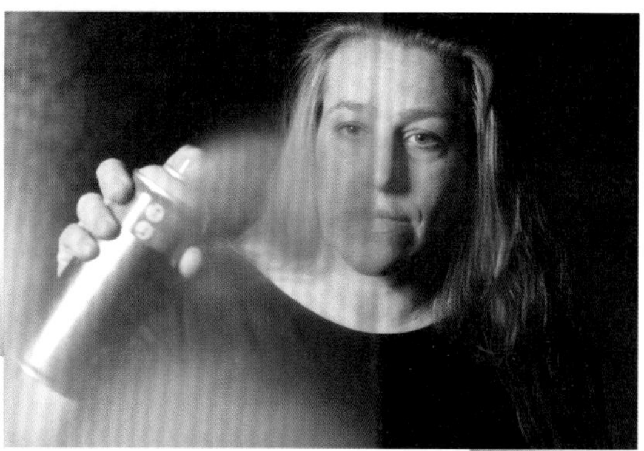
Silke Mattern-Specht

With our application we hope to offer you a truly unique option to reinvent the Professorship of Painting at the Kunstakademie Düsseldorf. An easy opportunity to get 12 for the price of one! Not only in the sense of an individual person and his or her individual achievements, but in the sense of having a self-sustaining collective approach on your faculty. We would be happy to answer any questions, and we look forward to receiving feedback from you.

Kind regards,

M. Sistig

Michael Sistig
(representing Freeters)

freeters

Michael Sistig
Vorstand

Lievelingsweg 82
D-53119 Bonn
www.freeters.de

M +49 171/7789963
@ michael.sistig@freeters.de

WANDERJAHRE
ART AS A CULTURAL UNIVERSAL

The collective idea encompasses the transregional interest in international cooperation, new artistic positions and approaches, as well as craftsmanship. As artists we are interpreters of our time, growing together globally through contemporary forms of communication while being divided and limited by political attitudes.

As the Freeters collective we find sources of inspiration and exchange abroad, the artistic research spirit drives us to seek Norwegian forests and quarries, picturesque areas in Italy and Spain, or urban life in Los Angeles, London, Tokyo, and San Francisco. At the same time we offer a place for guests and international exchanges in our workshop and our AiR Studio (in Bonn) and cultivate our international network with passion.

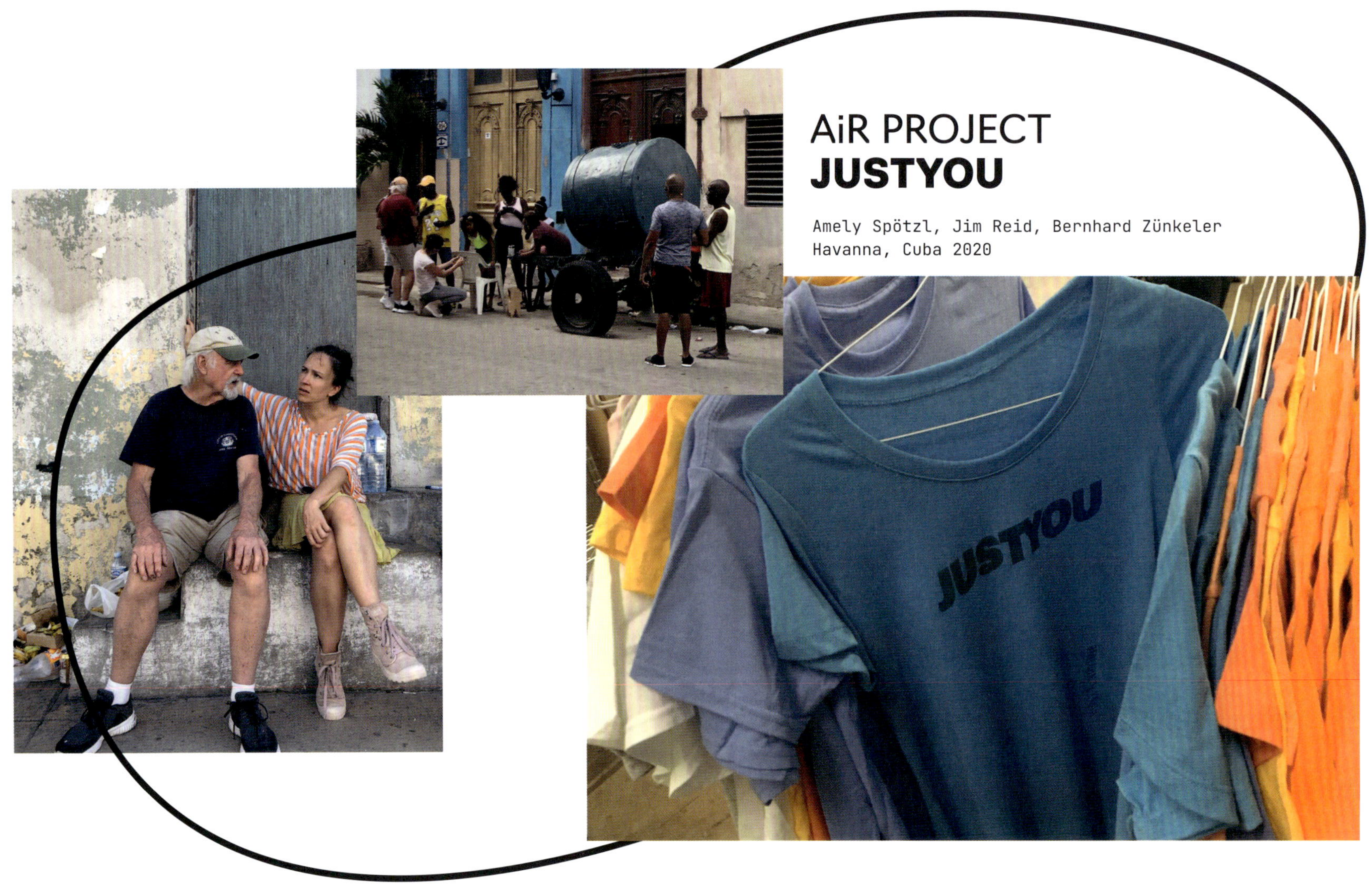

AiR PROJECT
JUSTYOU

Amely Spötzl, Jim Reid, Bernhard Zünkeler
Havanna, Cuba 2020

AiR PROJECT
ANTI ARK

Michael Sistig,
Los Angeles, USA, 2013

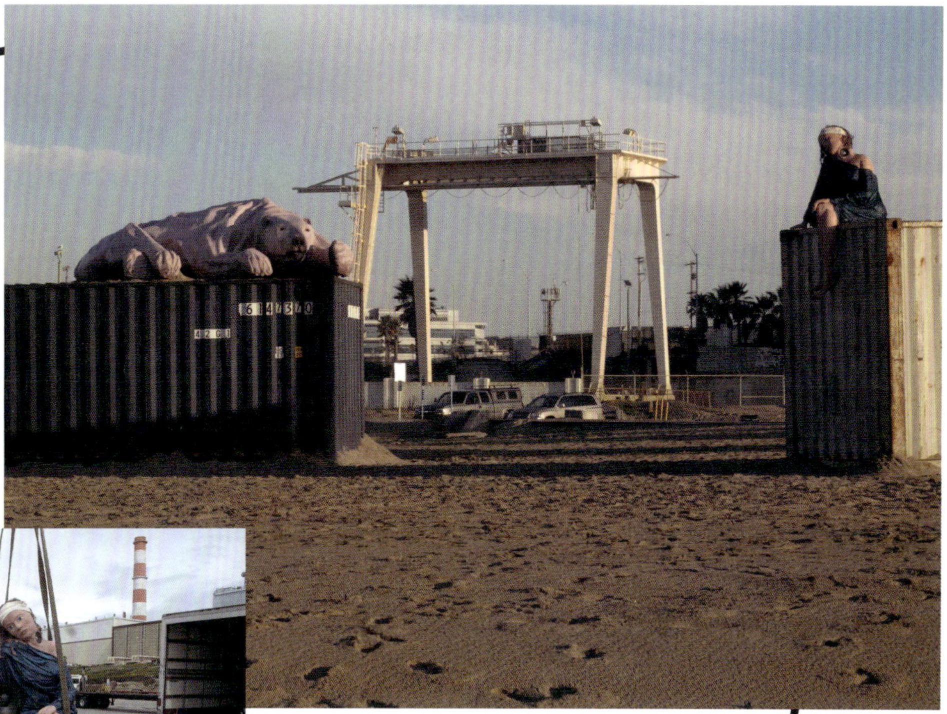

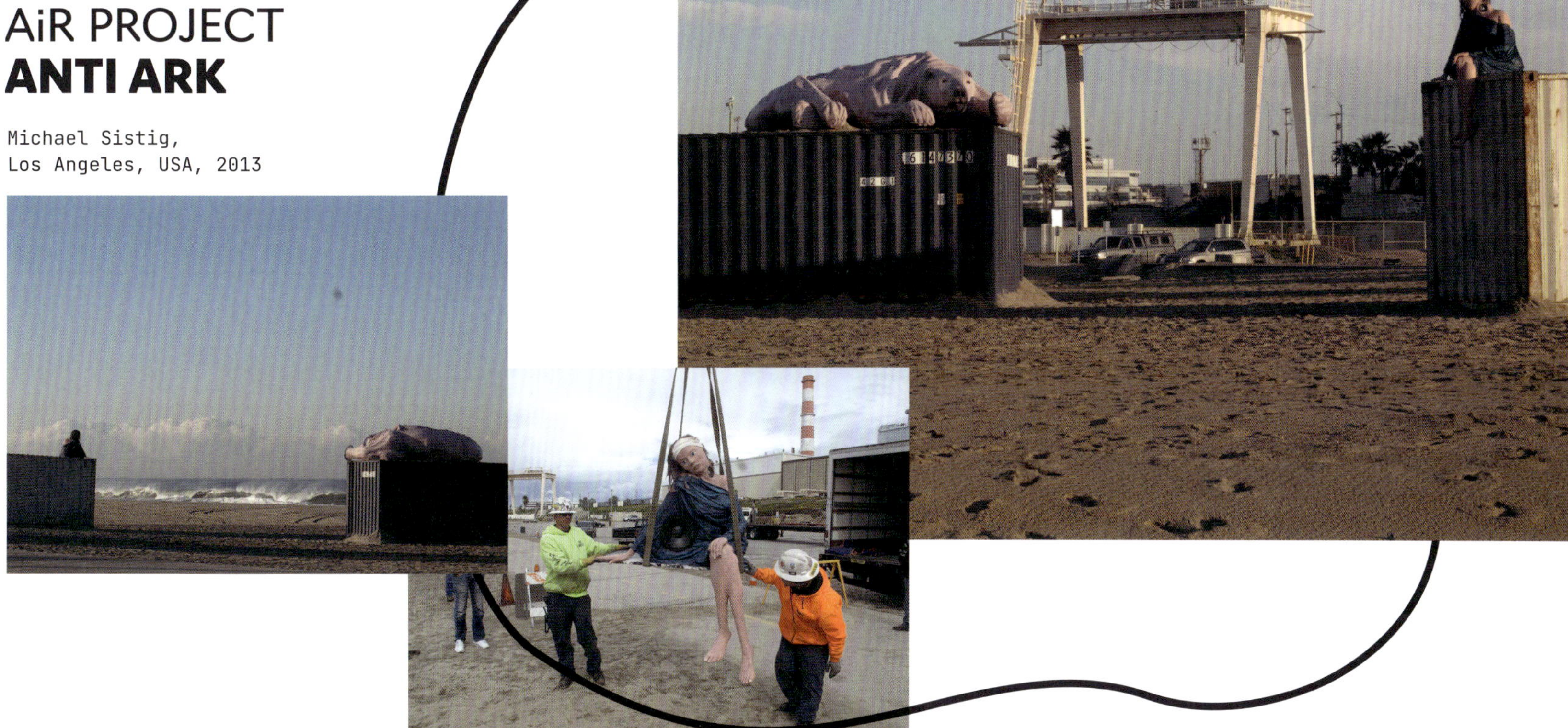

AiR PROJECT
GODESS

Pasquale Demeco,
Kleinsassen, Germany, 2006

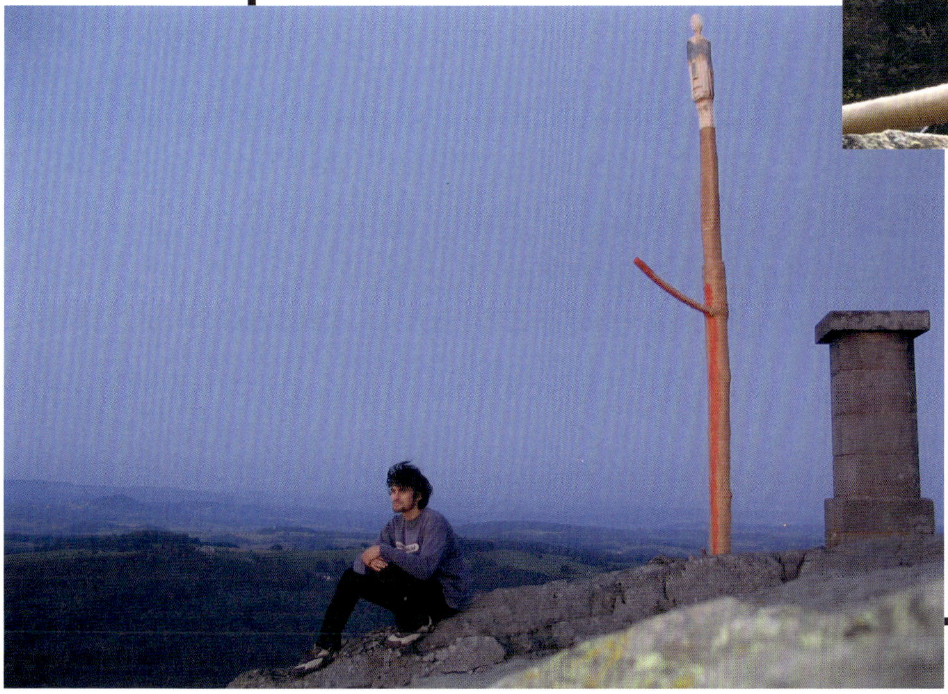

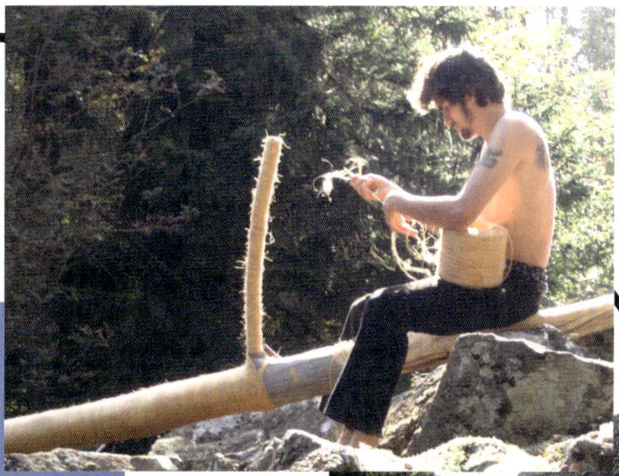

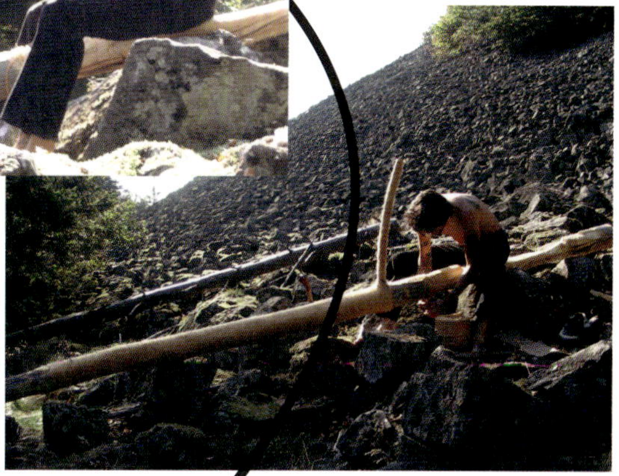

AiR PROJECT **ISLAND**

Ben Beyer,
Chile, 2018

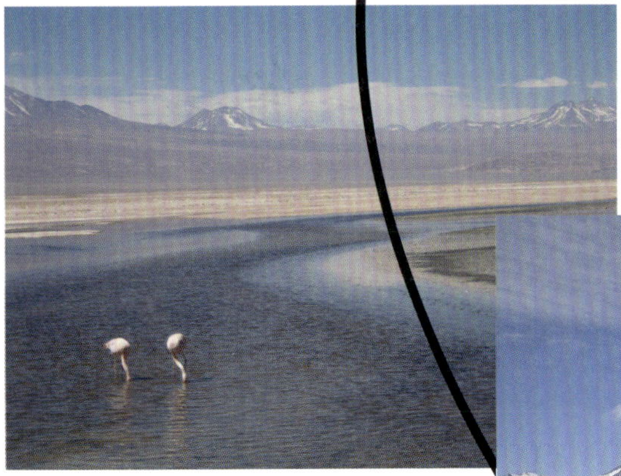

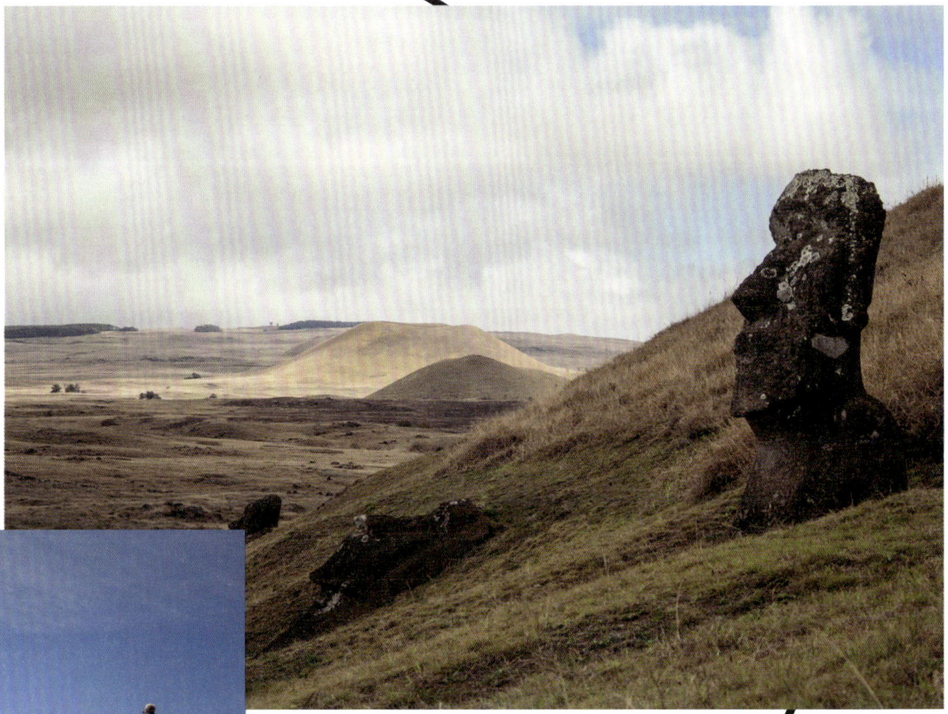

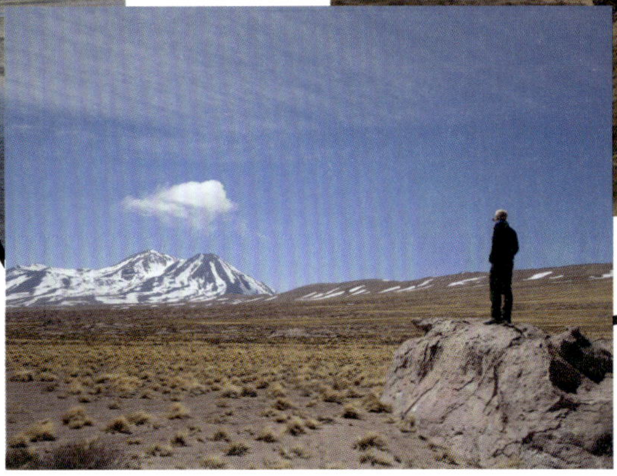

AiR PROJECT **ÅSGARD**

Miriam Nolte, Johanna Hendel, Johannes Hess,
Lukas Thein, Norway, 2016

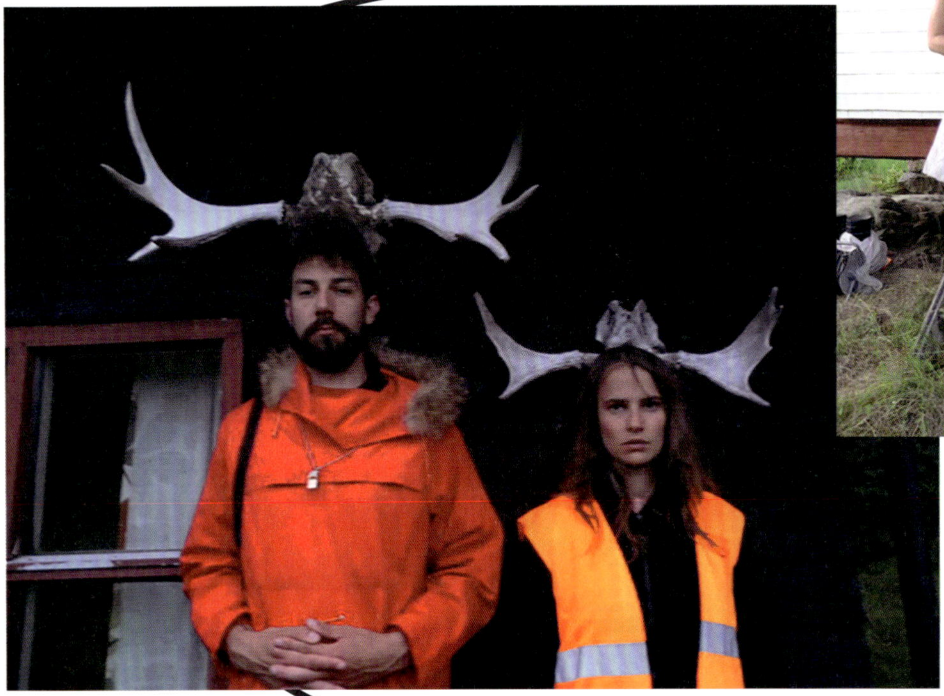

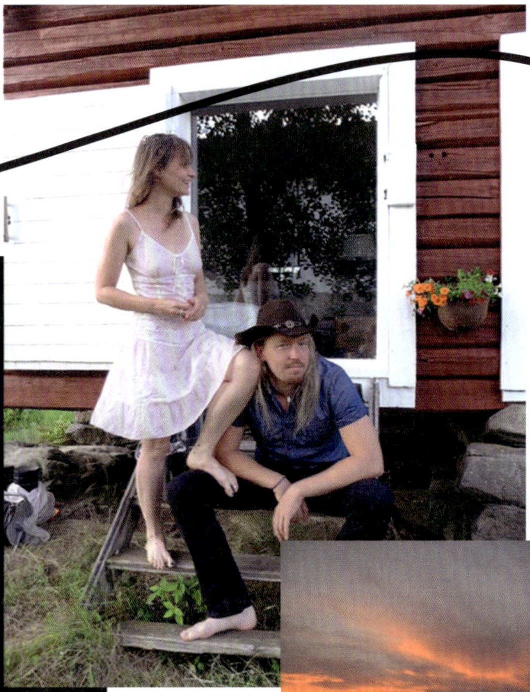

AiR PROJECT
FREETERS ARTISTS

Los Angeles, USA,
2013–2021

AiR PROJECT
ATLAS

Johannes Hess,
Larvik, Norway, 2013

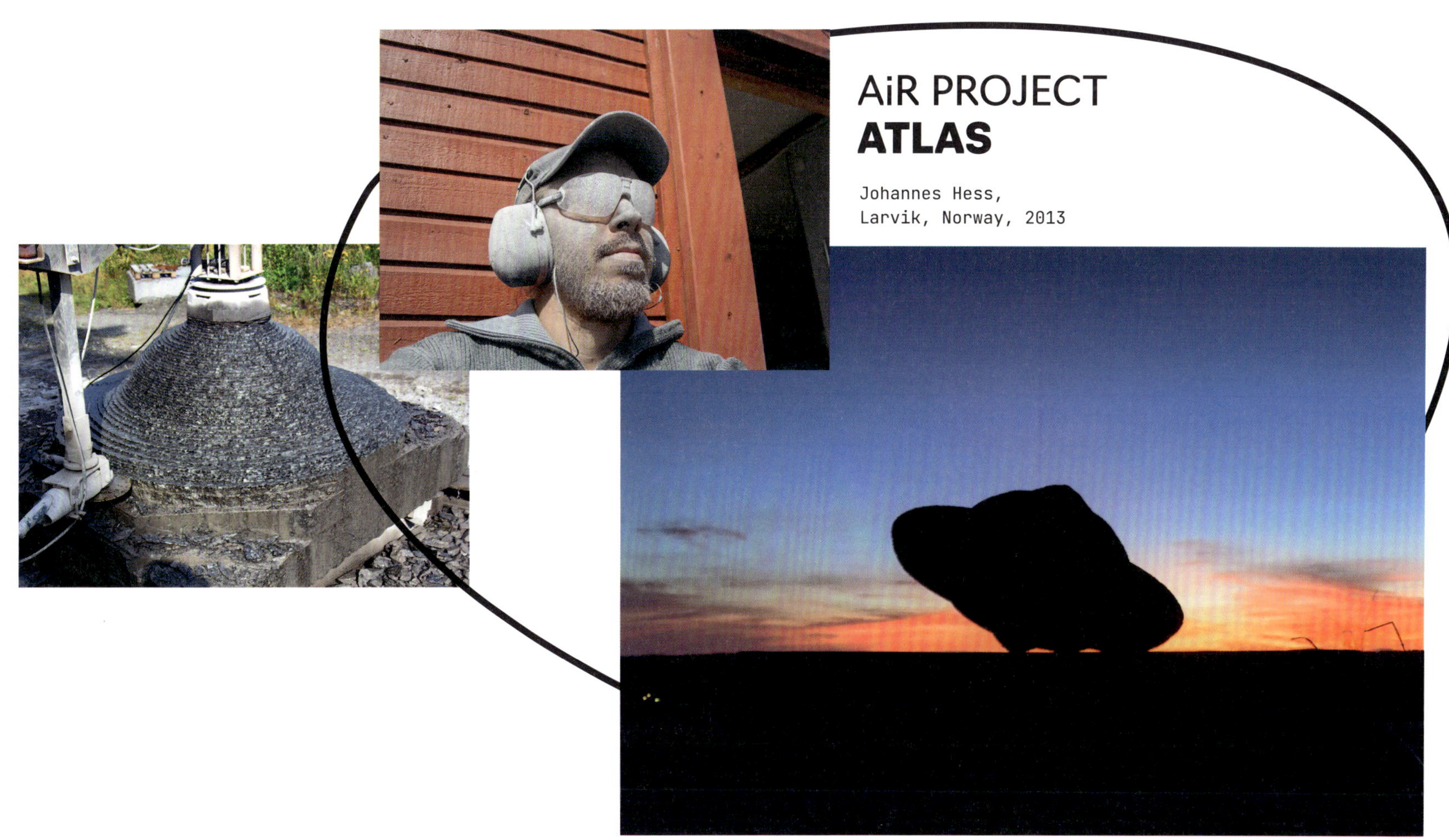

OPEN
ANNUAL EXHIBITION

The artist collective Freeters invites you to the annual exhibition the OPEN. The studios, production hall, and workshops are transformed into a cultural venue where people dance, make music, eat, and indulge freely in all aspects of art and creativity. The OPEN serves as an opportunity to build a bridge between independent projects and collaborations with clients. Thus, guests from all areas of collaboration are invited. Projects from the past year and independent works by the artists in the collective are on display. In addition, Freeters invites outside artists (regional, national, and international) to exhibit their work at the OPEN.

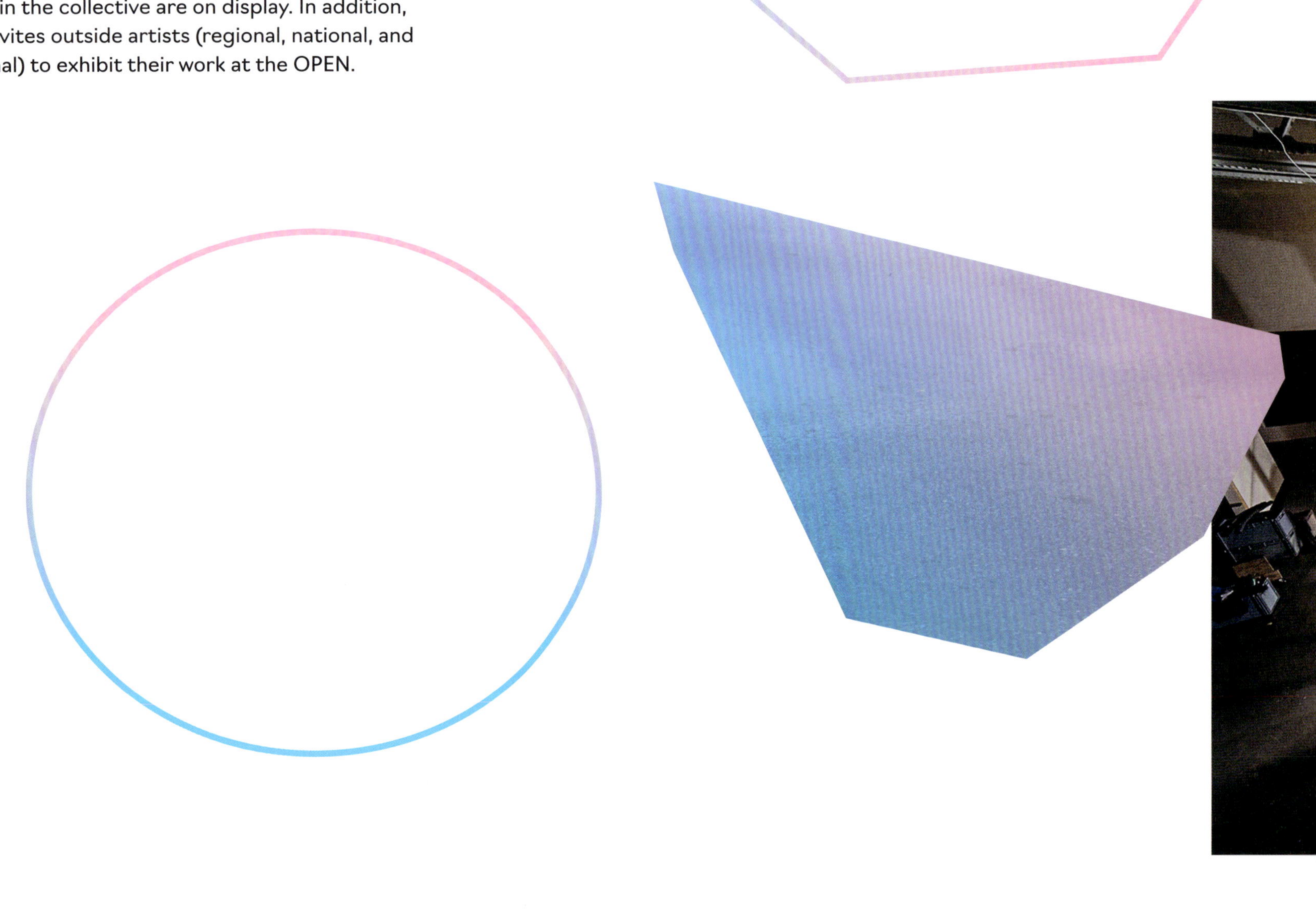

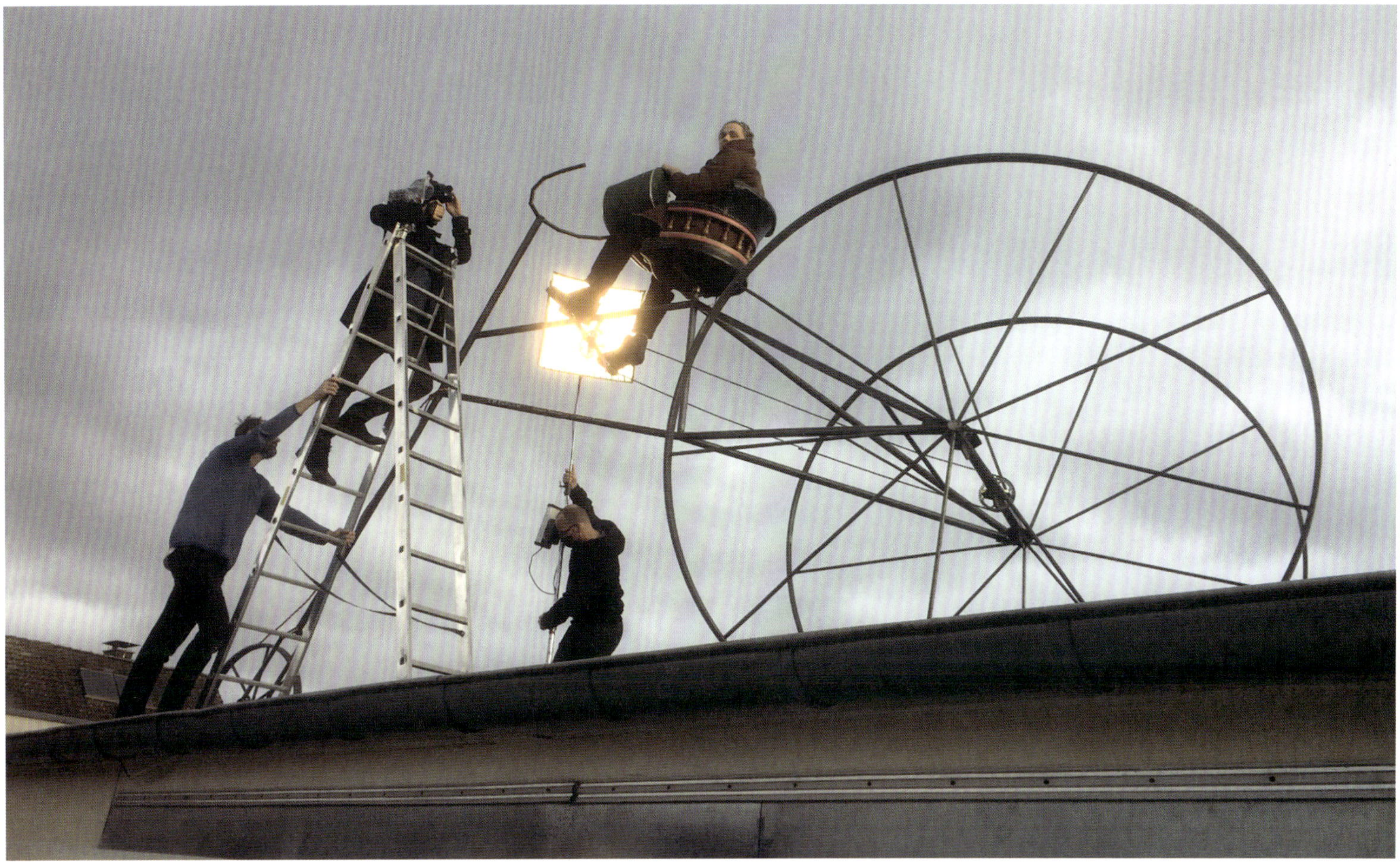

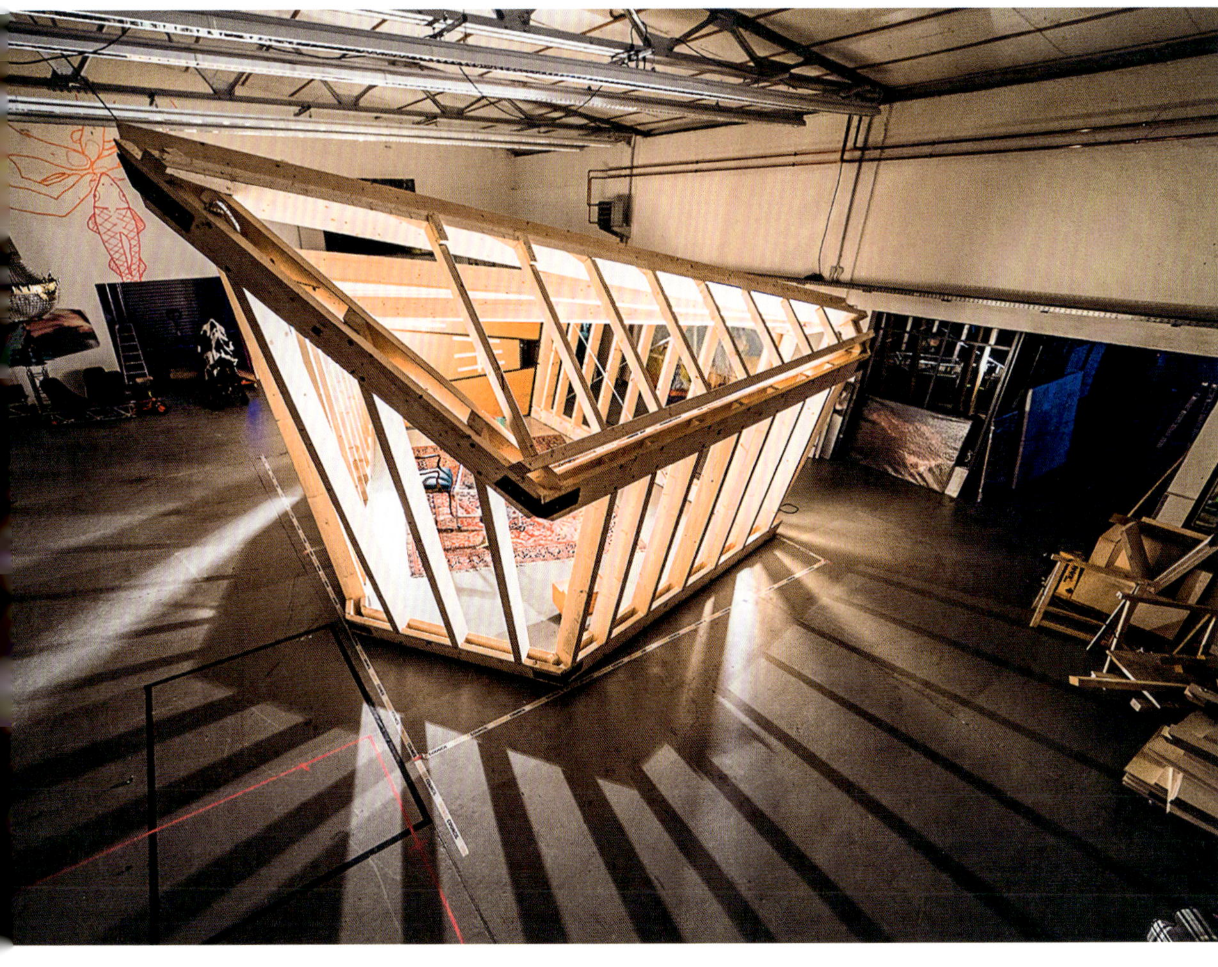

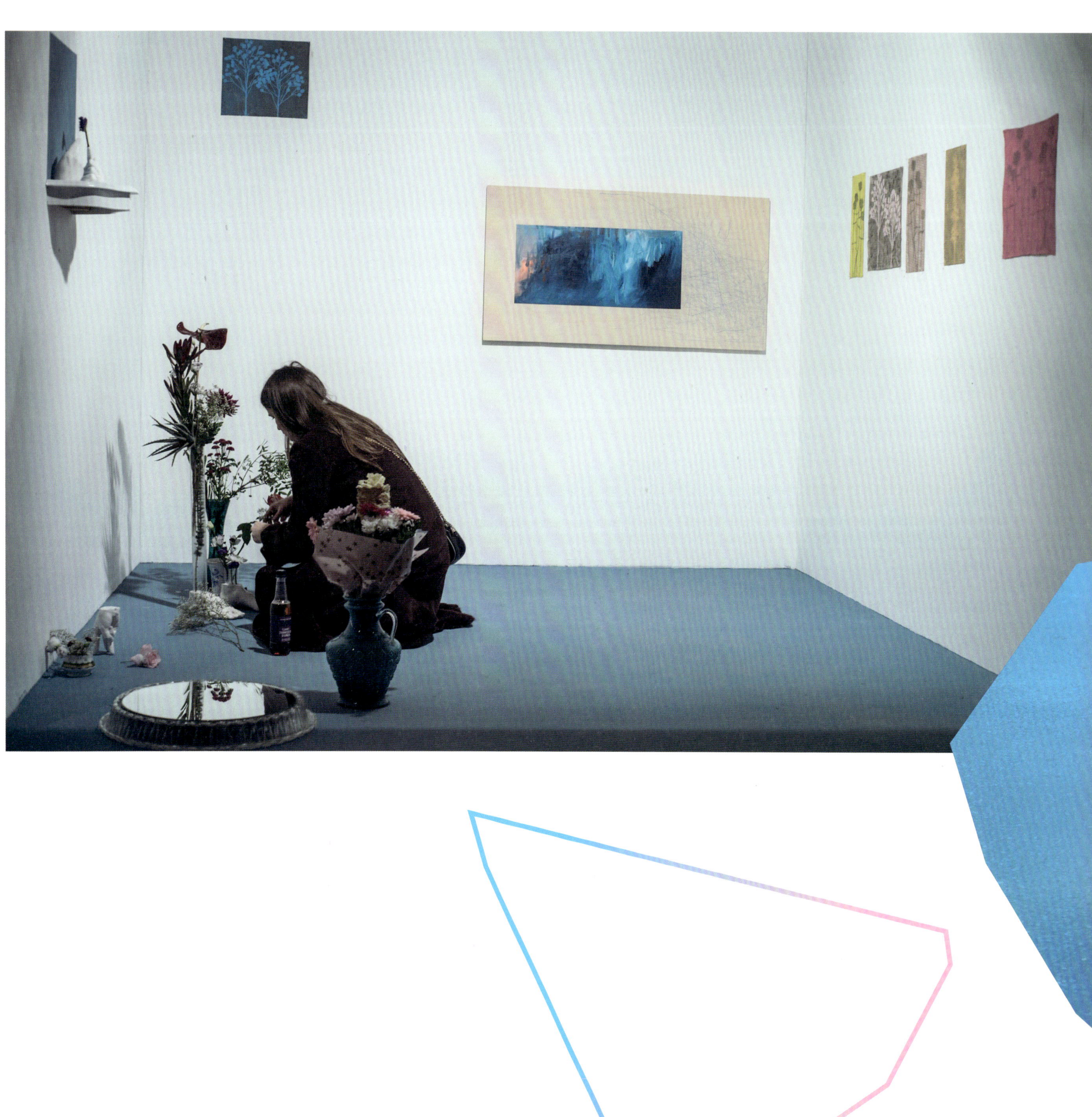

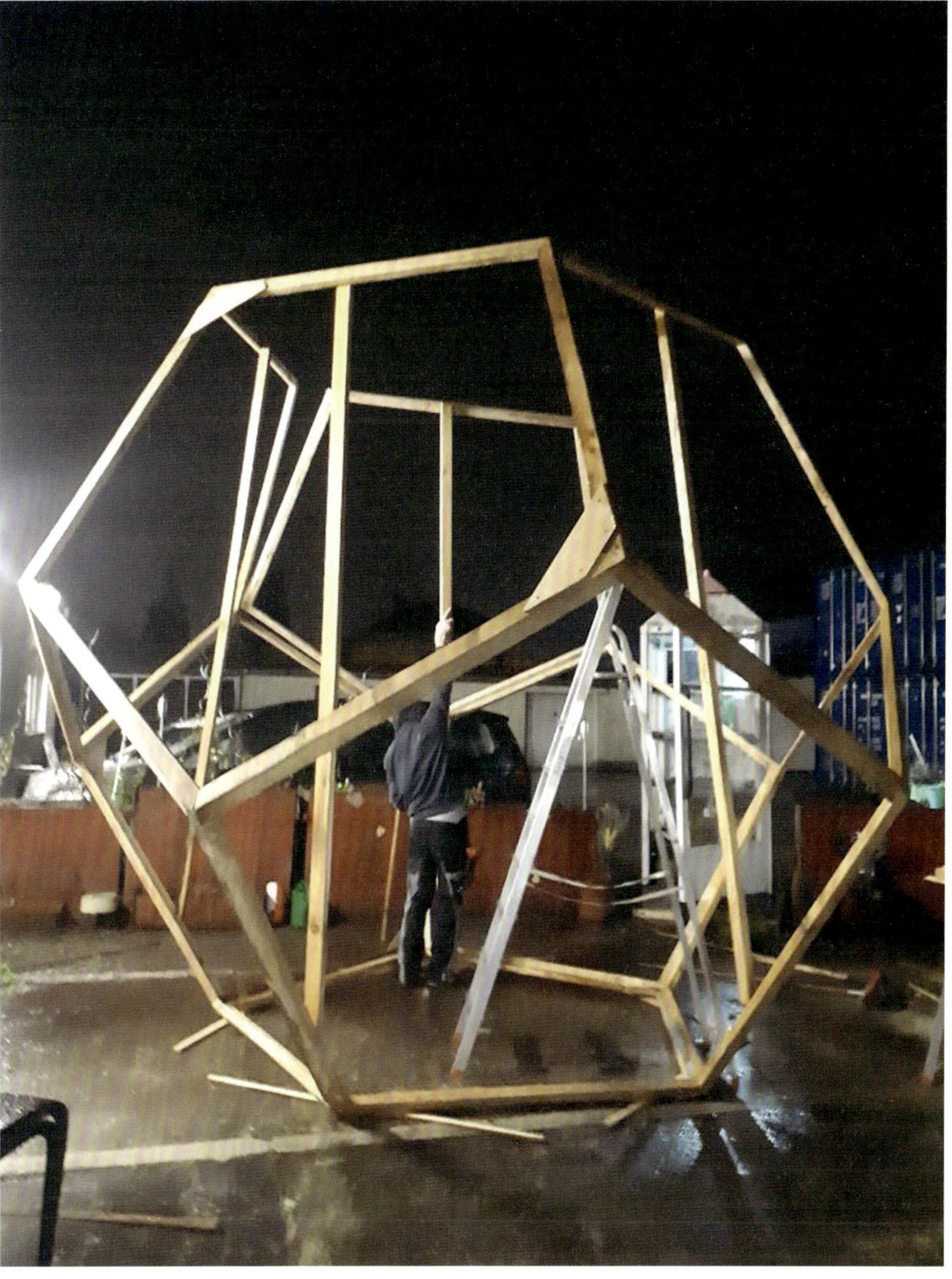

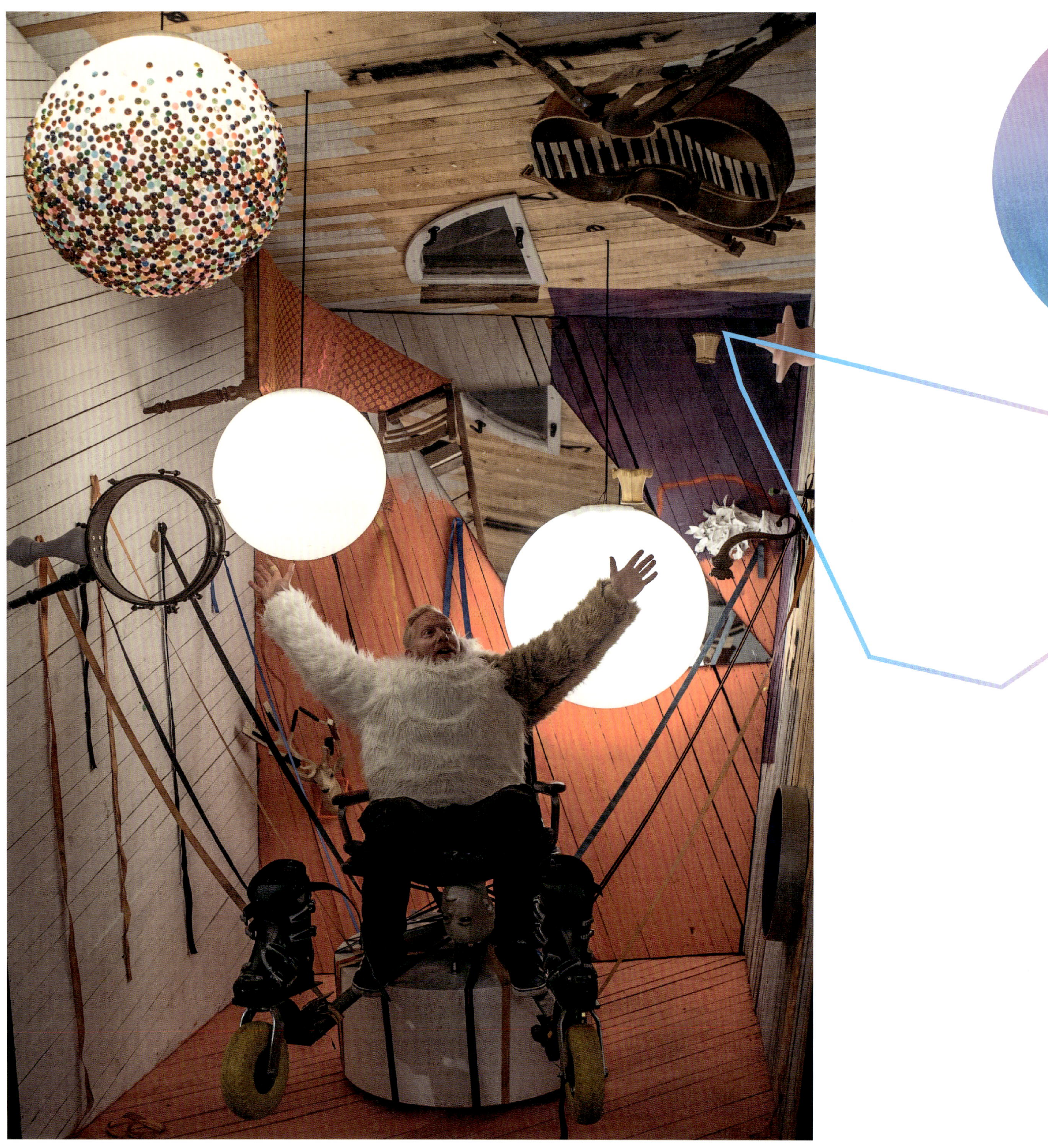

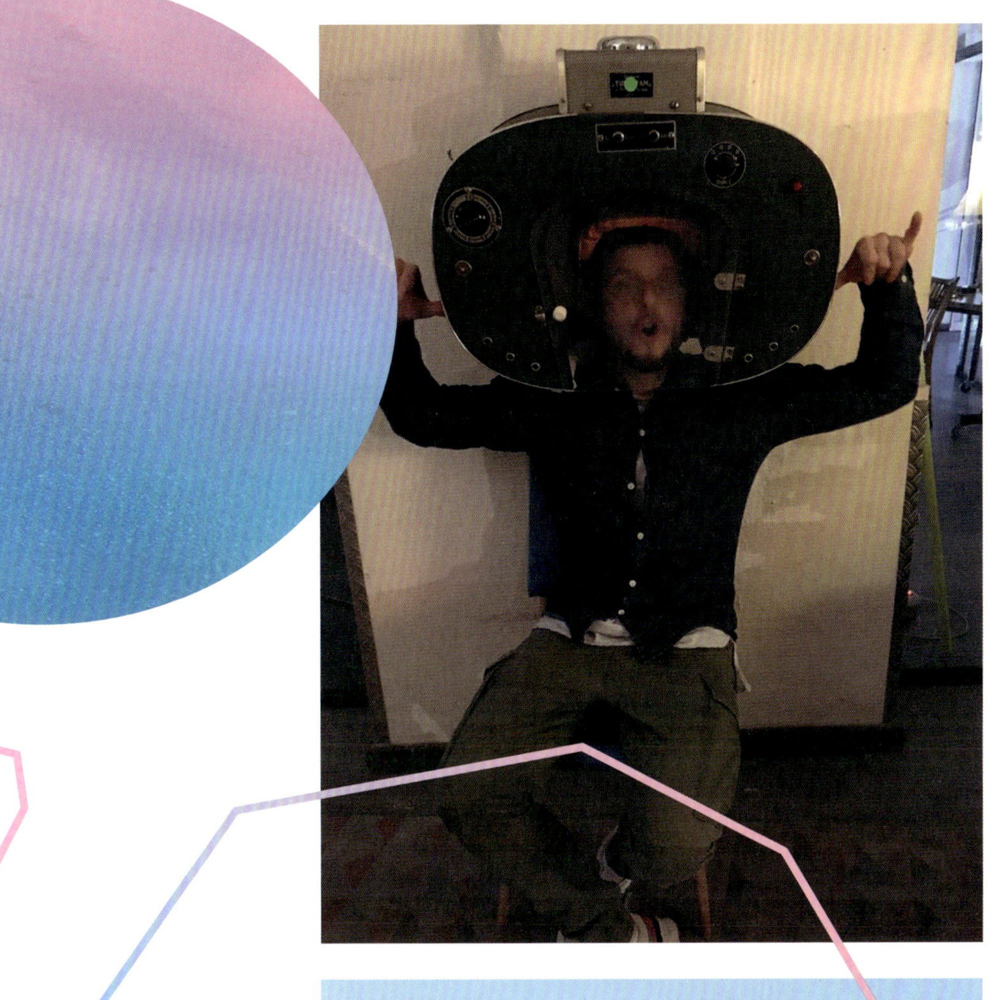

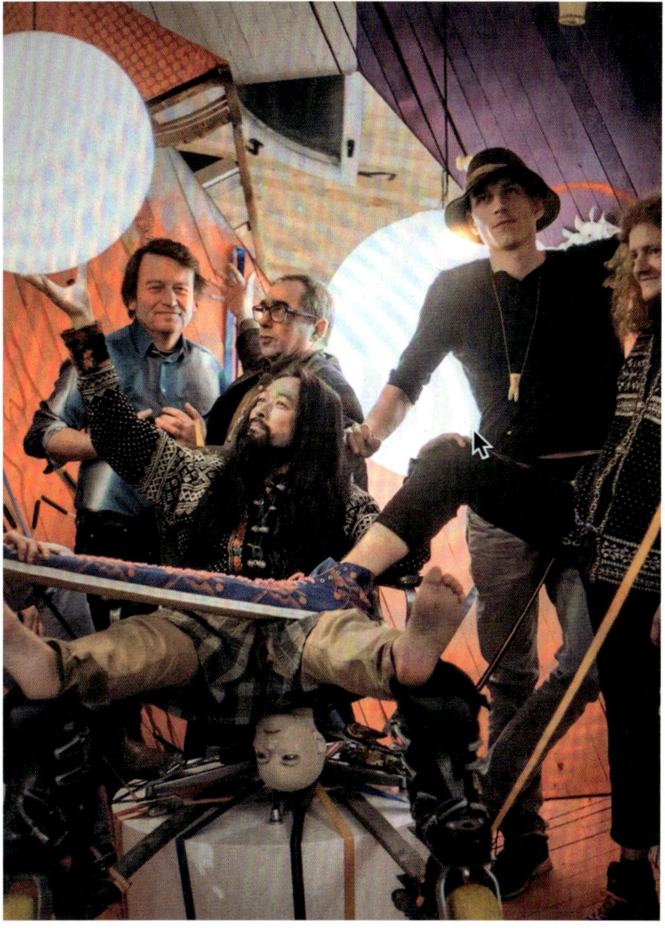

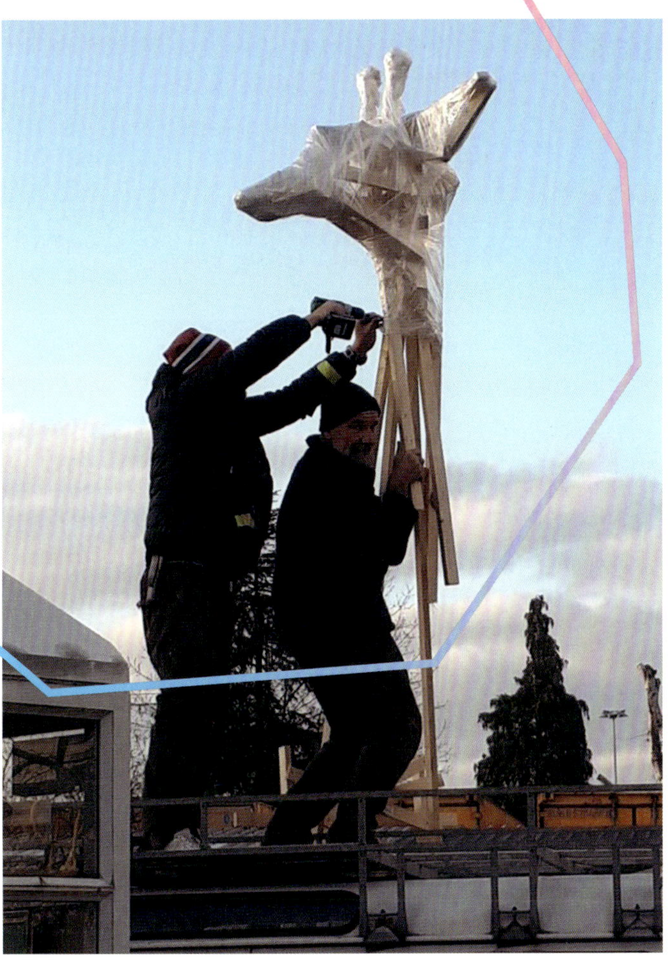

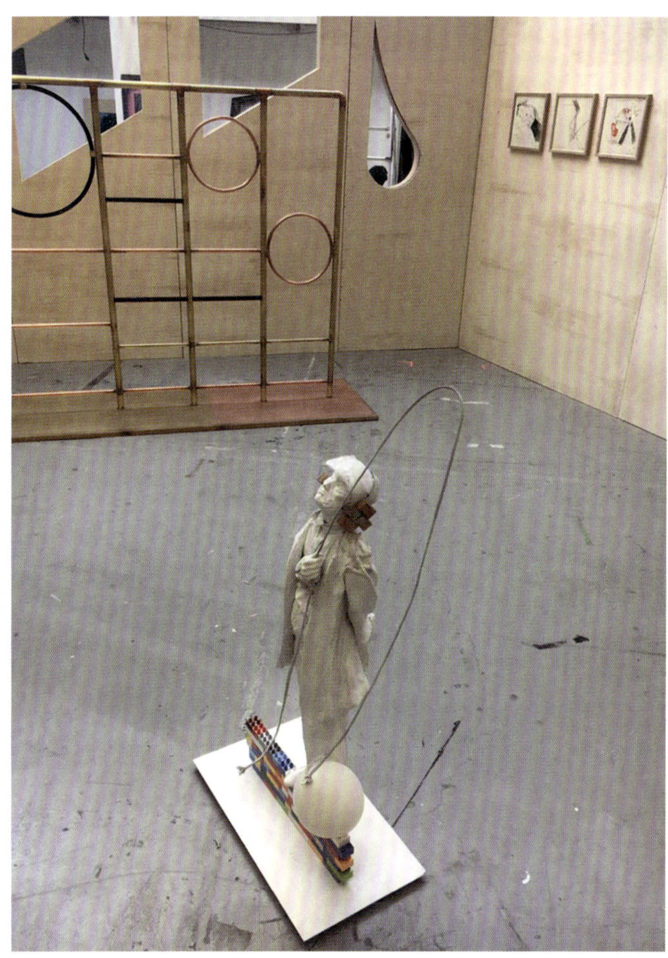

freeters SHOWROOM MAXSTRAßE 55

Since the approved S.Y.L.A.PPLICATION in 2019, this space is occupied by the artist collective Freeters and has, for the time being, been renamed Freeters Showroom.

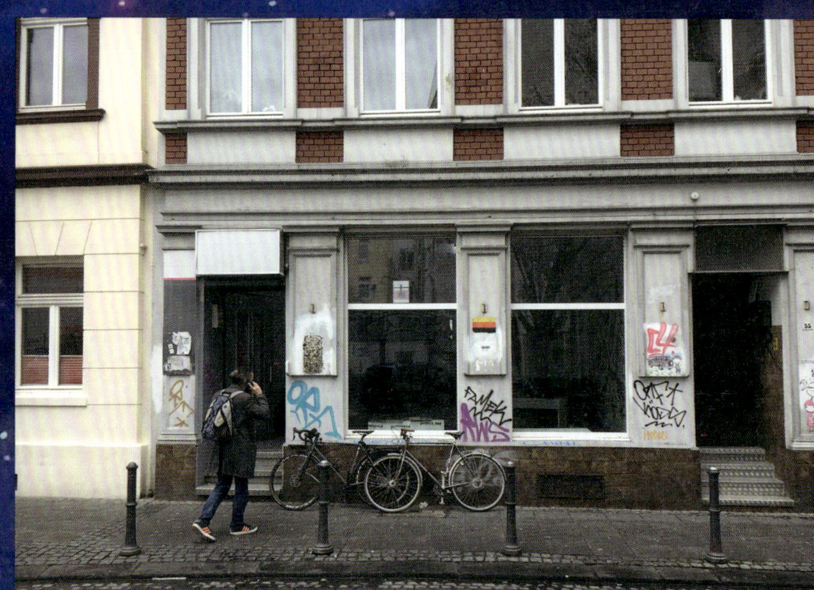

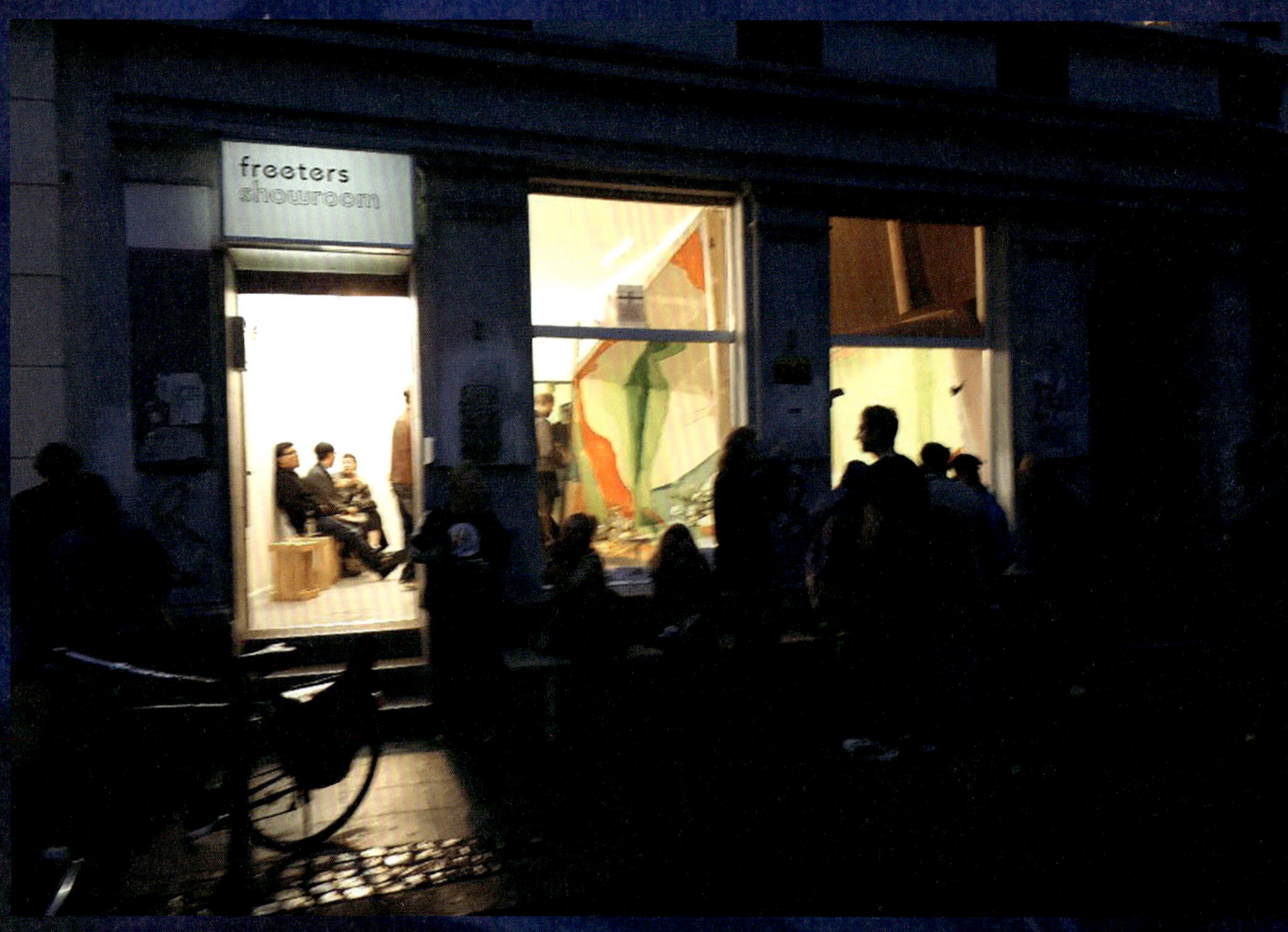

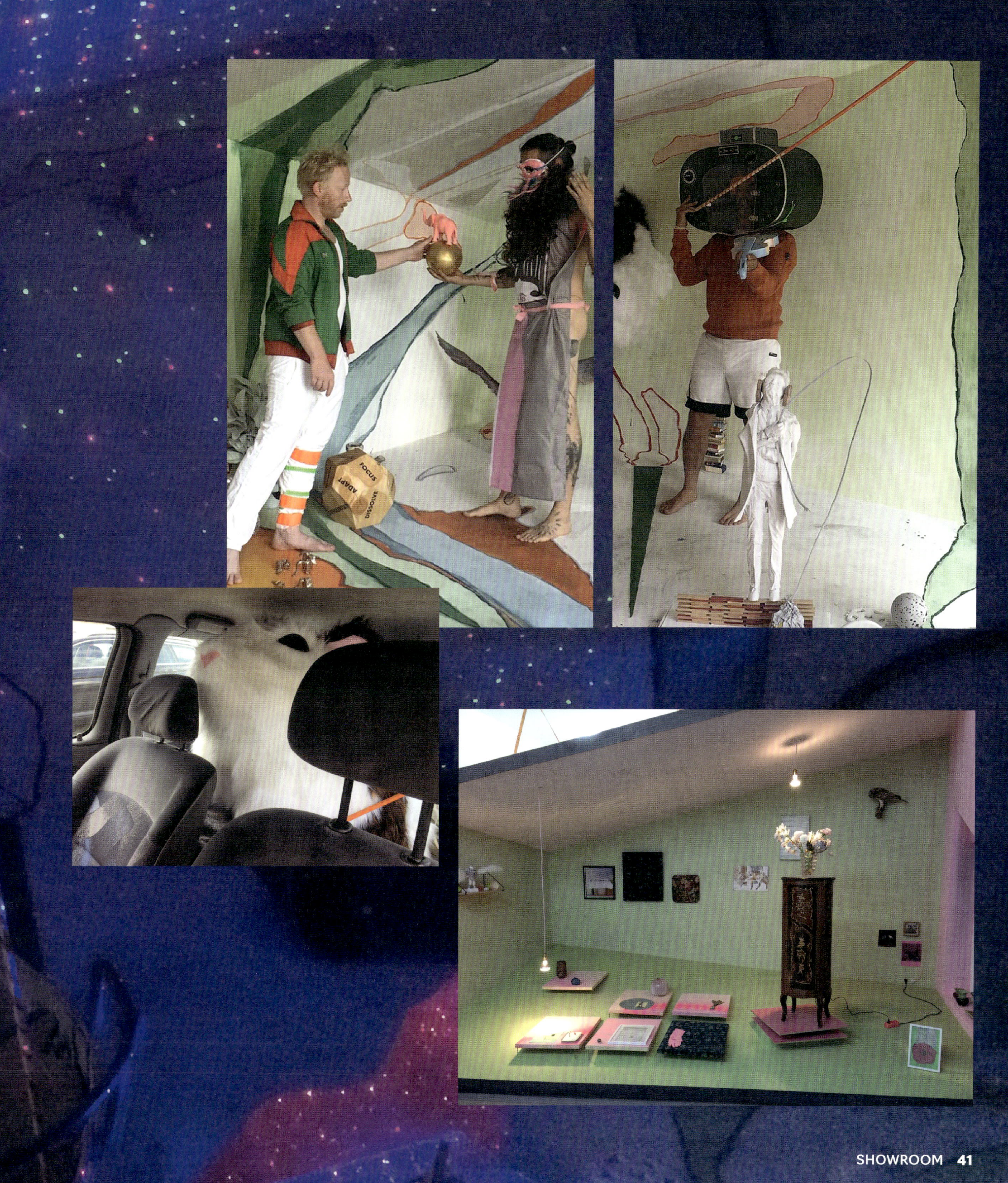
FOCUS
ADAPT
DISSOLVE

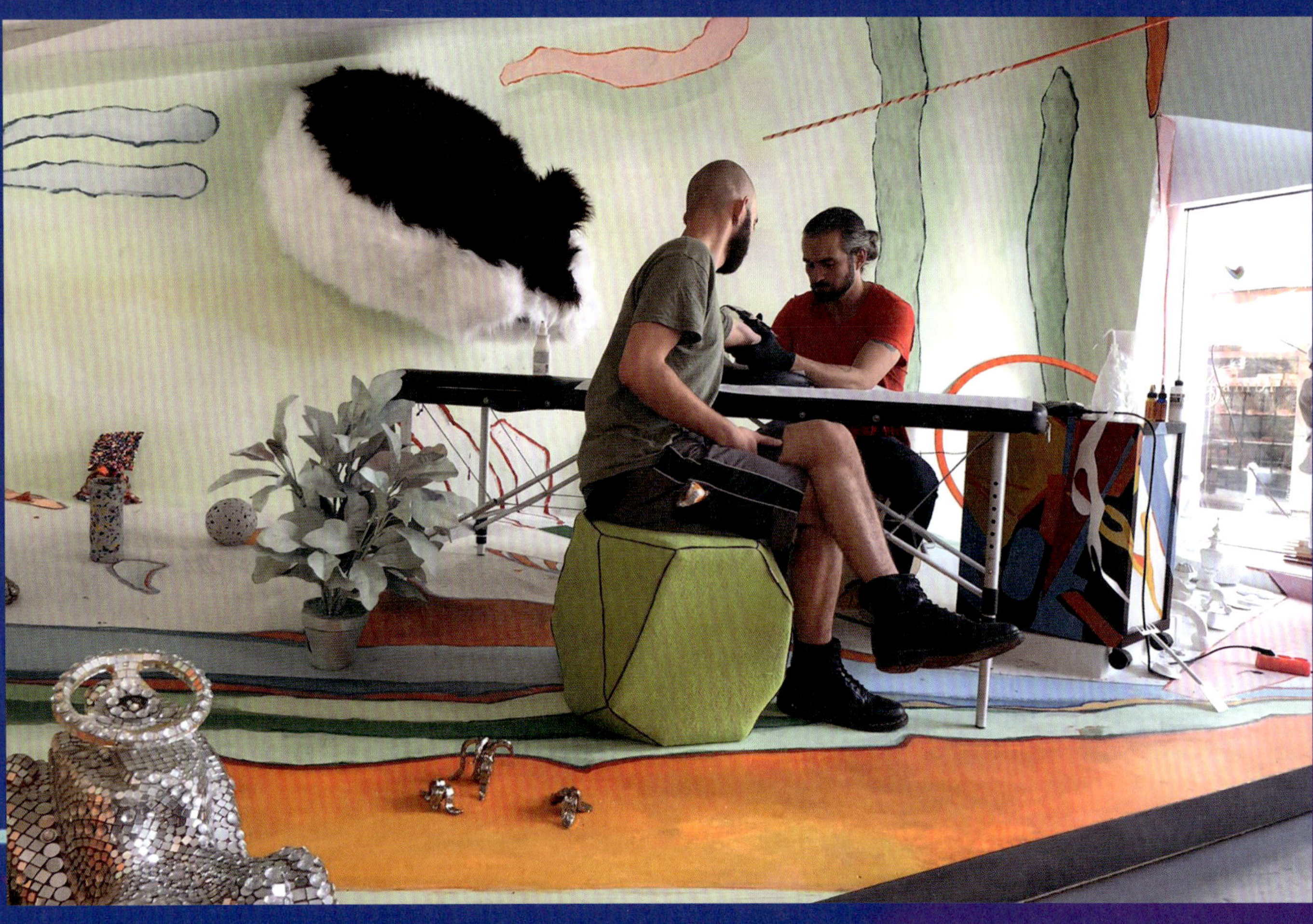

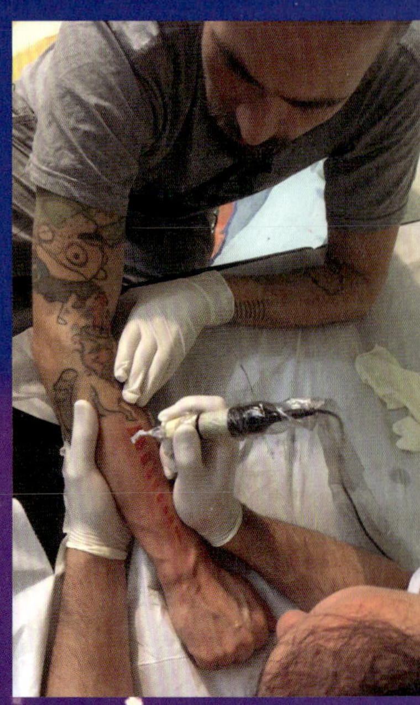

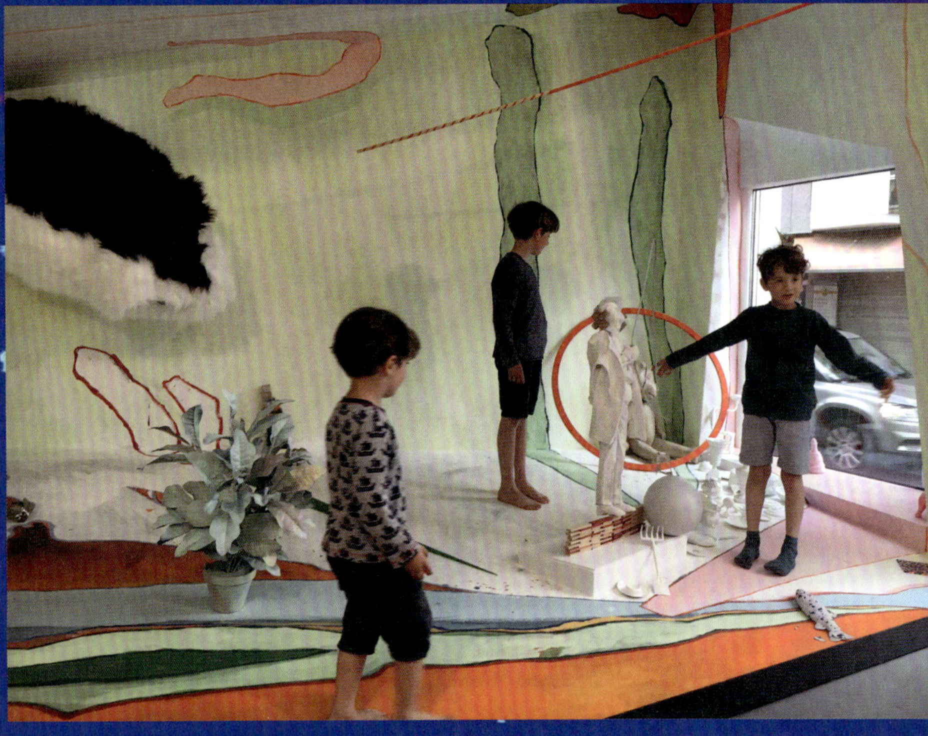

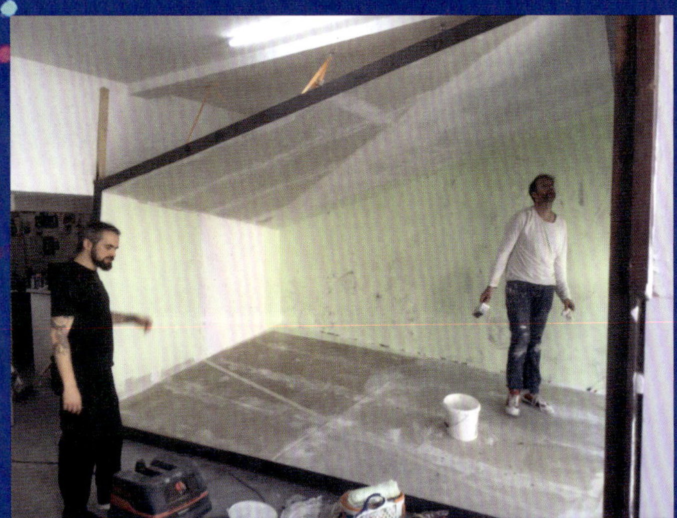

Art Supply Quarter in Bonn / Freeters Showroom

CONCEPT OF THE S.Y.L.A.N T E N H E I M

The central offering of S.Y.L.A.H.Q is S.Y.L.A. (Support Your Local Art). It offers unconditionally support for local artists in the form of space, organization and publication. Since April 2012, the project has been managed by DEMECO & PASQUALE.

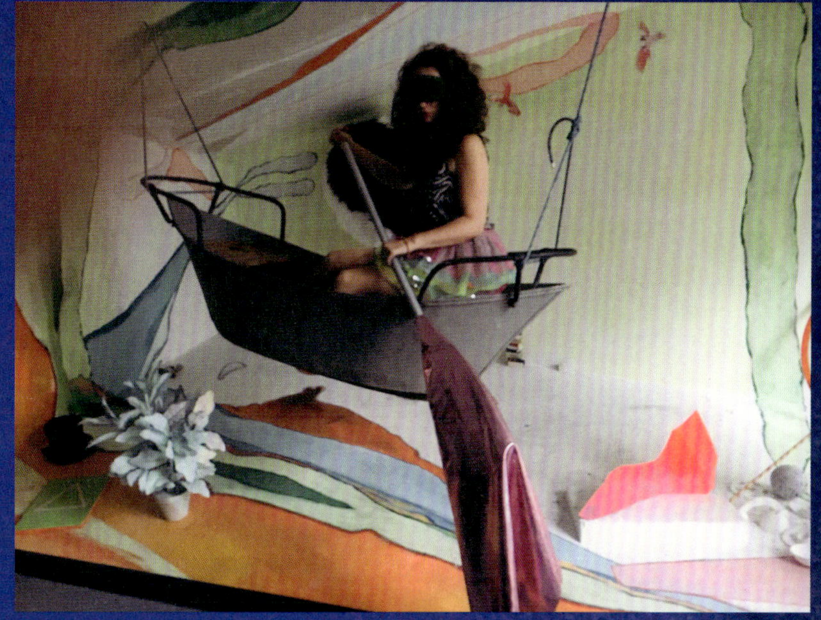

§1 Every person, animal, thing and community have, in the sense of art, a right to S.Y.L.A. (Support Your Local Art).

§2 Once a S.Y.L.A.PPLICATION has been submitted, a temporary right to reside is granted.

§3 There is no obligation to reside.

§4 Nos. 1 through 3 apply, under consideration of the freedom of art as set forth in the German Basic Law, Art. 5, Paragraph 3.

ART NEEDS ART

i need art.
you need art.
he needs art.
she needs art.
it needs art.
we need art.
you need art.
they need art.

i needed art.
you needed art.
he needed art.
she needed art.
it needed art.
we needed art.
you needed art.
they needed art.

i was in need of art.
you were in need of art.
he was in need of art.
she was in need of art.
it was in need of art.
we were in need of art.
you were in need of art.
they were in need of art.

i will have need of art.
you will have need of art.
he will have need of art.
she will have need of art.
it will have need of art.
we will have need of art.
you will have need of art.
they will have need of art.
i have need of art.

i will need art.
you will need art.
he will need art.
she will need art.
it will need art.
we will need art.
you will need art.
they will need art.

i have need of art.
you have need of art.
he has need of art.
she has need of art.
it has need of art.
we have need of art.
you have need of art.
they have need of art.

you have need of art.
he has need of art.
she has need of art.
it has need of art.
we have need of art.
you have need of art.
they have need of art.

i would need art.
you would need art.
he would need art.
she would need art.
it would need art.
we would need art.
you would need art.
they would need art.

FUNNY PRODUCTS

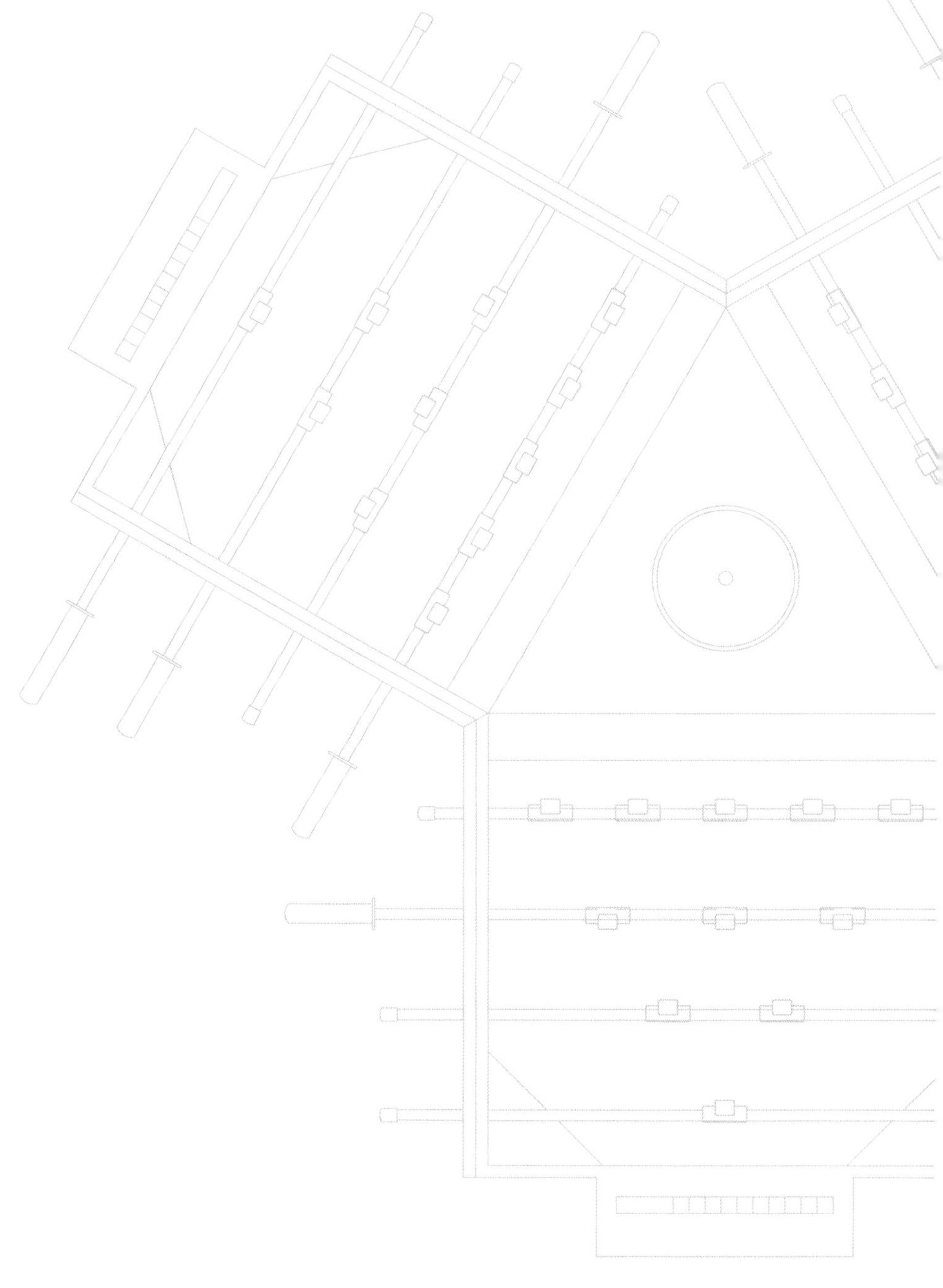

Funny Products are usually multiples that appear in very small editions.

Exceptions, however, are products that are ready for series production, such as the Y-Kicker, or immaterial works such as songs or jokes. They usually develop from spontaneous ideas but are based on serious questions posed during a working process with a client or for purely formal and aesthetic reasons. The answers or solutions to them can be sarcastic, irrational, or crazy. In any case, humor and jokes are the driving force of these Funny Products.

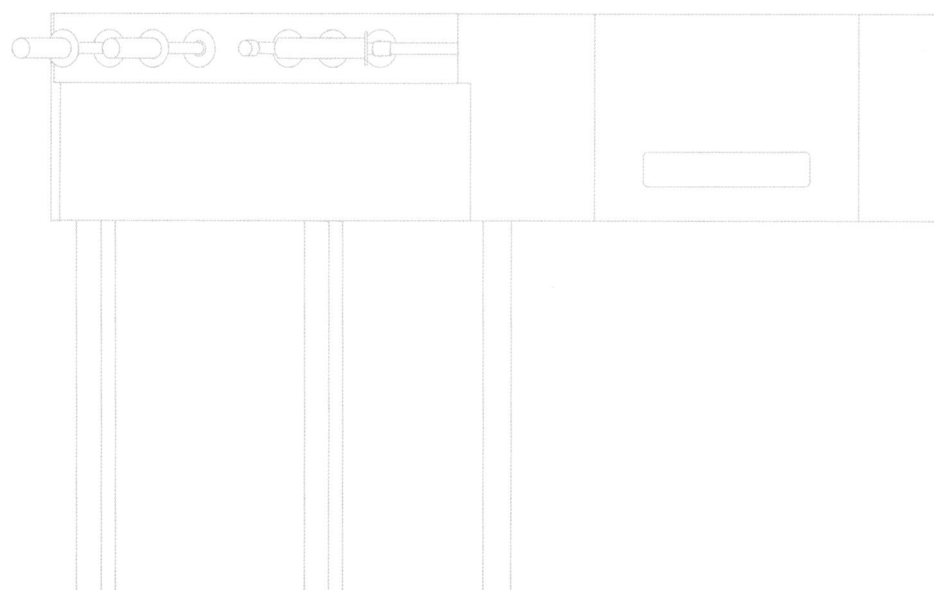

Y-KICKER

Thinking outside the box, playing out of bounds, or simply subverting a game by adding a third party – the Y-Kicker is a fascinating way to play around with these ideas. The Y-Kicker is an ingenious Y-shaped foosball table. The idea came to Ben Beyer spontaneously, but it was actually first conceived by the Danish Situationist Asger Jorn. In contrast to conventional foosball, in which the winner is determined by the most goals scored, in three-sided foosball the balls kicked into one's goal are simply counted. The team that allows the fewest balls past their goal posts by the end of the match wins the game.

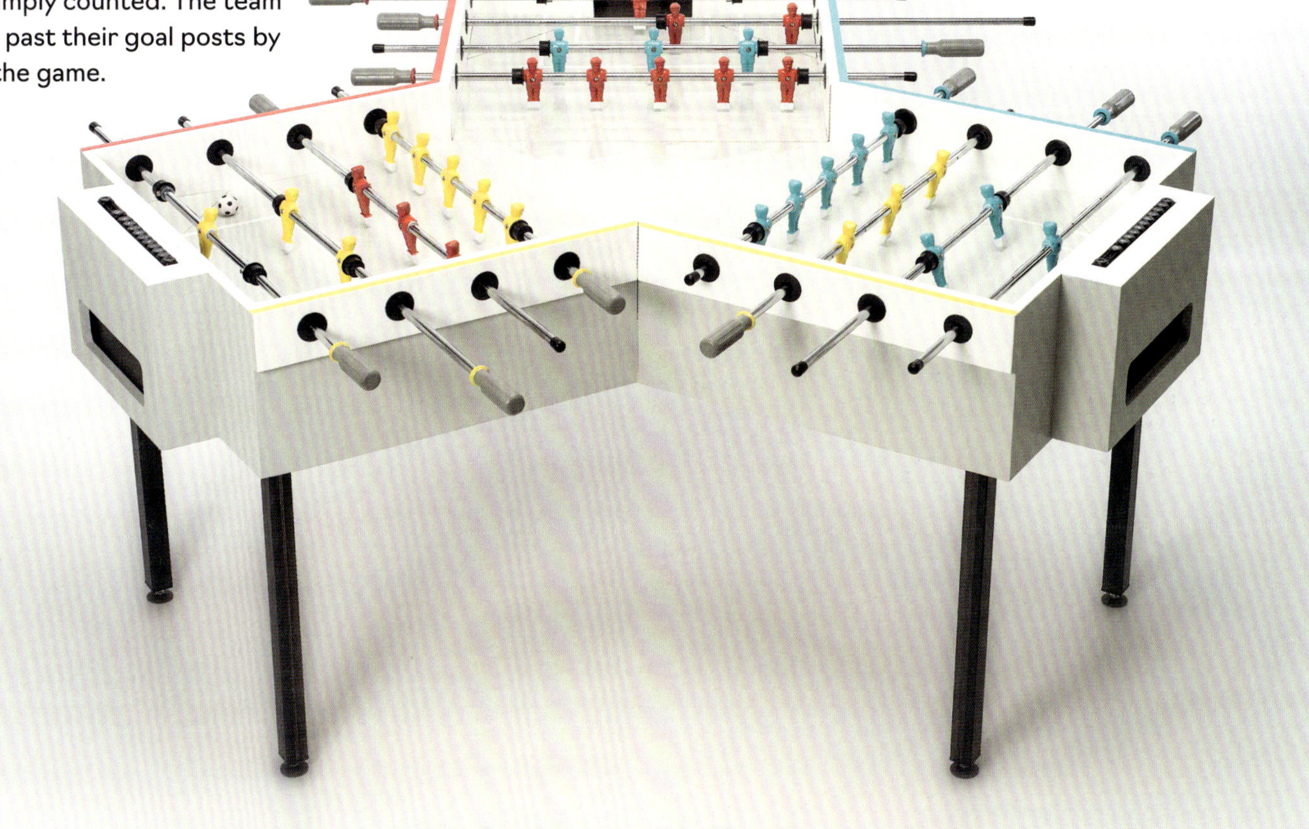

ESSENZ DES RIZZENWASSERS

How we came up with essence of this "essence" is no longer clearly traceable. Probably the idea developed over a long period of time until this multiple was added to the Funny Products portfolio. It was designed exclusively for internal applications but can be used externally at one's own discretion. It is a diluted concentrate of successful spiritual secretions, although the alchemical process of its production cannot be detailed here. After ingesting the Ritzenwasser, besides getting a euphoric, intoxicating, and stimulating effect, there is also the possibility for an increased color sensation, at correspondingly high doses. People under 18 years of age are advised not to consume it, unless in a homeopathic potency, e.g. D3.

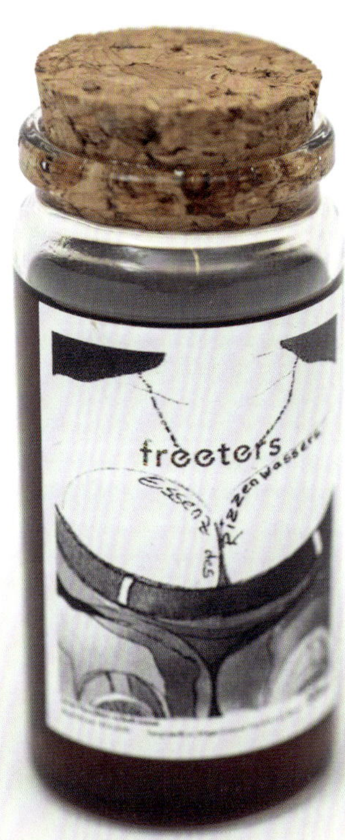

KANTENÖL

During the development of our objects, often a chair or a table, cooperating with safety officers is not always mandatory but often unavoidable. At least in Germany, the edge radius of a tabletop is checked by safety officers to help prevent injuries. The radius of a rounded corner must measure at least two millimeters so that the tabletop can be removed. Since, due to the safety officer's subjective decision, the radius was determined to be too small (although objectively the tabletop complied with the standard) a remedy was found through the development of Kantenöl. Any sharp edge, scalpel, or needle becomes smooth and dull by applying a little cutting oil.

In addition, it can be used as a perfume and of course helps in the treatment of blunt injuries and reduces the development of bruises. As a room fragrance it is especially good as it supports clear thinking and reduces prejudice. In addition, it is an excellent solvent and reliably removes dirt.

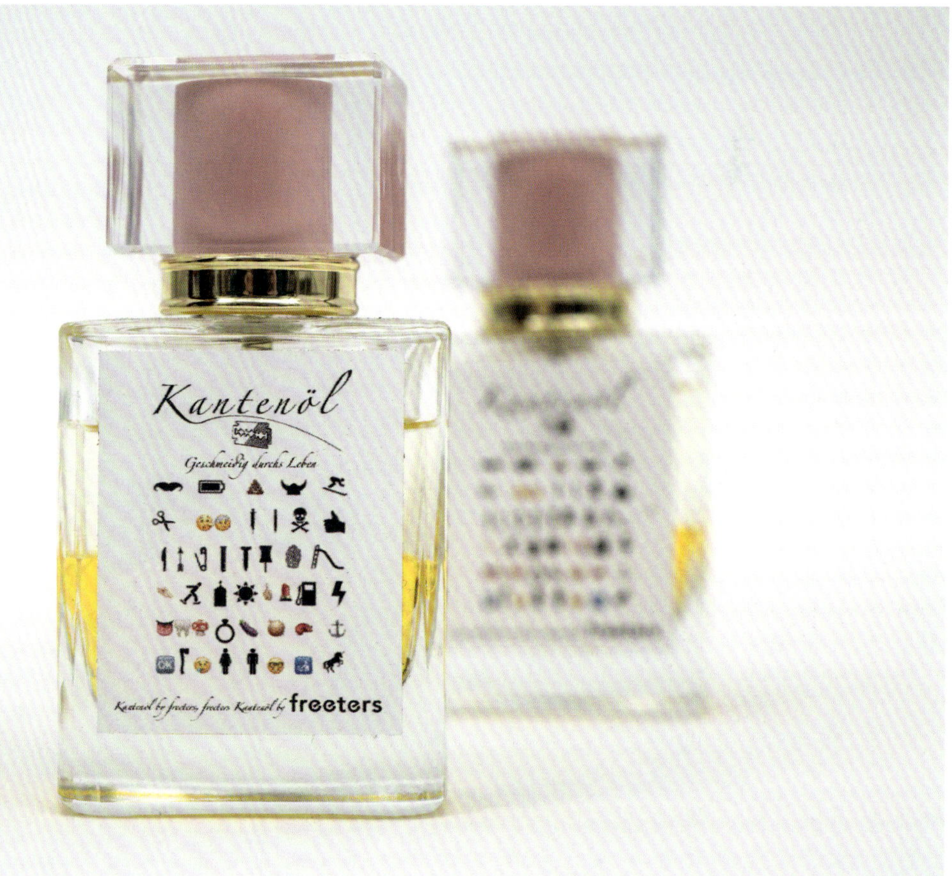

LOLLIPOP

When looked up in the glossary, the adjective "creative" and even the noun "creativity" are listed as "forbidden words." Therefore, in the following, these words will be referred to as "cr."

What at first glance may seem contradictory for an artist collective is in essence correct and important. The term "cr." has its origin in the Latin word "creare" which means to create, to generate, to choose.

This kind of activity is for artists unconditionally necessary and expedient for making a living. Artists make things. Things, concepts, music, solutions, and the absurd. "Cr." is, for example, nowadays demanded as a general solution approach in enterprises, as well as praised as an individual, desirable, and learnable ability. Whoever is a "cr." is "cr." Those who are not are left behind and without a future.

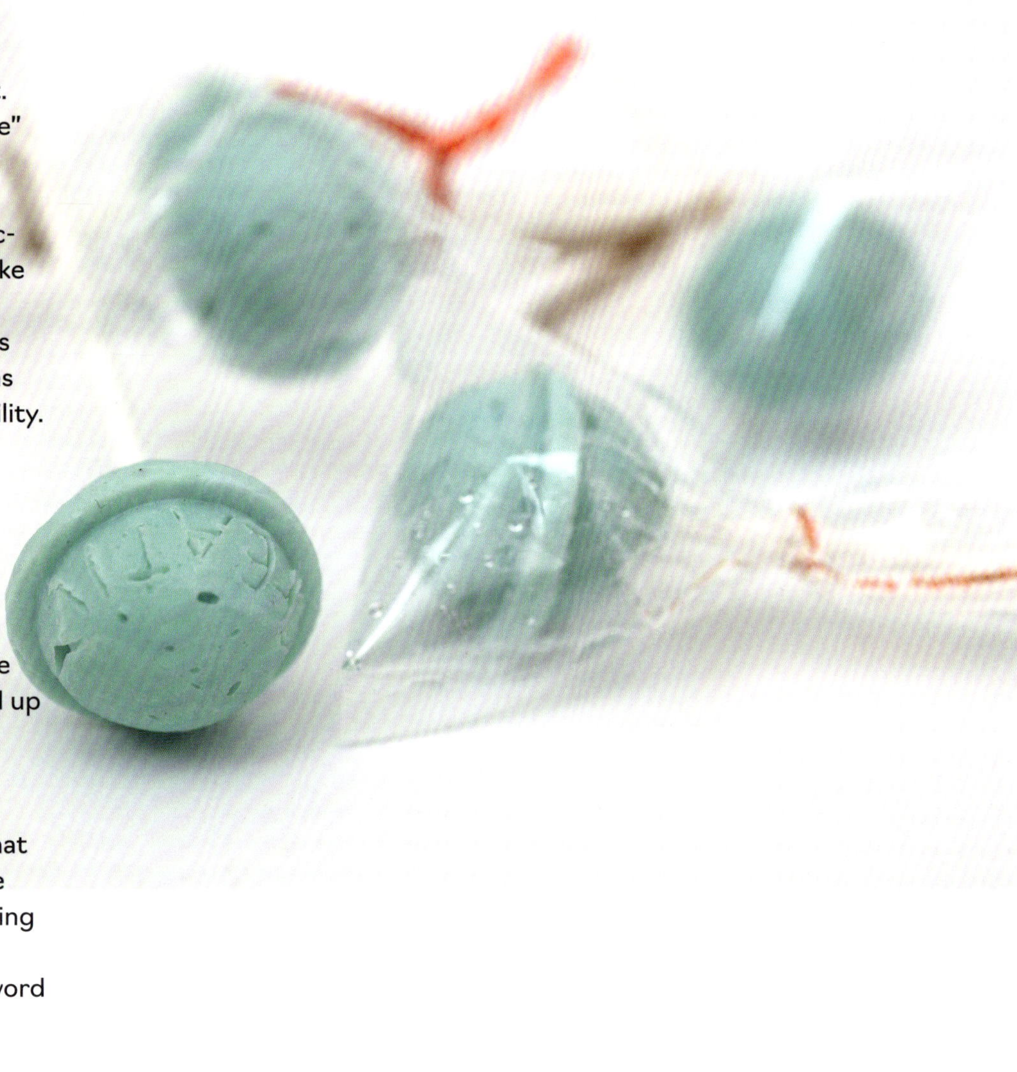

Besides, and here is where we find the origin of the ban, it is just a charming word that is mostly hot air. Like a spotlight, which directs the attention of the observer to the beam of light and distracts from the dark. It has degenerated into a shell of a word, used up in meaning and only a placeholder for vanity.

Children who utter a forbidden word are often told to go wash their mouths out with soap. Assuming that our ban on the word has little chance of success, we have developed the "Cr." Lollipop. A lollipop consisting of the best hard soap and high-quality hydrophilic pigments is sucked after the use of the forbidden word until the writing on the lollipop is no longer legible.

The effect of this educational invention can be summarized as follows: Freeters no longer hears more than the syllable "cr." in day-to-day discussions.

SIGNET RING

Not everyone gets or has a signet ring, for it is a symbol of the elite and of power, in short, it sets the wearer apart from the common rabble. Basically it can be used as proof of authenticity and as a safety precaution. As an ornament on the finger, it serves an aesthetic purpose as well as a practical one. The signet ring by Freeters is made by a 3D printer, and it bears the inscription “OB DU,” which means “whether you” in English. More specifically, “OB DU” is just the beginning of a question that is not asked.

Our work processes with each other or with clients are sometimes characterized by misinterpretations, misunderstandings, false assumptions, and, in rare cases, by obtuseness or even a lack of comprehension. The safety review process of our works does not always seem to make sense, and inquiries are sometimes not answered but are assertions to which we must be guided (even when it is a subjective assessment of a corner radius). Such a process does not always seem to be sensible and expedient. “OB DU” developed into the question of all questions, for people cannot be guided to a constructive discourse with good words and/or a patient ear.

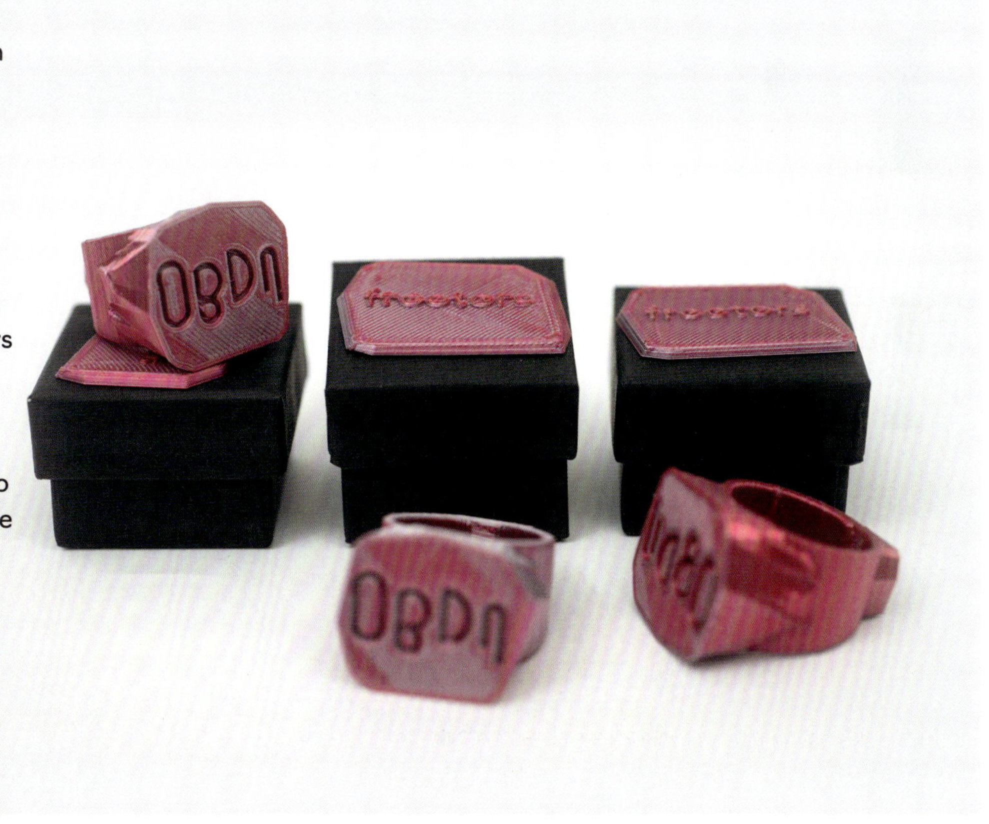

This has resulted in further puns that are unfortunately difficult to translate into English. However, the signet ring does not represent just a reactive desperation to label people who negate any constructive and process-oriented cooperation. Rather, anyone who has been subjugated by bureaucratic processes can wear such a signet ring. “OB DU / WHETHER YOU” is the question of all questions, a request for help, the beginning of cooperation. Everyone needs help with pressing questions.

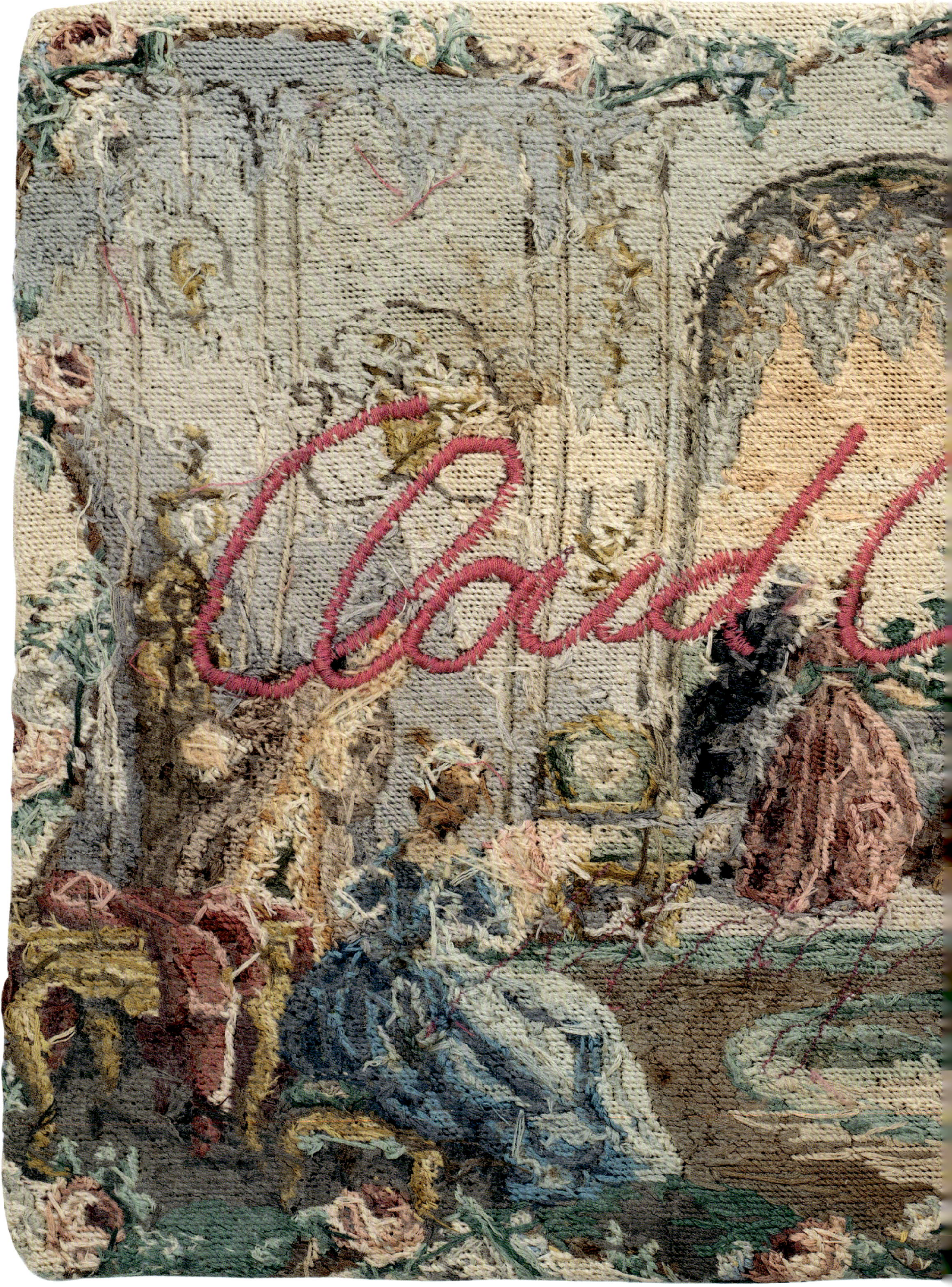

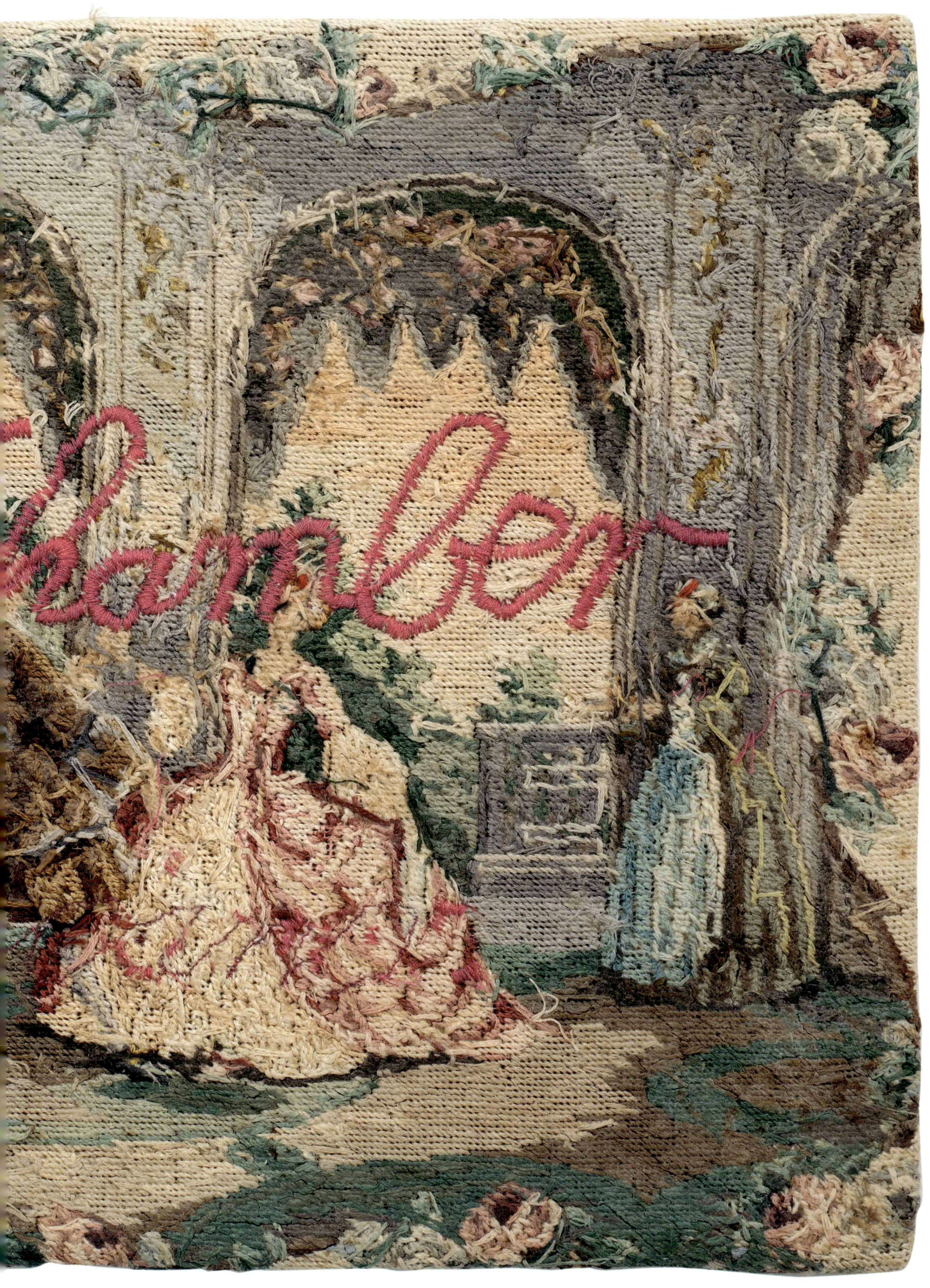
hamber

CLOUD CHAMBER

The Cloud Chamber is a real and fictional space, created by the artist collective Freeters, which serves in various ways as a source of inspiration, a community artwork, and a space for condensing and exploring different phenomena. Ideas on various themes are realized in an interdisciplinary way using different media and forms of expression, such as sculpture, painting, graphics, installation, photography, performance, and music.

Freeters is interested in opening the space to further artists as a platform for contemporary, participative, and innovative approaches. Across projects, the Cloud Chamber acts as a tool, catalyst, and driving force in all areas, such as the Process Art Thinking Projects, the workshop offerings, and the Artistic Intelligence Projects. It serves as a pure research field and stage for scaled and boundless imagination, providing space to create a number of different Cloud Chamber formats in recent years.

EPPUR SI MUOVE!

Thomas Lassner

Even if some admonishers currently fear a loss of importance of the sciences in society since the degree of social delusion and irrationality is increasing with the trend of current crises, there is rather little reason to worry that science could lose its role as a yardstick for rationality and truth. The paradigm of modernity holds unbroken that only what can be measured first and calculated second is true. Accordingly, what is only measured is considered ephemeral, what is only calculated is considered abstract. The conspiratorial belief in magic forces and hidden machinations is in the truest sense the reactionary turn against the general social principle of measuring and calculating values and people. What the individual misses in concreteness by being bound in the abstract principle of the commodity form, he recovers in superstition. At the same time, abstraction and the disciplines in which it is primarily cultivated enjoy an almost reverential standing in everyday life. What comes across as abstract is considered unimpeachable, almost sacred. Mathematics, philosophy, or even art are generally touched on superficially—for example, in friendly discussions—so as not to say anything controversial nor wrong. But it is art that does not do justice to those who think that it is the image-forming process of abstraction itself, just because cheap copies of some Kandinsky or Malevich hang in various bourgeois living rooms. As dishonest as it is to want to say anything general about "art," it is equally inaccurate to reduce it to abstraction. It shimmers in an ambivalent light, because the modern consciousness demands a definition that art resists. The supposed tendency to abstraction would elevate it to the rank of the sciences, while the shyness of definition would rather banish it to the realm of fiction. In the end, can the common distinction between art and science not be maintained at all?

Let's stay with art: in contrast to the pre-Enlightenment practice of aesthetic representation, today it is no longer clear what its exact subject matter is. The spectrum of possible subjects and techniques is wide and ever widening. Sometimes it almost seems as if the representation itself were the main object of representation. The old attempt to see the seeing. At the same time, on closer inspection, the principle of authorship is also dissolving more and more. This phenomenon is by no means a discovery of the 20th century. Even if Roland Barthes sums it up with the "death of the author," it can be assumed that aesthetic work has always been rather collaborative.[1] The genius, which is characterized above all by the fact that it can be marketed much better in the cultural industry, is first and foremost a kitschy exaggeration and not an adequate representation of artistic work. "Fine and good! But what is art now?" Someone might ask, but it cannot be grasped. Its charm lies in the fact that it keeps slipping through the fingers of definition. In analogy to the oversimplification of the answer to the question of what the world is, one could at most answer in a Dadaist way:

"It is a disk!"

The Cloud Chamber, addressed quite objectively, is neither simple, nor a disk.

It is rather a space of its own ambivalence. Originally conceived as a physical experimental setup to visualize tiny particles that cannot be seen with the naked eye, its artistic adaptation is a space where metaphors take shape. These figures are ephemeral and creatures of different authors, and thus condensations of communal activity. Each manifestation of the Cloud Chamber has an expiration date, its constellation is temporary. But these iterations are not arbitrary, even if it may seem so. As an aesthetic

1 **cf. Roland Barthes:** "The Death of the Author," in: Fotis Jannidis, Gerhard Lauer, Matías Martínez, Simone Winko (eds.): Texte zur Theorie der Autorschaft, Stuttgart 2000, pp. 185–193.

2 **cf. Artistic Intelligence.**

3 **cf. Zadie Smith:** "The I Who Is Not Me," in: Zadie Smith: Feel Free, London 2019.

4 **Walter Benjamin:** "The Work of Art in the Age of Mechanical Reproduction," 1935.

experimental setup, it is a chamber for making visible contexts of meaning that are only brought to light through collaborative work.

Its particular rationality, like artistic intelligence as a whole, consists in the ability to create ambiguity and allow for states of indecision.[2] Similarly, the British writer Zadie Smith describes her work as creating a space of nonidentity, for in the fictional world of her characters, they are at all times simultaneously identical with and distinct from the author.[3] Thus, every work lives from this indistinguishability—also for the receiver, because empathy with a character depends on identification and the tension of a developing story from the experience of the unexpected, the surprising. It is this tension that not only constitutes the quality of a good story but can also be transferred to any form of expression of aesthetic practice. The authenticity, or, to use Benjamin's term, the aura of a work always derives from the tense relationship between identity and nonidentity.[4]

Likewise, the relationship between art and science is not a trivial one. As methodologically opposed rationality practices, they nevertheless suffer loss without the other. Science without a fundamental understanding of the beautiful and sublime degenerates into a mere measuring station, art without a deeper knowledge of the mechanisms and structures of cosmic phenomena threatens to slide into arbitrariness and babble. What both spheres have in common is the curious mind that dares to ask uncertain questions, to let go of the familiar under certain circumstances, and to commit itself at the right moment.

CLOUD CHAMBER
LUDWIG VAN OR PARTITURA DEI LISTELLI

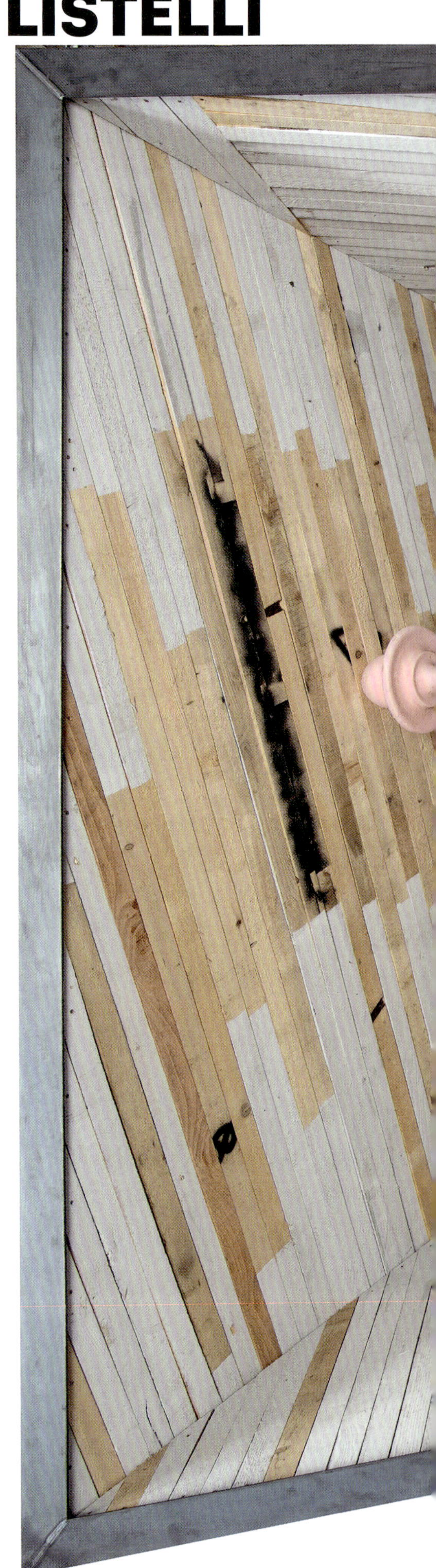

In 2020, the Beethoven Anniversary Year were celebrated with a Cloud Chamber Project.

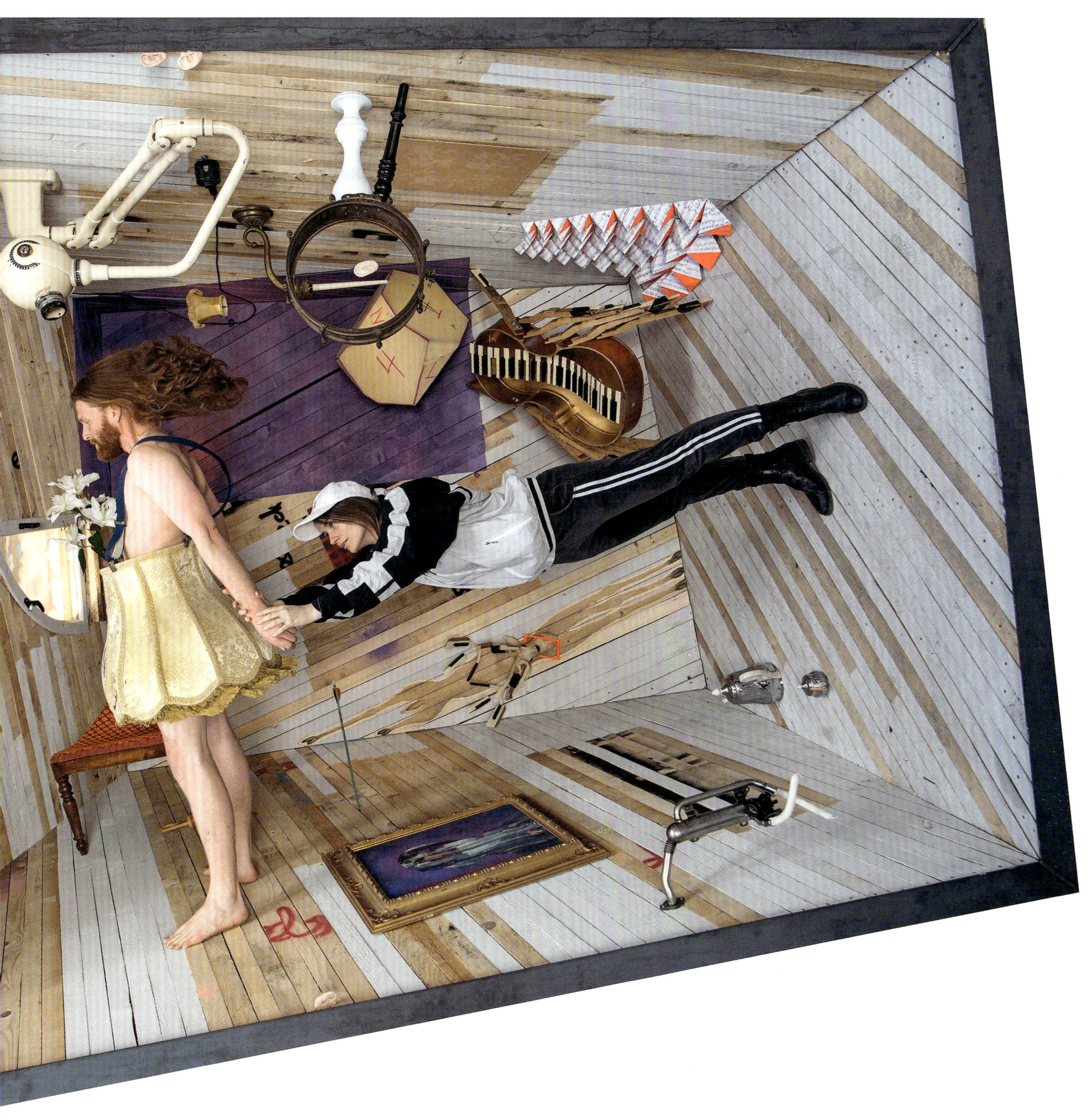

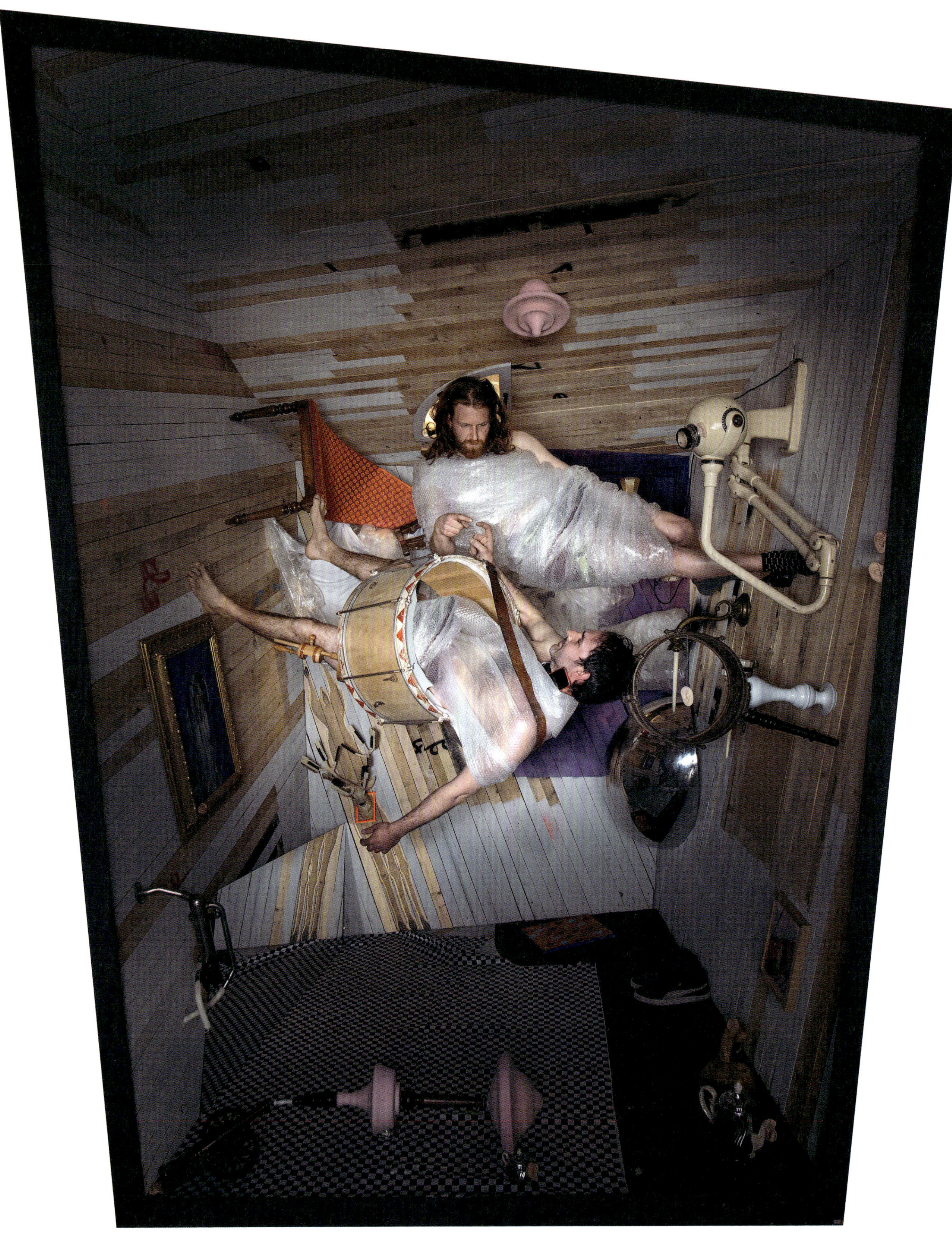

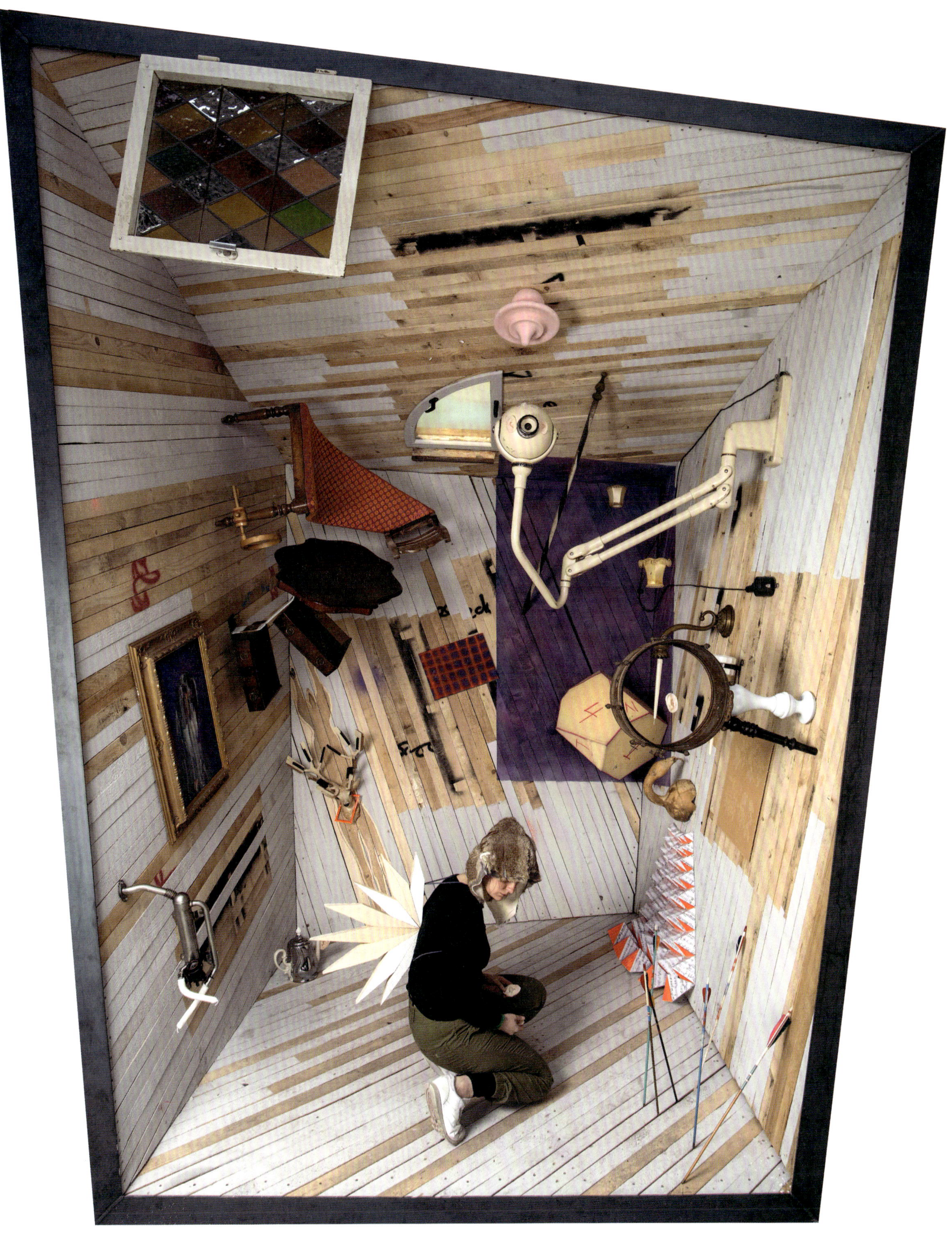

CLOUD CHAMBER
WALTERCHENS SPIELSACHEN

Exhibition project for the August Macke Festival. Inspired by August Macke's painting "Walterchens Spielsachen".

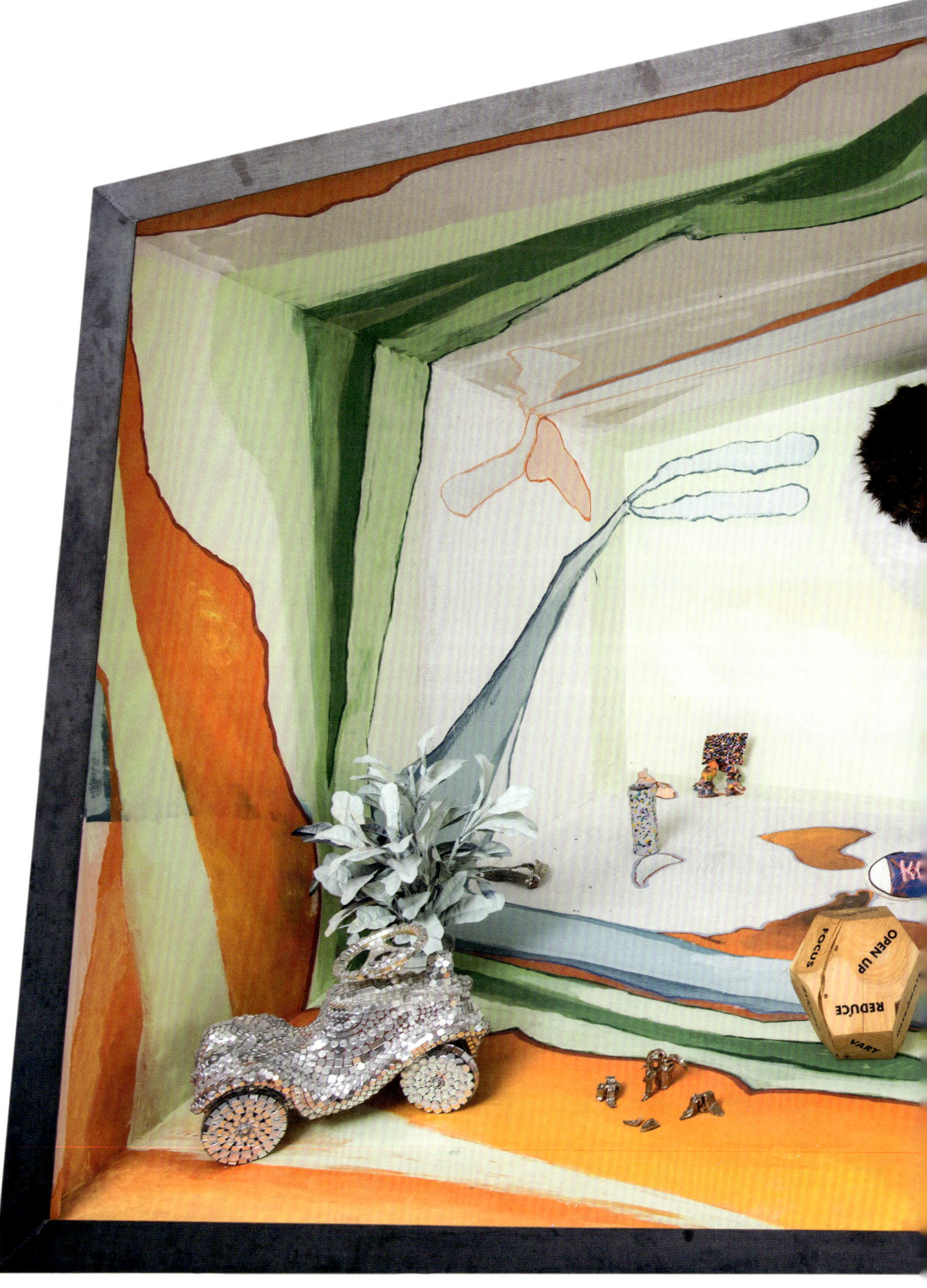

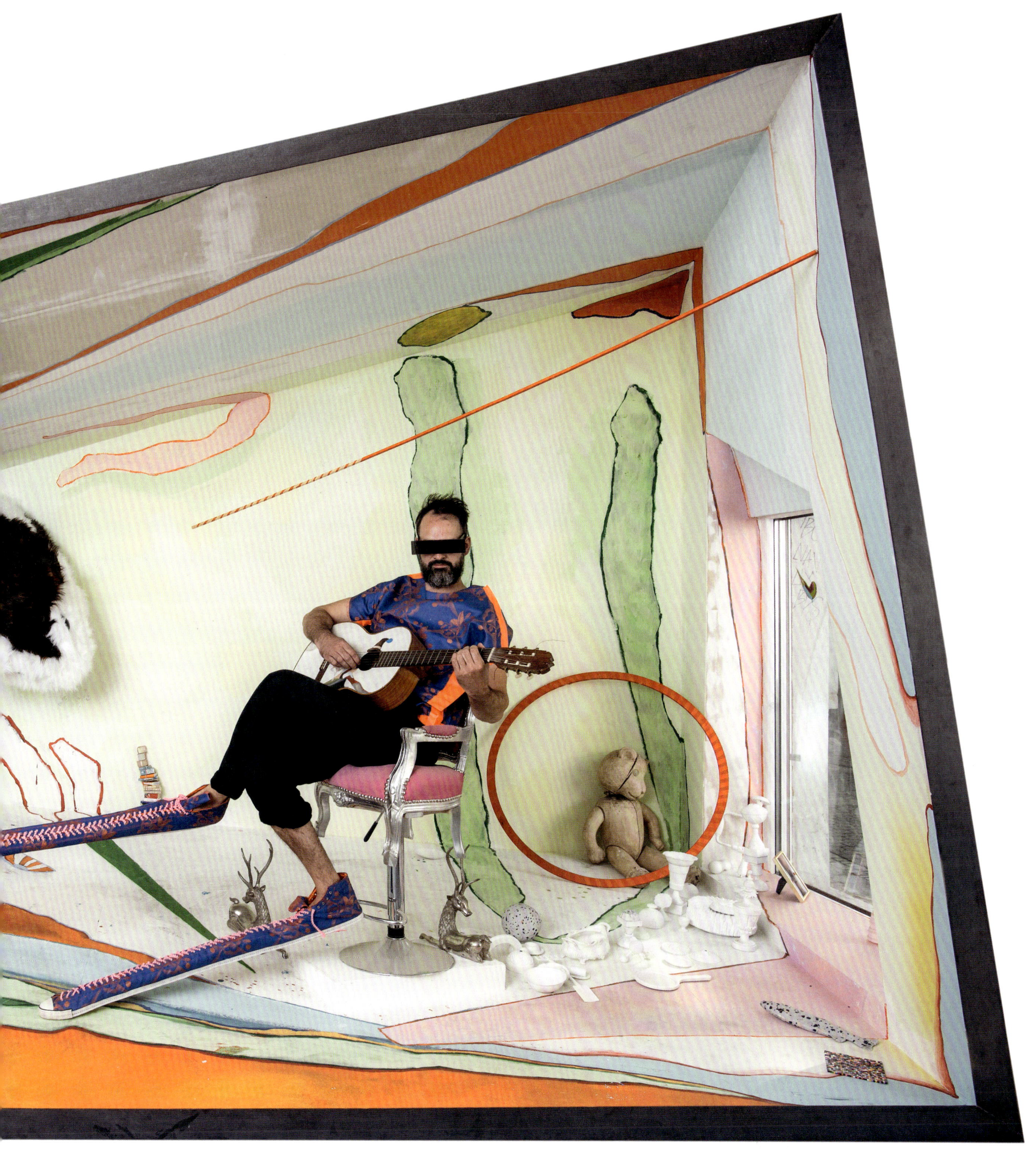

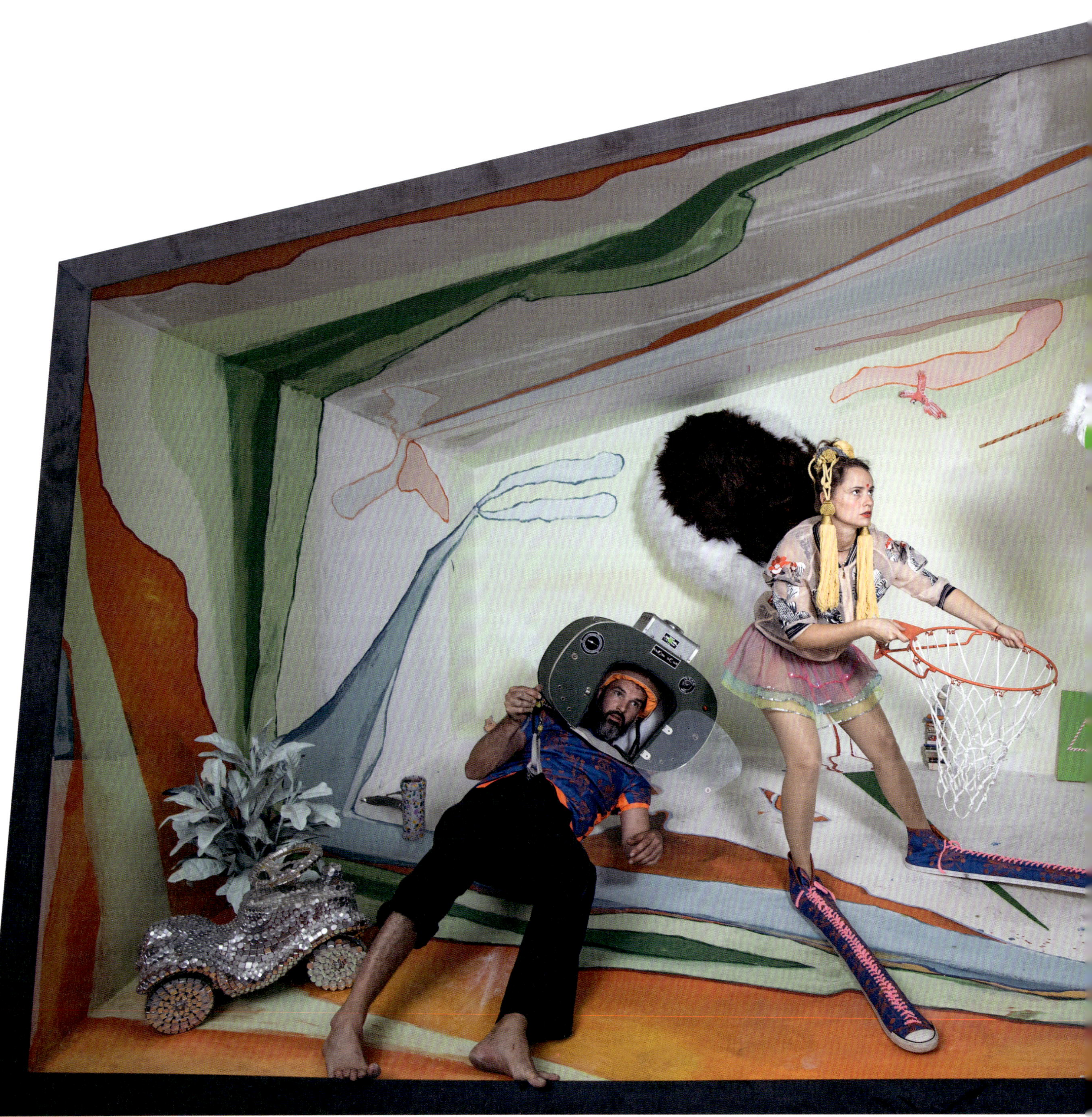

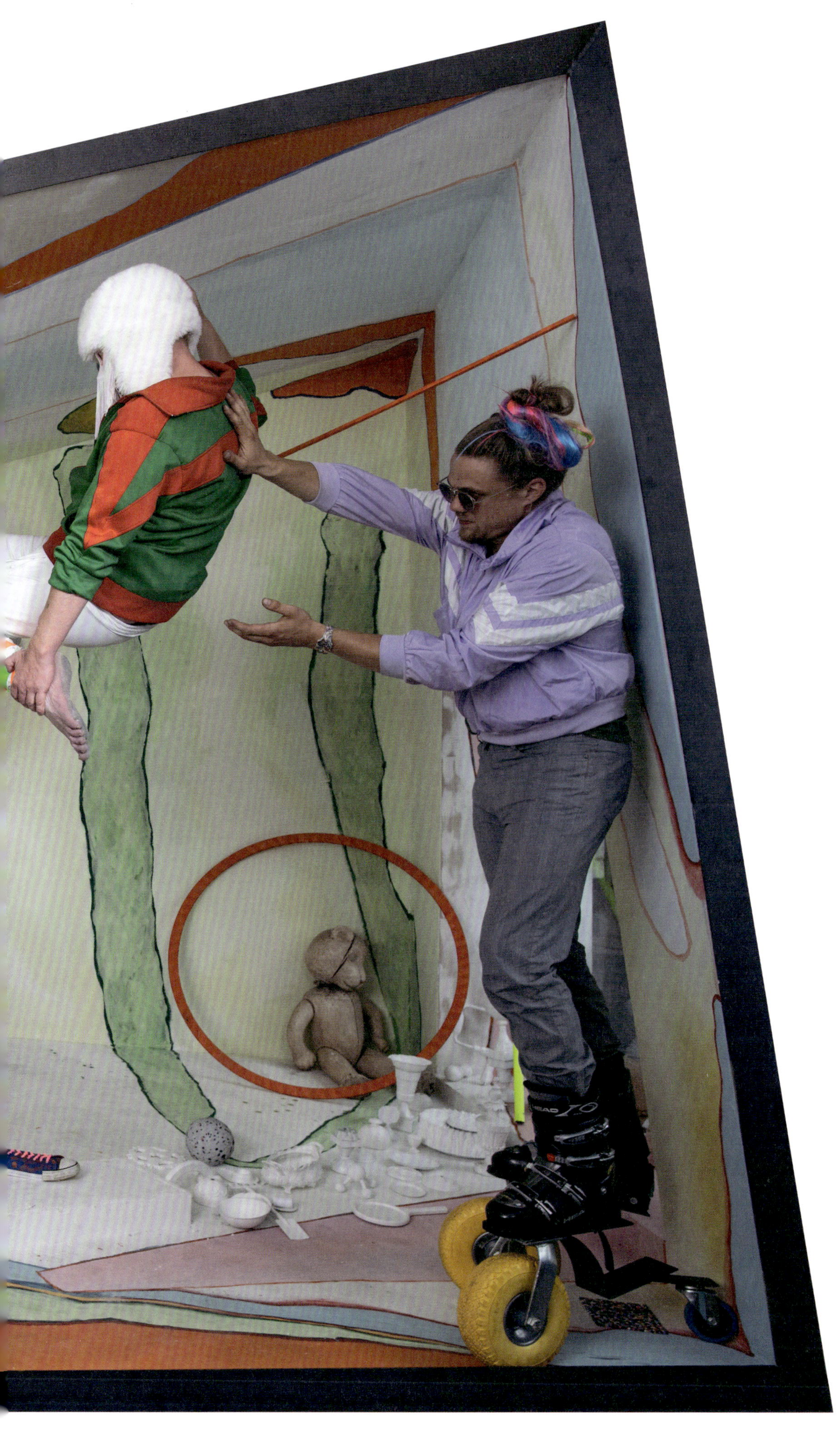

CLOUD CHAMBER
COLLECTIVE ISOLATION

2021

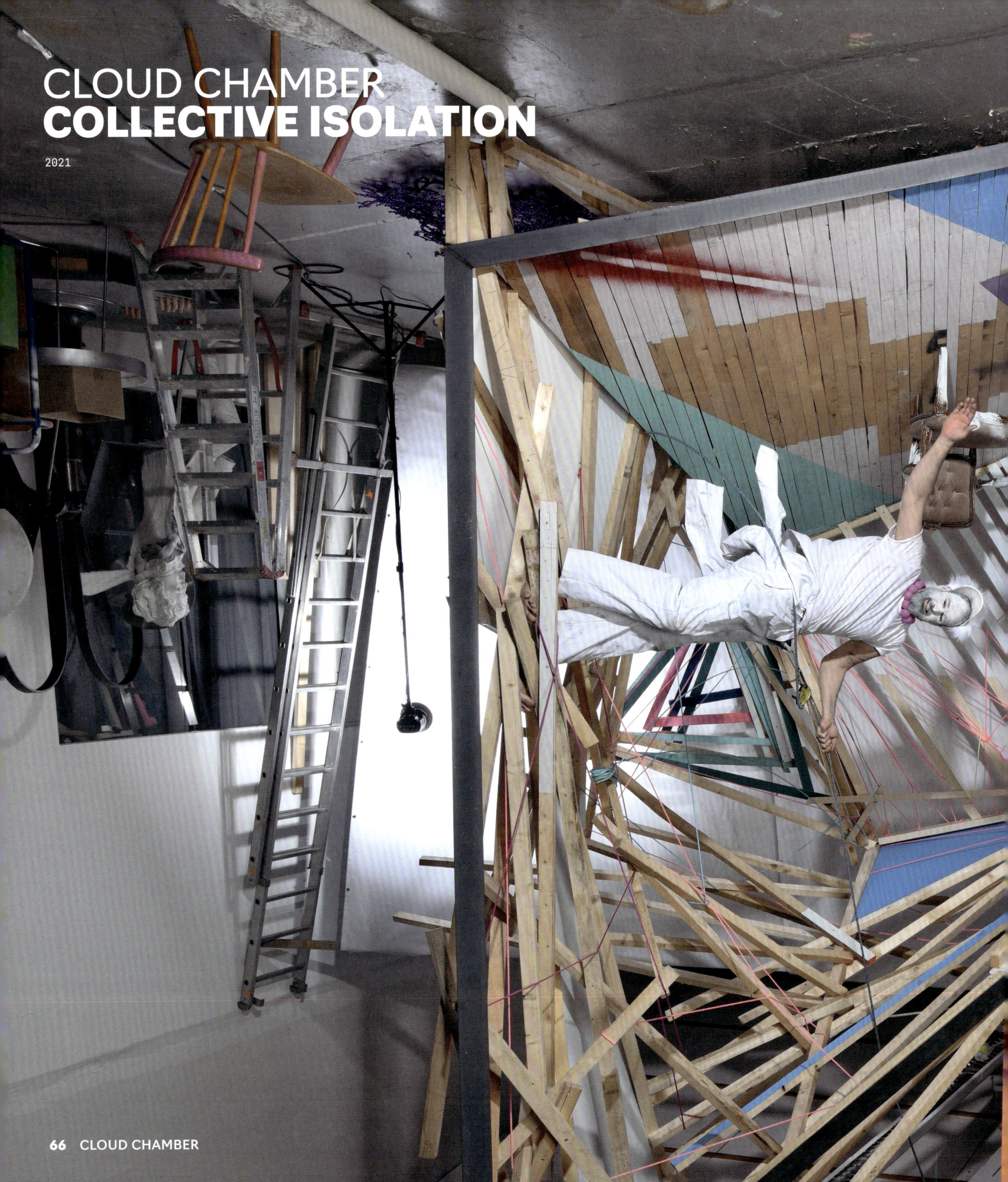

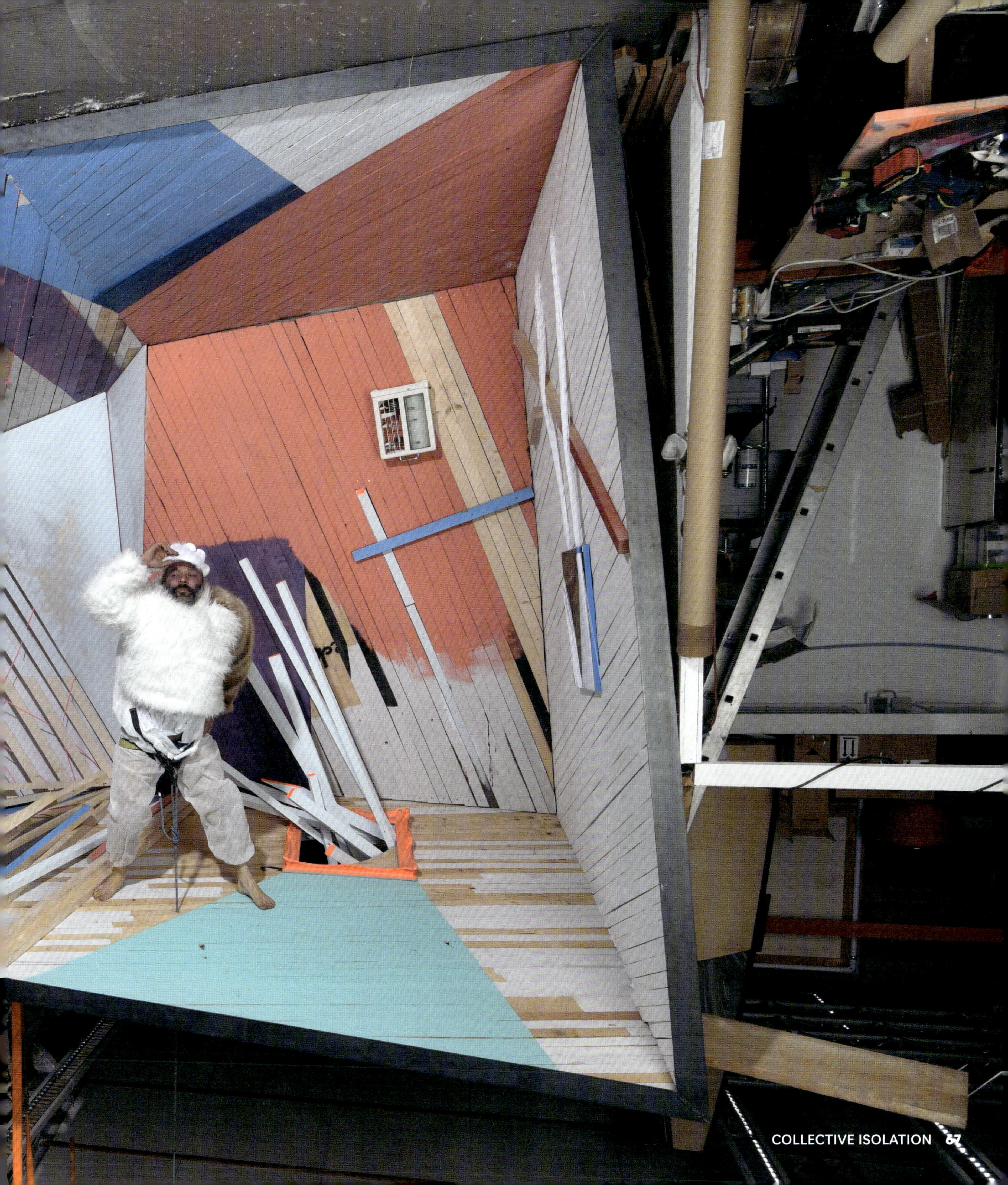

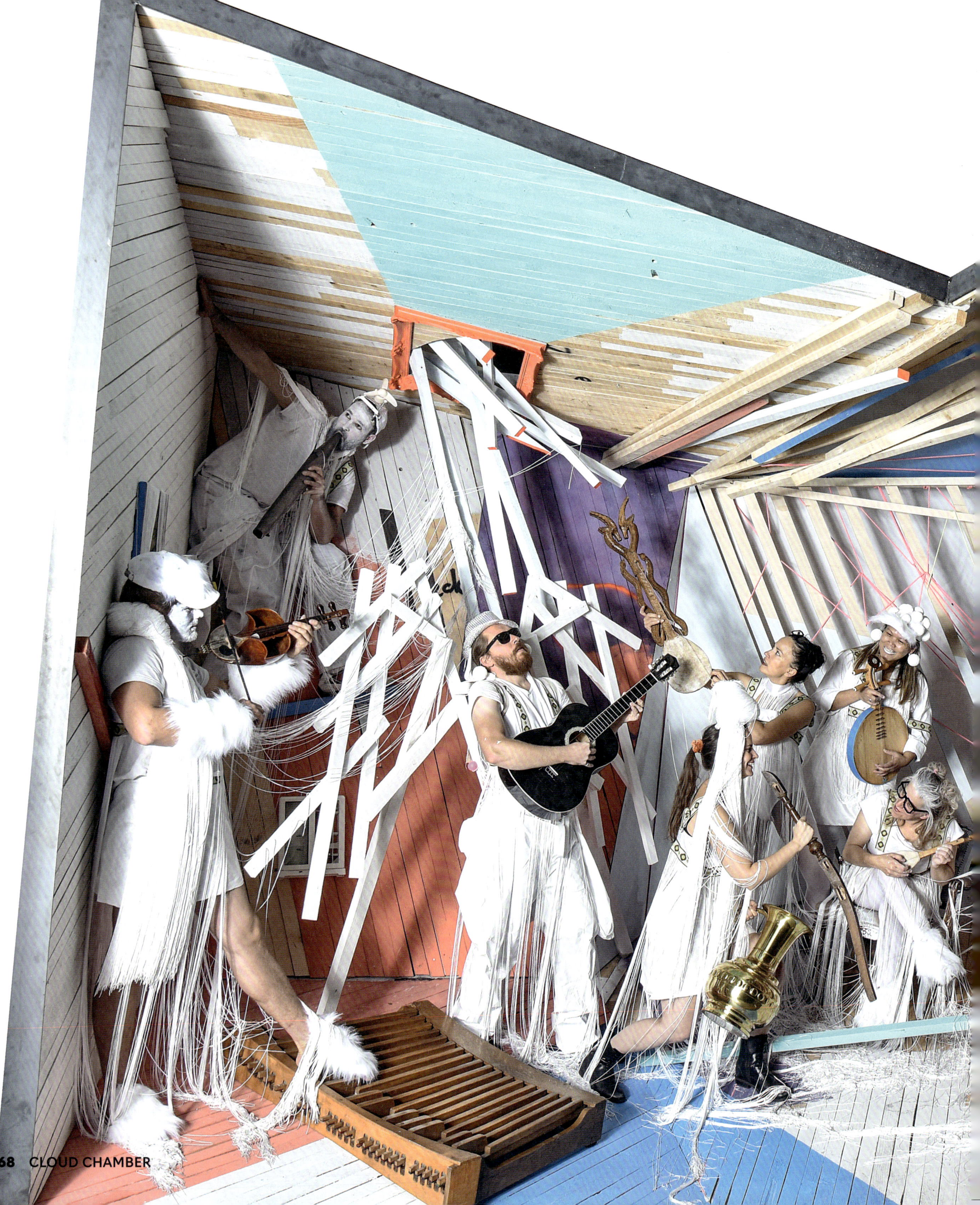

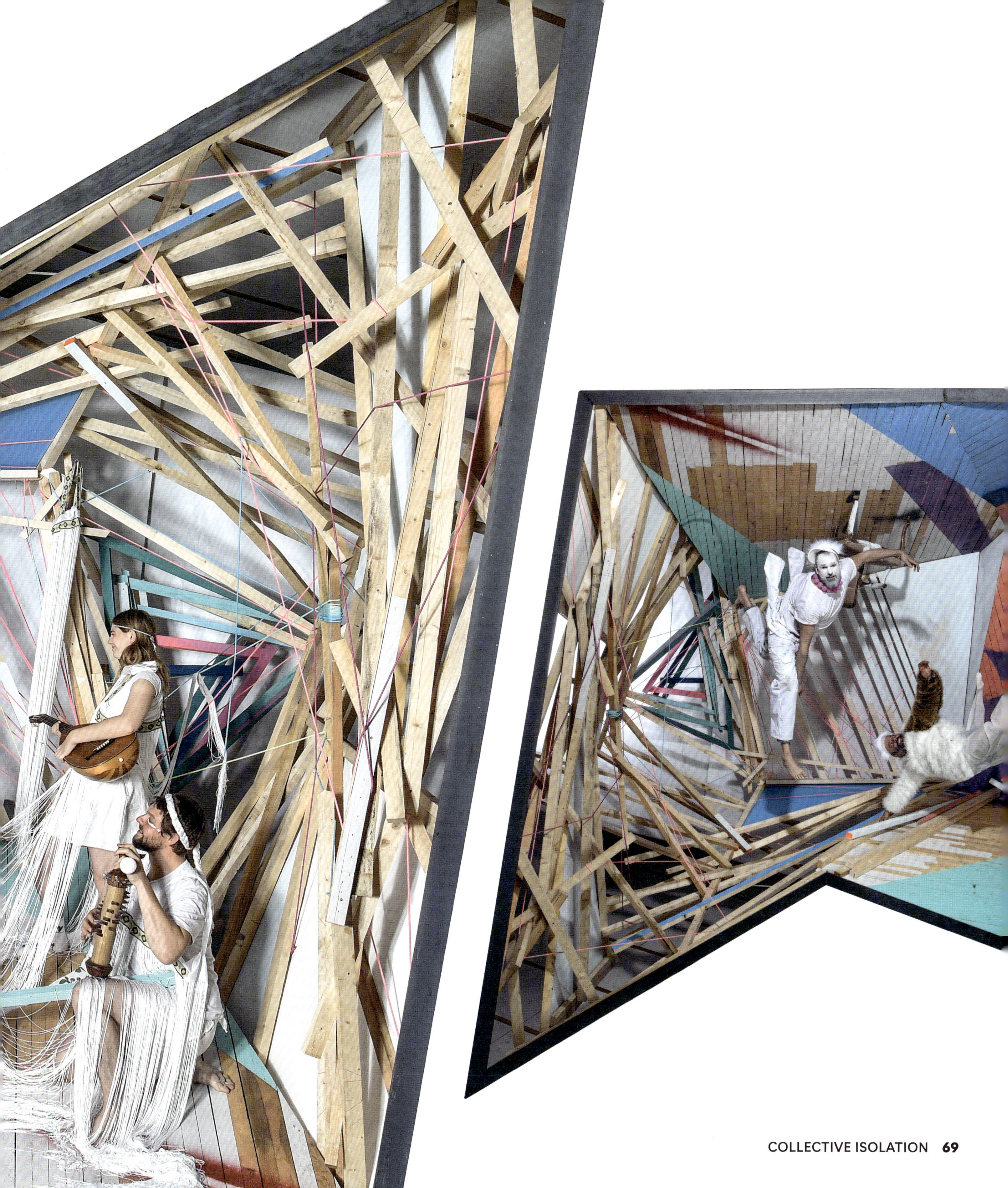

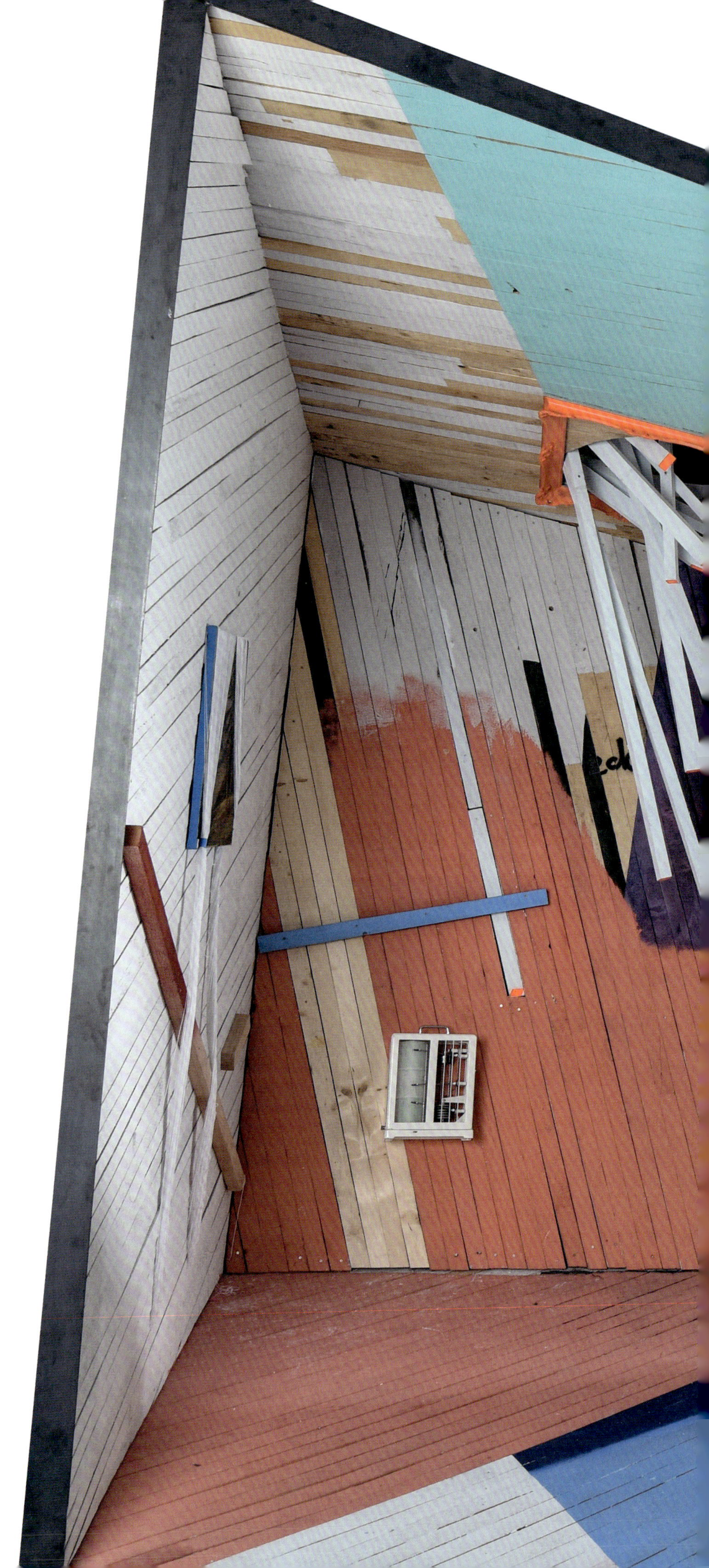

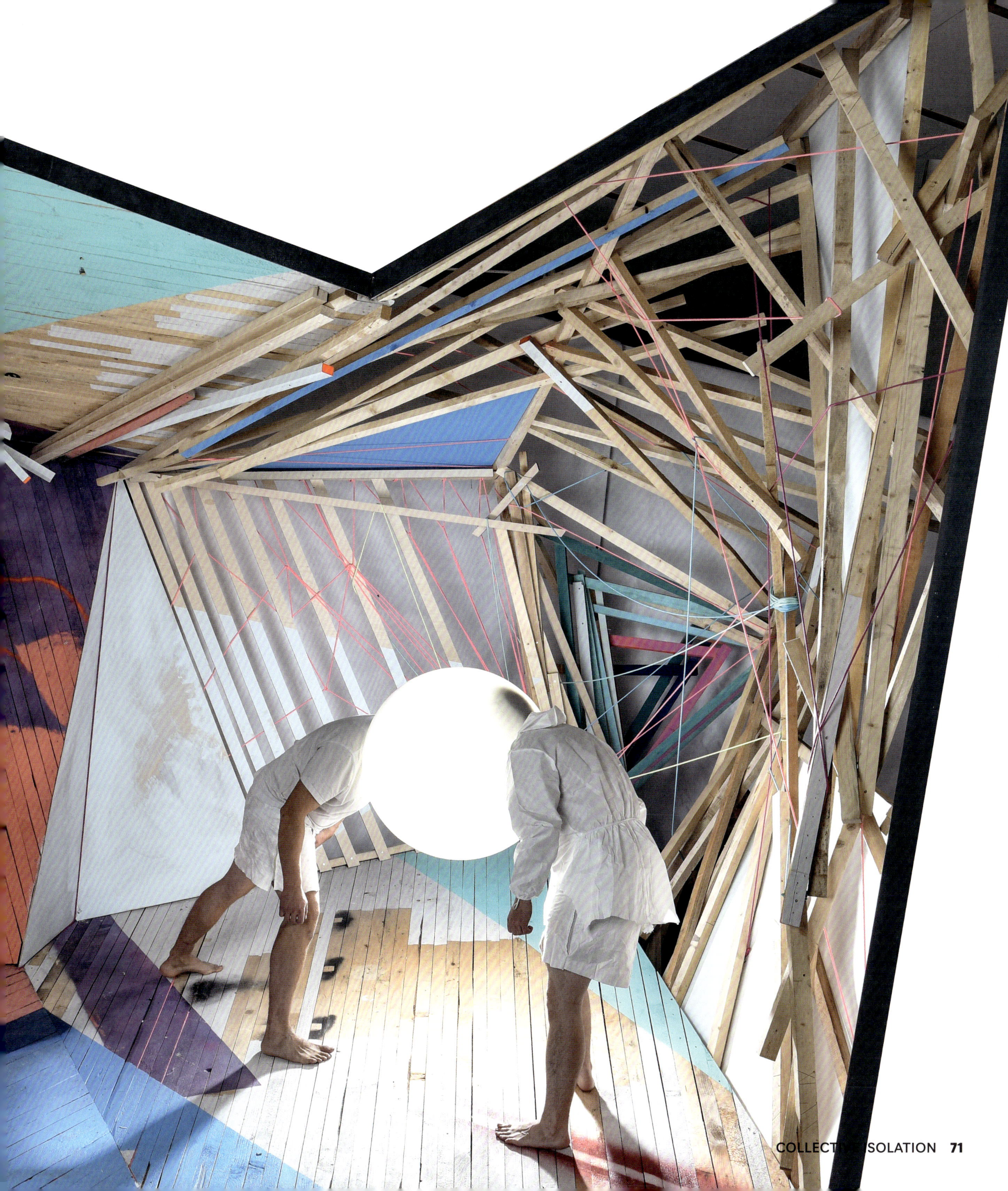

CLOUD CHAMBER
A FACE OF FIRE

2022

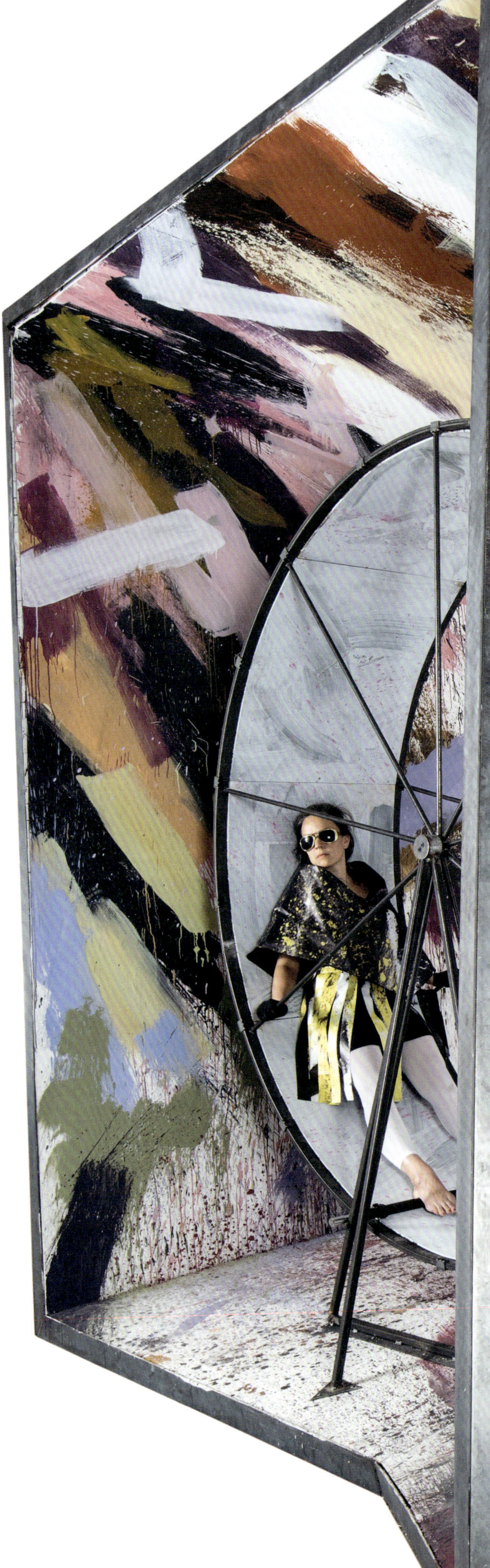

The resulting works show a parallel work to Cornelia Funke's short story. They are inspired by this and transform the core of the thoughts into a free work, which in turn could be inspiration for a new parallel work and hopefully develop into mutual back and forth play.

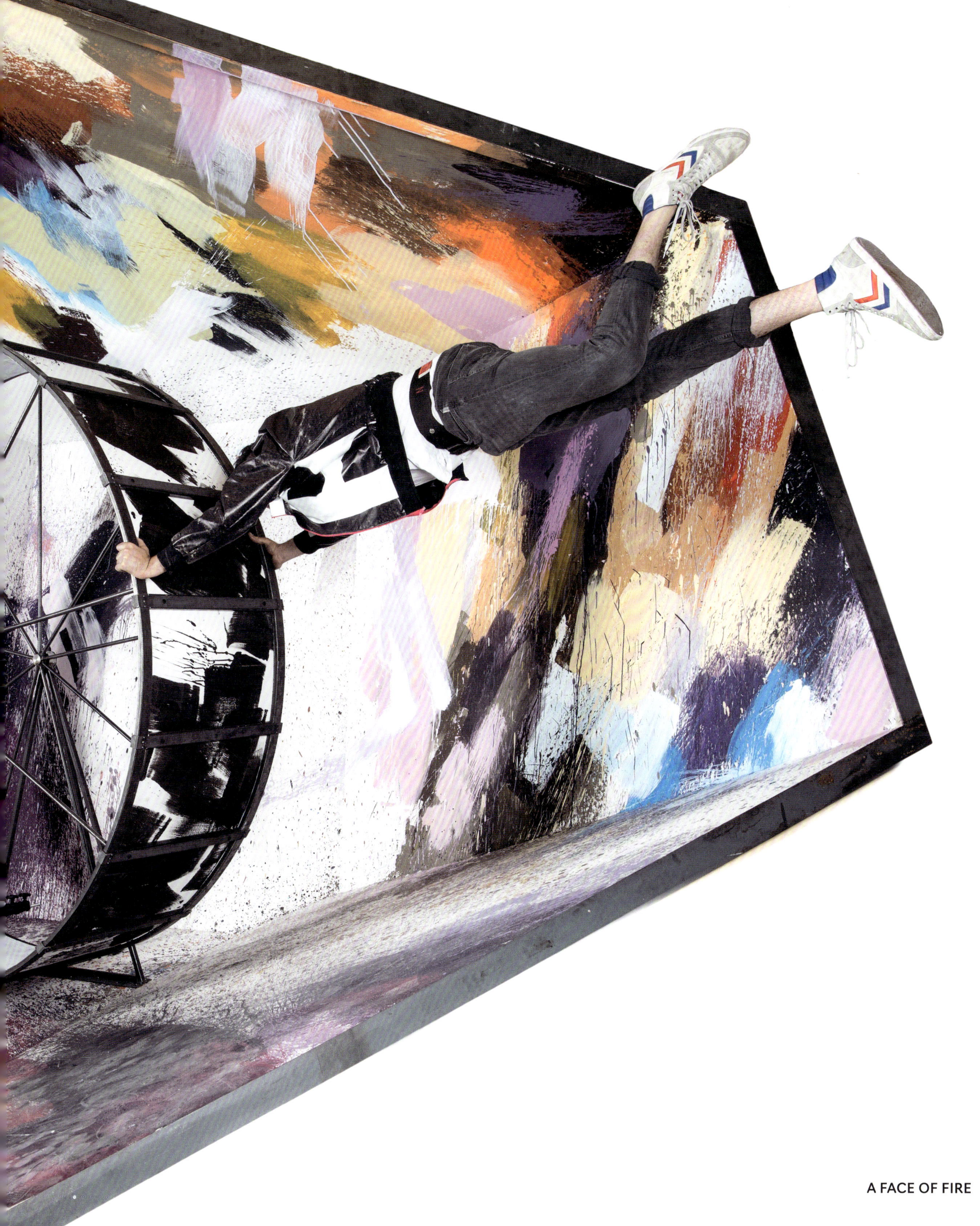

A FACE OF FIRE

Cornelia Funke

Mortal men. Soldiers, peasants, princes ... The lake showed them their faces like flotsam found on its shore. Some promised much, but when they lured them to the island, they fell for them so completely that in the end there was nothing left of them. The others liked that, but the Dark One wanted more, so much more. Maybe that's why her sisters called her the Dark One – because in the shadows of the night she dreamed of things they didn't understand.

The trees that grew on the shore of the island whispered to her that there had once been men who, like her, were immortal. They whispered that they had even been able to give them children. The Dark Fairy asked her sisters about them. "It's just a fairy tale," said one. "It was a long time ago," said another. "They stole from us and now they are gone," said the Red One, "we have wiped them out."

The Dark One carried her words to the lake and looked into the waves. The faces the water showed her drifted among the lilies as if they were glass, and the fairy stood there feeling the emptiness within her, all that terrible emptiness.

They had sown it themselves.

Her sisters filled it by breaking mortal hearts. Why wasn't that enough for her?

She took for herself a prince. A peasant. A soldier. Sometimes she didn't even know who or what they were. She didn't want to know their names, and none of them ever knew what name the water had given her. They stumbled onto the island like drunks. Most of them killed themselves when she sent them away, and returned to her still in death, to be lost as moths in her hair.

The Dark One, however, felt the emptiness each time worse than before.

So much cold.

And the endless flow of meaningless time.

She had to wait so long for him.

Of course, the red moon was over the lake when she first heard his name. The Dark One loved those nights when the water reddened as if the sky were on fire.

Kami'en. The trees whispered his name as if the wind had blown it here, from all the lips that screamed it, invoked it, sighed it, cursed it. Kami'en.

The lake did not show her his face this time. The water was too cold and damp for his skin of fire. She saw it in her dreams. As if they wanted to punish her for having stolen so often into the dreams of others.

Day after day. Night after night. Eyes of gold and a face of petrified fire.

How could she believe it would still be a game?

All those centuries nothing but moths in her hair.

Immortality made one stupid.

Would she have gone to him if she had known of the pain?

Yes.

Her sisters threatened her. How could she leave to find him? Men came to them, lured like children by the cake of sinister witches, only their bait was not sugar and cinnamon, but beauty. But the Dark One was tired of being like them. They knew nothing of the world and the world knew nothing of them. Immortal lives wasted looking at their own reflection in a lake and occasionally breaking a human heart. They were as useless as flowers without pollen, dead despite their immortality, lost in the cage they had built out of contempt, contempt for everything that was different from them.

Yes. She left her sisters, the island, and the lake to find him. She was the first to leave, the first in countless years.

The dreams showed her where she would find him. The bloody earth, the dirty tents, the fields covered with the fallen as if a farmer had sown dead bodies. The Jasper Goyl stood in her way. Hentzau. He hated her from the first moment as much as Kami'en would love her. The Jasper Dog knew immediately what she was. A fairy. His fear made him almost as weak as his hate. She passed through him like water through porous stone—and she knew all about him afterward. The moon was over the dead, and she still thought it was all a game.

Kami'en was alone.

He turned as she stepped into his tent.

His face was almost as familiar to her as her own, but he was seeing her for the first time. She had not visited him in his dreams, though he was in hers. She had wanted to stand before him when he was lost in the desire with which her beauty encompassed them all.

And she saw it.

Saw it all in his golden eyes.

But then it was she who was lost. In the untamedness of his heart. His strength. The echo of his own hunger for more, always more.

He was fire burning on water.

And the game was lost.

For the first time.

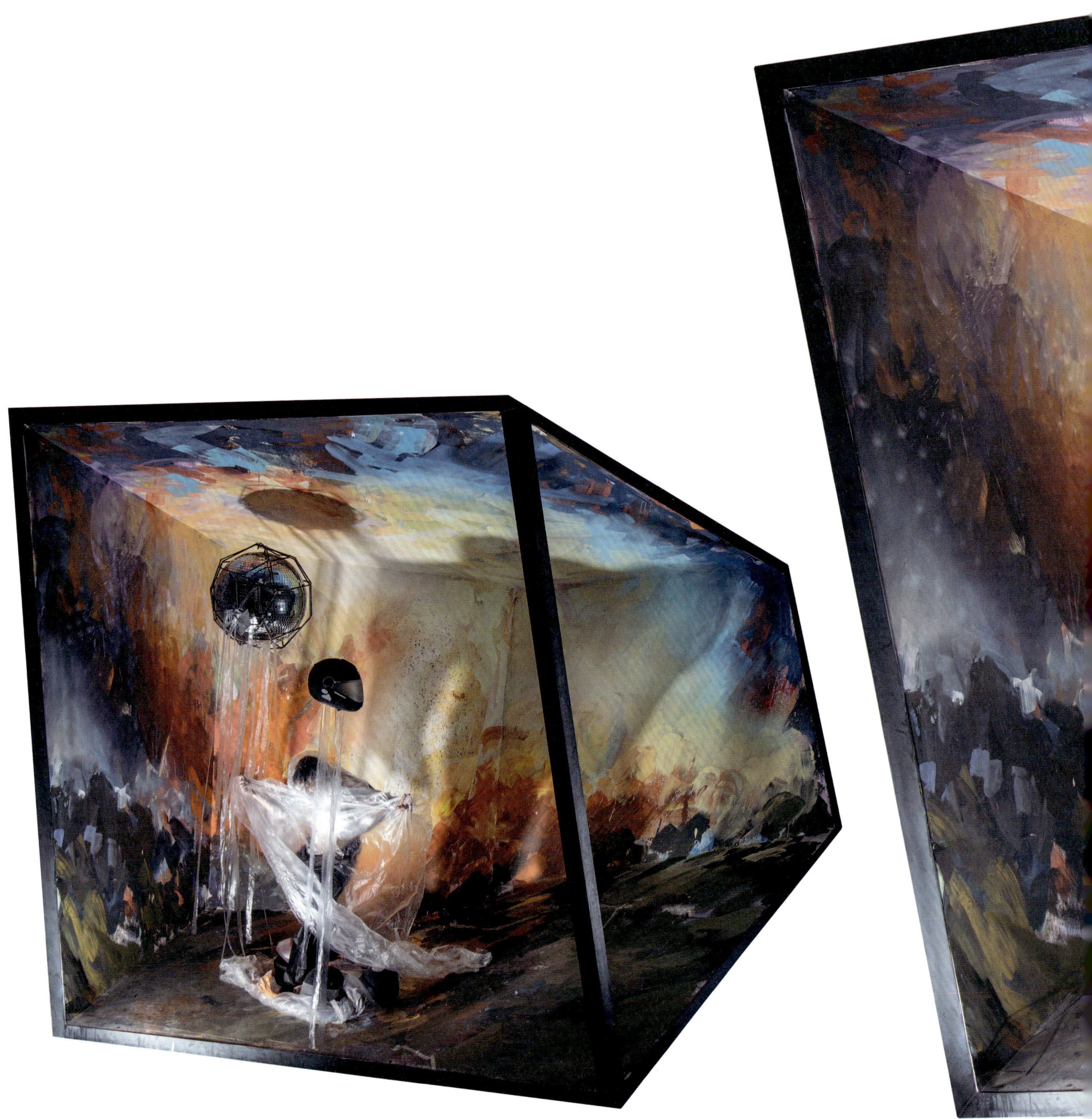

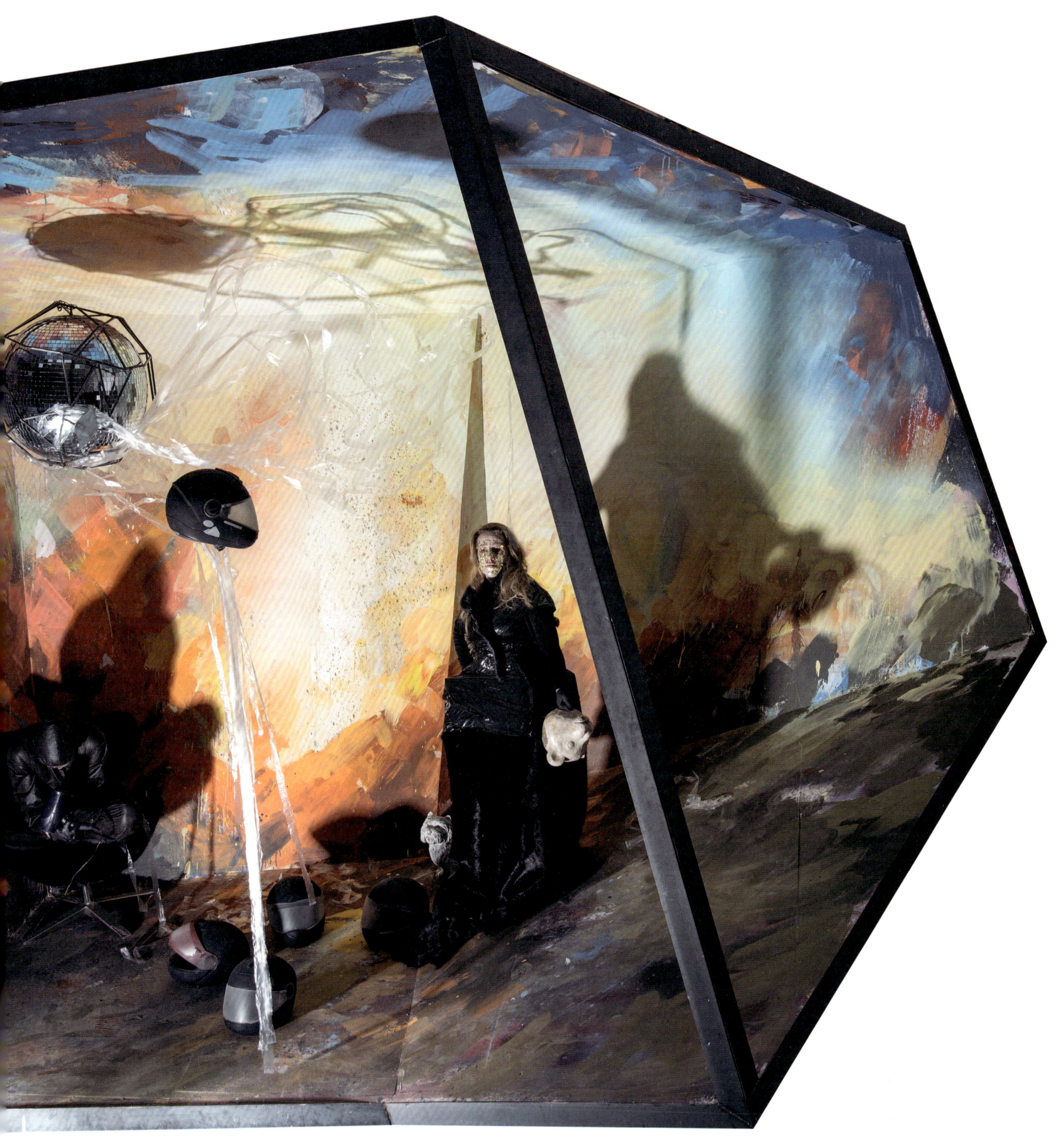

CLOUD CHAMBER
BACKSTAGE

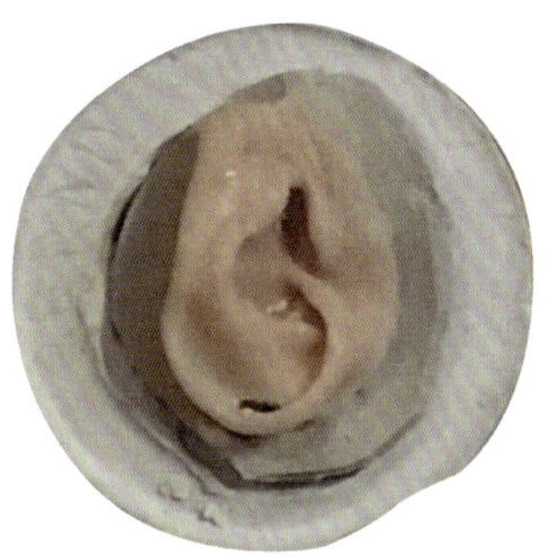

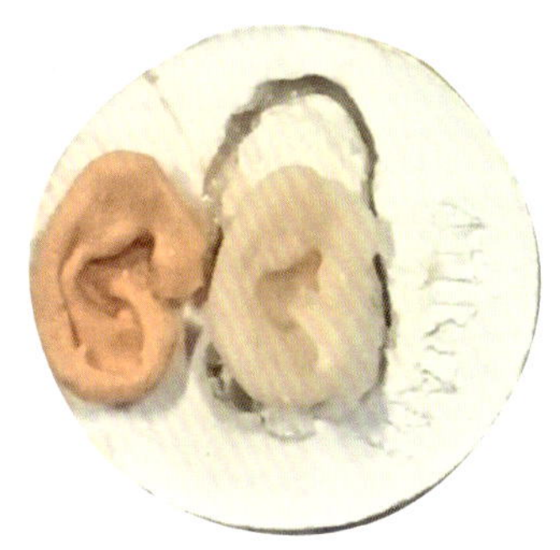

Here you can see things that happen around the Cloud Chamber. Works of different artists that are created before or after the photo session. Whether painting, sculpture, photography, literature, film, Tattoo or haute couture everything comes together in the Cloud Chamber and can also be used by the individual artists for their own work.

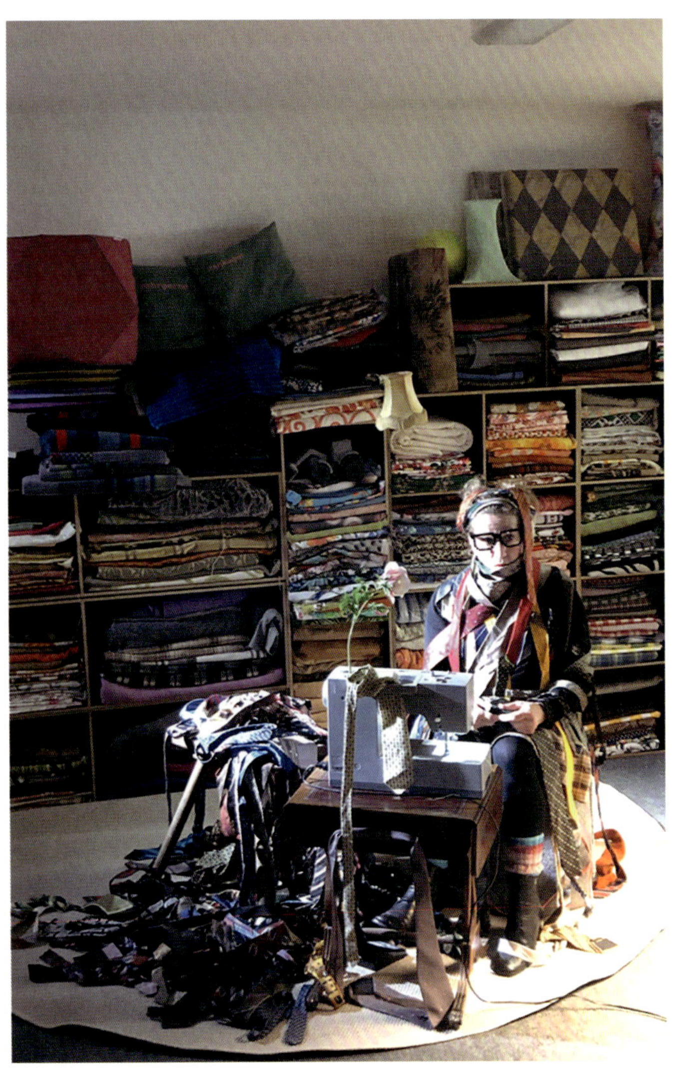

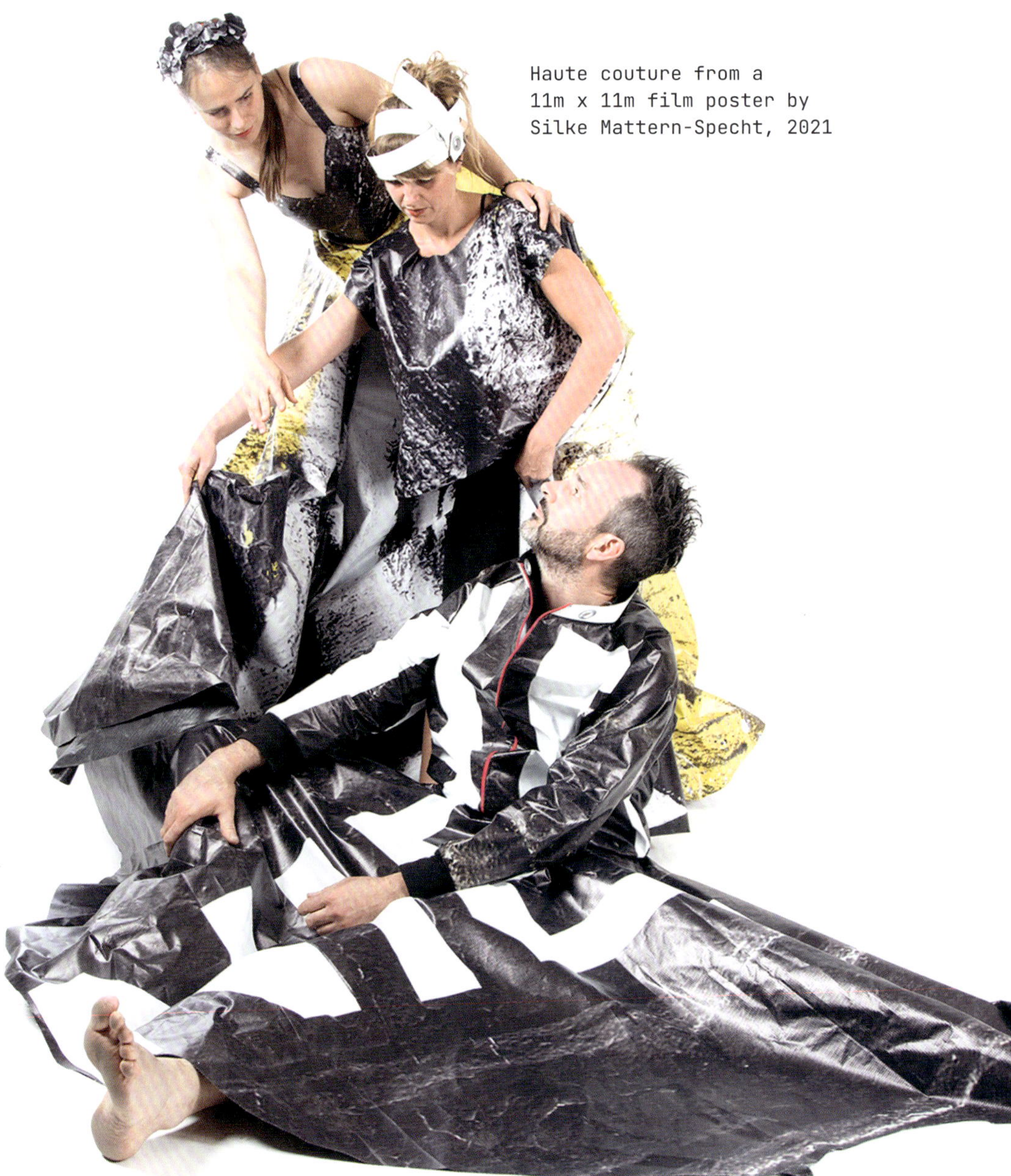

Haute couture from a 11m x 11m film poster by Silke Mattern-Specht, 2021

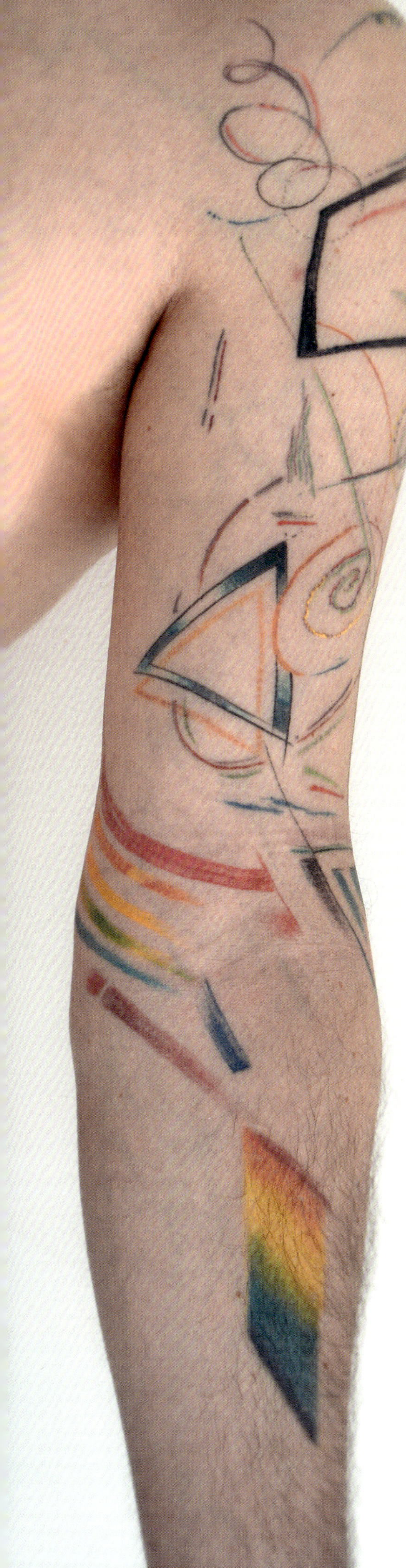

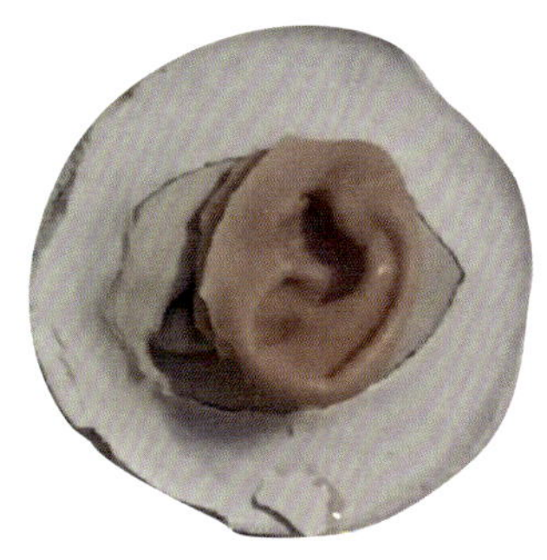

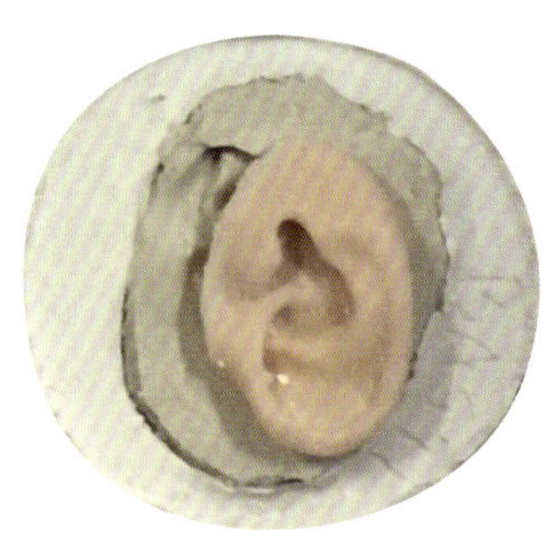

"Tattoed Cloudchambers"
(work permanently in progress)
Ink in dermis, 38 x 60 cm

Demeco & Sistig
2020 – open end

Portrait of Silke Mattern-Specht
to Cloud Chamber "A Face of Fire"
by Bernd Zöllner

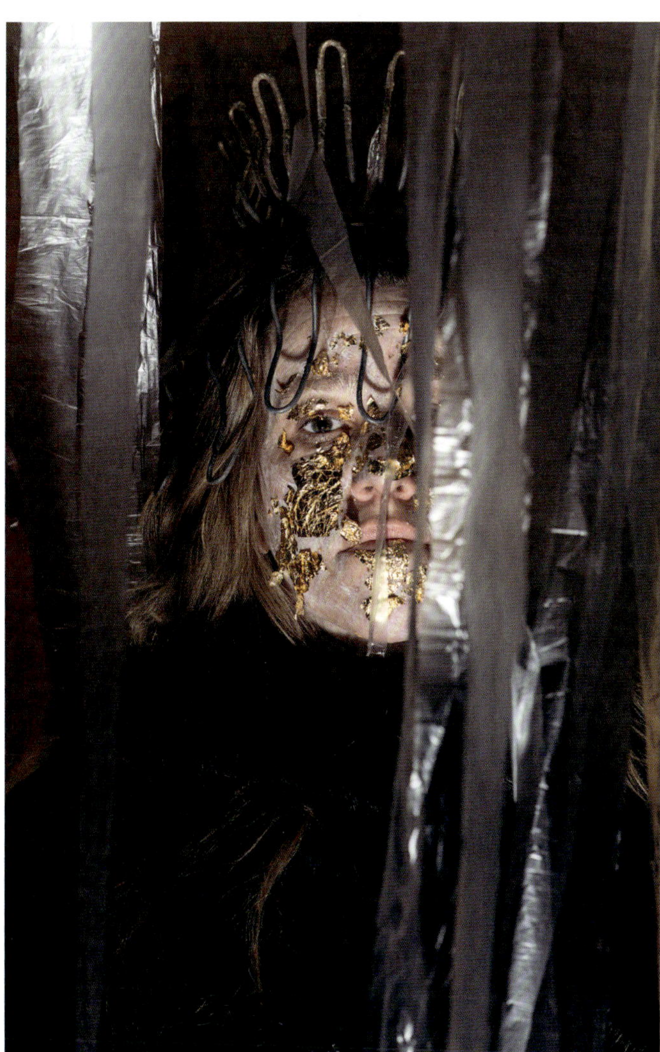

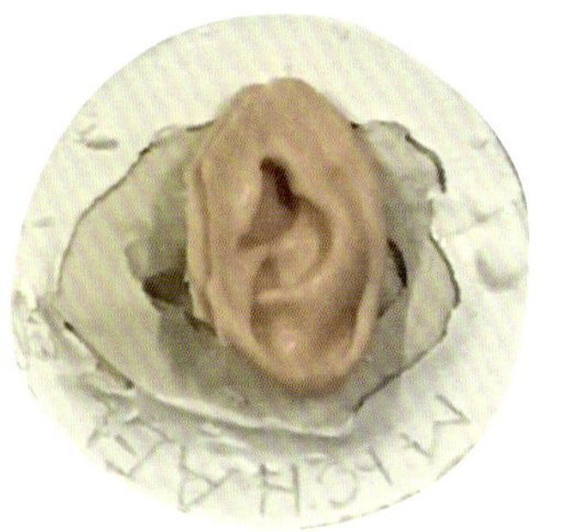
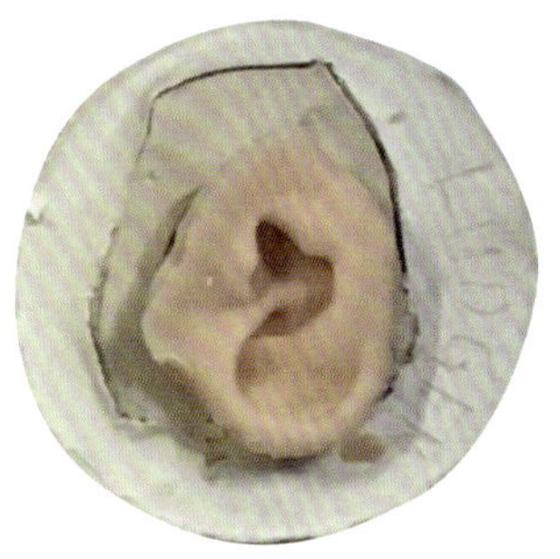
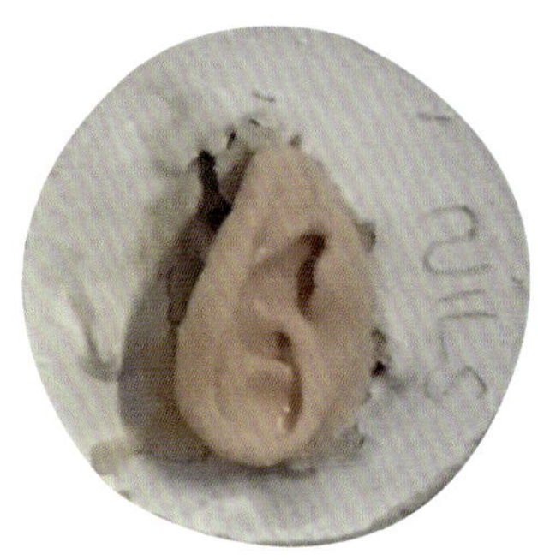

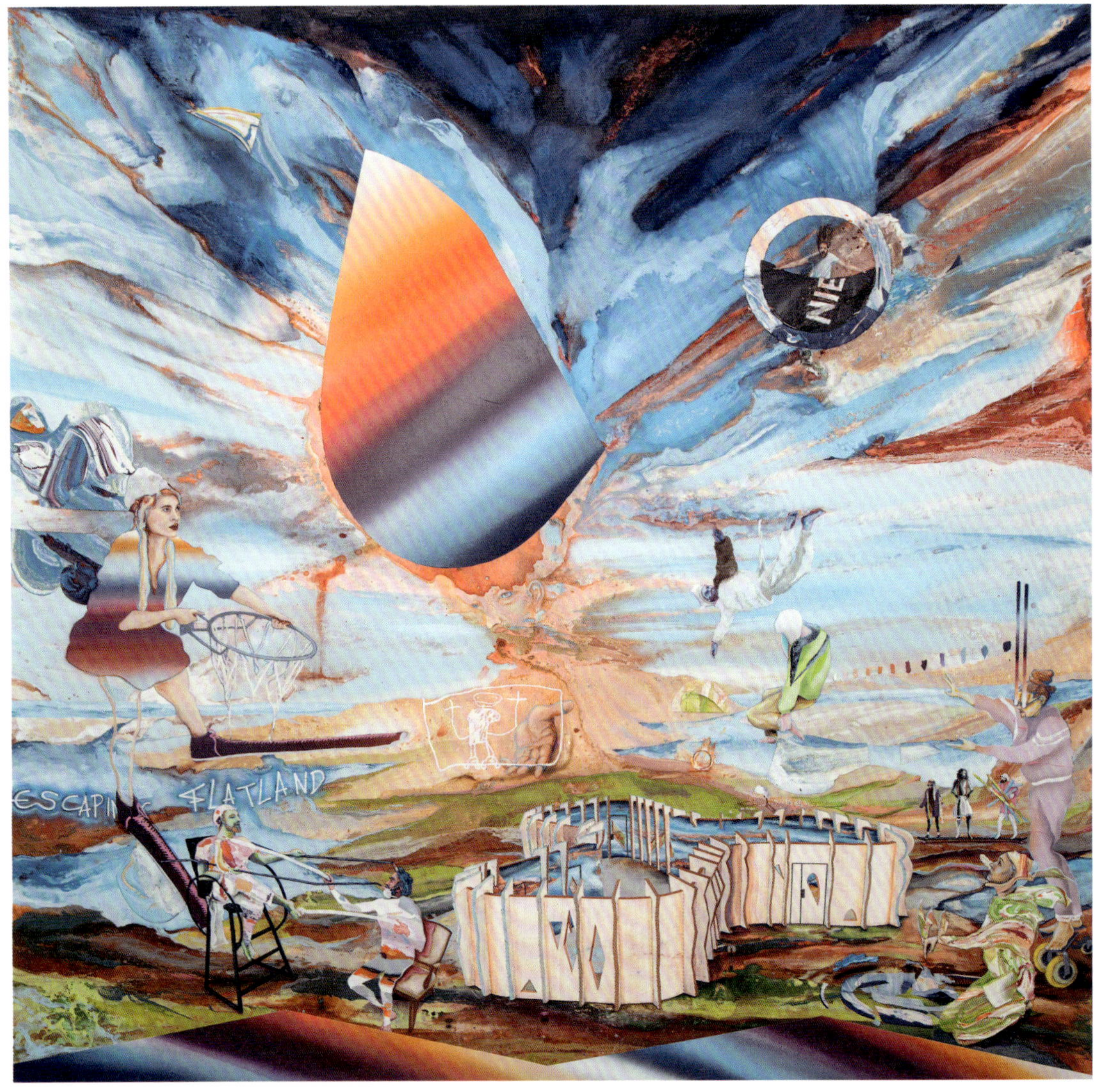

"Escaping Flatland"
Mixed technique on Canvas,
180 x 180 cm,
Michael Sistig,
2021

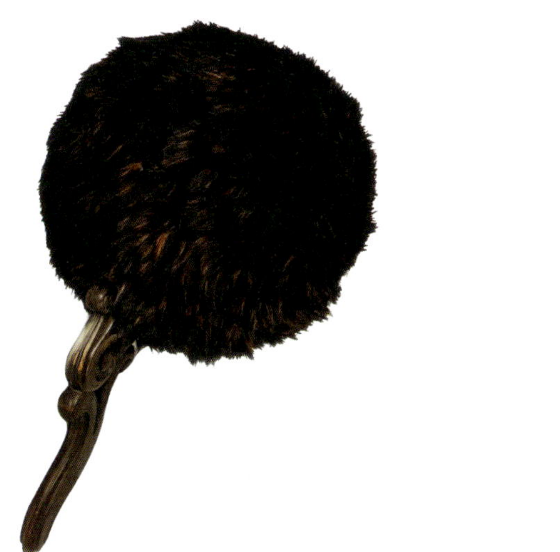

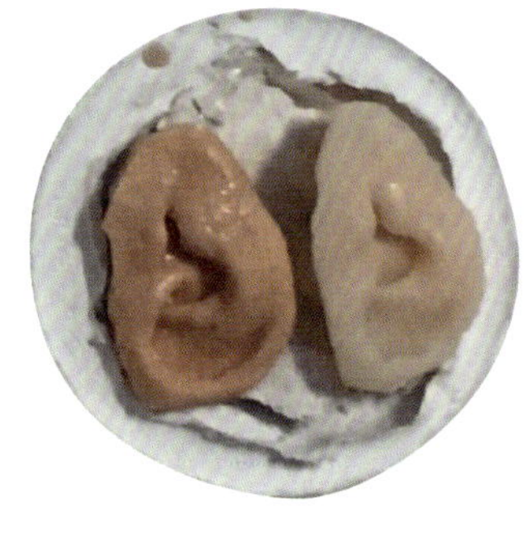

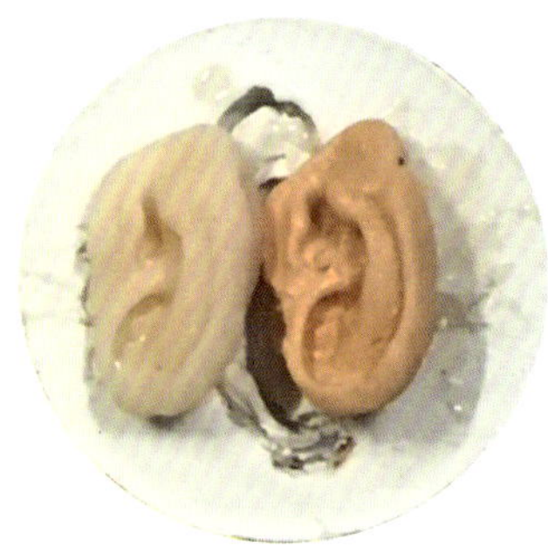

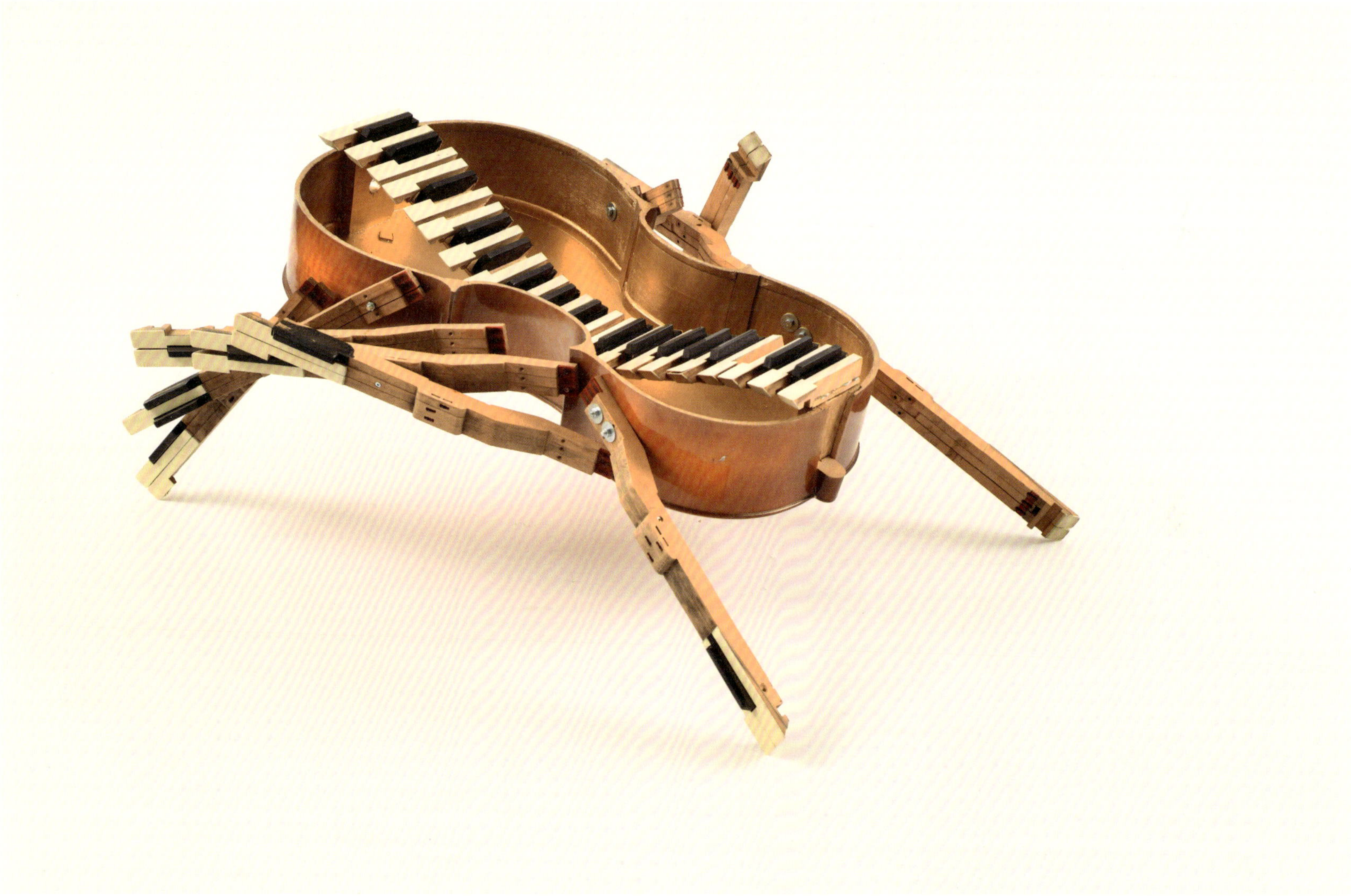

"Klartier"
Wood sculpture,
80 x 60 x 50 cm,
Rafael Maria Hildebrandt,
2019

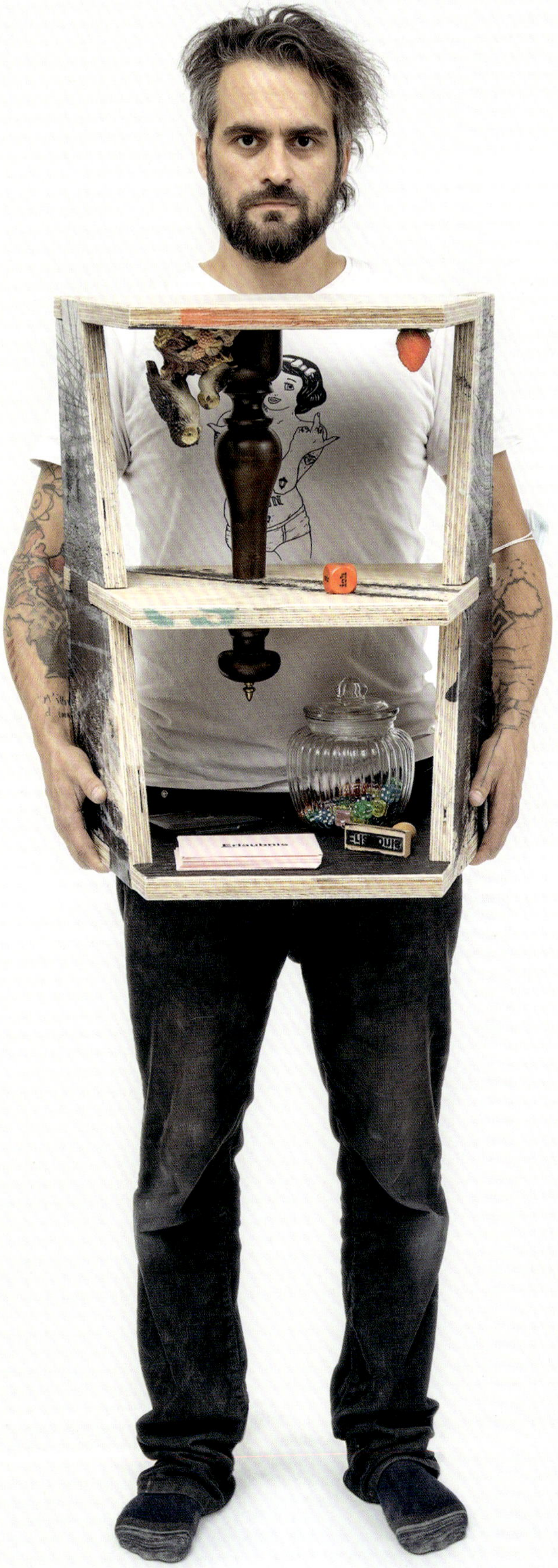

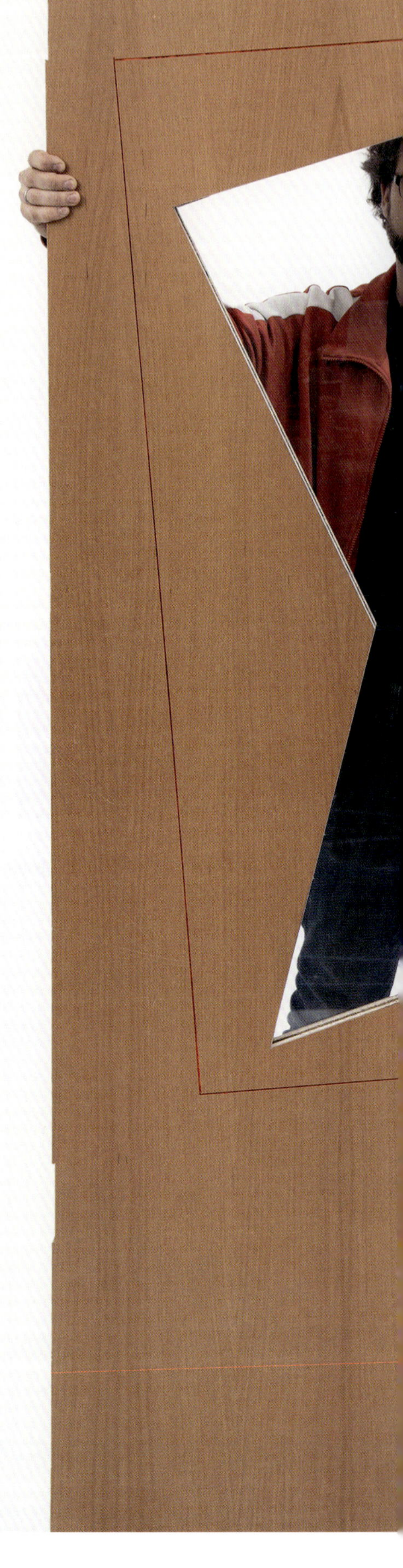

Pasquale Demeco,
Florian Benet-Riedel and
Ulrich Zünkeler
"The men who hold things"
by Bernd Zöllner,
2018-2021

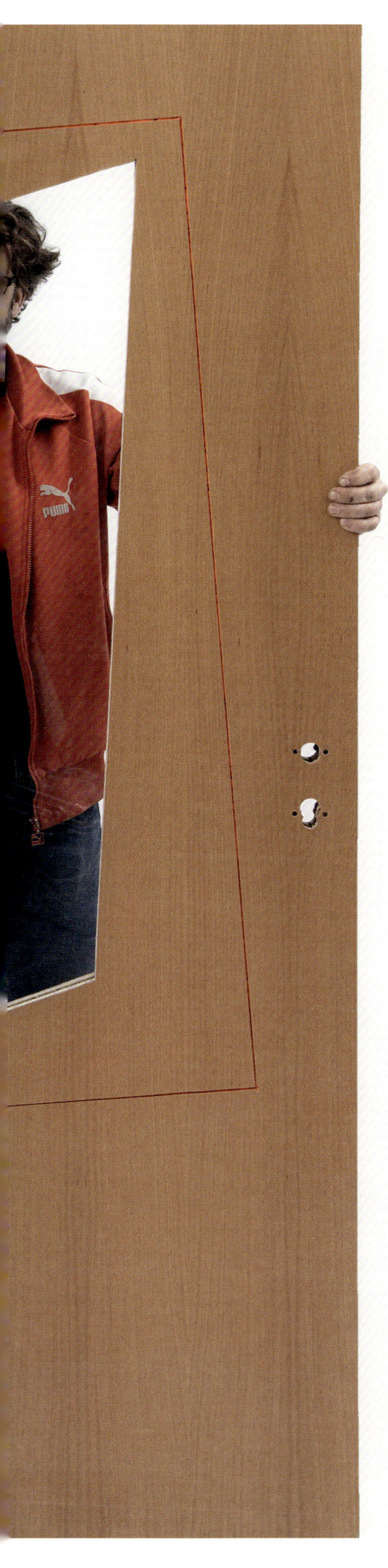
PUMA

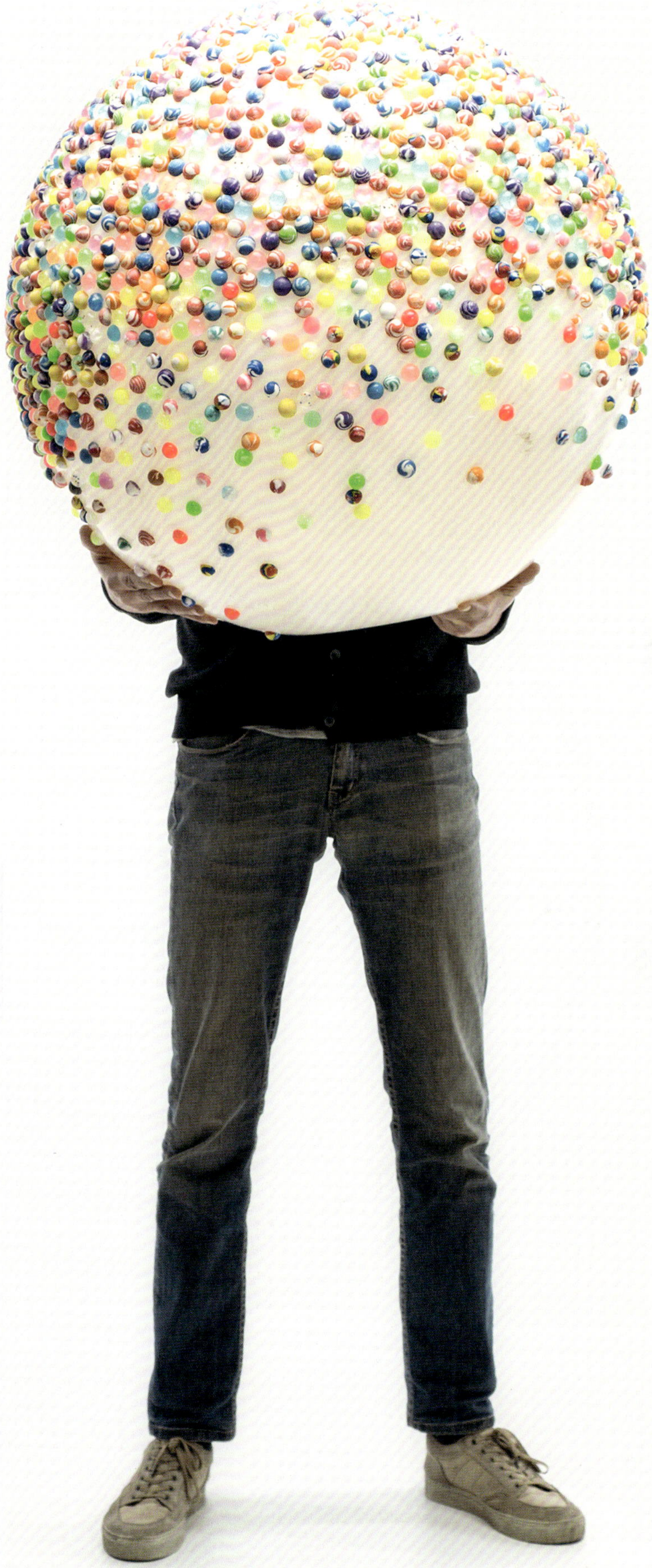

CLOUD CHAMBER **MINI**

November 7, 2019 – February 13, 2020

A package from Freeters collective to Ruangrupa collective. From Germany to Indonesia.

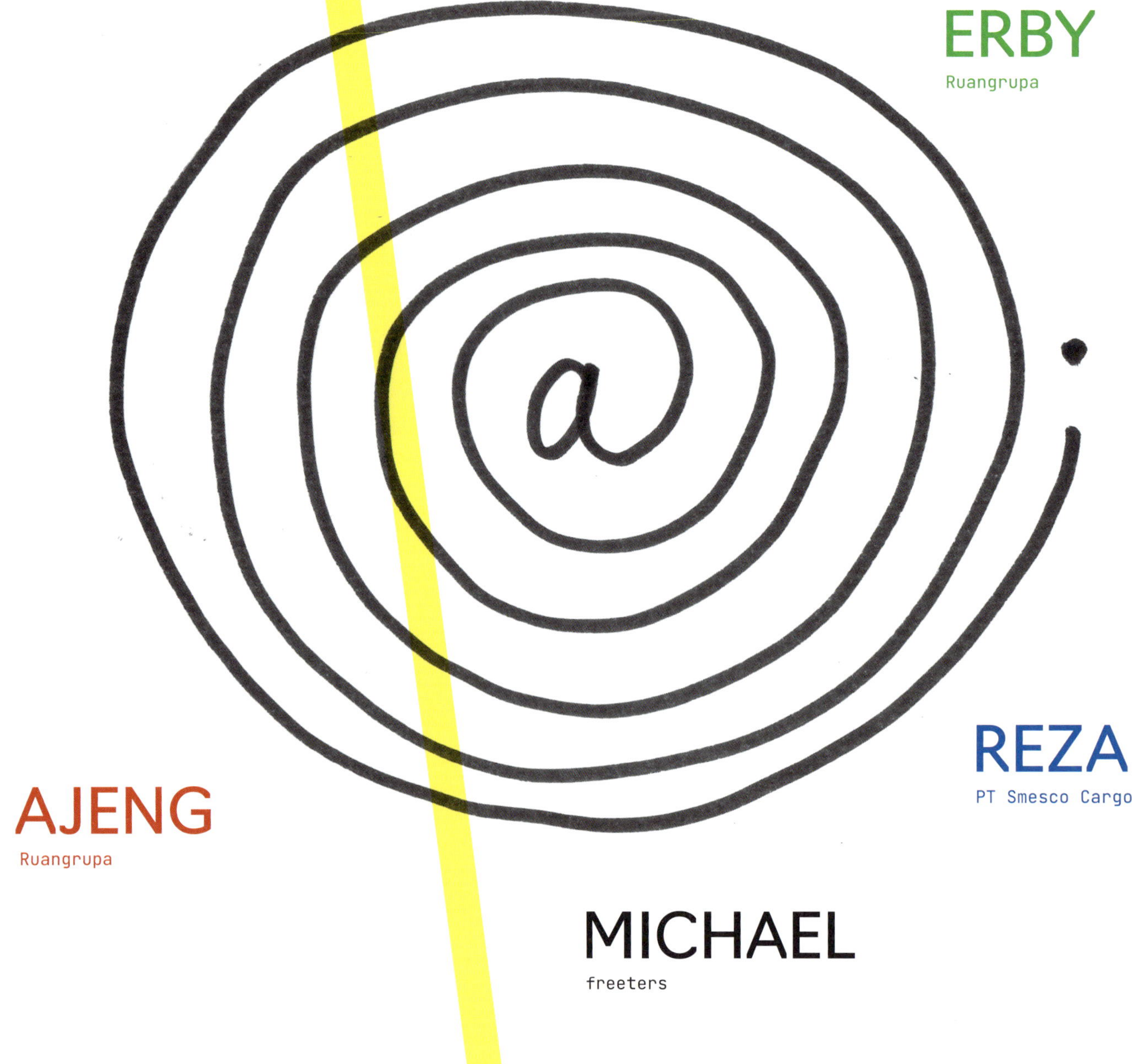

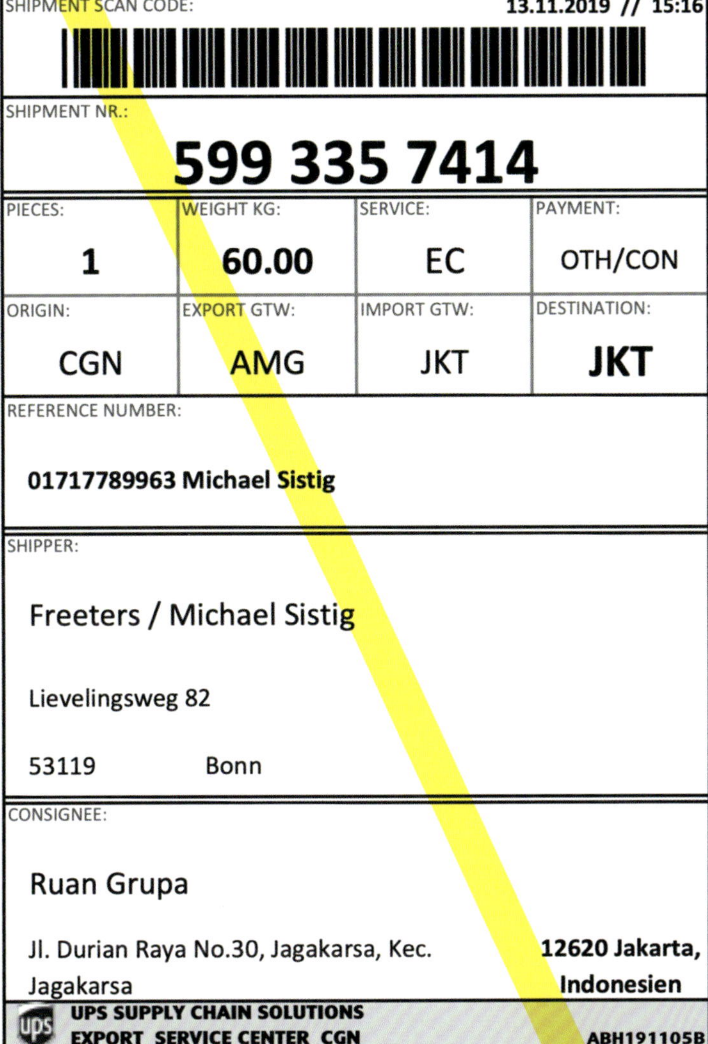
SHIPMENT SCAN CODE: 13.11.2019 // 15:16

SHIPMENT NR.: 599 335 7414

PIECES:	WEIGHT KG:	SERVICE:	PAYMENT:
1	60.00	EC	OTH/CON
ORIGIN:	EXPORT GTW:	IMPORT GTW:	DESTINATION:
CGN	AMG	JKT	JKT

REFERENCE NUMBER:
01717789963 Michael Sistig

SHIPPER:
Freeters / Michael Sistig
Lievelingsweg 82
53119 Bonn

CONSIGNEE:
Ruan Grupa
Jl. Durian Raya No.30, Jagakarsa, Kec. Jagakarsa
12620 Jakarta, Indonesien

UPS SUPPLY CHAIN SOLUTIONS
EXPORT SERVICE CENTER CGN
ABH191105B

On Thu, 28 Nov 2019,
Michael (Freeters) wrote:

Dear Ruangrupa,

we Freeters are an Artsist Collective from Germany and we were delighted that you were chosen as the artist collective to lead the Documenta. We wish you all the energy and ideas you need to make this documenta to something special. We know that it is not easy to bring sustainable themes back to art and art back into society, as the whole art apparatus has become a very exclusive club and is increasingly dominated by a few people and the gap is widening. You are a great motivation for us to continue to bring the passion and power of art back to where it is most needed, not just for a few, but art for many people. It was not until the press releases in Germany that we heard from you and through research we learned more about you and so it was just great to see how you approach the task and work together with the people of the city.

First and foremost we wanted to wish you all the best from collective to collective and express our joy.

This are some reasons why we wanted to send you a Paket to express our joy and inspiration and it should be a suprise for you, but now a days it is not possible to sent someone a suprise paket, because the delivery Service wanted to know an Emailadress or Phonenumber of the Receiver. This is the Reason why we contact you this way and we would like to know if it is possible that the Paket could be delivered to you.

We would be very glad if you would accept the Paket. We hope it does not sound confused, we just want to send you a suprise which is no longer a Suprise now. It is a gift for you.

We looking forward to hear from you.

With best wishes!
Freeters

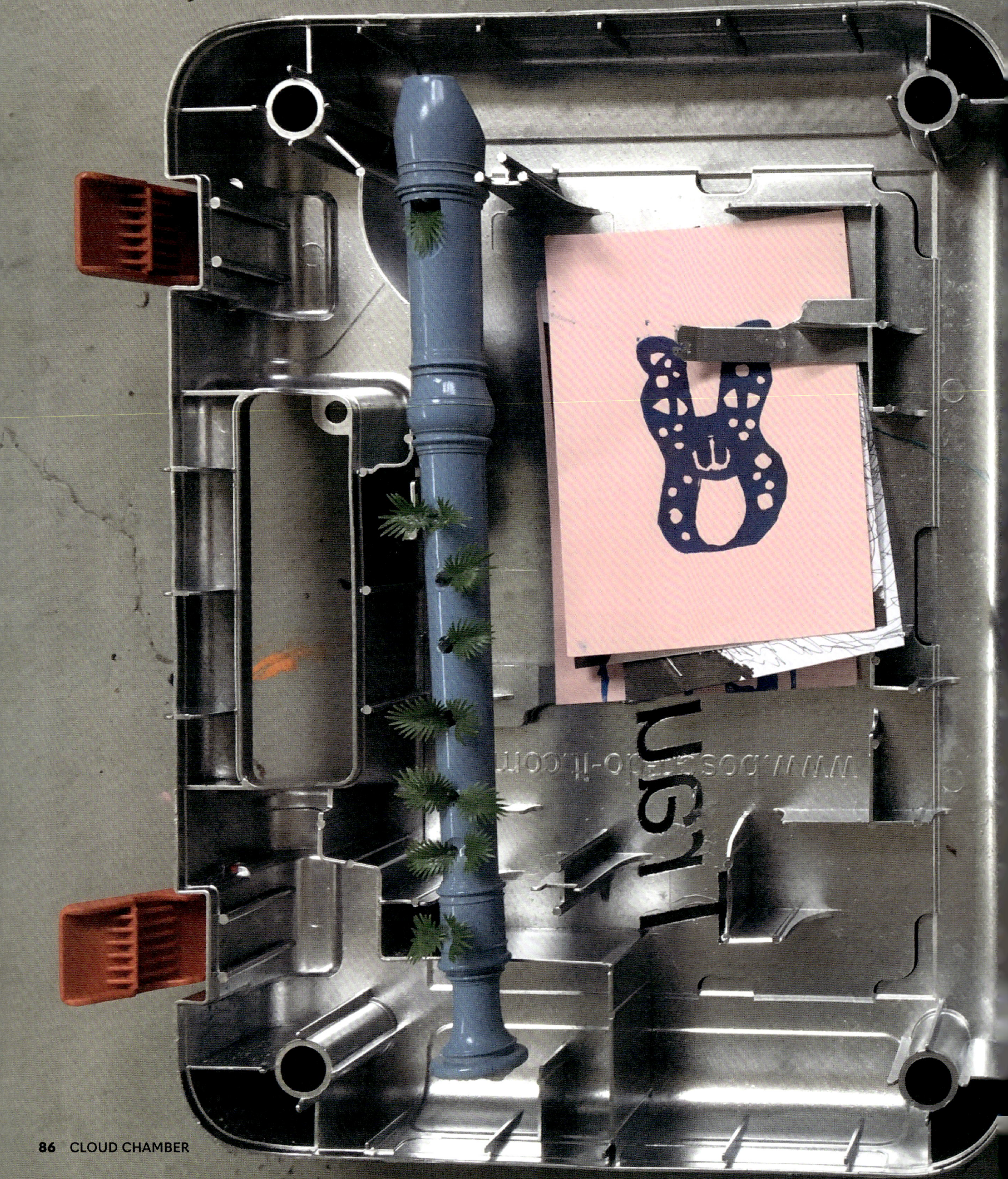

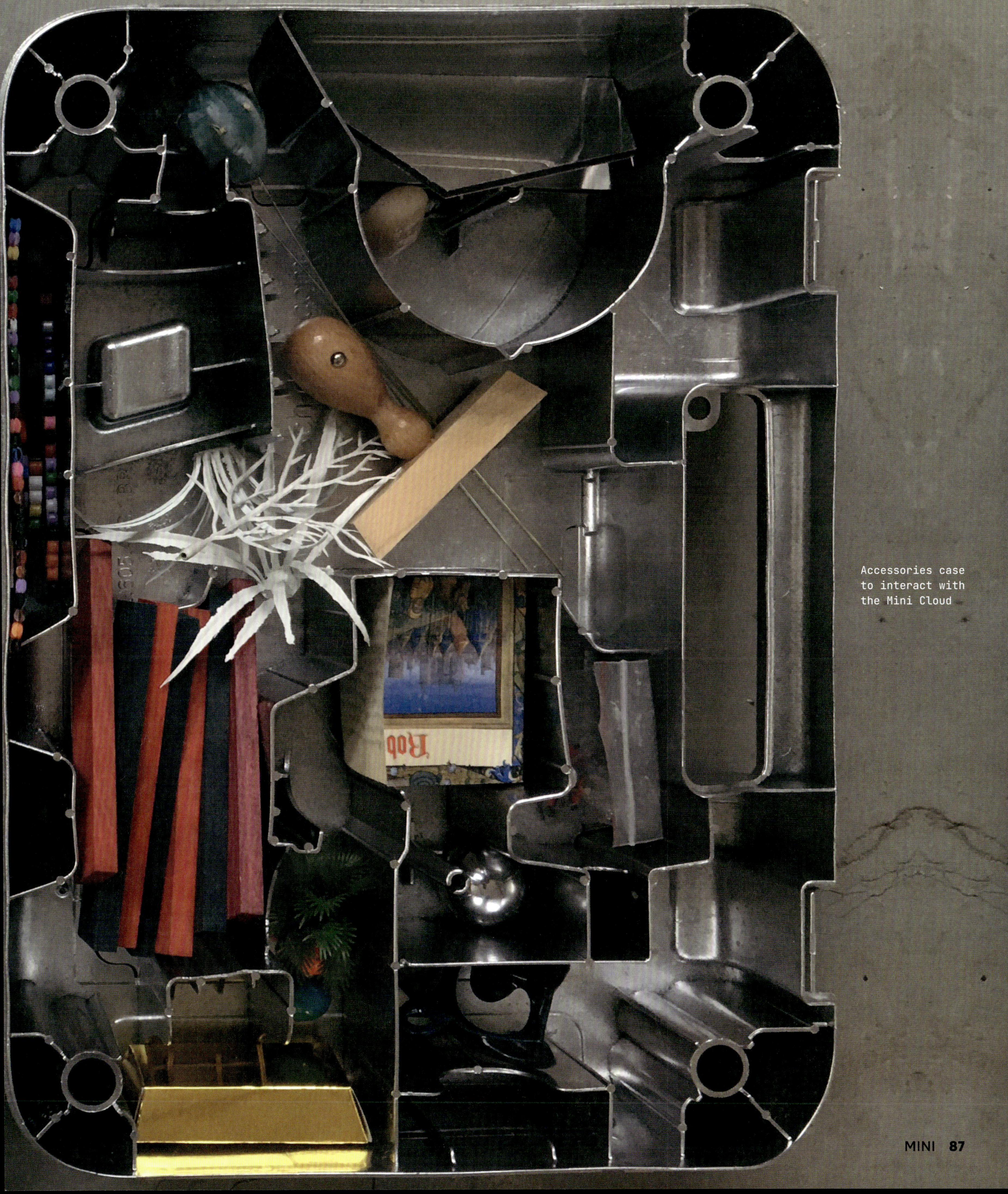

Accessories case to interact with the Mini Cloud

On Thu, 28 Nov 2019,
Ajeng (Ruangrupa) wrote:

Dear Michael and Freeters,

Thank you for the whises and really appreciate with this, we are surprised :)

Yes, it was me that ask to the delivery services to make sure about the sender because we didn't know anything about the package.

And to receive a package from outseas it is really straight and difficult sometimes regarding the policy and procedures.

Now I will contact the person from the delivery service, to continue the process.

Just to make sure we will inform all the cost that needed regarding this package delivery will be charges to the sender, hope it's OK with you.

We will keep you an update.

Once again thank you so much.

Best regards!
Ajeng

On Thu, 28 Nov 2019,
Michael (Freeters) wrote:

Dear Ajeng,

thanks a lot for the response, we are looking forward to your update.

Of course we will cover all costs for the package delivery.

Thank you and best regards!
Michael

On Tue, 10 Dec 2019,
Ajeng (Ruangrupa) wrote:

Dear Michael,

I have a called with the person from delivery services in Jakarta (PT Combi Logistic Indonesia) about the packages.

Unfortunately, for this type of shipping is require an import / export license code / number, which we don't have, because we are not an export / import company. Even though we have a case like this before too, but the process are very complicated, long and really need extra cost and time.

So she told me that the package will be return to the shipper and someone from the UPS will inform you.

You should to check again with them for this case and please let me know if there's anything that I can help.

All our best!
Ajeng Nurul Aini

On Tue, 10 Dec 2019,
Michael (Freeters) wrote:

Dear Ajeng,

thank you very much for your time and the informations.

I will try to manage that from here.

Maybe it helps, if you give them my Export-Number.

This is the EORI-Number:
DE465683246

I will try to send it to them too.

Thanks for your patience.

Hopefully it will work.

Best wishes,
Michael

On Thu, 12 Dec 2019,
Ajeng (Ruangrupa) wrote:

Dear Michael,

Thanks for your email, but what they need is the import license from us, which we don't have it.

It will take a long process to manage a non-import license in here.

But please keep me update the progress from you ya.

All the best!
Ajeng Nurul Aini

On Fri, 13 Dec 2019,
Michael (Freeters) wrote:

Dear Ajeng,

i'm so sorry that i have to disturbing you again, we didn't want that you have any troubles with this Paket. But UPS told us that the only way for delivery this Paket is to

get an Import License from you. I found some Informations in the Internet about undername Import License in Jakarta.

The Question is if you may could contact a business like this smescocargo.com in Jakarta today, if they can manage that problem? Otherwise they will destroy this Paket or send it back to us on Monday. If it is possible we would order this undername Import License Company from here and will carrying all costs.

It would be great help to us if you could call them and just ask if that is possible.

Thanks a lot.

Best wishes,
Michael

On Mon, 16 Dec 2019,
Ajeng (Ruangrupa) wrote:

Dear Michael,

Sorry for my slow response, yes case like this was happened twice, and as I said before the process could take more time and cost to process.

But let's try it again, I cc this email to my colleague, her name is Erby, she will follow up the process and hopefully everything will be fine.

All our best!
Ajeng Nurul Aini

On Tue, 17 Dec 2019,
Erby (Ruangrupa) wrote:

Hallo Michael!

I am Erby... nice to e-meet you.

I have contacted smescocargo.com / PT. Smesco Global Mandiri and they explained that in order to process this shipment the costs to be incurred were very high. it will cost around 20 million rupiahs (1281 euro). But, Tomorrow Smesco Global Mandiri will checking all the documents and recalculate. They will tell us exact amount that can be paid if you still want to process this shipment and I will let you know the update soon.

Best,
Erby.

On Son, 22 Dec 2019,
Michael (Freeters) wrote:

Hello Erby,

did you got new informations from Smesco Cargo?

Did they check and calculate?

We would like to process the shipment.

Thank you for your patience.

Best,
Michael

On Tue, 24 Dec 2019,
Erby (Ruangrupa) wrote:

Halo Michael,

Today Smesco Cargo confirmed about the shipment. They asked for Rp. 40.000.000 (2581 Euro) for clearance but exclude storage rental cost that you will pay after this process finished. I asked them for official invoice so we know the details. They will give us the invoice on Thursday Dec 26, 2020.

Best,
Erby

On Thu, 26 Dec 2019,
Erby (Ruangrupa) wrote:

Halo Michael,

Herewith I attach the invoice from Smesco Cargo. I will connect you directly with Smesco Cargo after you confirm the invoice.

Thank you,
Erby

On Fri, 27 Dec 2019,
Michael (Freeters) wrote:

Hello Erby,

wow that´s a lot, we didn't expect that it would be so complicated and so expensive to send a paket to Indonesia.

Over this year we did a non art project, just a renovation of a flat to save some money for this project, we will try to manage this shipment with that, just for the hope that it could be delivered to you.

So yes we confirm this invoice.

Thank you very much for your time and work on this, we will manage this with smesco after you made the connection to them.

We are looking forward that you will get the paket and hope you will enjoy it.

Best,
Michael

On Sat, 28 Dec 2019,
Erby (Ruangrupa) wrote:

Hi Michael,

Really sorry about the conditions, but that's the regulation and policy in here regarding import things, it's really strict and cost a lot.

There's also an issues that we have, 1) the receiver name is different with our legal name (Yayasan Ruang Rupa), it's makes an extra time to process, 2) we don't have any import licence that's why it's also affect to the cost, 3) and they will charge an extra cost for the warehouse as long as you still have your goods in the customs.

We try to contact our person that get used to take care this matter, but he refused according to the issues above.

But, its depends on you whether you want to process until delivery to us or return to you or even destroyed.

Hope you all the best,
Erby.

On Sat, 28 Dec 2019,
Michael (Freeters) wrote:

Hi Erby,

yes we want to process the delivery to you.

We confirm the invoice and will cover all costs.

Should i sign the Invoice or what would be the next step? Or do you give me the contact to smesco?

Thank you very much for your patience.

Best,
Michael

On Mon, 30 Dec 2019,
Erby (Ruangrupa) wrote:

Hi Michael,

I would like to introduce Reza from PT Smesco Cargo who has been in correspondence with me regarding the shipment of your paket to us. Reza will explain the next steps that you will take to complete this shipment.

Hi Pak Reza, I introduce Michael Sistig who sent the package to us. Please coordinate directly with Michael to get this item out of the warehouse, including about payment.

Reza and Michael, please cc me and Ajeng in your conversation so we can also find out the progress

Best,
Erby

On Mon, 30 Dec 2019,
Reza (PT Smesco Cargo) wrote:

introduce me reza,

for this work, we need funds in the beginning. 40,000,000 IDR. customs service. warehouse fees according to the receipt.

These costs are outside the warehouse costs.

For warehouse rental invoices not yet available, an invoice is issued when the goods are out

On Mon, 30 Dec 2019,
Michael (Freeters) wrote:

Hi Reza,

could you please send me the Invoice with your Account informations/Iban Number that i can wire you the money for custom service.

Thank you!

Best,
Michael

On Mon, 30 Dec 2019,
Reza (PT Smesco Cargo) wrote:

customs clearance fee is 40,000,000 IDR.

warehouse costs later according to the receipt.

On Tue, 31 Dec 2019,
Michael (Freeters) wrote:

Hi Reza,

we tranfered you the amount for costum clearence, yesterday.

Best,
Michael

On Tue, 31 Dec 2019,
Reza (PT Smesco Cargo) wrote:

The funds haven't arrived yet.

On Thu, 2 Jan 2020,
Reza (PT Smesco Cargo) wrote:

Dear

To process this item, we are waiting for funds to come to us first, because to process this item we need funds in advance,

thanks.
M. Reza

On Thu, 2 Jan 2020,
Michael (Freeters) wrote:

Dear Reza,

we wired the amount of 2600€ on Dec. 30th 2019, it is an international Banktransfer, that is the reason why it will take some time before it will arrive on your account.

Best,
Michael

On Thu, 2 Jan 2020,
Reza (PT Smesco Cargo) wrote:

ok I'll wait for the funds to arrive, then I will process the customs clearance

On Fri, 3 Jan 2020,
Reza (PT Smesco Cargo) wrote:

yeah right, later when it has been transferred, please send the proof

Sent from Android device

On Sat, 4 Jan 2020,
Reza (PT Smesco Cargo) wrote:

Dear Michael sistig

To this day funds have not arrived.

Thank you
M.reza

On Sat, 4 Jan 2020,
Michael (Freeters) wrote:

Dear M. Reza,

i called our Bank yesterday, they said it should arrive on Monday. The funds left our Account two days ago, hope it will arrive asap. In Germany we had some public holidays around new year maybe this is the reason why it takes so long.

Best,
Michael

On Sat, 4 Jan 2020,
Reza (PT Smesco Cargo) wrote:

Ok I will check again on Monday.

thank you michael sistig

On Tue, 7 Jan 2020,
Reza (PT Smesco Cargo) wrote:

Dear Michael

The funds have not yet arrived, please check.

thank you

On Wed, 8 Jan 2020,
Michael (Freeters) wrote:

Dear Muhammad,

i checked it again and all things from Account, Banknumber etc. are right. The funds are gone from our Account, we just can wait until the money arrive on your account.

Thank you for your patience.

Best,
Michael

On Wed, 8 Jan 2020,
Reza (PT Smesco Cargo) wrote:

Dear Michael.

I have received the funds with a nominal value of Rp. 39,644,920 IDR.

On Wed, 8 Jan 2020,
Michael (Freeters) wrote:

Dear Muhammad,

that's sounds great. So you can start the costum clearance now?

I'm wondering if you can tell me the weight of the paket if you have the paket in your storage?

Because i weighed it here and it was 60 kg and now UPS told me it is allegedly 275 kg and this is not possible or not our paket, it should be around 60 kg. It would be great to get this informations from you if you have the possibility for.

Thank you very much.

Best,
Michael

On Wed, 8 Jan 2020,
Reza (PT Smesco Cargo) wrote:

I checked the data, it weighed 110 kg,

and for customs processes after the required data is available.

On Fri, 17 Jan 2020,
Reza (PT Smesco Cargo) wrote:

Dear Michael.

The customs clearance warehouse rental to be paid is 65,000,000 IDR,

These costs for today, day by day, are increasingly rising

On Fri, 17 Jan 2020,
Erby (Ruangrupa) wrote:

Halo Michael and Reza,

Yesterday Reza gave us the invoice for rental storage is amount Rp. 65.686.445 (invoice attached). We know is really really expensive and more than cost that you already paid.

But, we already contacted the storage to apply cost relief because this package is a present not commercial things.

Let you guys know soon the progress

Erby

On Fri, 17 Jan 2020,
Erby (Ruangrupa) wrote:

Halo Michael,

We already talked with storage. It seems so hard to make cost relief. You have to pay the storage cost first and then write down the cost relief form. Your application to storage could be agreed or not depends on the reason. If agreed they will do refund the difference. But, the difference is not will be much. If we stop the process , you don't have to pay the storage cost but we will never get the paket.

Sorry for this. Hope you can decide soon.

Thanks,
Erby

On Mon, 20 Jan 2020,
Michael (Freeters) wrote:

Halo Erby,

after some days of Phonecalling to get financial support, we are happy that we will get the money for the final Invoice.
The El Segundo Museum of Art ESMoA from Los Angeles will support us.

But we have to do the application for costs relief after you got the paket, in hope that we will get something back. Hopefully you can send that formular for application to us and maybe you could help us with it?

We would like to transfer the Amount today, but we need the international BIC Swift Code from the Mandiri Bank. Could you send this Code to us, please?

Best,
Michael

On Tue, 21 Jan 2020,
Erby (Ruangrupa) wrote:

Dear Michael,

Great to hear that! Hopefully all of the the things will going well.

The Storage gave me a draft letter in Bahasa with the data that had to be filled out. Unfortunately, they don't have the English version. So, please make a letter and put the data below and reasons to reduce costs and sign it.

The letter is addressed to the PT. Bangun Desa Logisindo.

MAWB: 235-33672741
HAWB: 5993357414
Weight: 275,5 Kg
Item: DIsplay Case/Toys
Airlines: Turkish Airlines Arrival
Date: 17. November 2019

In the letter also stated that this letter was known to
PT. Combi Logistics Indonesia.

Please send it back the letter to me first and I will send it by completing the documents that are already with us and I will cc you.

For Swift Code Mandiri :
BMRIIDJA

Best!
Erby

On Wed, 22 Jan 2020,
Michael (Freeters) wrote:

Dear Erby,

attached you can find the Application for costs reduce.

Thank you a lot for your help!
Please let me know if i can do anything else.

Best,
Michael

On Wed, 22 Jan 2020,
Erby (Ruangrupa) wrote:

Dear Michael,

this is invoice that i gave from storage today. Please transfer the money as soon as possible and give us the evidence. Everyday the cost is increasing.

Thanks
Erby

On Wed, 22 Jan 2020,
Michael (Freeters) wrote:

Dear Erby,

we transfered the last Invoice two days ago, but it is an international Bank Transfer and this is the reason why it takes some time at least 3–7days before it is wired to the account. It will be endless if the storage is not exepting that we pay the Difference to the last Invoice after you got the Paket. We wired Combi Logistics 65686445,00 and we will pay the rest of 5days when you got the Paket, because it is not possible to do a one day transfer from Germany to Indonesia.

The Difference between this Invoice and the today Invoice is not that much.

It would be accommodating if Combi Logistic excepting that, they will get the difference immediatly if you got the Paket.

Thank you!

Best,
Michael

On Fri, 24 Jan 2020,
Erby (Ruangrupa) wrote:

Dear Michael,

I already forward your application for costs reduce to PT.Combi Logisindo and the storage . Let you know soon the progress.

Best,
Erby.

On Thu, 13 Feb 2020,
Michael (Freeters) wrote:

Dear Erby,

how is it going?

I just would like to know if you got the Paket?

Best,
Michael

On Thu, 13 Feb 2020,
Erby (Ruangrupa) wrote:

Hallo Michael!

Yesterday the paket had arrived.

We just open today! Finally,
Thank you for paket! We're so
excited when the paket opened.
Is the artwork can interact?

Best,
Erby

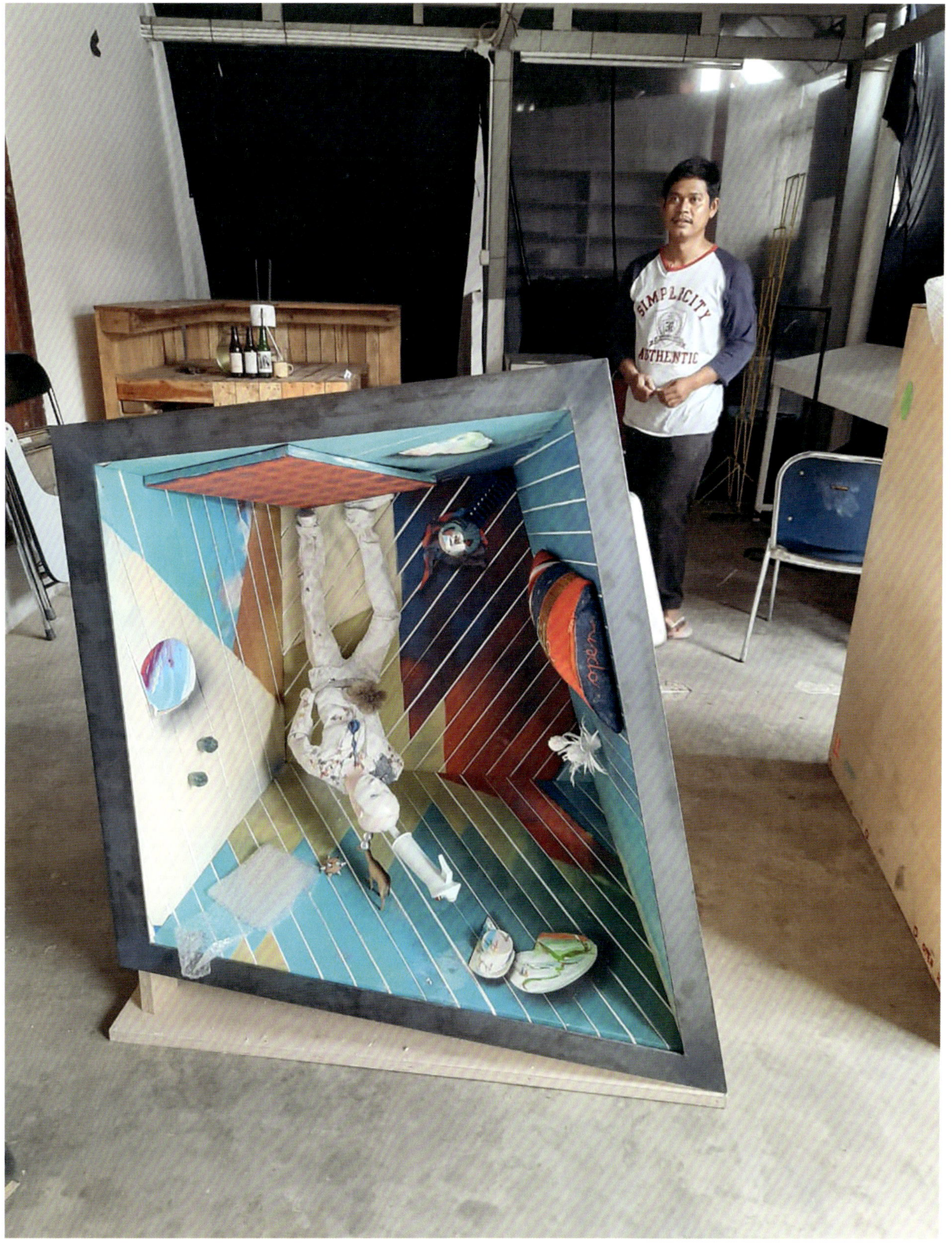

ESMoA COLLABORATION

One of the most interesting projects of freeters is the permanent collaboration with the art laboratory ESMoA. ESMoA is conceived as an urban catalyst in the South Bay of Los Angeles. Here, artistic processes are connected in their immediate form and are changed through engagement with the community. ESMoA focuses on aspects of shared understanding and exploring, and in its Experience projects, continuously builds bridges into contemporary issues through collaborations in science, research, and art. Artists of the freeters collective have been involved in further developments of ESMoA through the curatorial support of founding member Bernhard Zünkeler. There is a constantly renewing participation of Freeters artists in the ongoing Experiences at ESMoA. These include, in particular, the group initiatives ELSEGUNDISSIMO (2017) and STARDUST (2020) and also the individual projects of freeters artists Amely Spötzl, with PHYTOMAGNETIC (2014) and PLANT (2019), and Michael Sistig, with ANTI-ARK (2013) and MATTER (2016).

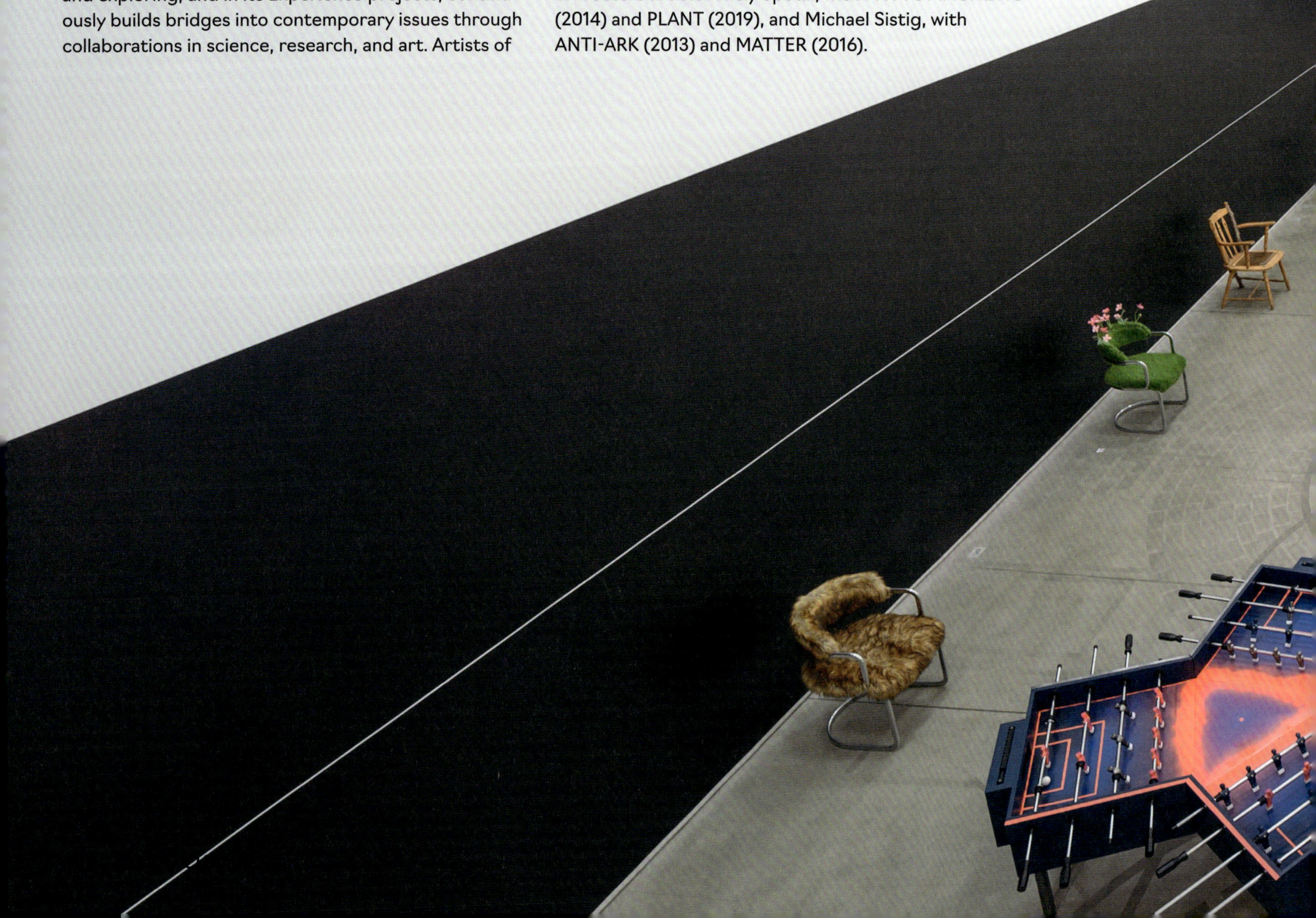

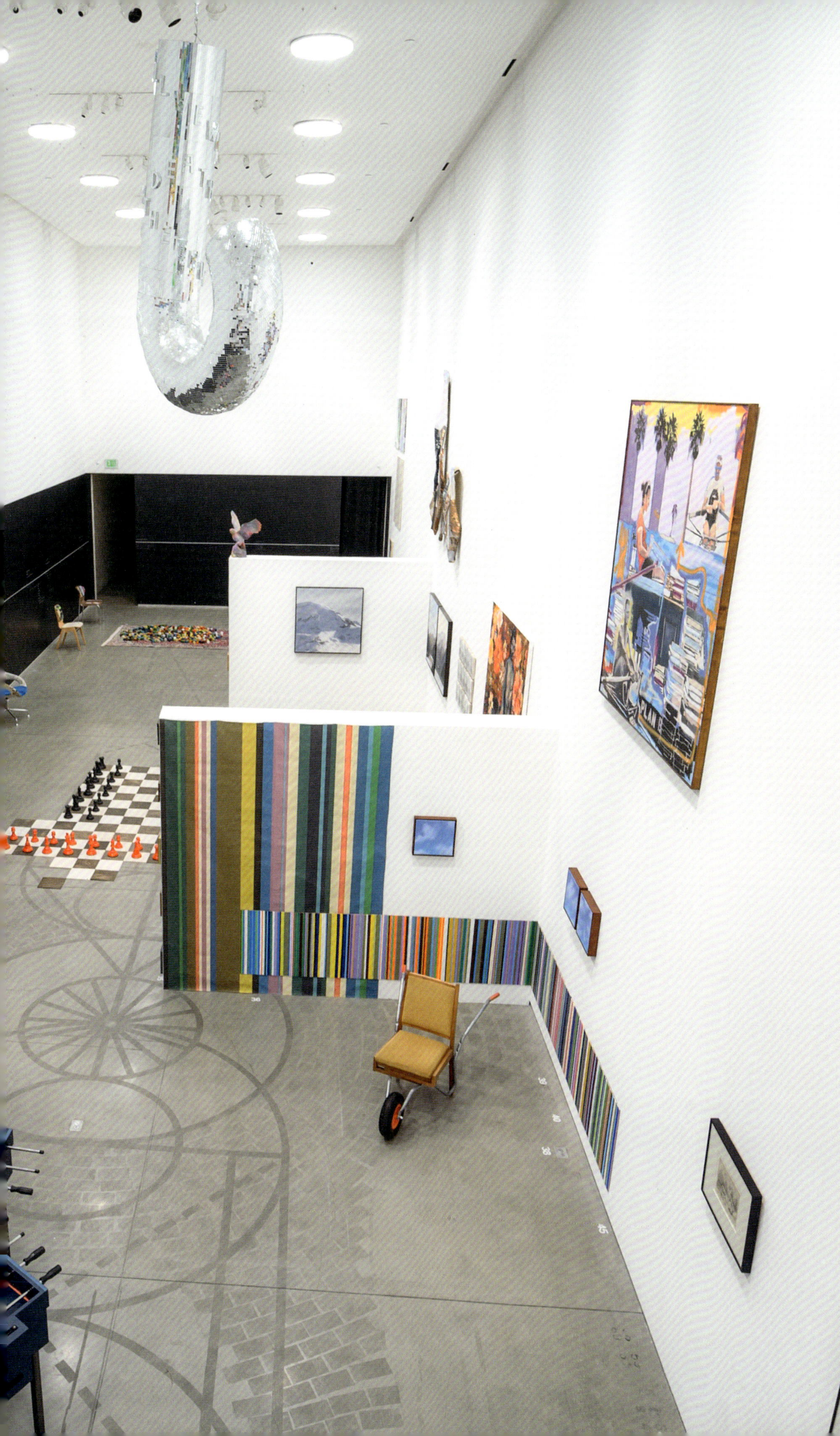

ESMoA COLLABORATION
MATTER

Michael Sistig, 2015

MATTER aims to stimulate curiosity about the myths of life. Mythology and science have historically been intertwined, as people throughout time have used mythology to understand the natural world. The new ESMoA Experience explores the convergence of mythology and modern science, with its constantly changing theories, through the eyes of young German artist Michael Sistig. In his first solo show in the United States, Sistig will invite us to take a glimpse into his approach of negotiating modern science through the media of painting and sculpture.

While we are used to seeing scientific theories translated in numbers, symbols and words, rarely do we see them presented like this as inspirational, confusing, yet somehow still comforting images. With Experience 23: MATTER, a new form of dialogue will unravel, challenging our mystified knowledge of modern science. Through the enchanting art of Michael Sistig, MATTER will reinvigorate in us a sense of wonder and magic toward numbers, geometry, and heroic archetypes.

What are scientific theories? Why do we create these theories? How do we make sense of things we don't understand? To what degree are we enlightened by new knowledge? Do our values develop based on this new enlightenment? How does scientific language affect our lives? How can we understand the world, when science wants to explain it in binary codes of 0 and 1? When we try to understand the world today, do we create myths, like the ancient Greeks did? Have those myths ever left us? Do technological advancements actually make us smarter, or more able to find awareness?

Paradox disposition: Since his childhood, artist Michael Sistig has repeatedly encountered the same, simple aesthetic questions that he could never answer. Through painting and the intensive study of philosophy, he began to find answers, and he felt himself getting closer to Truth. Today, he is engrossed in the achievements of physicists and hopes thereby to come even closer to answering these open, elemental questions. He has become fascinated by the language of physics and scientific formulas, and he loves to create enthusiasm for modern science in others. With his interdisciplinary approach, Sistig allows himself to be inspired by various scientific facets. For the length of MATTER, the artist will transform ESMoA with his incredible, intuitively created imagery that explores the relationship between myth, magic and modern science.

Begin Exploration: MATTER will show that you do not have to be a scientist to be inspired by the grand magic of science. Maybe the source for curiosity and scientific progress is not only to be found in numbers and formulas. Surprisingly, maybe art is the vehicle through which to understand science. Rather than explaining life through scientific theories, perhaps the way to understanding is through finding visuals for worlds no one has ever seen.

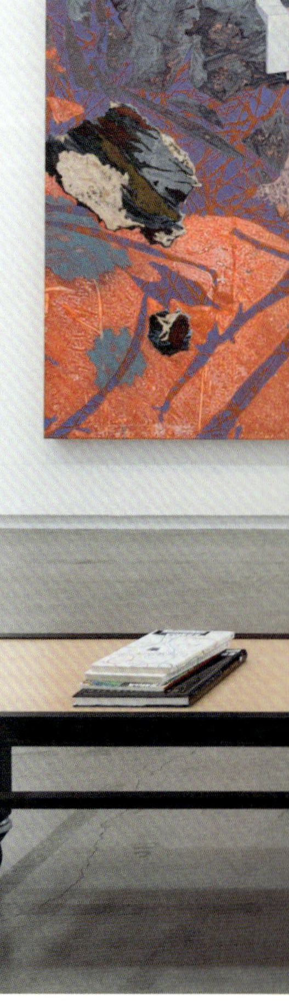

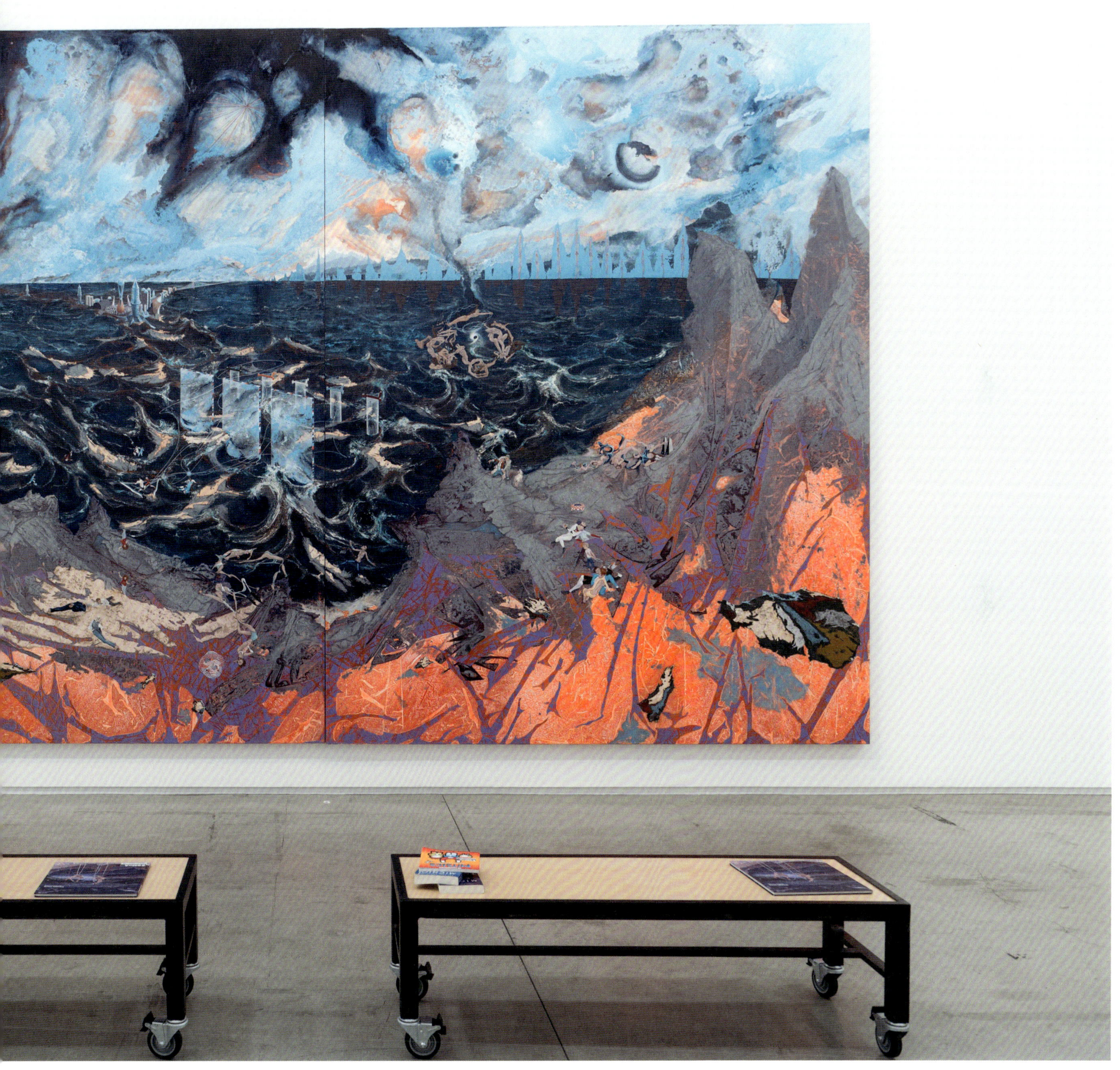

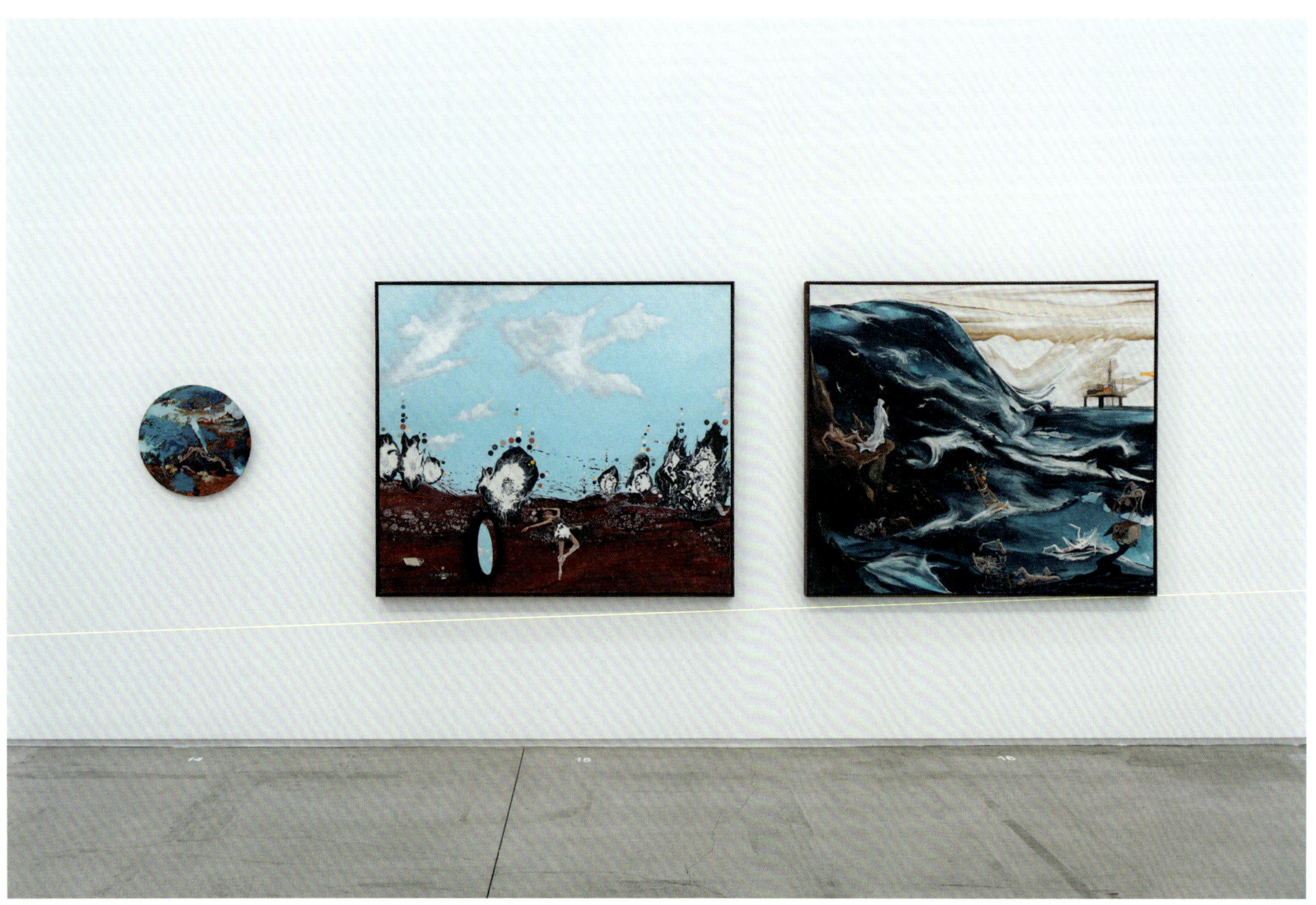

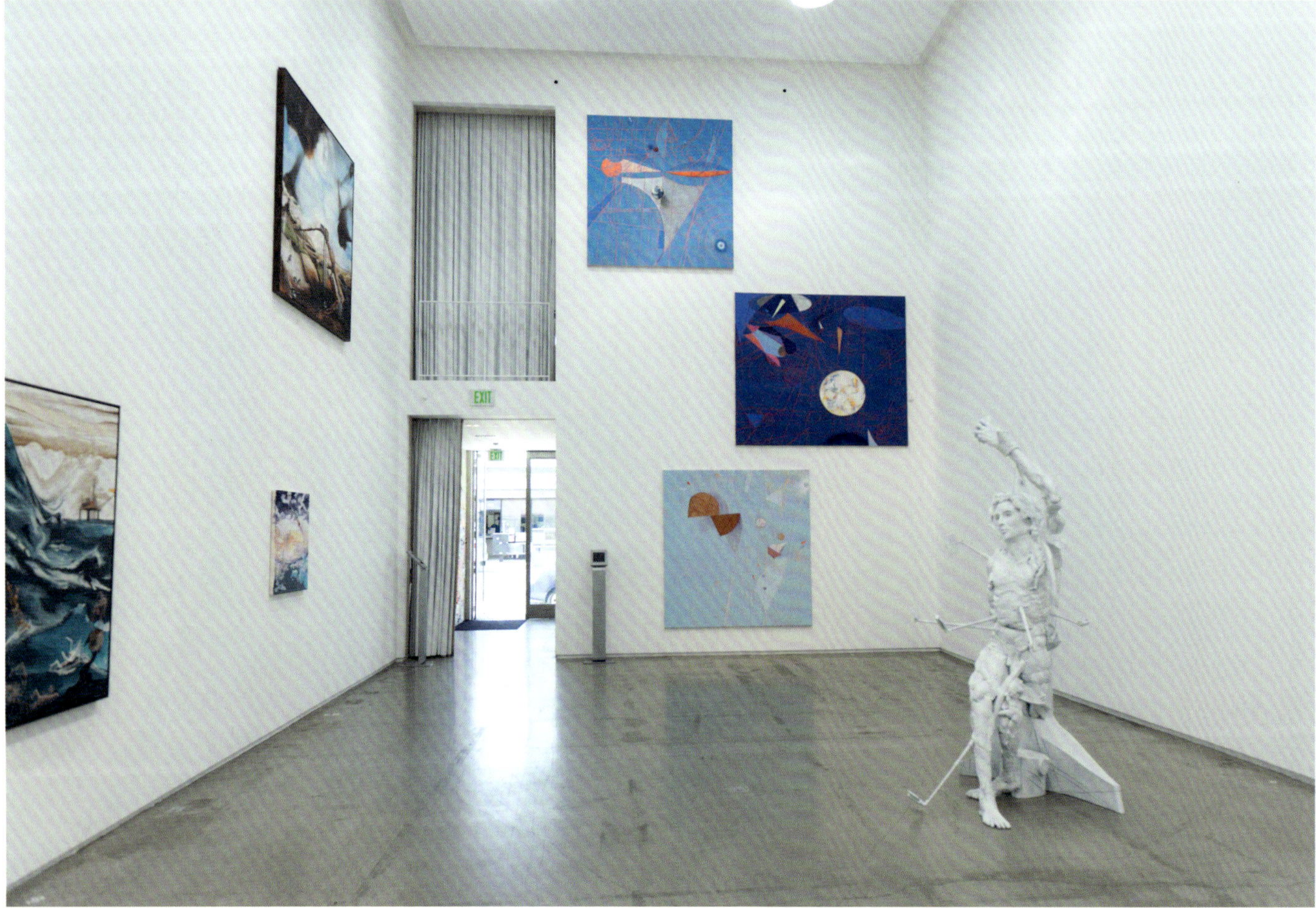
EXIT

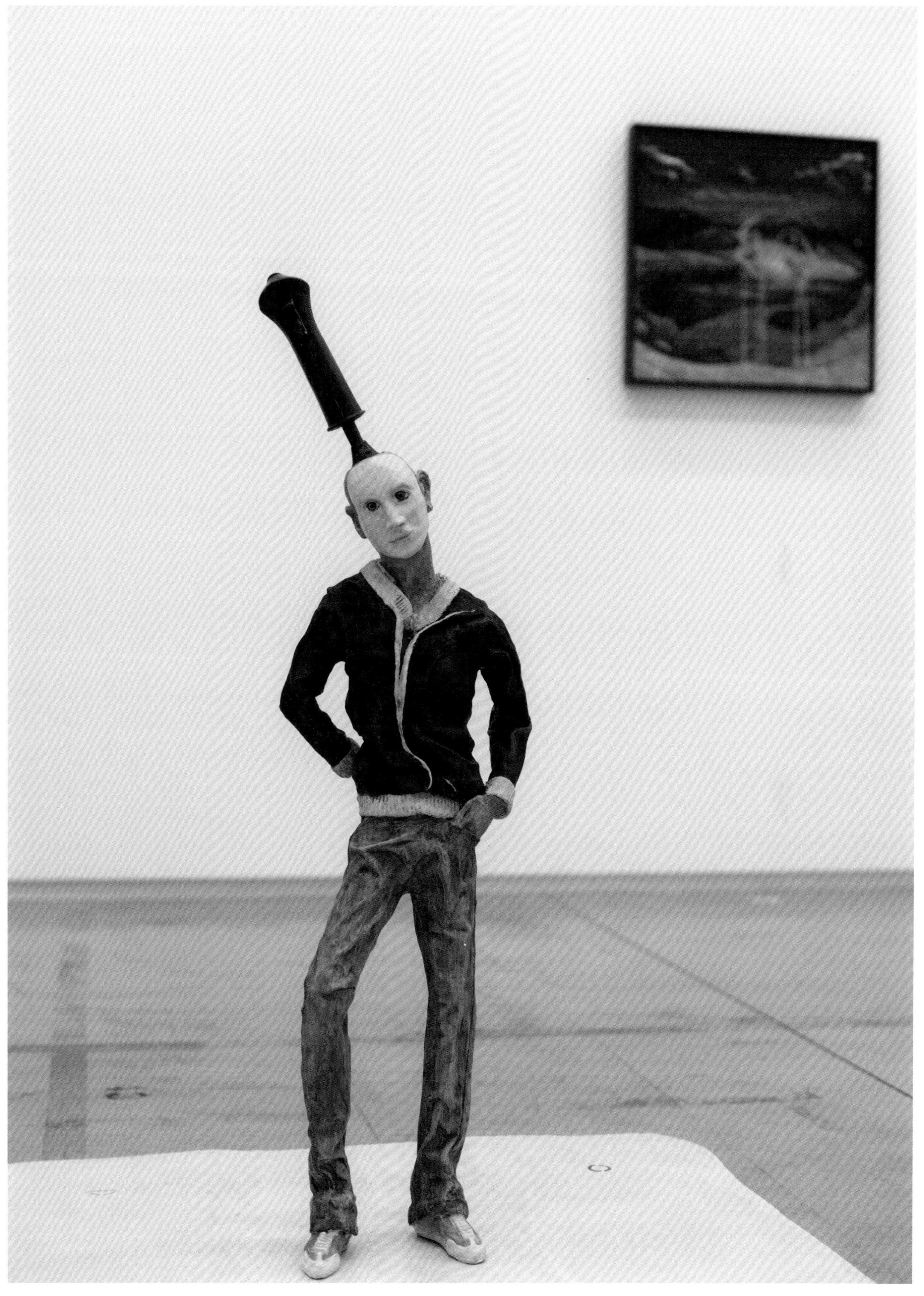

ESMoA COLLABORATION
PLANT

Amely Spötzl, 2019

ESMoA presents Experience 43: PLANT, the first solo exhibition of German based artist Amely Spötzl, on view from October 24, 2019 through January 25, 2020. The Experience invites visitors to peek inside her studio and experience the ephemeral nature of plants.

Since childhood, Spötzl has played with, and been intrigued by, plants and structures found in nature. In her public interventions, the outline of a plane leaf becomes a silver live drawing on the side of a building in El Segundo (Phytomagnetic, 2014) and strategically placed acrylic boxes filled with flowers on L.A.'s Westside inspire spontaneous actions and reactions by passerby (Just a Moment, Please, 2009). For her sculptures and drawings, Spötzl often incorporates dried flowers and plants, creating geometric artworks that replicate number sequences and repetitive systems. On view for PLANT will be 20 artworks that Spötzl has documented and created as part of her evolving study of nature, including but not limited to photographs, drawings, and sculptures. Her latest work, Chapel of Process will be reveled for the first time as part of the Experience.

A replica of Spötzl's studio will also be built into the gallery providing guests with further insight into an artist's laboratory based on fascination, connectedness, play and curiosity.

Additionally, PLANT will include an interactive artwork, Thicket, where visitors can actively contribute to its formation using drawing tools created by Spötzl. Also on view will be photographs of Spötzl's artworks created in collaboration with photographer Bernd Zoellner.

Born in 1975 in Biberach on Riss, Germany, Amely Spötzl resides and works in Bonn, Germany. She studied sculpture at the Alanus University of Arts and Social Science, Bonn / Alfter Germany. In recent years, she has lectured, drawn, sculpted and worked in mixed media there.

Spötzl has shown in Germany and the United States, including the Montalvo Arts Center. ESMoA has previously shown her work in Experiences DESIRE (2013), SILENCE (2014), SPARK (2015), and EAT (2019). Spötzl's work appears in collections in the U.S. and Germany.

The ESMoA Experience Award recipient for PLANT is Jasmine Nyende. Nyende is a new media artist from South Central Los Angeles whose work explores the fields of fiber, music and community-based social practice using poetry, plays, and experimental performance. Her work has been shown at institutions throughout Los Angeles including the Hammer Museum, Human Resources, and Sade Gallery. Nyende's installation, Experience 22: A Love Letter to the California Coast is a large-scale embroidery work on burlap that will be installed in ESMoA's Entry. Visitors will have the chance to add to the installation during the run of Experience 43:PLANT.

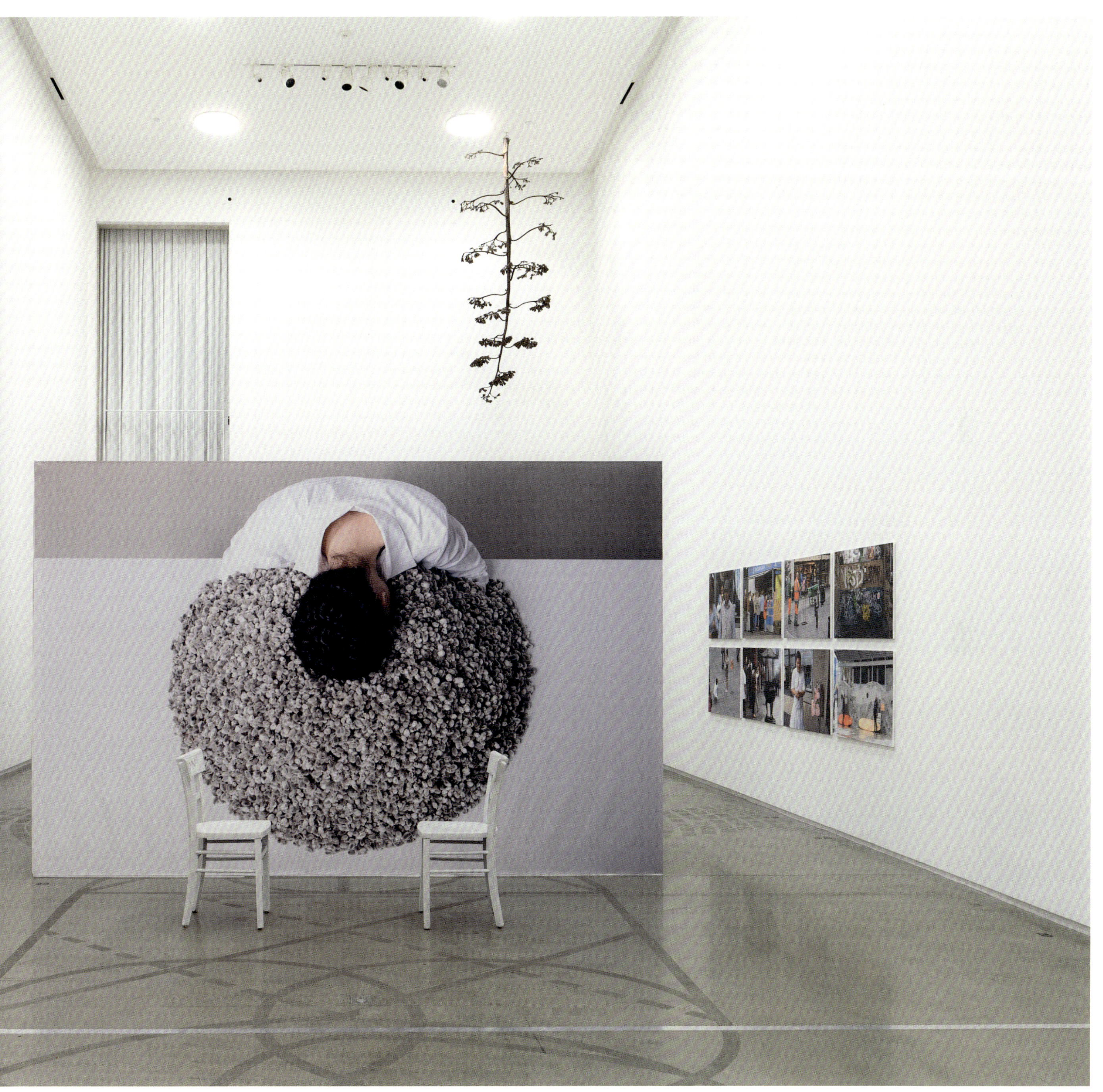

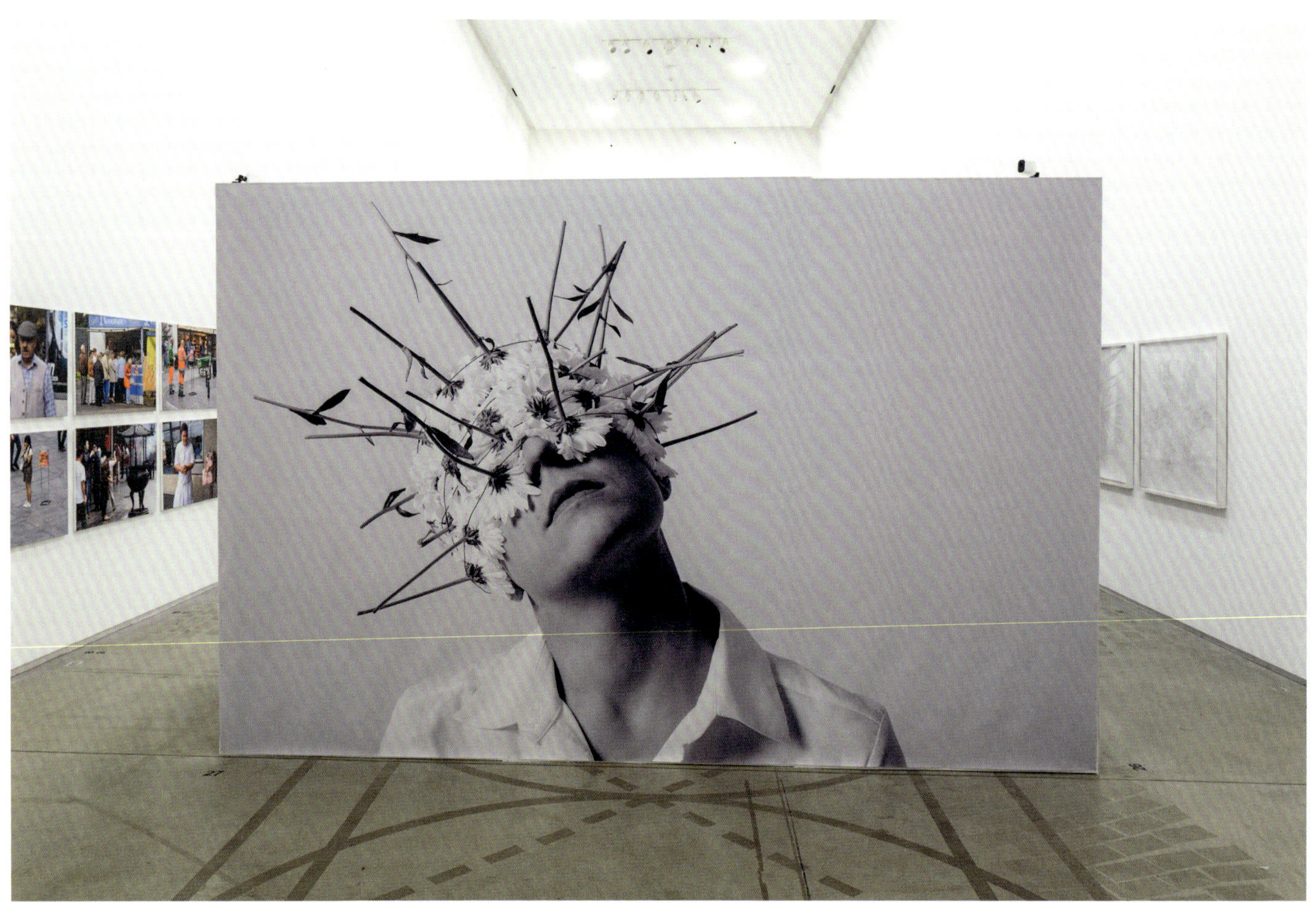

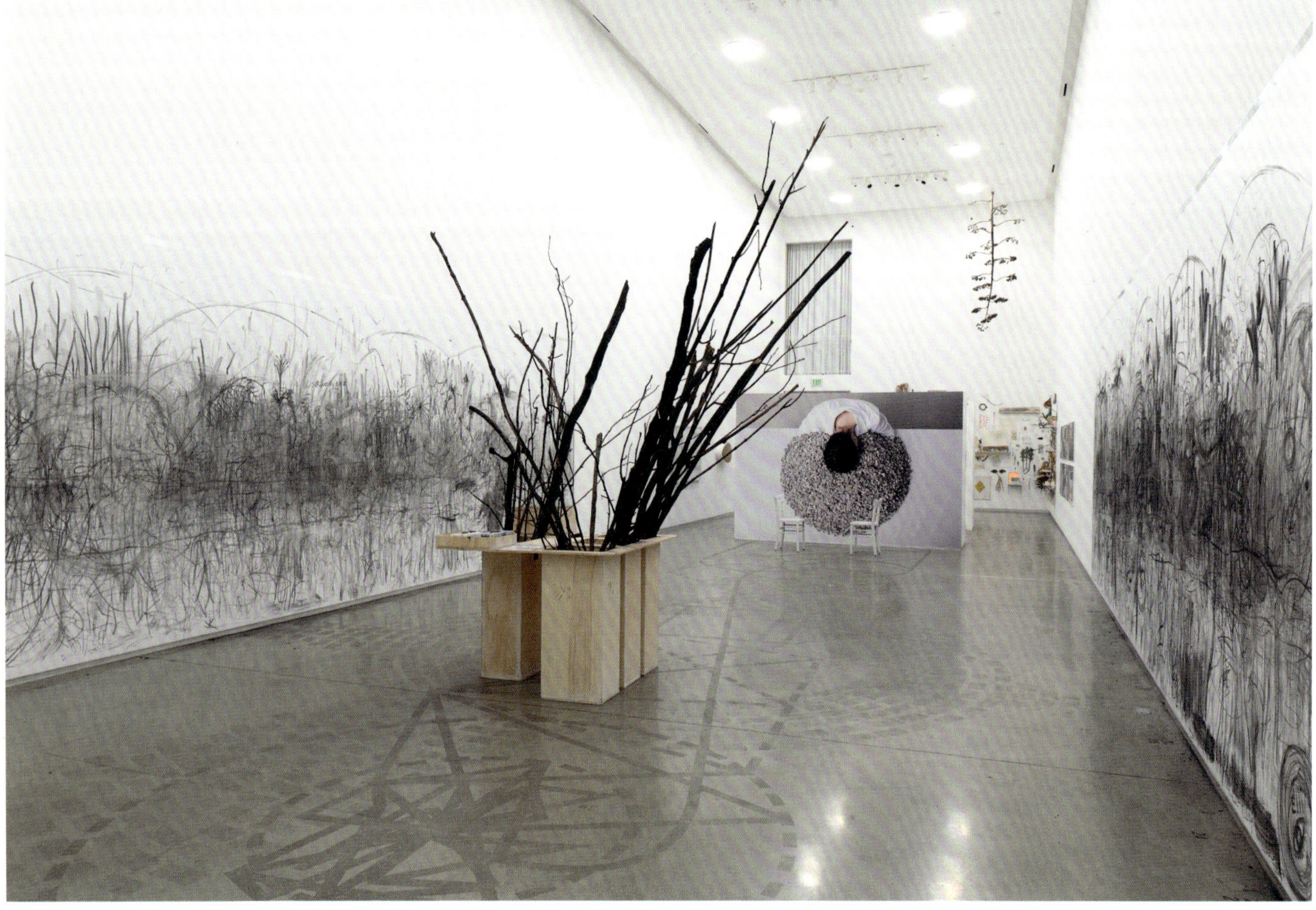

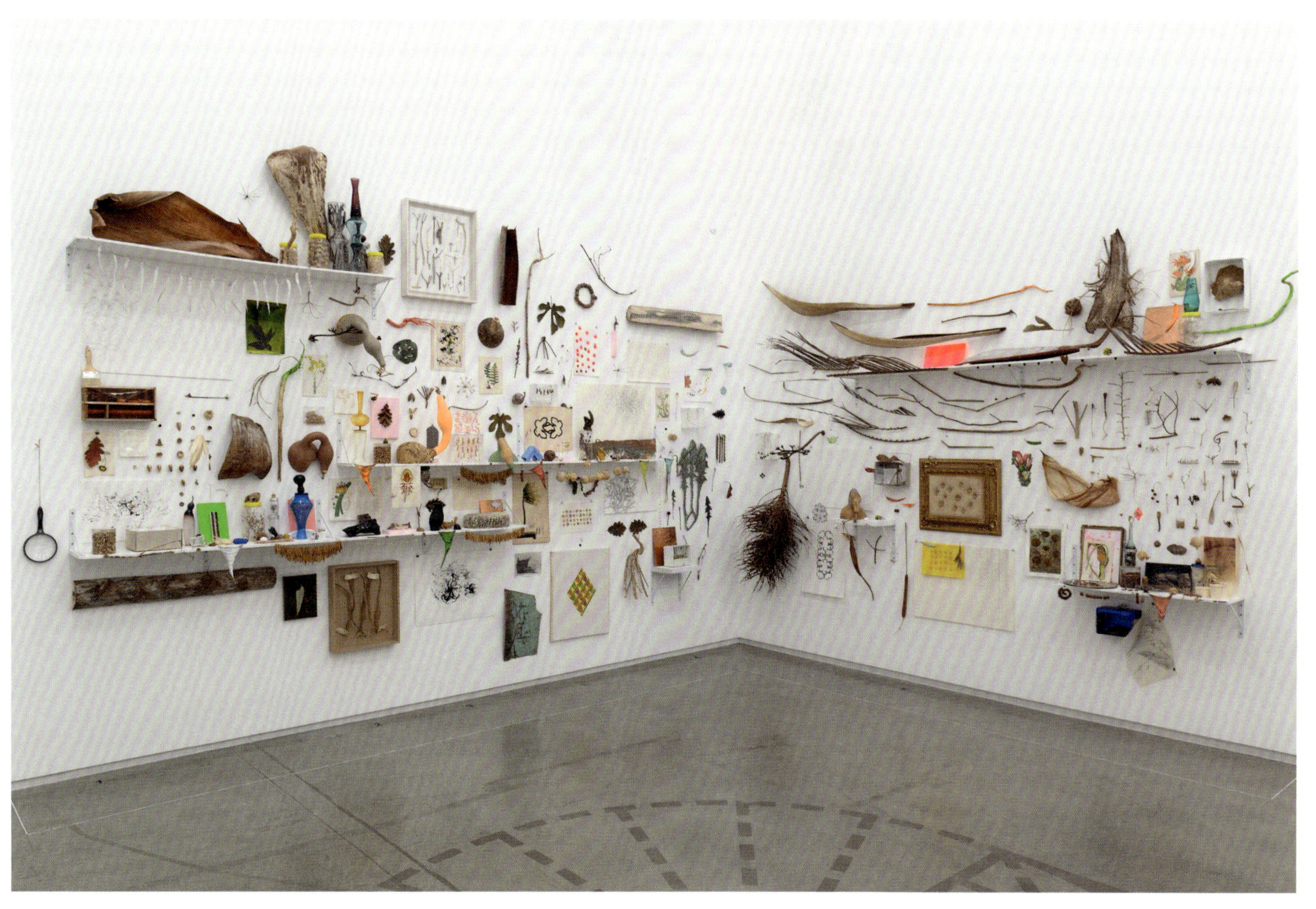

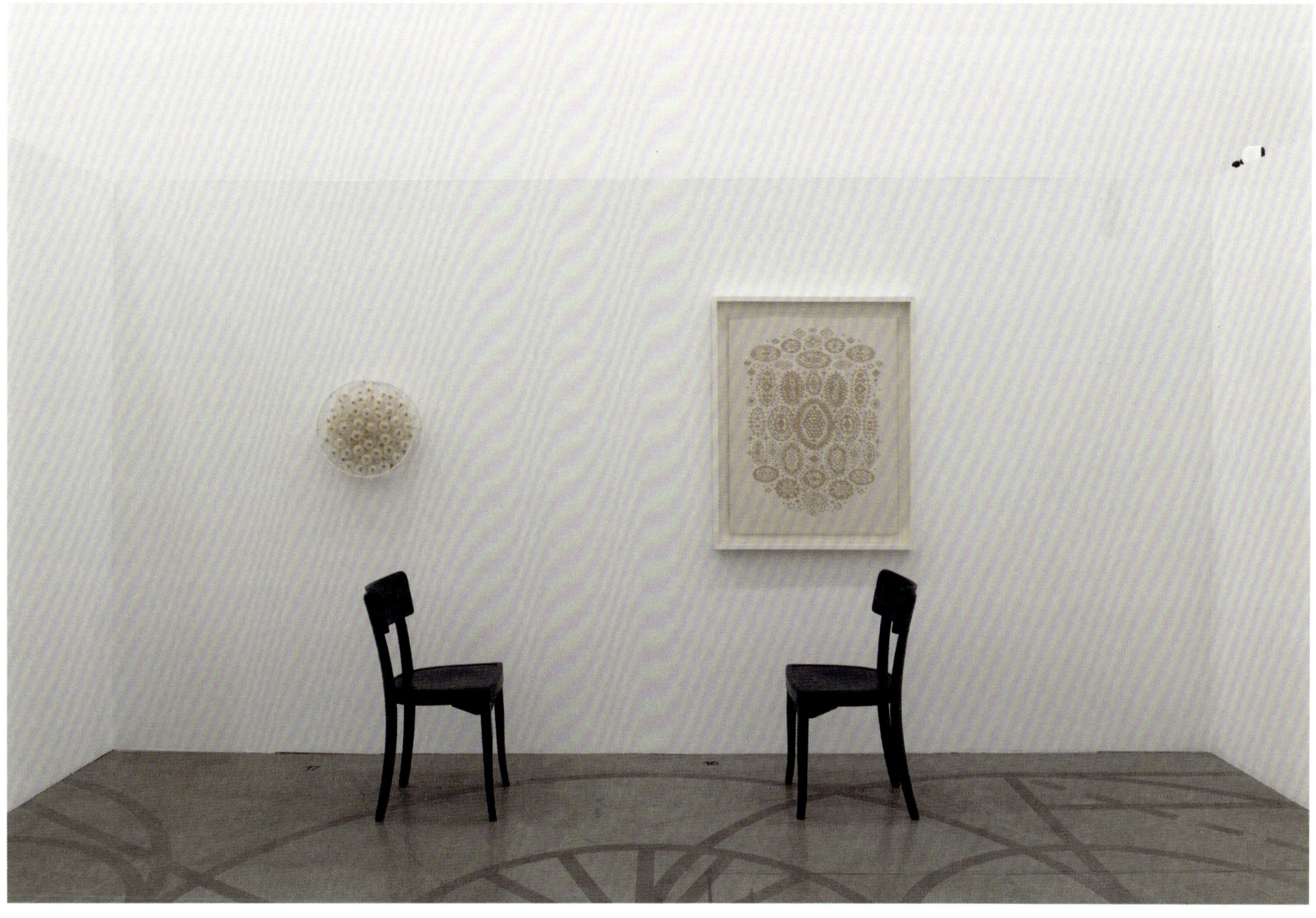

ESMoA COLLABORATION **STARDUST**

Bernhard Zünkeler with Freeters and more, 2020

STARDUST explore the different pathways of thinking. Art is a state of mind. Artworks are able to prime and inspire your brain activity. They can wake you up, where intuition has put you to sleep. Through STARDUST the visitor will experience the underlying laws of creative thinking. STARDUST is a backstage pass to the world of artistic stimulation and a showcase of the power of an artist collective.

The ESMoA Experience Award recipient for STARDUST is Rachel Reid, a Los Angeles based artist, transforming stardust into a sequence of ceramic variations. Rachel Reid is an artist and master printer. She received her BFA in sculpture from the Pacific Northwest College of Art. Heavily influenced by the simplicity of form and color, Rachel navigates both 2D and 3D media, most extensively in lithography as well as stoneware ceramics.

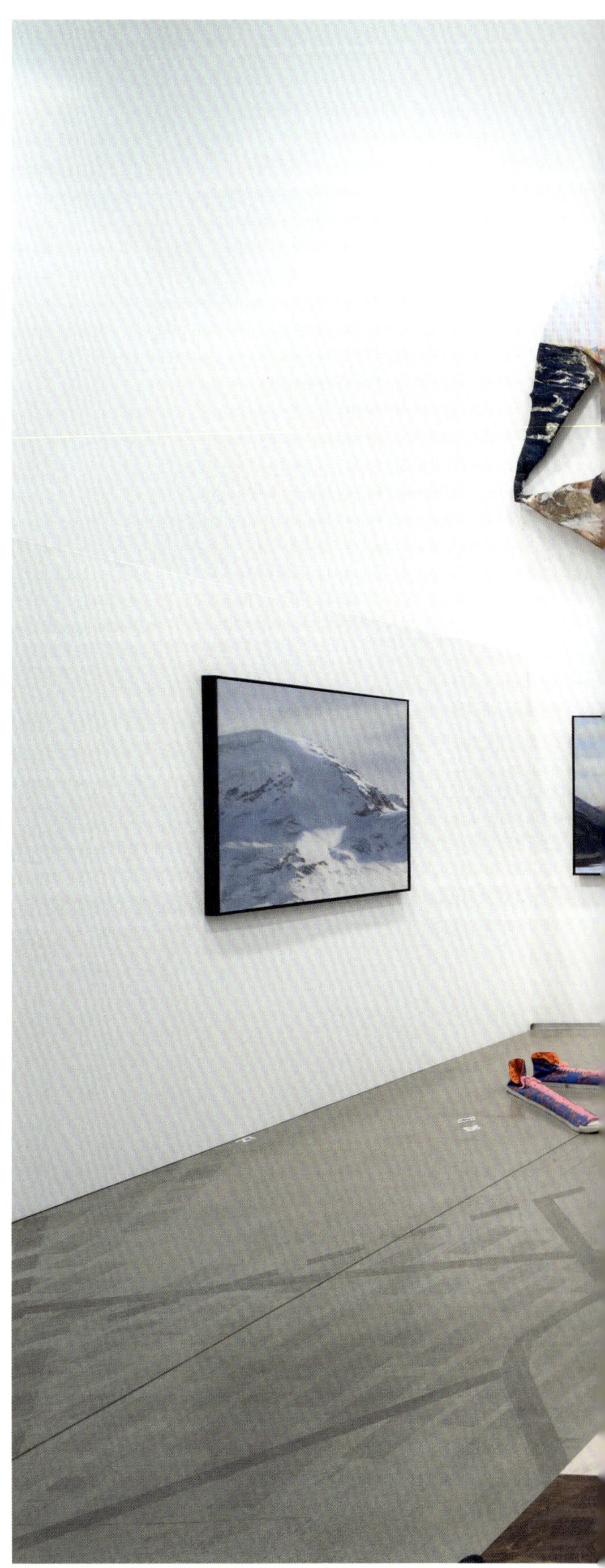

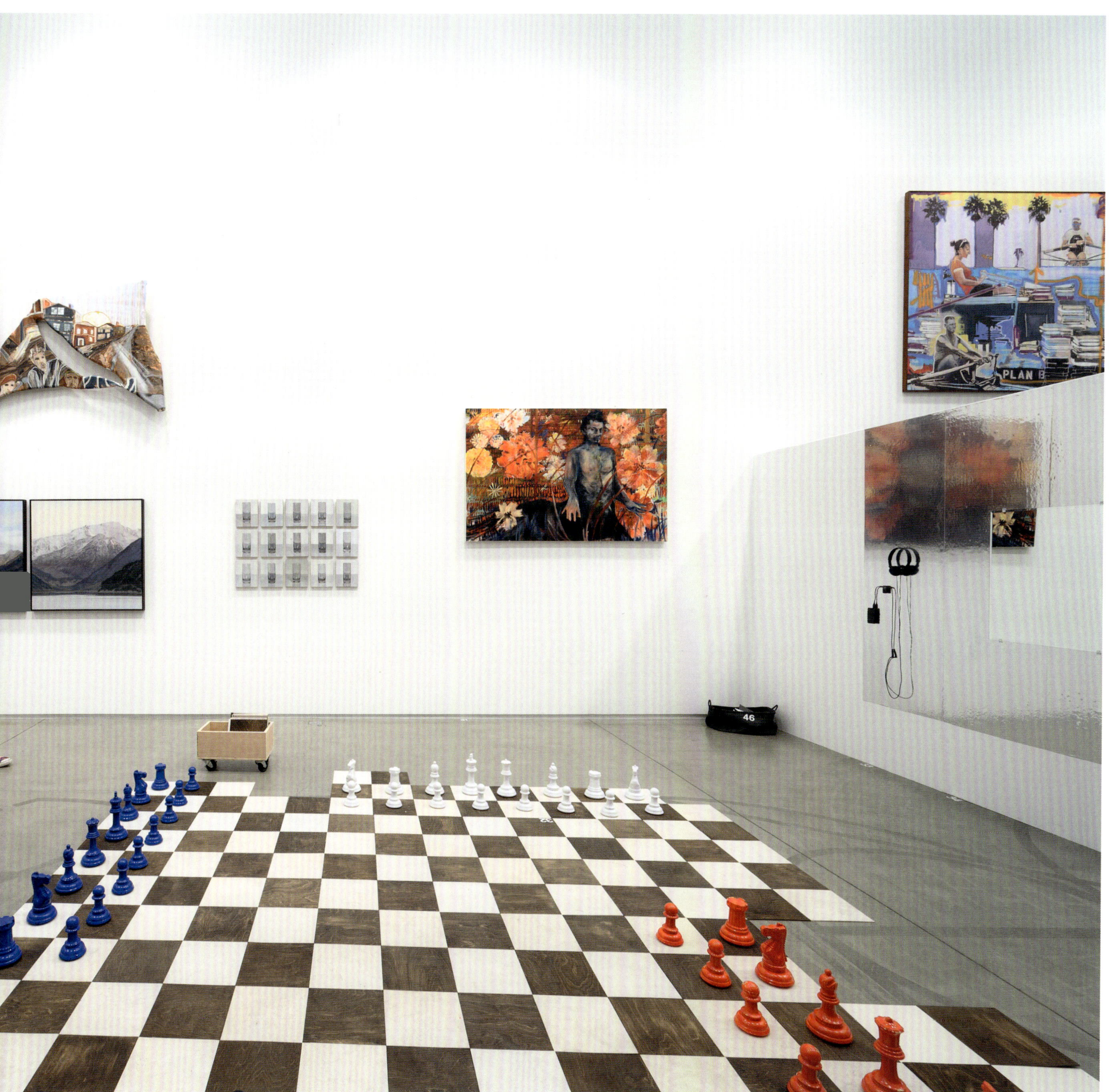
PLAN B
46

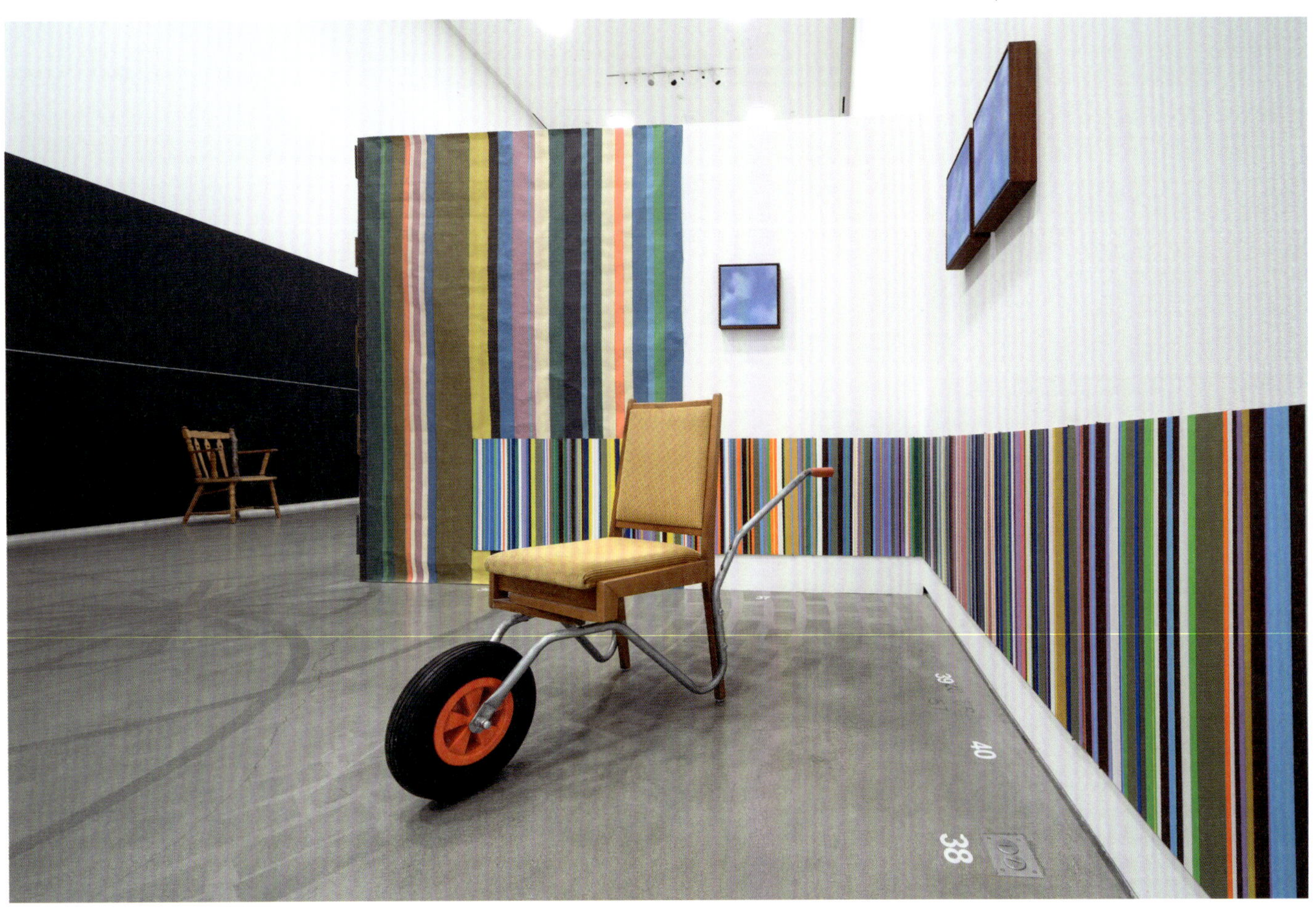

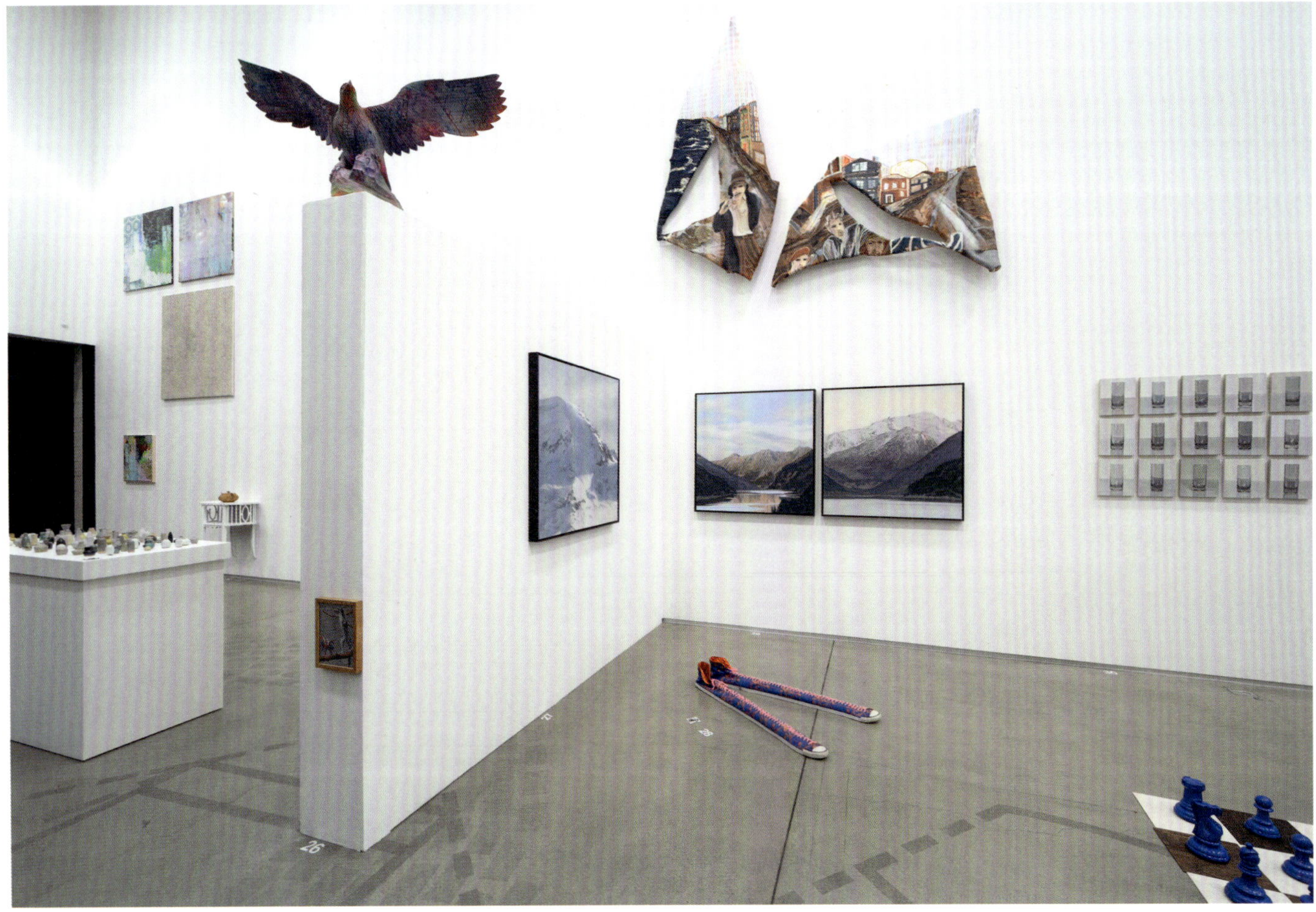

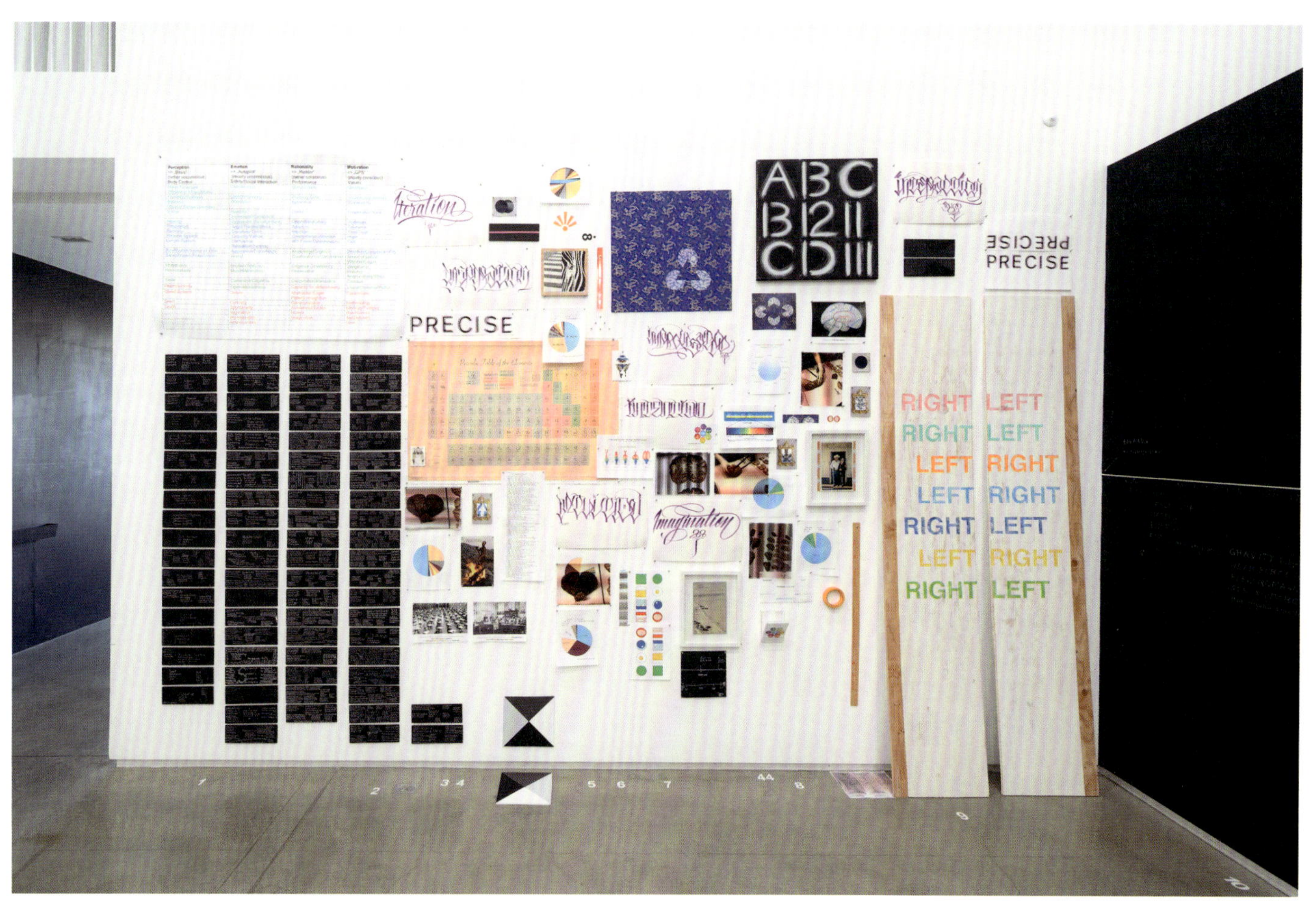
ABC
B2II
CDIII
PRECISE
PRECISE
RIGHT LEFT
RIGHT LEFT
LEFT RIGHT
LEFT RIGHT
RIGHT LEFT
LEFT RIGHT
RIGHT LEFT

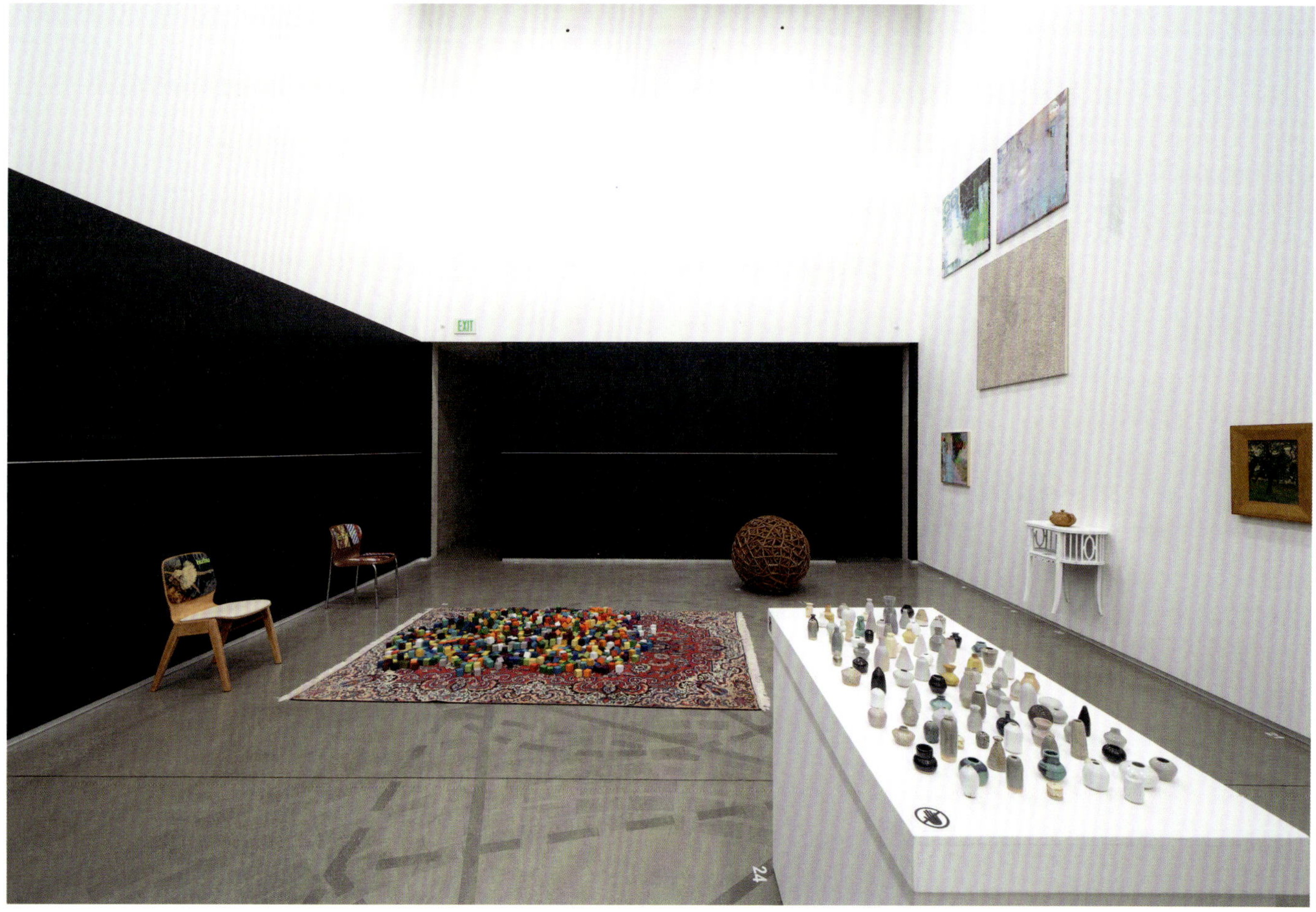
EXIT

ESMoA COLLABORATION
ELSEGUNDISSIMO

Collective Exhibition, 2018

Experience 27 is about you, the citizens of El Segundo, as you celebrate our city's 100th anniversary. And it is about you, visitors from all parts of the world, coming to LA. ELSEGUNDISSIMO* will be a crowd-sourced Experience, based on your feedback. What could be done better in our city? What are the sore spots, the sticking points, the areas that need improvement? How can we strengthen the connection between the east and west sides of Sepulveda? Whatever you can think of will be addressed.

Would you like to put a smile on your face when you enter the City? What would put tears in your eyes when you leave town?

In fall 2016, ESMoA collected your thoughts and wishes, and in a unique democratic process will ask local, national and international artists and architects to come up with solutions. When Experience 27: ELSEGUNDISSIMO opened its doors in March 2017, visitors were able to vote for the best ideas.

Ideas are born from ideas! Let's make this a combined effort! Let's make it ELSEGUNDISSIMO!

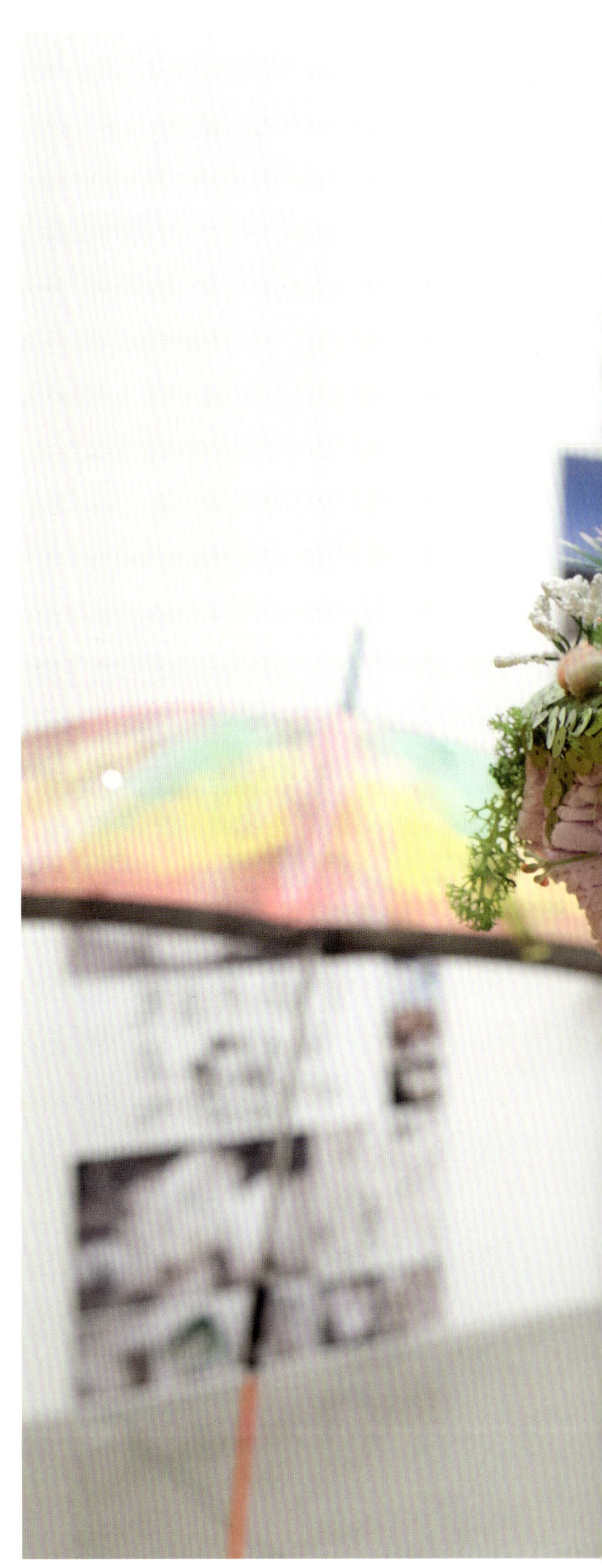

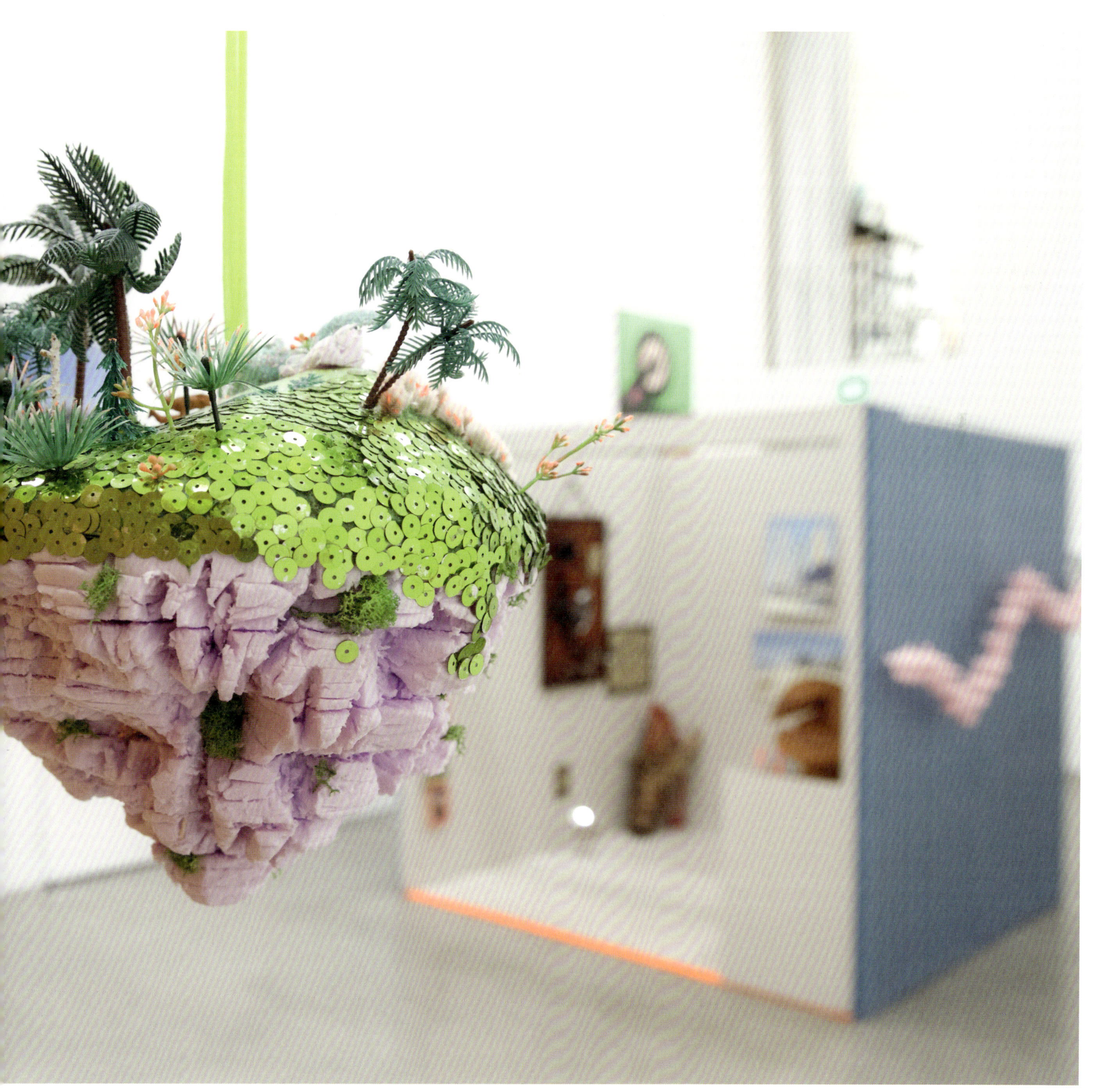

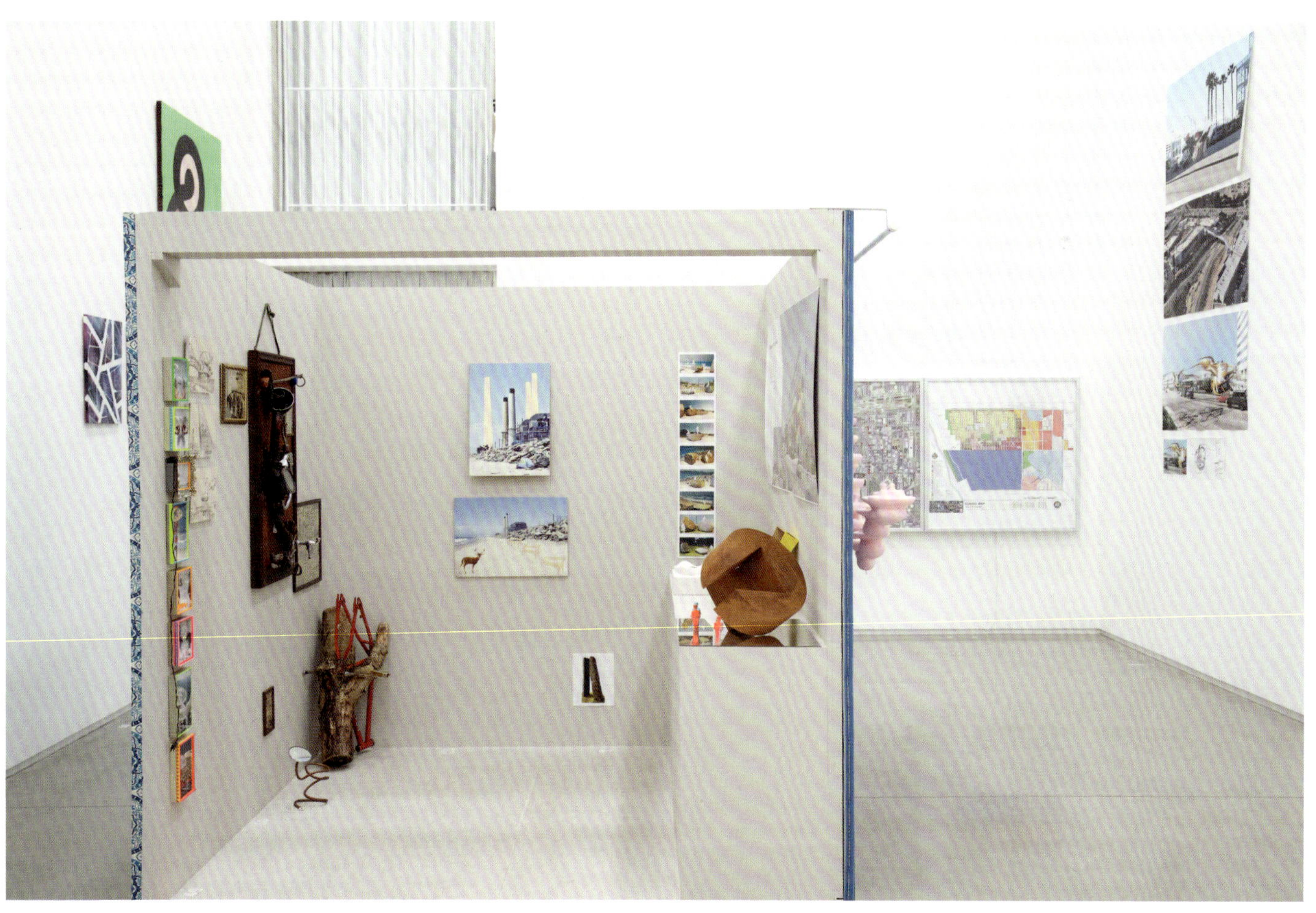

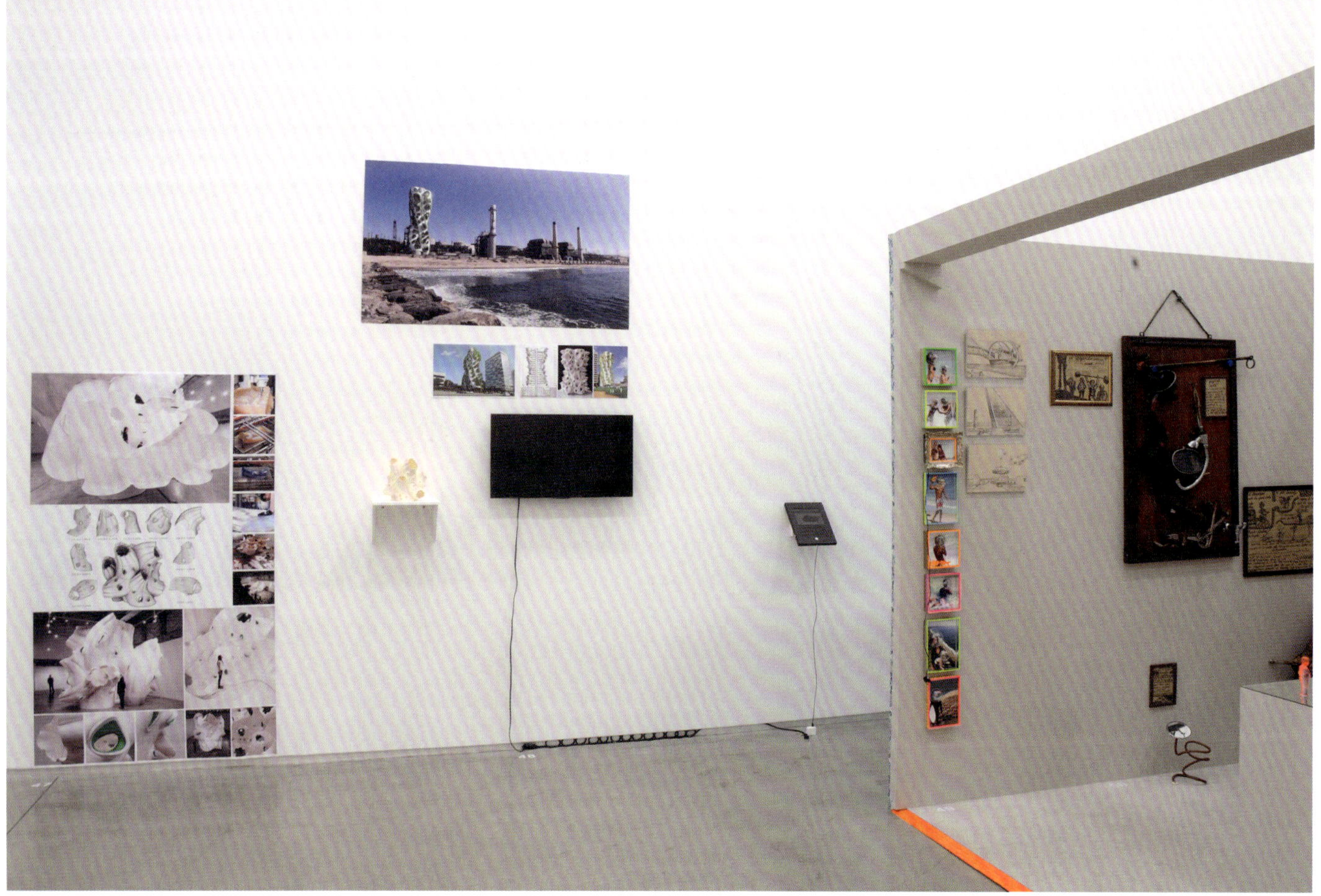

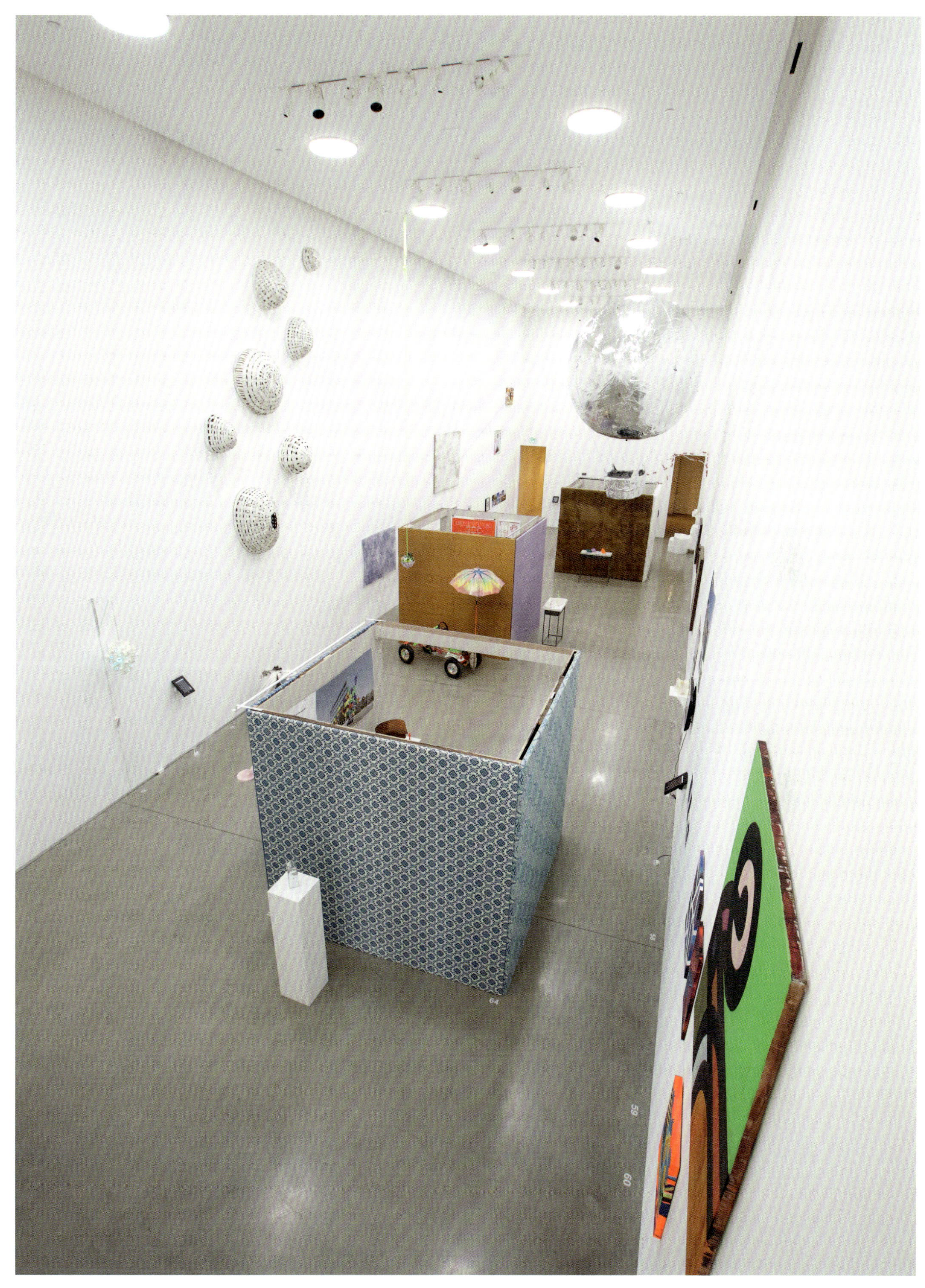

FEEDBACK FILMS

Cologne, 2020
Cooperation with Nikolas Jürgens and Feedback Films Production.

Zamma Summa

Meanwhile

Gabriel –
oder Mein Haus, mein Block!

Ach wie gut,
dass niemand weiß …

Rio Reise

Smooth

Fach C2

Touché

Unbegrenztes
Halteverbot

5G war
gestern

Rumkugeln

Nikolatte

Banana

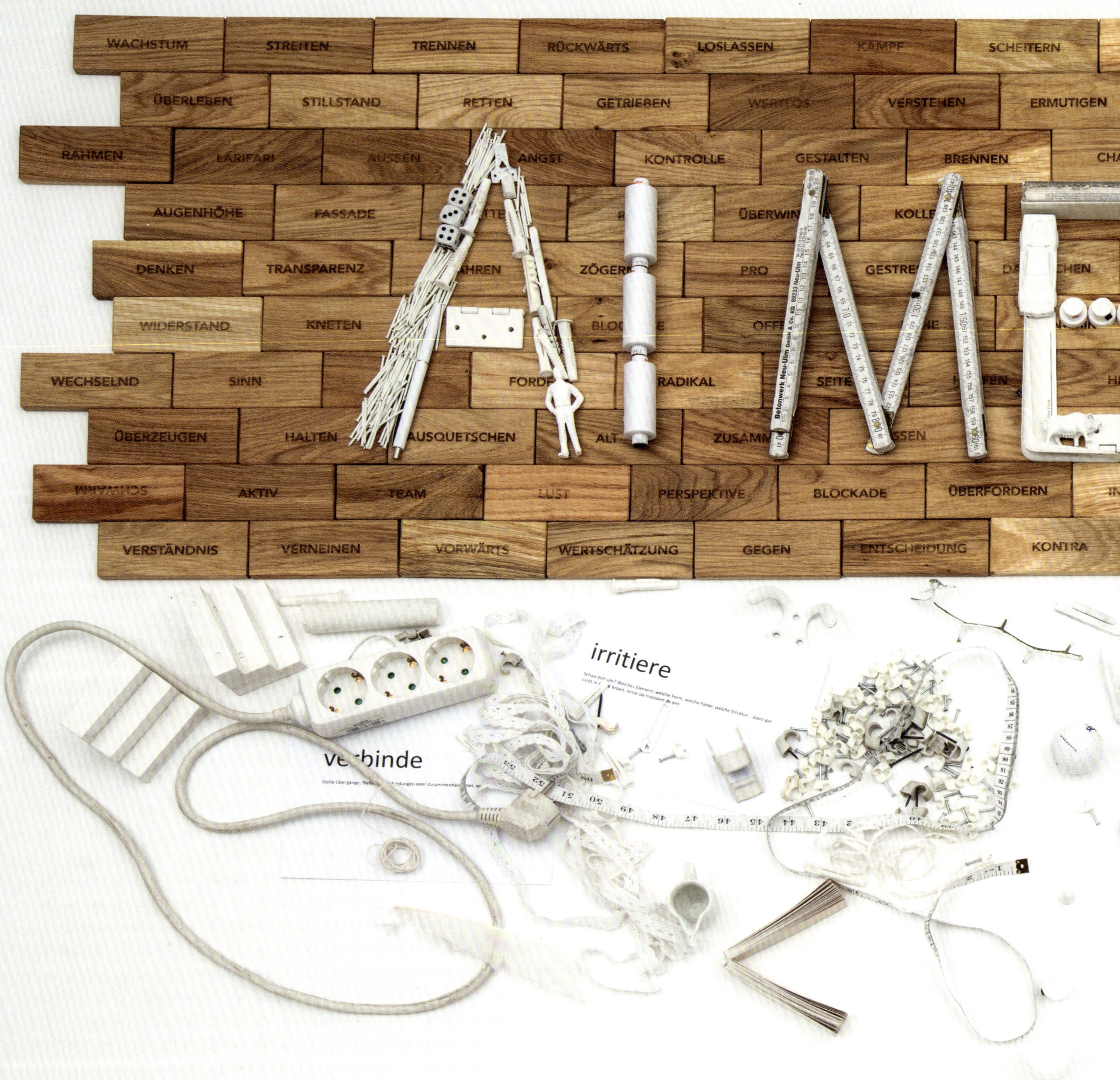
WACHSTUM
STREITEN
TRENNEN
RÜCKWÄRTS
LOSLASSEN
KÄMPFE
SCHEITERN
ÜBERLEBEN
STILLSTAND
RETTEN
GETRIEBEN
VERSTEHEN
ERMUTIGEN
RAHMEN
LARIFARI
AUSSEN
ANGST
KONTROLLE
GESTALTEN
BRENNEN
AUGENHÖHE
FASSADE
DENKEN
TRANSPARENZ
PRO
WIDERSTAND
KNETEN
WECHSELND
SINN
RADIKAL
ÜBERZEUGEN
HALTEN
AUSQUETSCHEN
ALT
AKTIV
TEAM
LUST
PERSPEKTIVE
BLOCKADE
ÜBERFORDERN
VERSTÄNDNIS
VERNEINEN
VORWÄRTS
WERTSCHÄTZUNG
GEGEN
ENTSCHEIDUNG
KONTRA
irritiere
verbinde

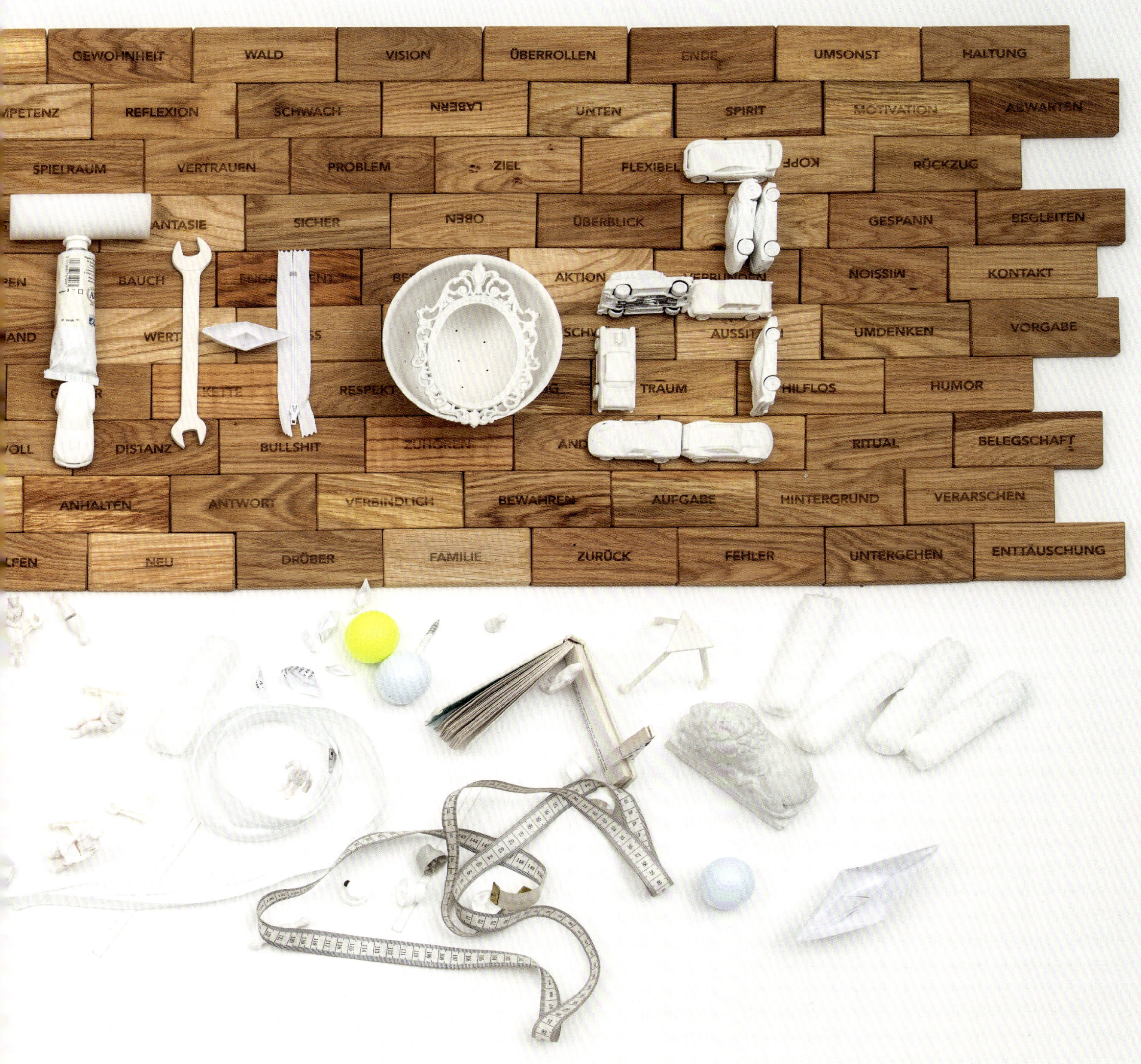
GEWOHNHEIT
WALD
VISION
ÜBERROLLEN
ENDE
UMSONST
HALTUNG
REFLEXION
SCHWACH
LABERN
UNTEN
SPIRIT
MOTIVATION
ABWARTEN
SPIELRAUM
VERTRAUEN
PROBLEM
ZIEL
FLEXIBEL
KOPF
RÜCKZUG
SICHER
OBEN
ÜBERBLICK
GESPANN
BEGLEITEN
BAUCH
AKTION
MISSION
KONTAKT
UMDENKEN
VORGABE
RESPEKT
TRAUM
HILFLOS
HUMOR
DISTANZ
BULLSHIT
ZUHÖREN
RITUAL
BELEGSCHAFT
ANHALTEN
ANTWORT
VERBINDLICH
BEWAHREN
AUFGABE
HINTERGRUND
VERARSCHEN
NEU
DRÜBER
FAMILIE
ZURÜCK
FEHLER
UNTERGEHEN
ENTTÄUSCHUNG

AI METHOD
LEARNING LAB

The Learning Lab is a space of possibilities, experimentation, irritation, play, and learning. It is a space for unusual workshops and tools. What kind of learning? Subtract all conventional experiences from what you associate with learning, and you have the Learning Lab. Change of perspective, interdisciplinarity, improvisational skills, creativity, and tolerance of ambiguity are key concepts in dealing with the time-defining factors of uncertainty and not-knowing.

But how do we acquire all these future-relevant competencies? We are convinced that by providing space, time, and stimuli, uncertainty and not-knowing may not be eliminated but can be worked with. There are no recipes nor standardized formulas for this. We understand not-knowing as not-yet-knowing and provide workshop concepts and inspirational tools in the Learning Lab, making it possible to explore the potential within it. Thought-provoking methods drive the search for new solutions and the optimization of existing ones.

ON THE CONSTRUCTION OF SPACES OF POSSIBILITY AND (S)TOOLS

Sandra Freygarten

Freeters' spatial designs include not only physical constructions but also spaces in which the Freeters' method can be experienced. They are experiential laboratories, problem-solving stations, and spaces of possibility for new things. Tools are constructed that break down barriers to thinking and help illuminate topics from unusual perspectives. Materials are at the ready to pose impetuous questions and provide fresh insights. Because an experimental approach is an essential, innovation-generating component of professional artistic activity, methods that provoke experimentation have been developed. They are derived from the creative processes of Freeters' spatial transformations.

That chair over there, it's squiggly and robotic at the same time. It oscillates between bright airiness and dark ostentation, between science fiction and rustic tradition, between raw pipes and antique woodwork. Worlds collide. The rupture is obvious. Apart from the technically qualified work undertaken, the connection there is seemingly none but contrast. The character of the parts remains. They enhance each other in their otherness. And this squiggle in the middle, a question mark without a dot, an inverted S? Irritating. Many people have sat on this chair, on the robust wood-framed leather surface, leaning against the triple-curved solid oak. The aluminum construction, a so very different, sturdy supporting structure. Comfortable, ergonomic, well-proportioned, balanced.

How might this chair have been created? In the mind of the artist? It is more likely that this unique bar stool came into being through active, hands-on play with concrete materials. By experimenting between deconstruction and construction, the goal, namely a chair, became apparent and something new emerged.

First there was a massive curlicue chair, its design no longer up to date, but solidly crafted. Individual scaffolding poles were also around. As was a curvy wooden fragment that had once been the ornament of a dresser. All these things in a room full of other furniture and objects. The gaze was allowed to wander, the imagination to take up space, something was taken out and rearranged. Or each part had to be found first, peeled out of each different context, and brought together. This finding required a certain form of perception—elements were examined on the basis of their expressiveness, aesthetics, and ability to combine with other elements; investigated for their impact and possibilities. Seemingly unrelated parts were combined. Things were transformed. What had previously been scaffolding now became part of a chair. What was a seat remained so, but only half of it. A found object corresponded with a part of a chair—related in color and carved from the same wood. What was special about the form, the color, and the material was given prominence and became even more apparent in contrast with the other qualities. Fragments became a whole.

The processes of creation of artifacts like this chair proceed nonlinearly and in dialogue with material. This can be anything—stone, text, color, sound, plasticine, toothpicks, or aluminum rods and chairs. The material is taken into consideration and taken in hand, examined, arranged, reduced, formed, and reshaped. It is not a shaping according to a given plan, but rather a discovery of possibilities by doing.

With this special kind of doing as a basis, spaces, workshop concepts, and tools for companies and institutions have been created. With and within these companies, artistic design paths can be traced and their own channels to innovative power and creative passion can be tapped. Multifunctional tools break down the development of this chair into experimental stages as an illustration and thus make this complex artistic action tangible. This process is not for cultivating amateur artists or for integrating creative downtime, it is for utilizing experimental thinking and action for non-artistic tasks. For thinking of mission statement work in terms of breaks, contrasts, and contradictions. For analyzing a company from the perspective of a paper clip. For bringing chance and playfulness into employee communication. And for developing an organization through complementary strategies.

In contrast to the explanatory and action models of many methods and tools, the AI Method does not have a simplifying and limiting effect, but rather breaks down barriers and channels ideas and potential.

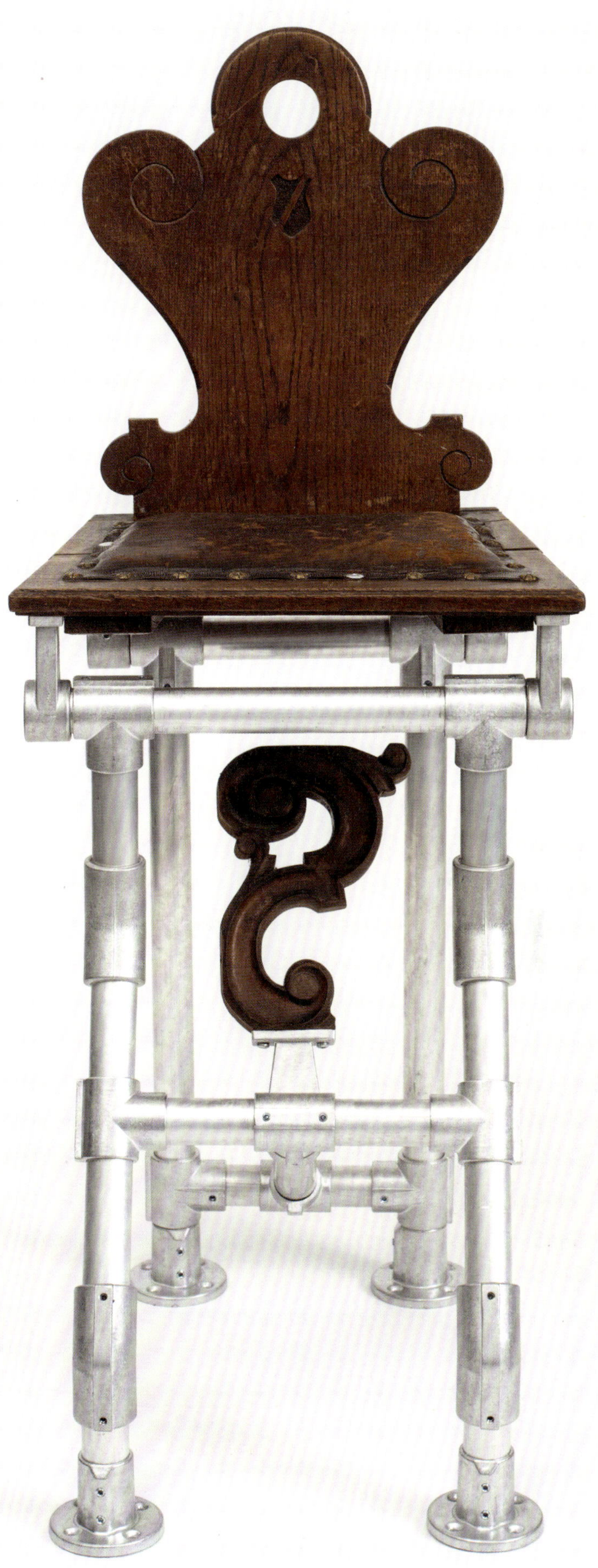

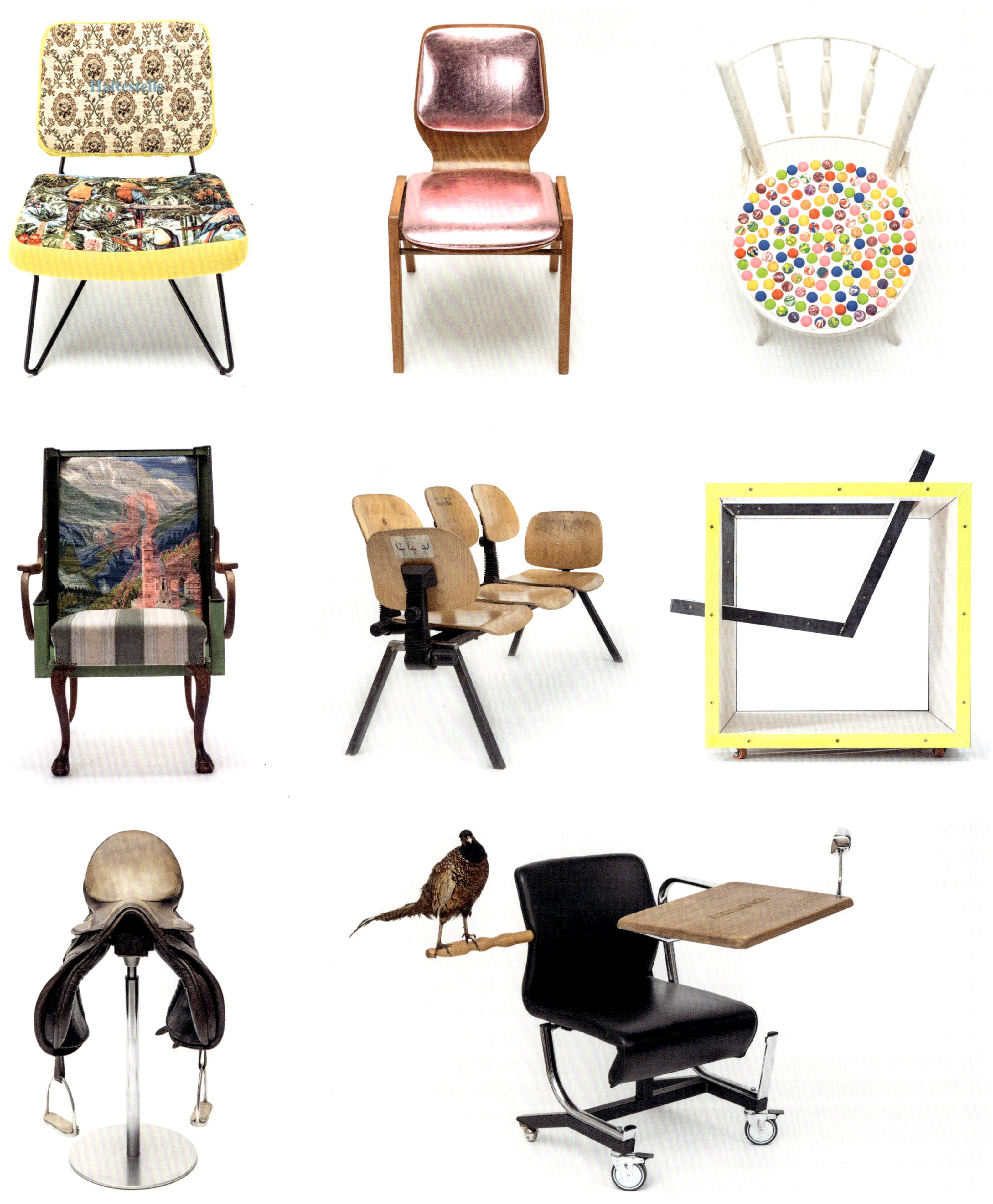
Haltestelle

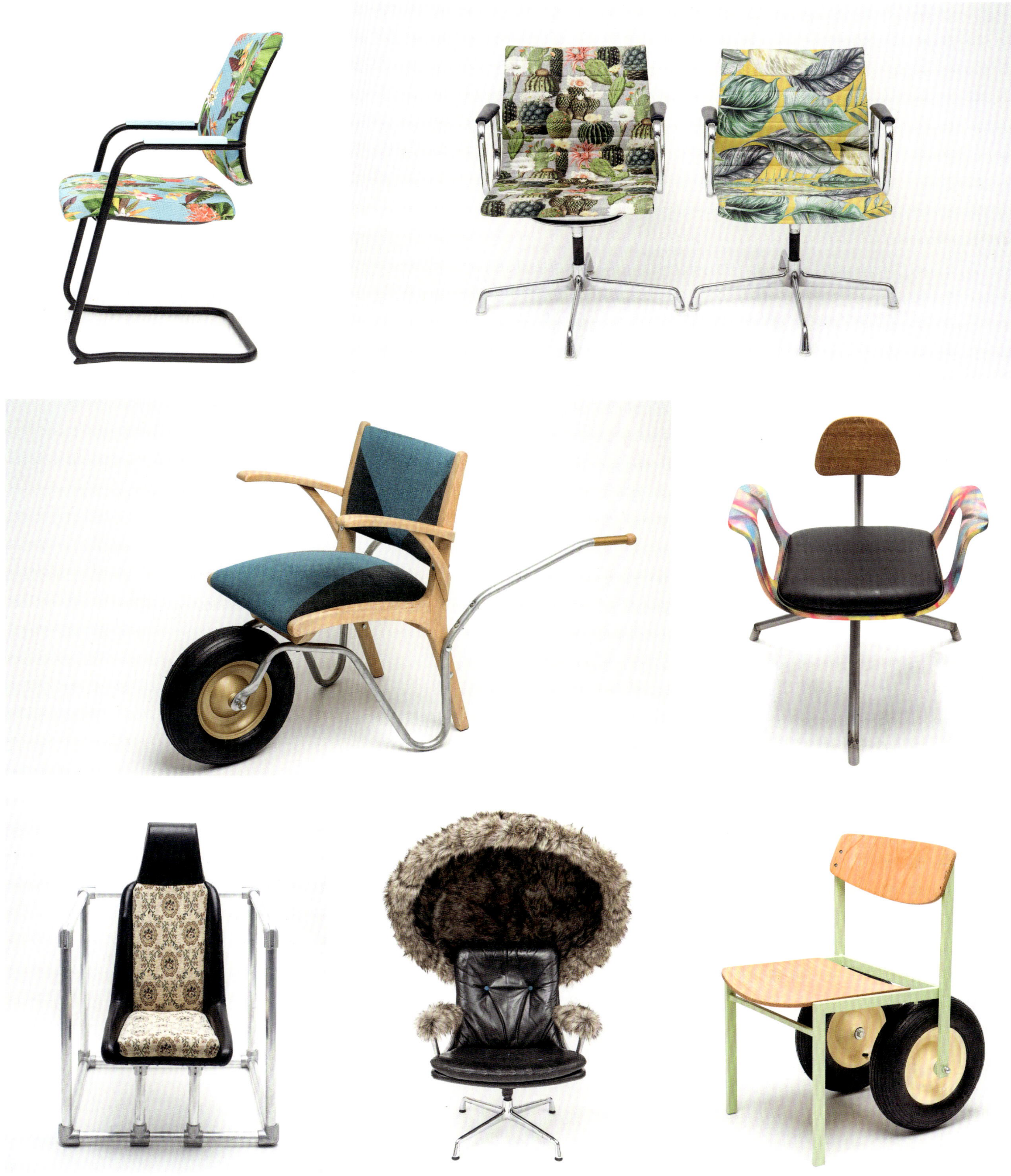

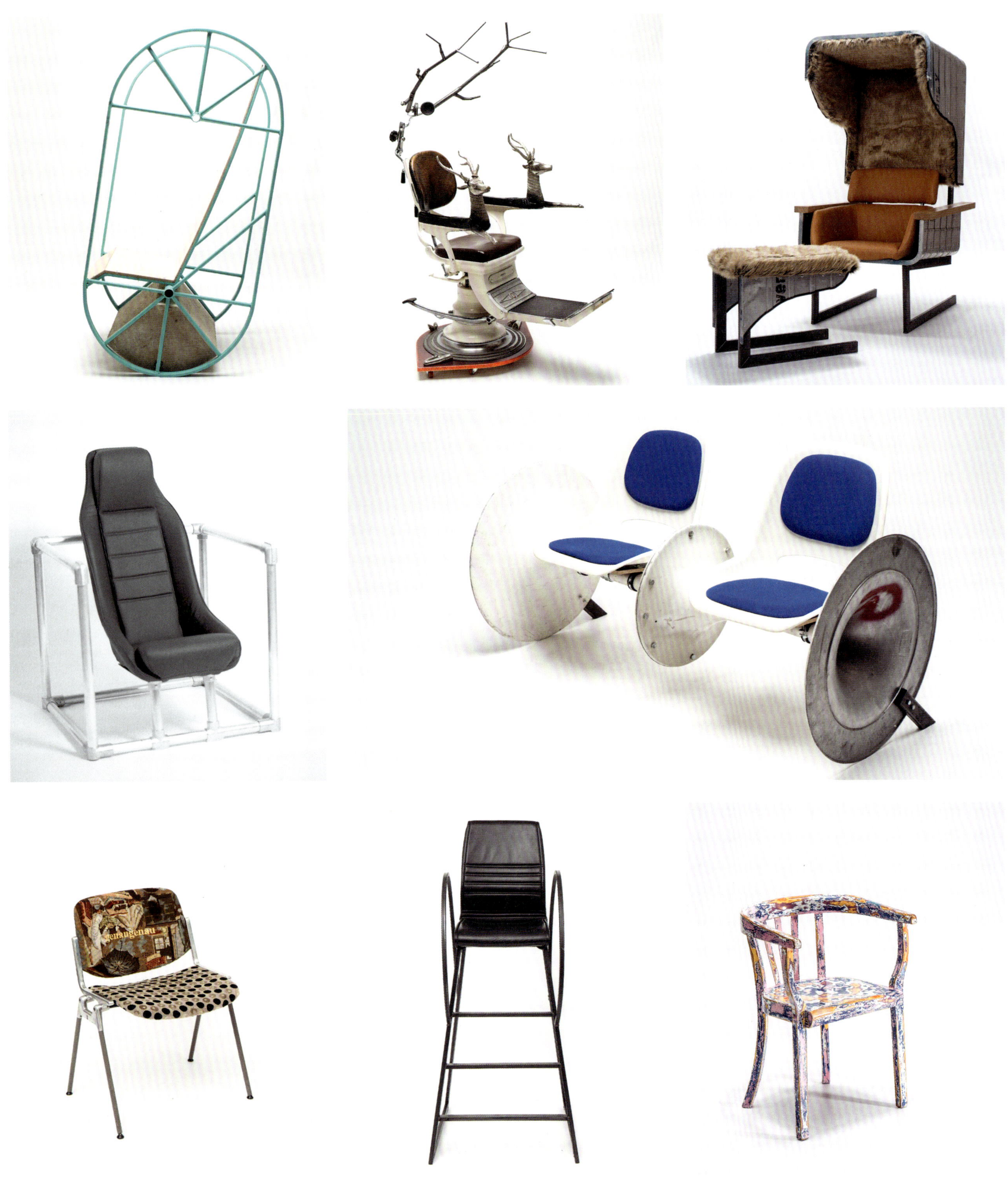
genaugenau

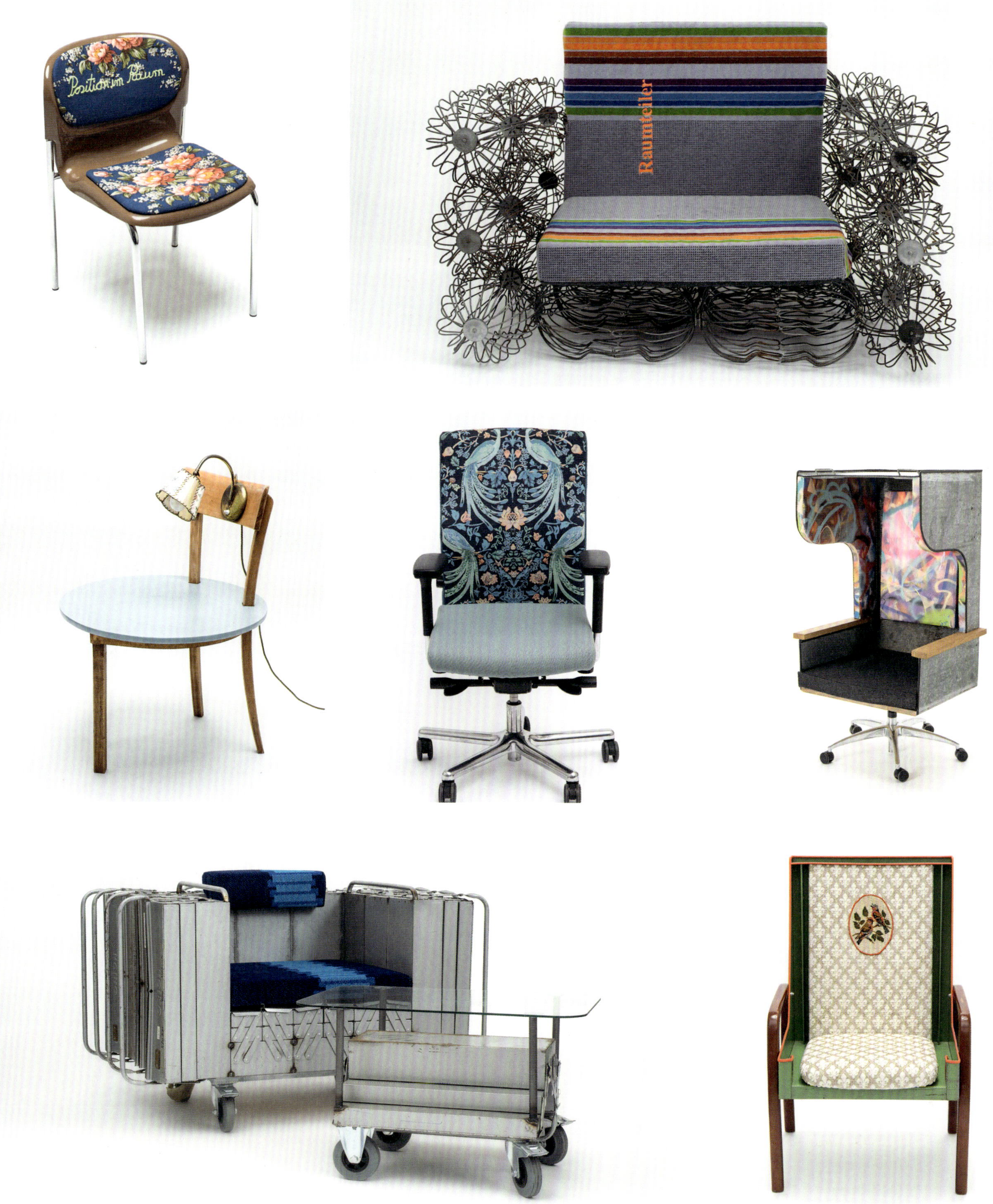
Position im Raum
Raumteiler

TOOL
TAKE WORDS

A collection of terms around the topics of work, attitude, team, and cooperation.

This process tool offers unusual gateways to topics, opens experimental approaches, and lets you think and talk differently about issues.

Example: A team would like to discuss the topic "How can we make better use of our skills?"

SELECT
Each person draws two words for each of the following questions:
- Which concept is central for me to fully utilize my skills?
- What is the most effective way to keep me from using my skills?

SHARE
Come together in small groups, share the words you chose.

IMPROVISE
Turn over all remaining words and shuffle them. Each person draws a third word to put alongside the two original words.

COMBINE
Combine the words by changing their order. What thoughts and ideas emerge?

ASSOCIATE
Think of more words and make up words related to art. Write them down.

CONNECT
Look for relationships between everyone's words. Make families of words.

DEMONSTRATE
Think of concrete scenarios that promote your skills.

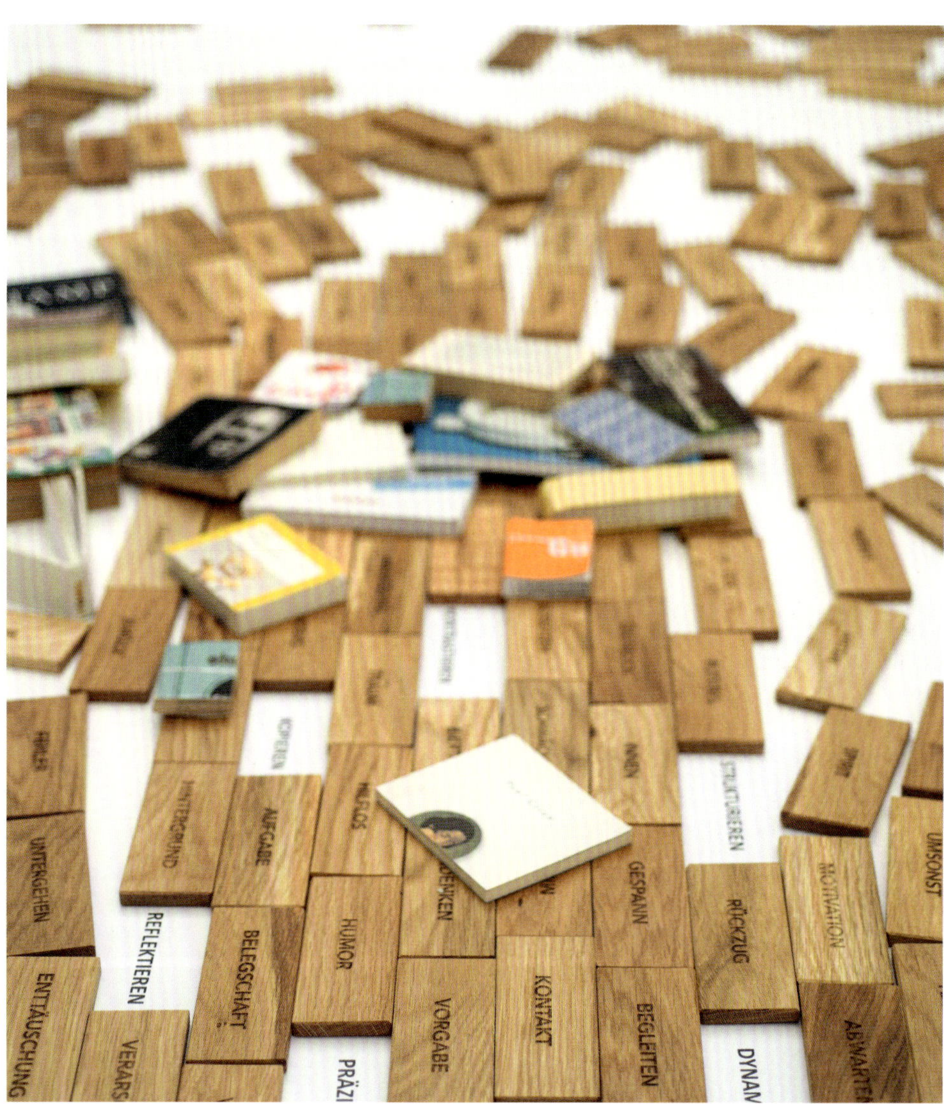

TOOL
MAKE ATTIDUDES

A method for exploring your attitudes and positions.

Design and transformation processes can be experienced through fragmenting, constructing, and rebuilding objects. When you think with your hands, unusual results are produced, which simultaneously activate a three-dimensional examination of personal perspectives and places of longing.

Make Attitudes is designed specifically for each new situation and context.

DECONSTRUCT
Take apart what is already there.

PLAY
Arrange fragments and pieces of material into new temporary shapes.

PERCEIVE
What effects do the resulting combinations, shapes and contrasts have?

CONSTRUCT
Build an unique.

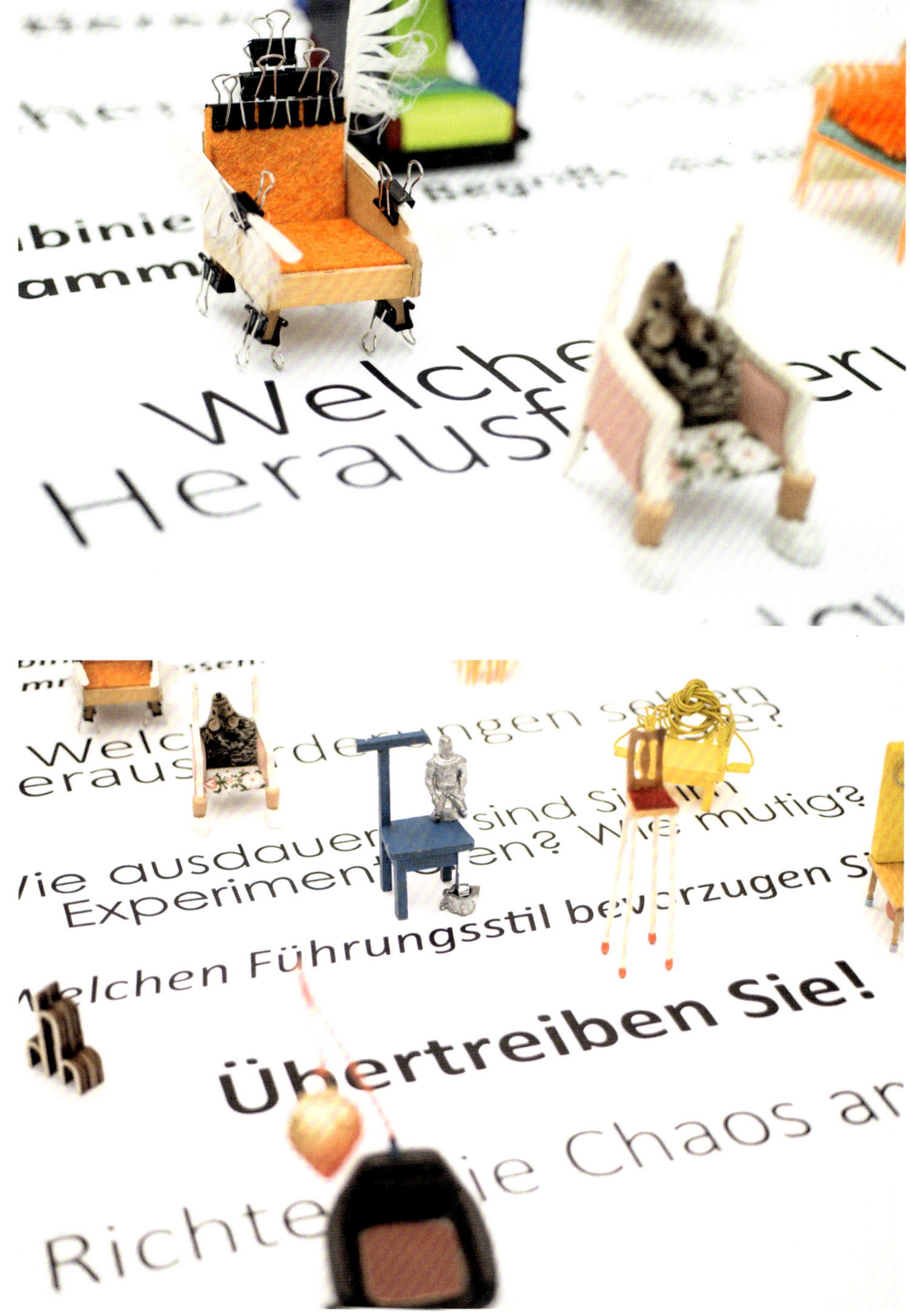

TOOL
TAKE DICE

An inspiration tool that opens up surprising new directions and twists. With its action-based nature, it gets groups moving. Even topics stuck at dead ends gain momentum.

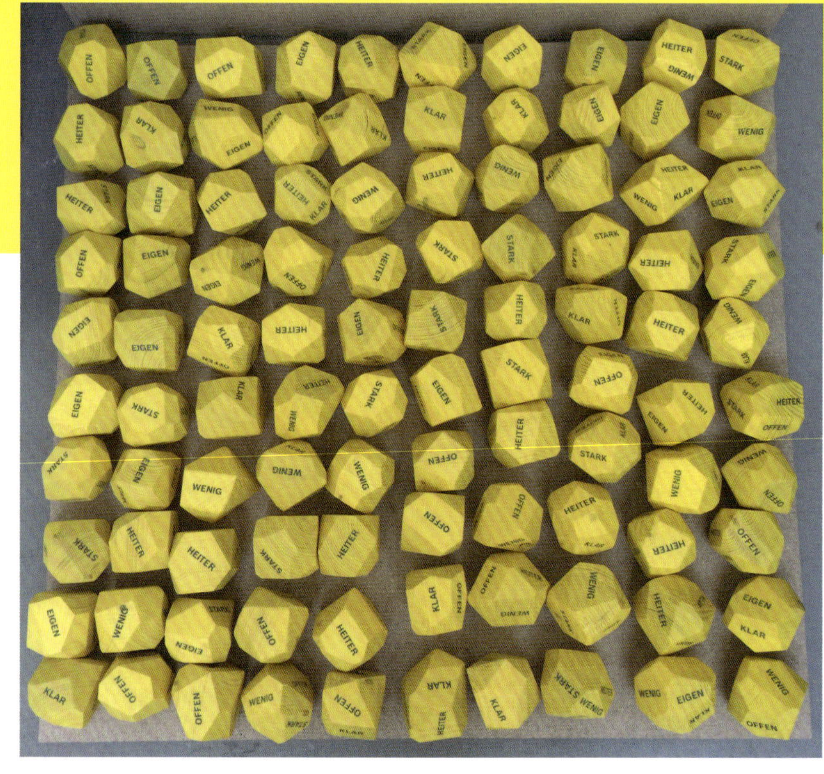

This process tool promotes improvisational competence, sharpens resourcefulness, and encourages spontaneity.

Example: A team looks back on a phase of collaboration.

INITIATE
One person rolls the dice and gets the term "integrate."

CHANCE
What does the term "integrate" have to do with the person rolling the dice? In what situations does the person relate to this concept? Does it bring up any specific memories? The other participants make a list of any associations that come to mind.

REPEAT
The dice are rolled and associations are made until each person has had a turn.

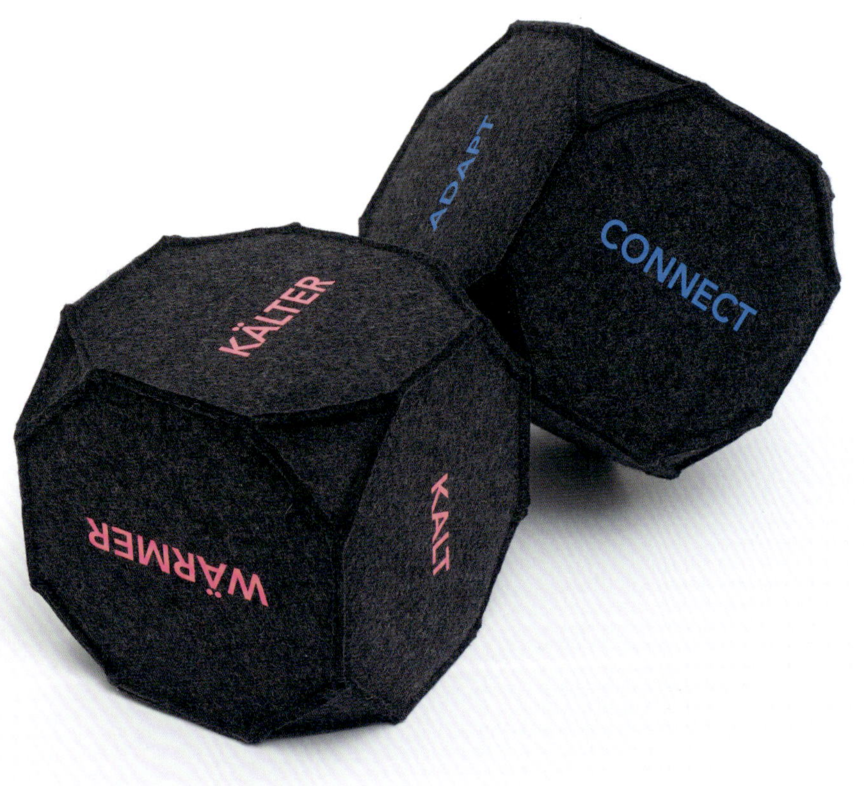

TOOL

WHITE DRAGON

An associative tool that addresses attitudes, styles, and playful ways of acting.

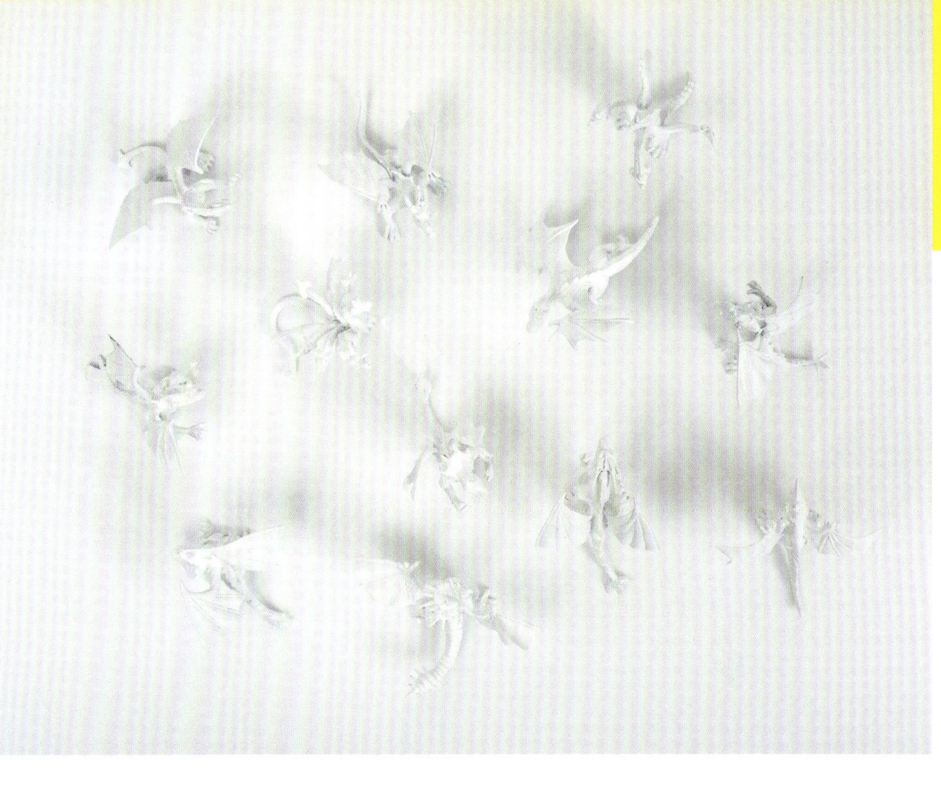

This process tool opens up new perspectives, is tremendously stimulating for the imagination, and encourages visualization.

Example: A group works on the topic of leadership styles.

FANTASIZE

Each person chooses a dragon associated with a leadership style they have encountered in their professional life. The participants tell each other which characteristics of the dragon they each associate with the chosen leadership style.

VISUALIZE

Using the dragons, the participants define the characteristics of a desirable leadership style. Is there already a dragon among the 12 who has the right skills, the right attitude? Share your vision with the group.

SUMMARIZE

Agree on characteristics of the leadership style you favor. Record the essential aspects.

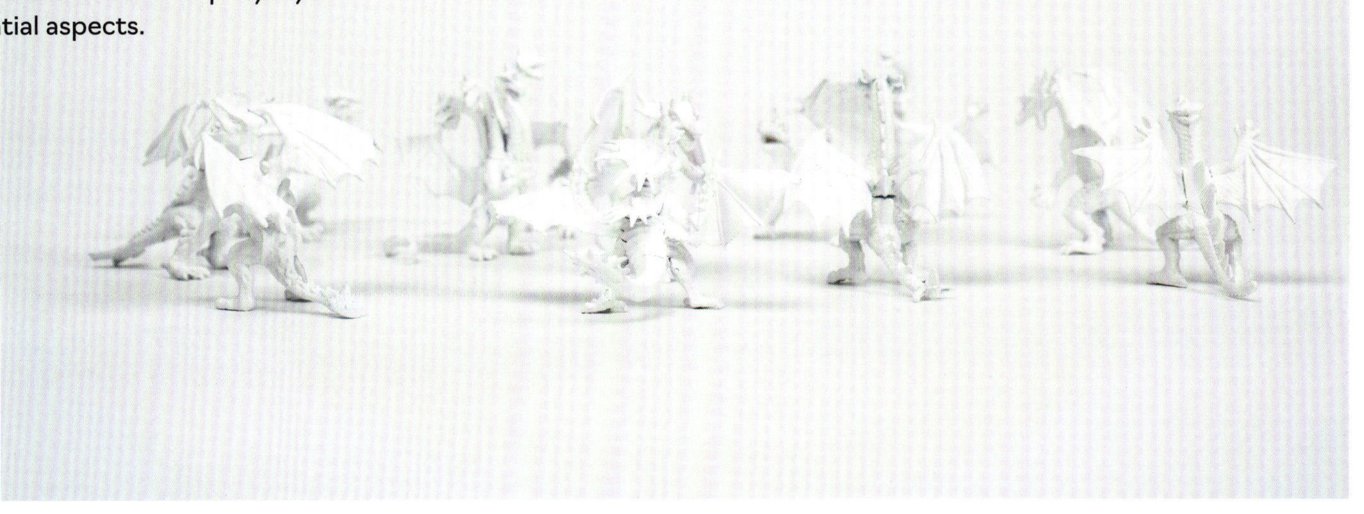

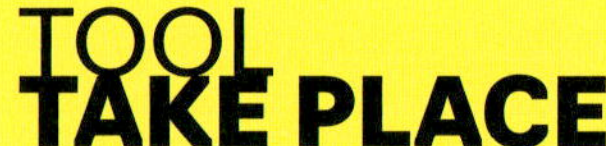

TOOL TAKE PLACE

Take Place is a dynamic communication tool for working in teams, groups, and organizations.

Take Place offers inspiring approaches, breaks down dead ends in thinking, illuminates polar points of view, and allows new perspectives to emerge from multilayered reflections.

PROCEDURE

The team leader or coach introduces the topic.
For example: The use and design of workspaces.

SEARCH

Each participant draws a card and searches for the participant who has drawn the matching card.
For example: You draw the "today" card. Now look for the participant with the "tomorrow" card.

FIND

The participants with the matching pair of cards sit down opposite each other. For example: You sit down with your "today" card facing your colleague with the "tomorrow" card. For the time being, make sure there is enough distance between you.

FROM THE KEYWORD TO THE TOPIC

Duration: 2–3 minutes

Concentrating on the word on their card, each participant makes associations with the topic in the form of keywords. For example: The word on the card is "today": the participant thinks of other words and phrases like modern, current, state of affairs, status quo, relevant, momentary, changeable, old, outdated, etc. and comes up with associated statements or questions like "Today everything is better," "What can we do today?" "What you can do today, don't put off until tomorrow," "Colleagues ask what they are missing today," etc.

FROM THE TOPIC TO THE POINT OF VIEW

Duration: 2–3 minutes

Each participant deepens the topic in their mind based on the keyword on their card and writes down their ideas.

For example: What are workspaces like today? What do you notice today? What do you need in order to work effectively today?

INTERWEAVING POLARITIES

Duration: 10–15 minutes

The participants with the matching pair of cards describe to each other the point of view they have developed. Learn your topic together against the background of this polarization. Think big!

For example: Today the workspaces are cozy, still it has become too cramped since the team has grown. The open atmosphere and privacy of the spaces should be maintained. We need more room for creativity: rent new spaces, work from home more, etc.

THE BEST OF THE PAIRS

Duration: 2–3 minutes

In pairs, the participants decide which of their observations and thoughts are the most interesting.

Keywords can be highlighted and combined. Likewise, points of view, ideas, and wishes from each opposing position can be further articulated.

For example: We need areas that are free of electronic devices so that we are able to think in peace.

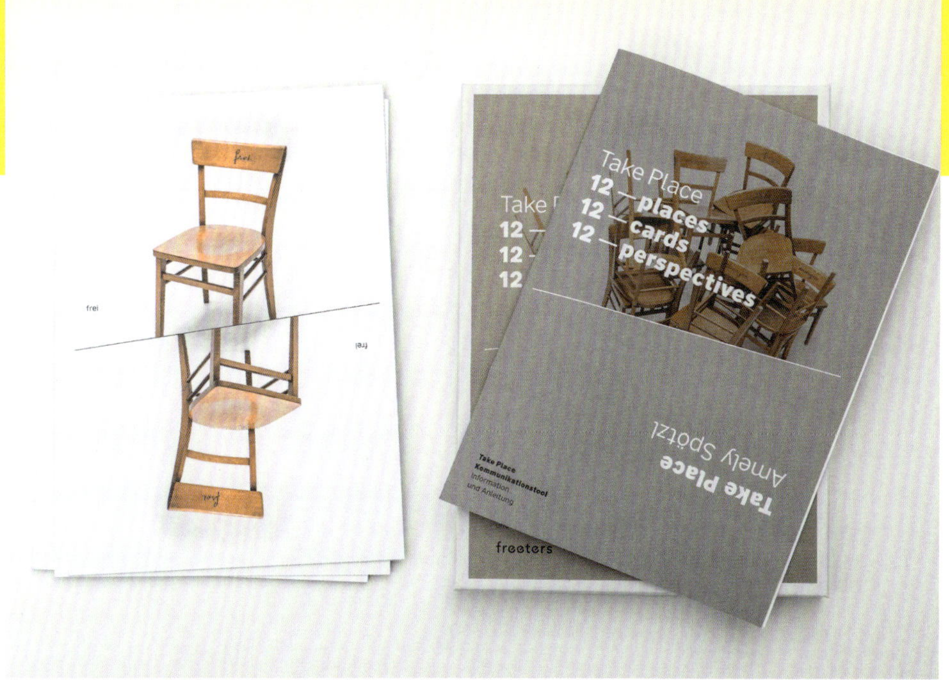

THE BEST OF THE TEAM

All participants come together again in a big circle. Each pair of participants briefly presents their most surprising key points.

For example: Identity / authenticity have come up as a question. What could make the workspace more conducive to this? What does a good working atmosphere mean?

SHOWDOWN

Duration: 30 minutes is reasonable

Now open a discussion on the topic. Determine the points to be discussed. Include all points of view that have been developed. Determine the duration, 30 minutes is reasonable. Visualize and document the process with a large mind map, index cards, or sticky notes.

For example: The team leader has noted that the items Priorities, Roles, Renewal, Change, and Position are to be discussed. You can use the pair of words "today and tomorrow" to emphasize that your priority is to preserve what is good today and to change what no longer fits. To do this, you would like all of the colleagues to have a say. You suggest an email survey.

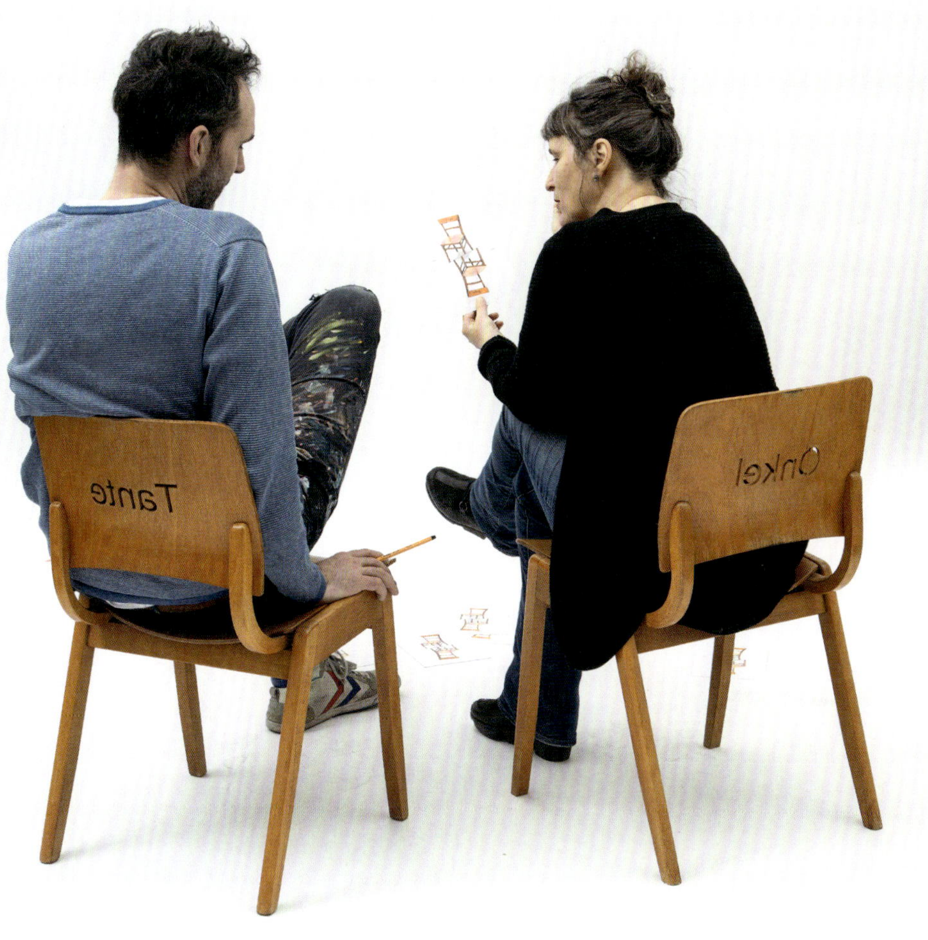

FINAL

The team leader closes the discussion and summarizes the most important findings. What new concepts have resulted? Each pair agrees on a new term that emerged during the discussion in relation to their two words. These 12 new words either serve to further develop the theme or represent the outcome of the workshop.

For example: "Today and tomorrow" have produced the new term "flexibility." They will have a different relationship to this term in the future.

WORKSHOPS

ATRUVIA

Bonn, 2021

Some people say artists are ahead of their time. They sense the future and engage in transformational processes in a natural and playful way. Working, acting, and thinking artistically mean perceiving contexts anew and making immediate use of unexpected dimensions and possibilities. Topicality, renewal, and transformation are the core events in this process. The social and heartfelt motivation from this practical and intellectual experience creates space for the inspiration and skills that are really needed in times of change: presence, spontaneity, courage, and creativity.

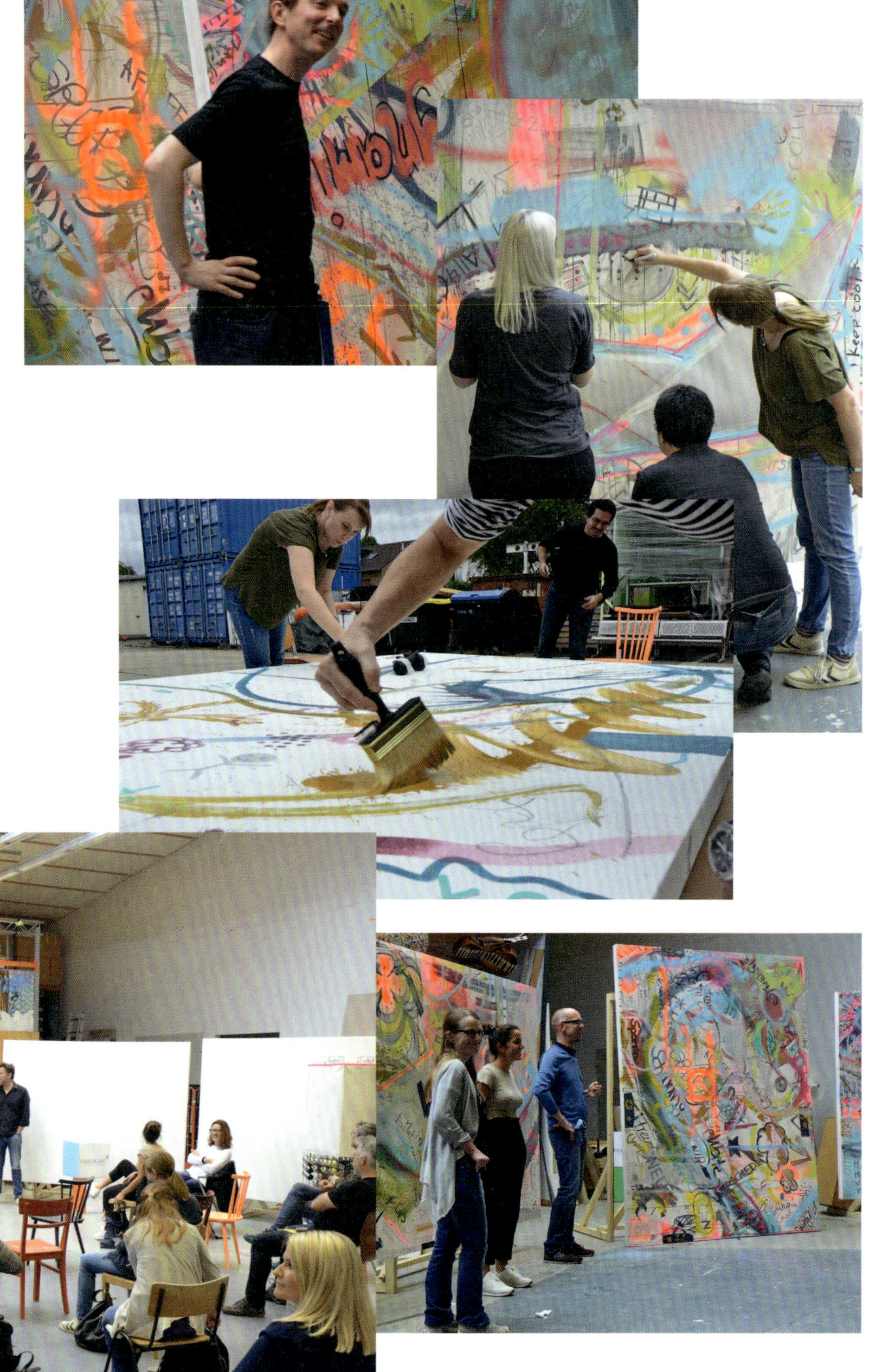

ORGATEC

Cologne, 2018

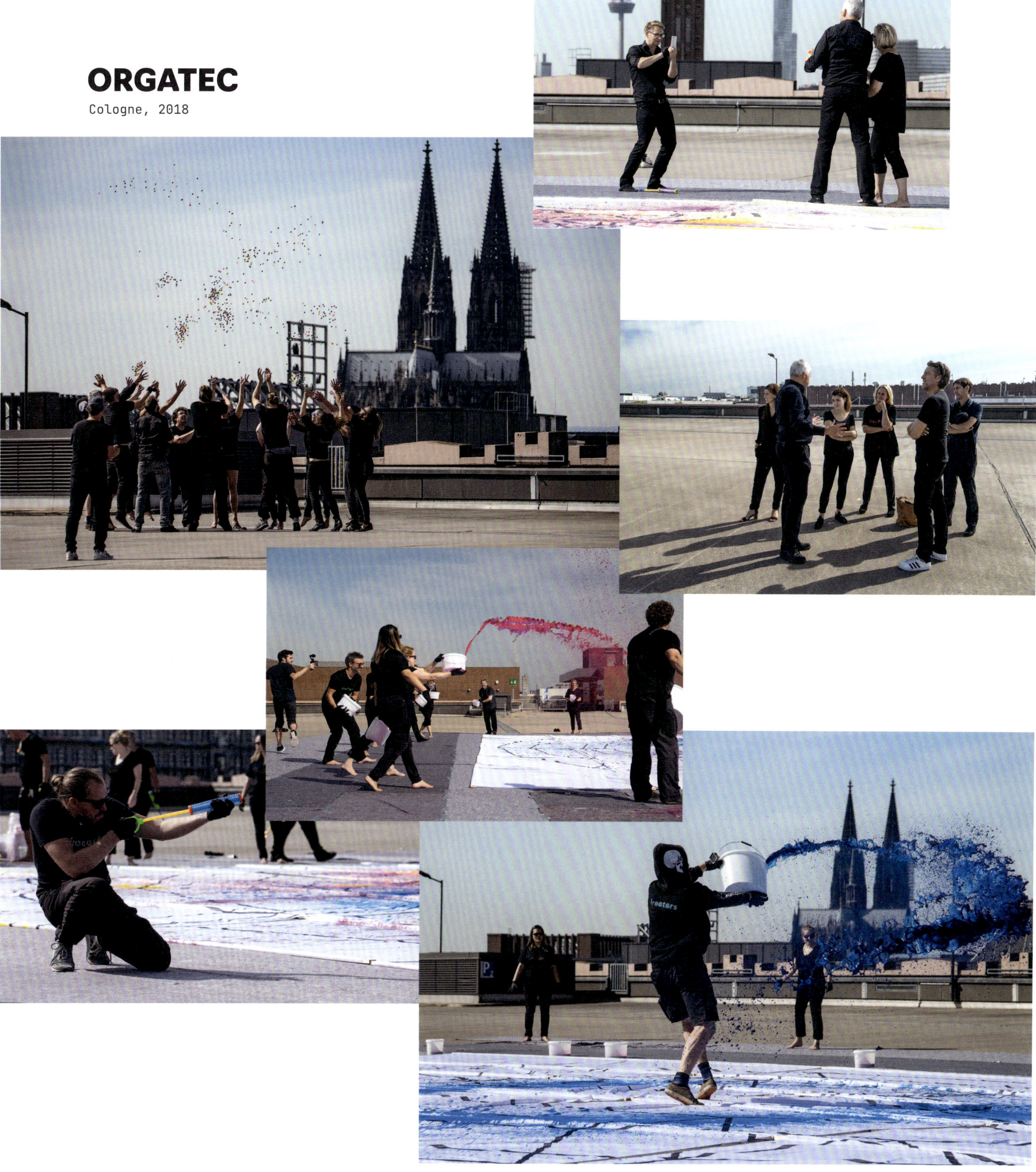

RUB MAKERSPACE

Bochum, 2022

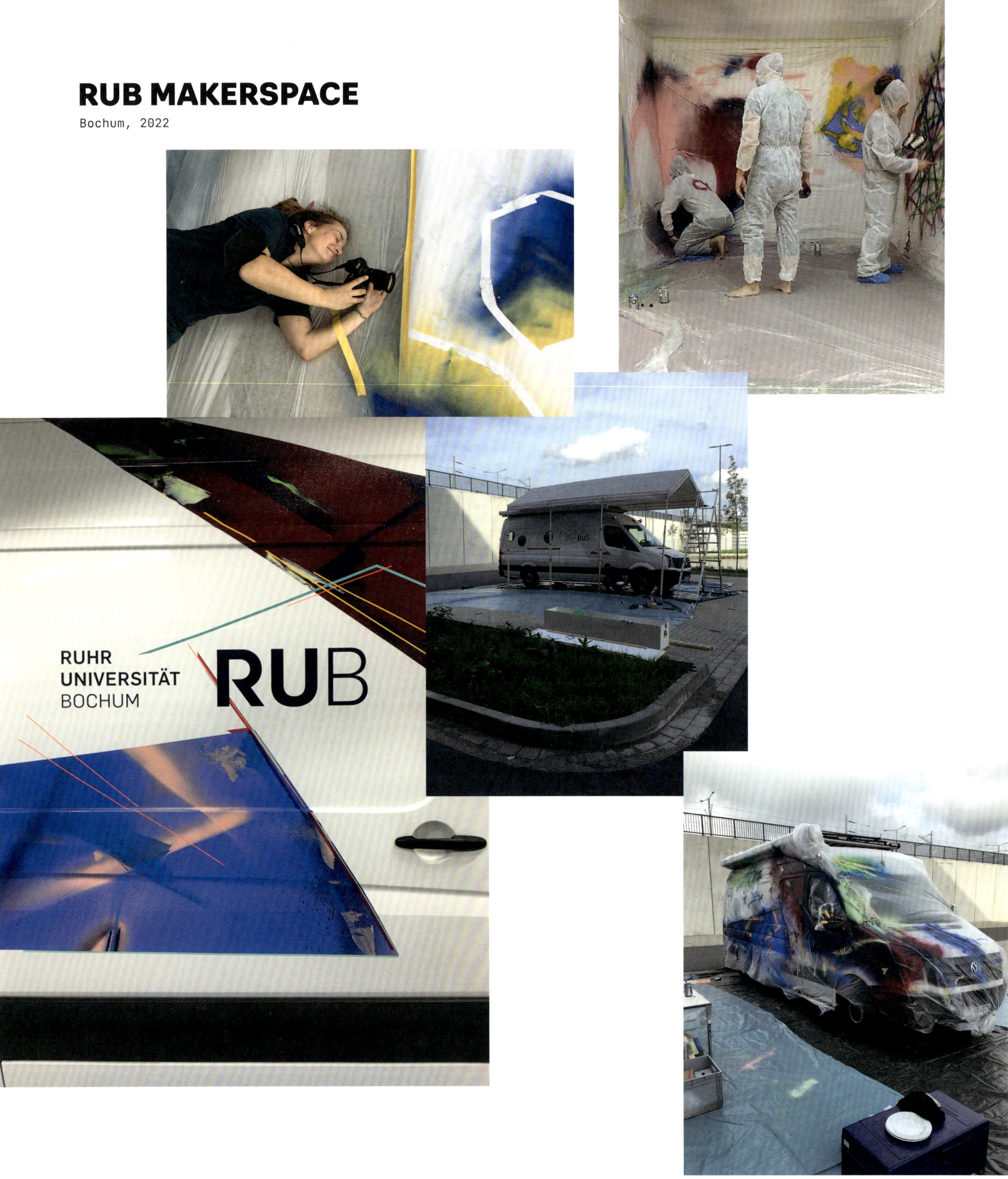

HELLO, WE'RE STUCKED.
WE NEED SOME AI!

Melusine Reimers
former founder,
project coordinator WORLDFACTORY Start-up Center

If you have Freeters do a workshop, a design, a consultation, or even if you just spend an afternoon with them on-site (at Magic Ground), you can be sure that you will lose your sense of certainty there. In the most positive sense, the approach of Freeters confuses and unsettles the original ideas or plans one has made. So if you are only looking for obedient interior designers, you will not be happy with Freeters. But if you are ready to be thrown back to your own workspace and convictions, to take them apart neatly, to confront yourself with relentless openness, and in the end to come out with incredible results—then Freeters are your first choice. Those who have a tendency to micromanage or even to be cautious should not focus on the creative process of Freeters in detail, but should instead let themselves be amazed by the results. Since Freeters are guided and inspired by the spaces, materials, and people they encounter in the process, "chaos" can break out from time to time.

The art then lies in presenting a qualitatively enormously high-quality complete work at the end, whose origins remain visible and yet represents a transformation of the given circumstances. Perhaps it is only in the final result that you find out something about your own company, your day-to-day workspace, or yourself (in it?). Possibly one already has an inkling about these things, but only through being confronted with Artistic Intelligence can some insights emerge from beneath layers of assumptions. Each individual in Freeters is a kind of seismograph for the vibes and realities that float around in our spaces. The act of translating the invisible to the experiential takes place in the process of editing and confrontation mediated through various materials.

I was fortunate to be able to directly experience Freeters' space for a time. My largely remote team came together there and had a home that changed every time we closed the door. And even outside the door, objects appeared and disappeared, new ones grew or transformed into others. We could hardly have wished for a more stimulating and creative environment, and we could never have made it ourselves. "Outside the Box" was definitely yesterday, because the boundaries of our minds may well be temporarily transcended, but they still take hold in the end. If Freeters were with you, you might run in circles for a while afterwards, but you won't find yourself safely back in your box.

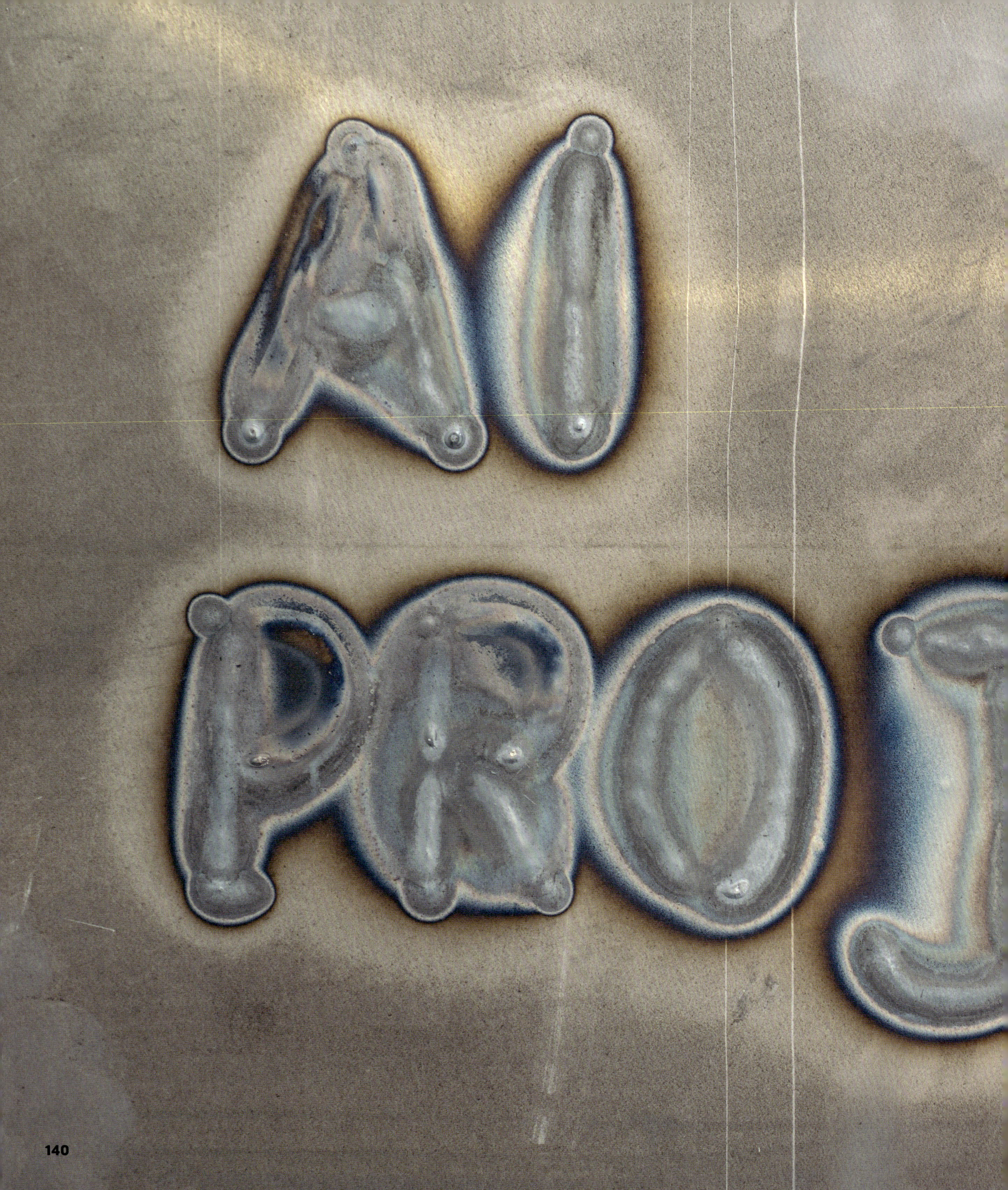
AI
PROJ

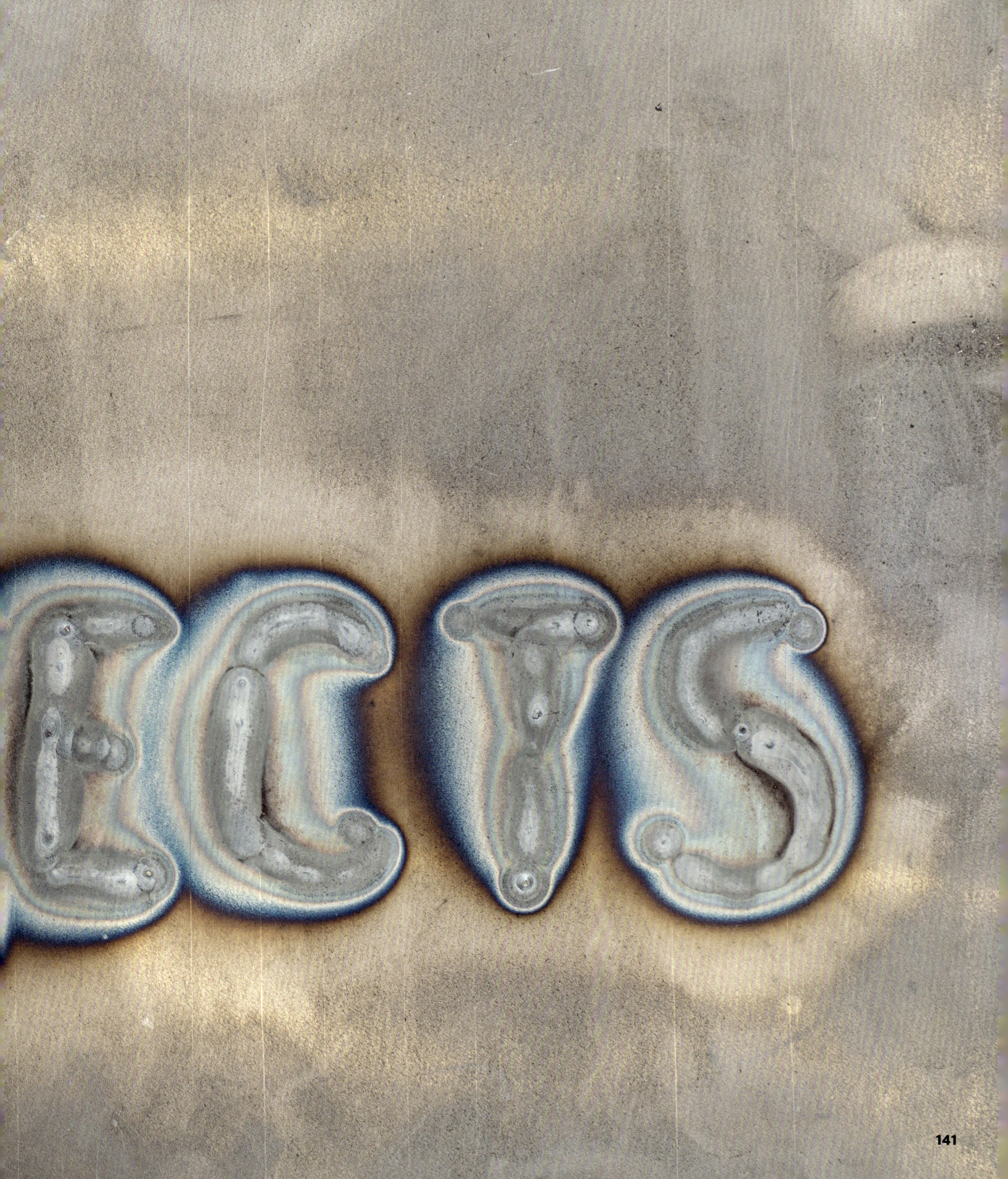
ECVS

AI PROJECTS

Freeters' AI approach should be understood less as a scientific methodology and more as a call to not reduce our intelligence to just rational thought processes with functional utility. Of course, AI has already made impressive progress in many areas of our public services via the hard components of reinforced machine learning. However, it is doubtful whether this approach alone can really give rise to a universal superintelligence that will one day create a resource-saving paradise on earth. Nor is it guaranteed that we as human beings will be assigned a place in this paradise by such a unilaterally gifted superintelligence. Cognitively, this machine will be superior to us in any case — as can already be felt now — but the necessary feeling of happiness of a consensual coexistence does not seem quite conceivable.

In this respect Freeters wants to help with their own version of an Artistic Intelligence model if it ever comes to the development of actually helpful superintelligences, i.e., an intelligence beyond pure cortical control that also has the abilities of our limbic system and our holistic sensory-driven control. So we can at least hope to get the benefits of a superintelligence while still staying connected to the rest of the evolutionary development on this planet. Freeters' AI model is thus the modest beginning of enabling universal superintelligence with minimal onboarding while anchoring basic evolutionary parameters. Industrial and administrative processes are at the center of our startup efforts. After all, they take up a large part of our daily lives.

Our action model starts with six basic modules, which in turn are composed of different building blocks. In this way, we want to start to reveal the emotional and sensory aspects of our actions in companies, administrations, and other institutions. Because in our experience, a meaningful project rarely crumbles because of failed logic. Rather, the lack of integration of emotional and sensory framework parameters means that we usually end up getting in our own way.

The modules with their corresponding building blocks are not to be understood as linear work packages, but can be varied flexibly and accumulatively according to actual needs. In the following, the individual modules are briefly explained and the most important building blocks are addressed. Everyone is welcome to experiment with these modules on their own and of course with us:

AI MODEL

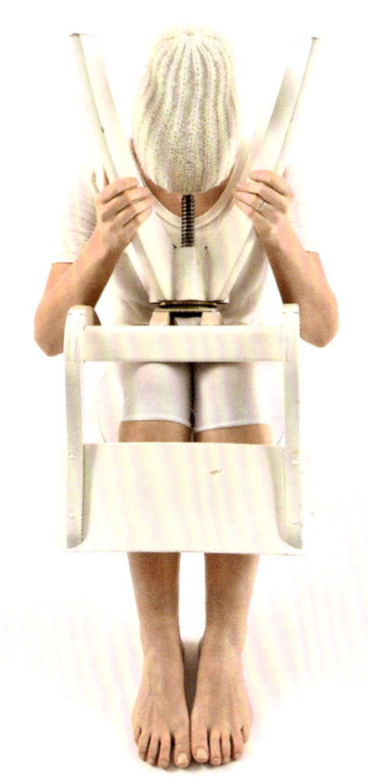

ORIENTATION 1

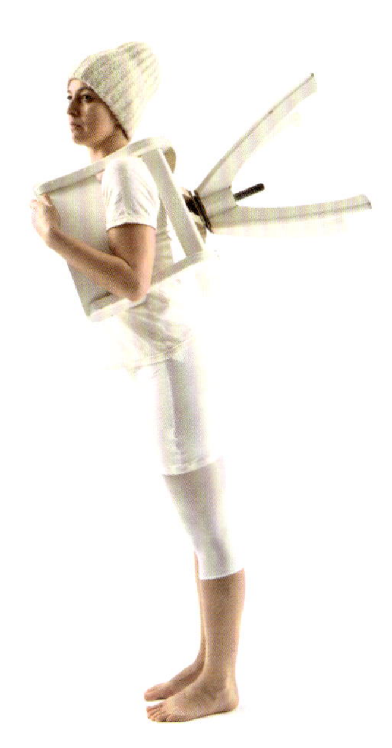

DIGITISATION 6

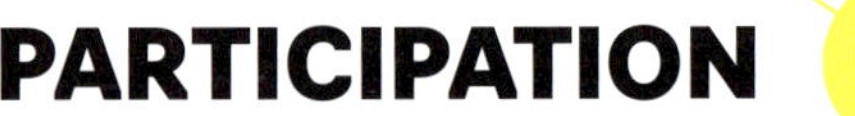

PARTICIPATION 5

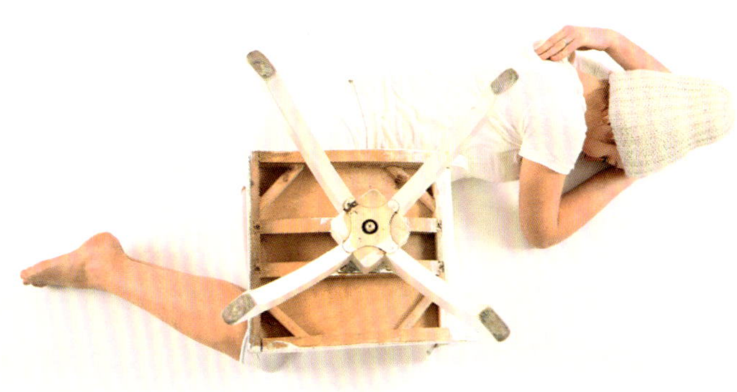

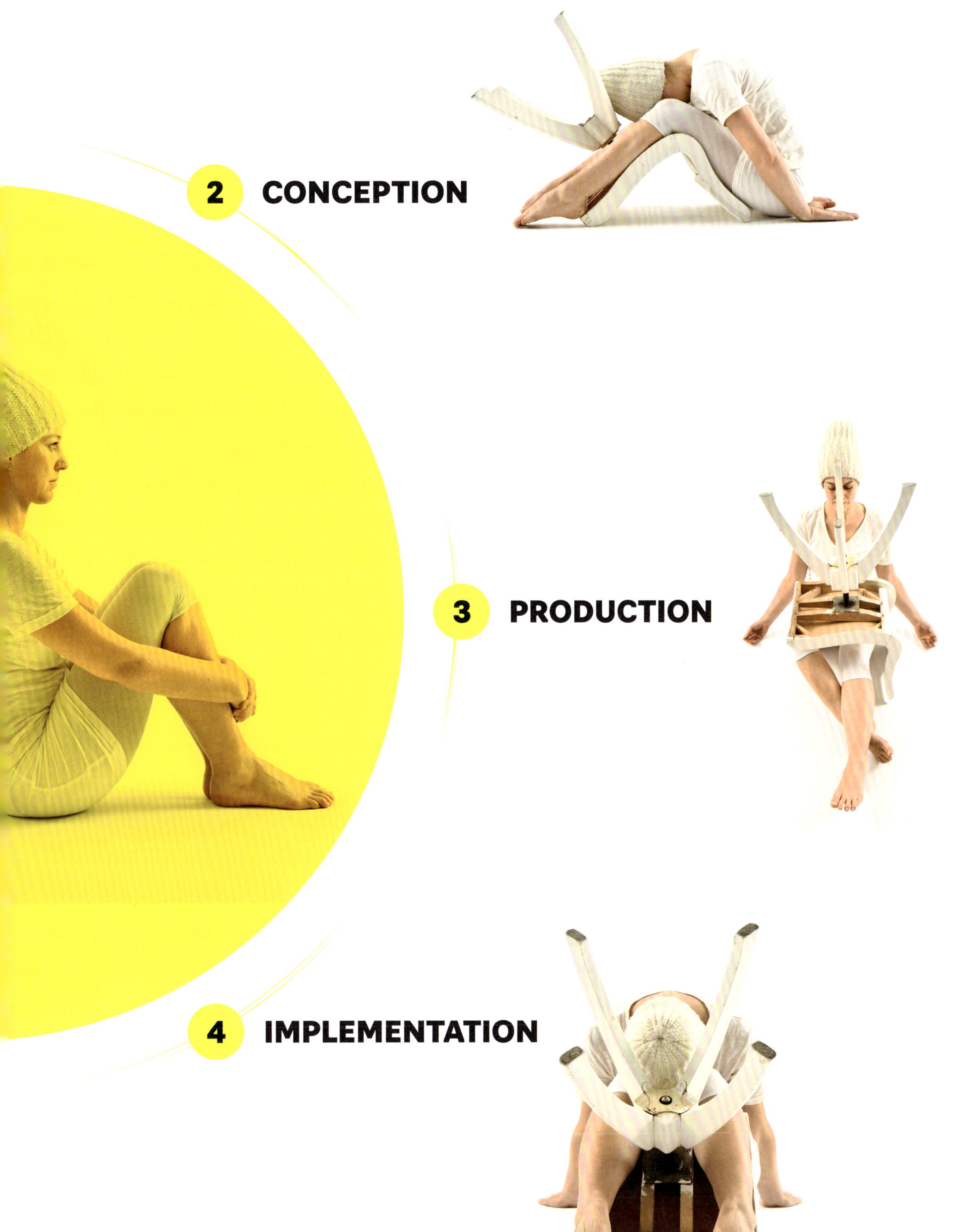
2 CONCEPTION
3 PRODUCTION
4 IMPLEMENTATION

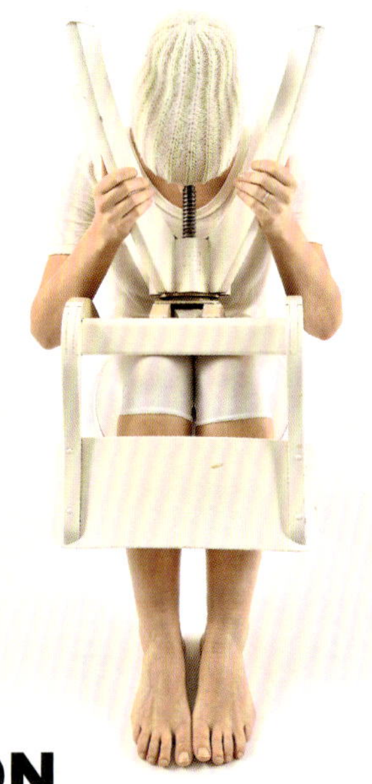

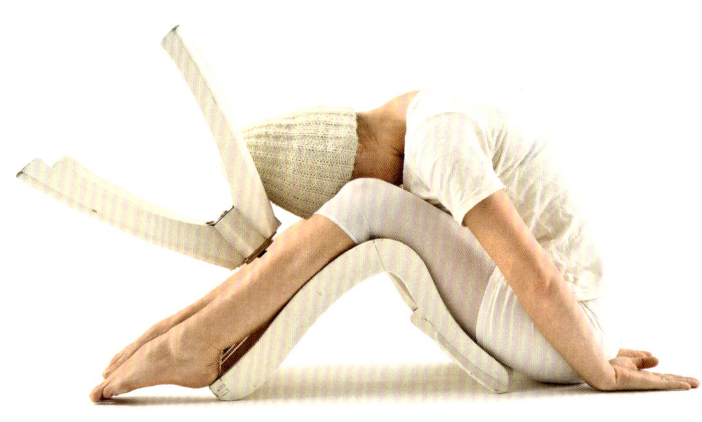

1 ORIENTATION

The basic module of Orientation is intended to be able to locate oneself in real life outside of a "flatland" perspective that is usually created on the computer. It is about creating a 360° image in addition to the notorious "paper layer," which above all also includes the dimensions of emotion and sensory perception. We are firmly convinced that the assessment and decision-making of essential processes is mostly one-sided and rather remotely based on economic or technical functionalities. Thus, an essential orientation aid is missing in order to successfully support empirical project approaches inductively, especially in the case of missing experience. Currently, we are in the process of further developing the following building blocks:

A TREASURE HUNT: A search in the positive for emotional "silent reserves" that can be lifted and in the negative for "black holes" that suck energy and should be transformed.

B JOB SHADOWING: A guided expedition of the employees to uncover the real existing, perceived operational reality and thus also to experience the highly subjective view of implemented cases and workflows beyond mission statements, job profiles, and brightly polished advertising brochures.

C ECOSYSTEM SCOUTING: An inventory of the immediate environment of organizational units.

D MYSTERY SHOPPING: A real journey of experience that takes on a customer perspective that is as unbiased as possible, in order to place overall emotional and sensory experiences in the foreground here as well, since usually only these are really "stored" within the customer.

E 3D SCREENING: The optical data recording of spatial environments, in order to be able to fall back again and again on as real a basis as possible in follow-up discussions and evaluations.

2 CONCEPTION

The module Conception serves to transfer a fictitious basic assumption into a real tangible basis of experience in order to achieve tangible progress in empirical iterations as fast as possible. Due to the speed of spontaneity and a conscious "fault tolerance," we also want to open the possibility of working with open-ended approaches, which elude normal reason and logical experience and thus usually fall away from the outset in the context of "normal" project organization. We are convinced, however, that it is precisely these approaches that can create essential conditions for discovering truly original innovations. The following building blocks are in development:

A MIND MAPPING: Creation of a vision landscape, which can include all artistic techniques and in this way can lead illusions with one's own imagination into completely new areas.

B STORY BUILDING: The attempt at a first fiction, which is suitable both as a coherent narration as the starting point of a progressive development, but also as "breadcrumbs" to create crystallization points for a game that is constantly being recreated.

C MODELING: Creation of a spatial sensory basis for deciding further process steps.

D RAPID PROTOTYPING: Core approach of any conception, since only through the real tangible and perceptible preproduction is the transition from fiction to realization clarified in order to create a comprehensible meaningful conception.

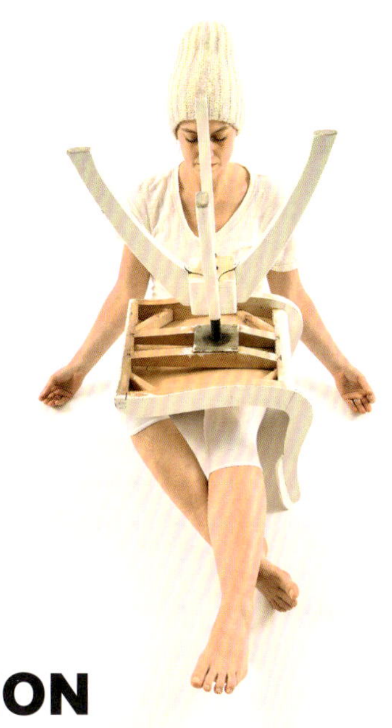

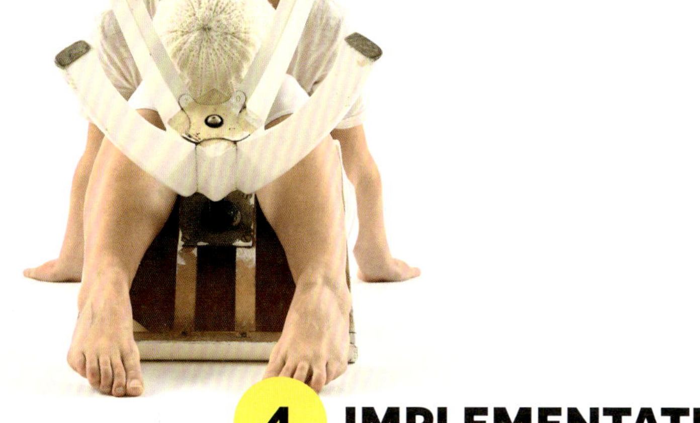

3 PRODUCTION

In the area of Production we concentrate on a manufactory approach, which can be focused on specific themes and values. Industrial duplication and mass production can ultimately also be the result, but is not the focus of our actions, because in each case we also want to see and preserve the power of the unique and special in its immediate form. In a way, this is where the luxury of everyday life can best show itself, because the specialness can lie in every detail and moment. The currently practiced building blocks are based on the following focal points:

A SUSTAINABILITY RULES: The Gestalt transformation of objects into new functionalities so as to support the cyclical consideration of life realities and to counter the "throw-away" and "after-the-flood" reflex of today's productions.

B WORDS MOVE MOUNTAINS: Clarification of the power of words beyond the currently often encountered supposedly neutral and objective use of words in one language at a time.

C POWER OF PICTURES: Declination of pictorial worlds and overall visual experiences that can go beyond the fixed and moving image.

D SPACES ARE INTERFACES: Concretization of the experience that space not only contains a physical dimension but above all a psychological dimension that is far too often neglected.

E DIGITAL DISCOVERY: The attempt to rediscover digital space as a real existing space for action.

4 IMPLEMENTATION

While Conception and Production can still move somewhat outside the organism in which it is to be realized in the end, the basic module of Implementation represents the segment of the circle of forces in which direct contact with context is necessary. The main goal is to test the interrelation of work and environment and to replace a "planned situation" with an actual perspective that can be experienced as quickly as possible. Our approaches, which are currently primarily applied, are the following:

A SPEED CURATION: Rapid merging of the most diverse partial productions into a meaningful whole.

B GUERRILLA INSTALLATION: Immediate integration of individual productions into the reality of life, with simultaneous connection of spontaneous and planned elements.

C EMOTIONAL EVALUATION: New formats of documentation and evaluation, which elude conventional procedures or provide new insights (e.g. poetic recording).

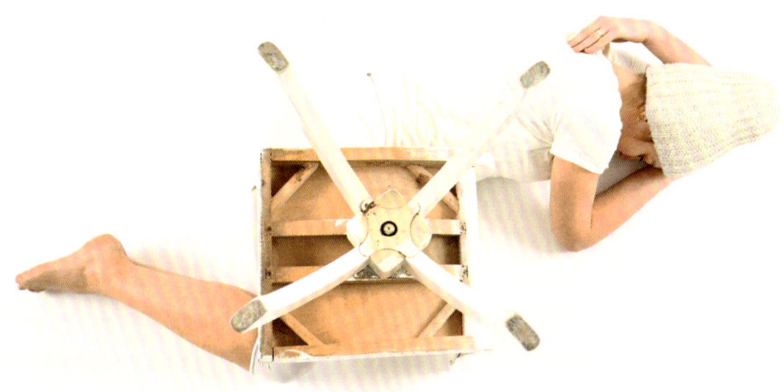

5 PARTICIPATION

How do I boost our energy? How do I stay awake and alive? If the company knew what it knew and entrepreneurial spirit was lived by everyone, all performance could be increased. Pure energy! Pure wishful thinking? Mostly yes. Because two important obstacles stand in the way of interdisciplinary cooperation, know-how transfer, and autonomy awareness: silo thinking and service-by-direction behavior. These two factors will not disappear as a result of New Leadership or New Work. They are an expression of a corporate structure that has been strongly hierarchical for decades, with a corresponding top-down decision-making culture. In short, they are still preferred today as focused actions and are promoted unilaterally by increasing standardization. Within this, employees have simply forgotten how to open up at lightning speed, how to pass on their knowledge, and how not to answer critical issues with worrywart automatisms but to see them as a source of inspiration. In addition, today's planning processes seem to be a systematic attempt to replace the unloved coincidence with deliberate error. In a time of maximum speed of change, openness, improvisational power, and spontaneity are the immediate key sources to constantly revitalize the company's energy balance and not to constantly frustrate the workforce by changing goals. This requires practical exercises and not theoretical managerial games: we don't make a plan but create something physically tangible.

Together with employees, we create MVPs (minimum viable products) that literally make all previous procedures at your company look old. We have developed the following methods for rethinking collusive co-creation:

A PLAYFUL CO-CREATION: Engaging in an open(-outcome) game to increase the enjoyment of each other and the willingness to work together in general beyond immediate business goals.

B ART WALKING: Joint inspiration tour in order to see things through the eyes of others.

C FACING TRUTH: A test of honesty that brings hidden dissent to light so that it can be confronted.

D BUILDING PURPOSE: Search for a common intrinsic basis for motivation.

E CREATIVE JAM SESSION: The power of immediate interdisciplinary collaboration.

6 DIGITISATION

How do we balance the powers of the digital and analogue world? In the past it was said: "If you can dream it, you can make it!" So we believed in the power of ideas and translated them into plans and then into action. It was a highly intellectual process. However, the thoughts of those days are today's data sets, which can be realized much faster in the near future via 3-D printing and robotics than we dreamed of at the time. Even if we, as half Neanderthals, are only beginning to understand the power of this digital world of thought, it is time to take a close look at the interface between the analog and digital worlds in order to combine the best of both and move more easily between them. To this end, we have developed some scouting products that will make everyone want to come along on this exciting journey into hybrid land. The digital space is an entity that is evolutionarily foreign to us that we have to let into our psyche from the ground up in order to be able to understand both its opportunities and dangers in our daily interactions. For the discovery of personal access we have developed the following development formats:

A CONQUER DIGITAL SPACE: Development of access and shaping techniques of digital spaces.

B HYBRID SHOPPING: Holistic balancing of analog and digital experiences.

C GAMIFICATION: The chance to discover new abilities and possibilities playfully with the help of avatarization and game elements.

D DIGITAL CLEANSE: A targeted fasting cure to recalibrate and recover one's senses.

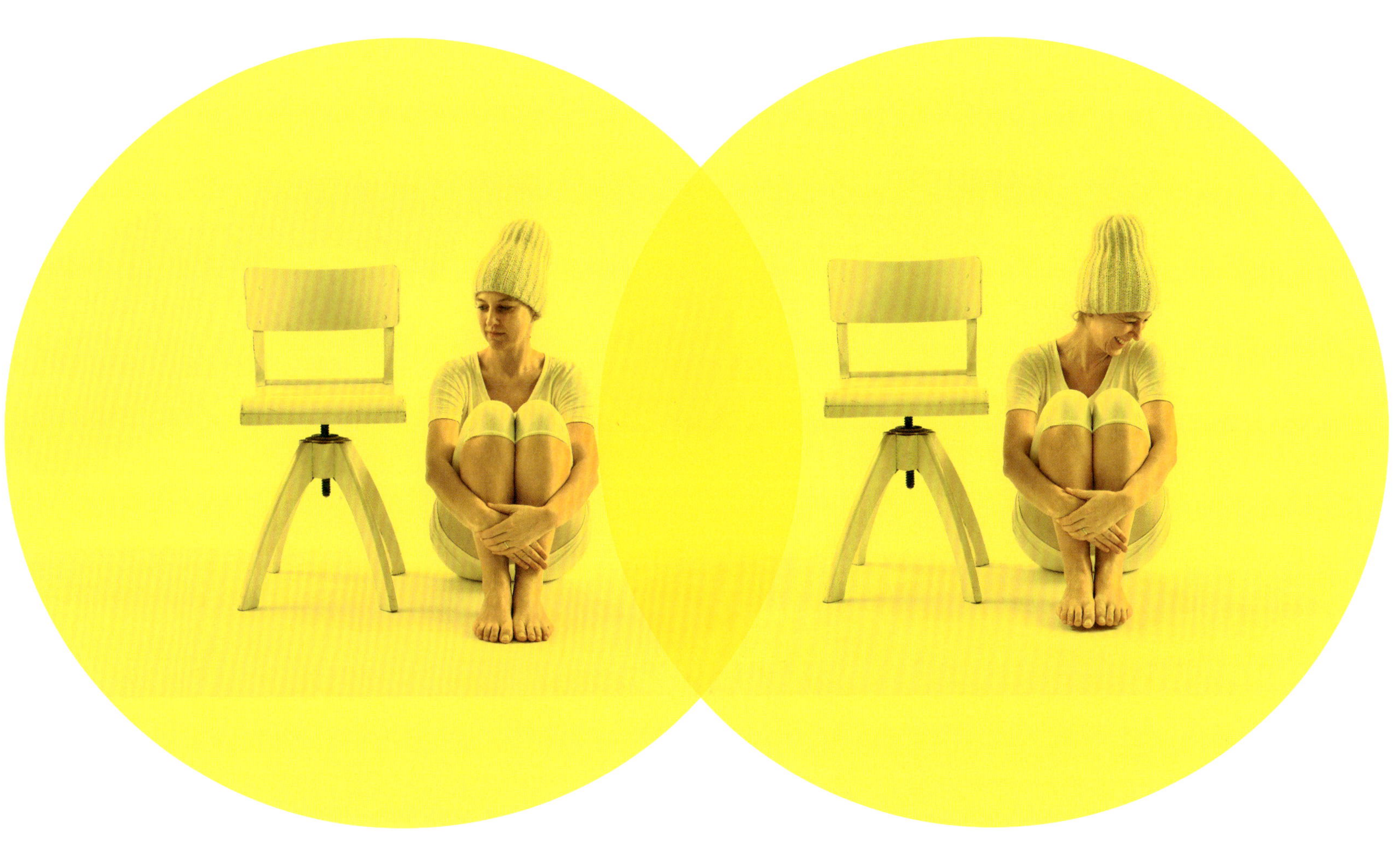

PILOT PROJECT PROPELLER
WITNESS REPORT

Ulrich Zünkeler

Without wanting to go into more detail about myself, I will now tell you a little true story that is not written down anywhere else. But be assured that I was deeply involved in the whole thing from the beginning. In addition, it must be mentioned that the client may not be named for security reasons and will simply be called "client" in the following to protect her anonymity.

It all began with a commission from the Cologne Trade Fair for the last prepandemic Orgatec in the fall of 2018, which, as is well known, is one of the world's largest trade fairs for everything to do with offices, with exhibitors coming from around the globe. The brief was to design a special area of approximately 600 square meters as an alternative inspiration area and to give the visitors a better understanding of the power of art in the office sector beyond the usual decorative ideas. Taking the role of a deliberately aggressive and disruptive trendsetter was fully successful, also when retrospectively assessed against the expected headshakers. Were there only headshakers? No, certainly not. The client in question was the most courageous and open-minded. An invitation to her office followed, with a request to develop ideas for creative solutions for a trial area during general remodeling work. More about this in a moment.

Initially, a small cooperative group of people was responsible on our part: the management consulting firm Detecon, the architectural firm as-if, the Freeters cooperative, and two brothers who were still at that time managing partners for the agency Orange Council, which acted a marketer for Freeters.

The whole process up to the awarding of the contract in summer 2019, in summary: two design concepts were in the running, of which the Propeller project, a room-within-a-room installation, was ultimately chosen alongside other installations in the space. What was behind it?

The client's own internal IT department, until now a staff scattered across the company's premises, was finally to be given a home base. It should be inviting to everyone in the company who needs their services (in other words, everyone!), inviting for interdisciplinary collaboration with product development, inviting and functionally calm for concentrated programming, invitingly open for agile work in temporarily assembled work groups, inviting for informal encounters and exchange, as well as identity-creating and inspiring surroundings with a high feel-good factor. All this was to be realized on an open T-shaped 800-square-meter space in a completely renovated old building. Does this sound like a pie in the sky kind of project? It was, more or less, if it weren't for the Artistic Intelligence, particularly in the loving attention to the smallest detail.

Let's get to the eponymous heart: the propeller. The Irish would perhaps sooner associate it with a cloverleaf, because its construction consists of a central part and three wings or blades projecting into the T-shape of the base. The wings give the 800 square meters rhythm in an organic way: they divide the Quiet Area for concentrated programming from the Agile Area for flexible use and from the Welcome Area as an informal meeting place including a kitchen area. The Propeller houses three workshop and meeting rooms with everything you need (from huge magnetic whiteboards and projectors to individually combinable table and seating situations), plus a technology and materials room. And in the center, an experimental space called the "permission room." All of this under highly effective, artistically designed acoustic sails to dispense with noisy ventilation systems. The entire Propeller is a modular structure that can also be dismantled and rebuilt elsewhere. It consists of insulated wall elements and standing frames that provide indestructible stability.

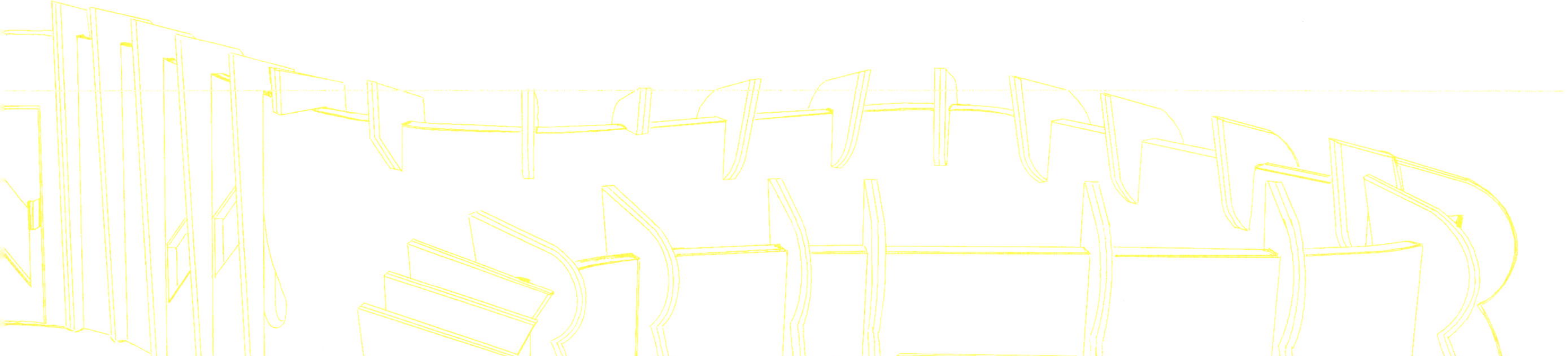

Parallel to the design development of the Propeller, a kind of "treasure hunt" took place on the client's premises. With the request to "give us everything you want to discard that is rooted in the history of your company," two truckloads' worth of furnishings made the journey to the Freeters' workshops in Bonn for artistic upcycling. This resulted in countless objects, some extremely functional, with a humorous connection to the client's old and new DNA. Because identity is best established not with the dictates of branding, but with emotion, authenticity, humor, and surprise as esteem, gained through listening lovingly and genuine joy in the matter.

In addition to the large-scale installations Propeller and Kitchen, a total of around 700 individual works were created for this pilot project: from furniture to wall-transforming artworks and many accessories to completely new inspirational tools for workshops of all kinds. Not all objects and ideas made it into the space. The better is simply the enemy of the good.

The pandemic has prevented a real evaluation so far as the company has been generally working from home since then. Everyone hopes that this can take place soon. A full report will come later, perhaps in the next book.

Thanks for the interest and extra thanks to the client for her courage and patience, especially to all involved from the facility and IT. Everything is going to be fine.

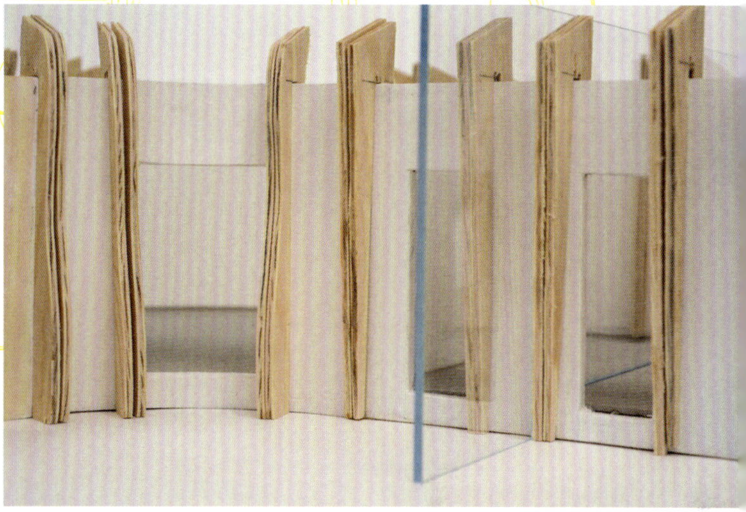

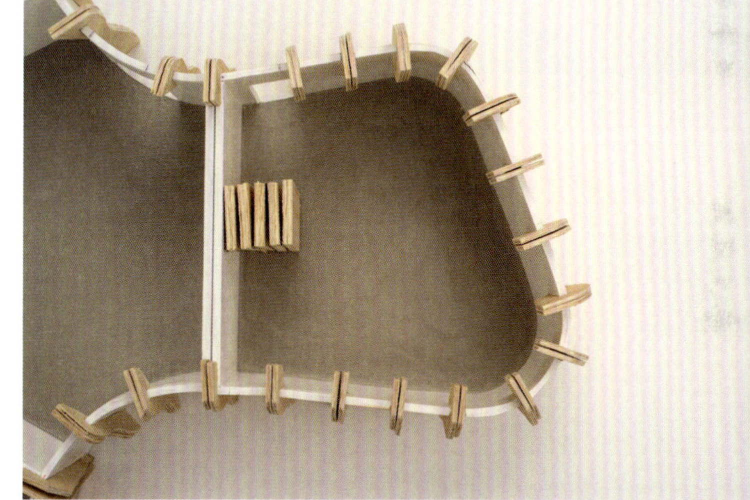

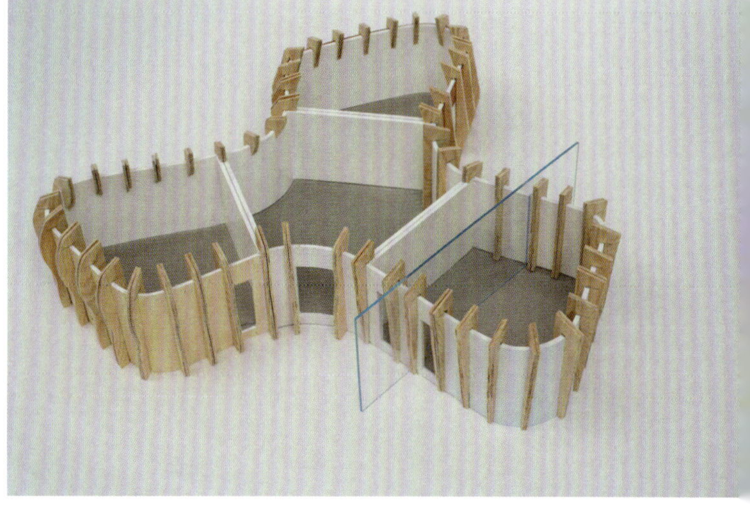

1:10 model of the room in room sculpture "Propeller" Concrete, wood and plexiglass.

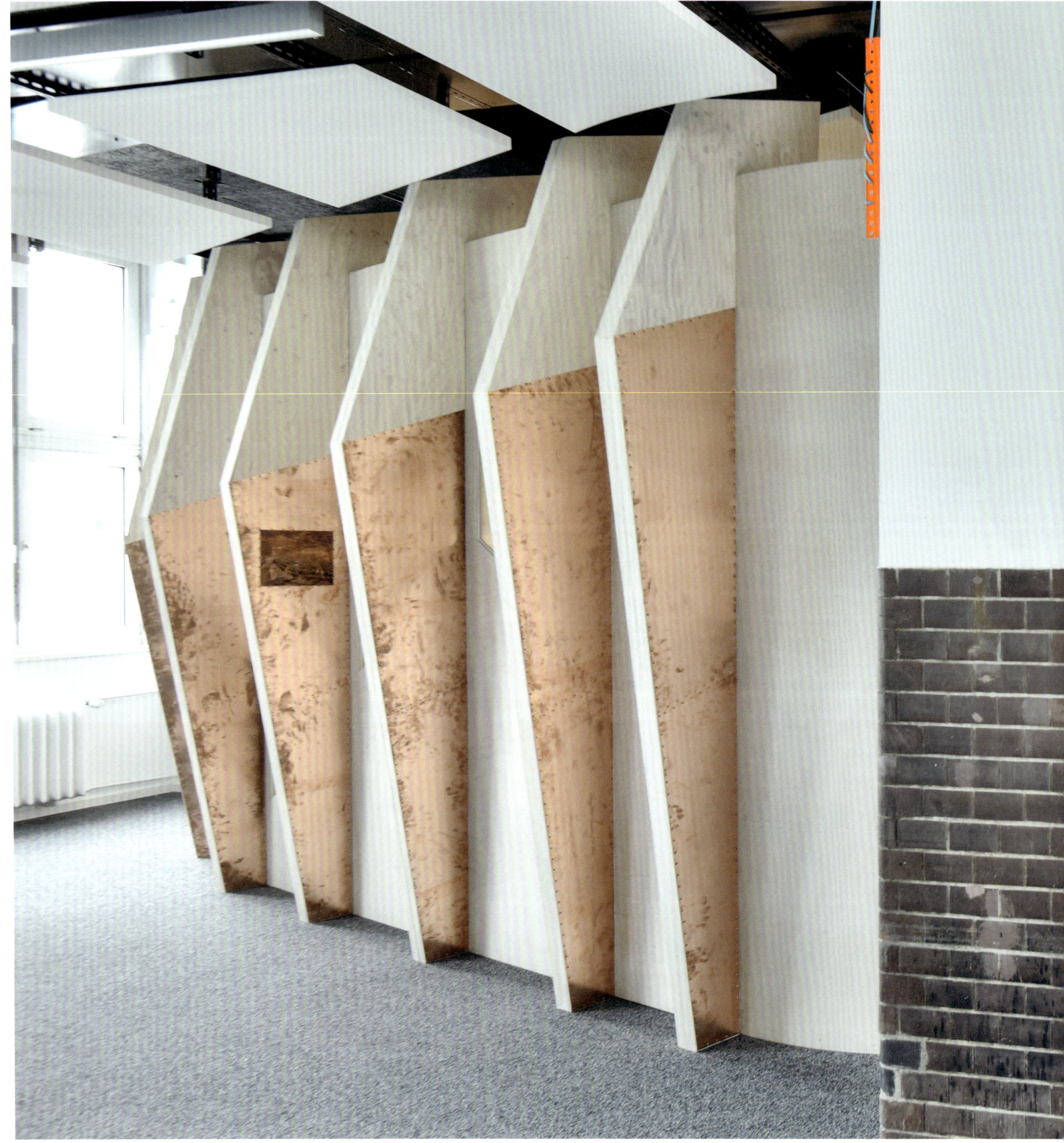

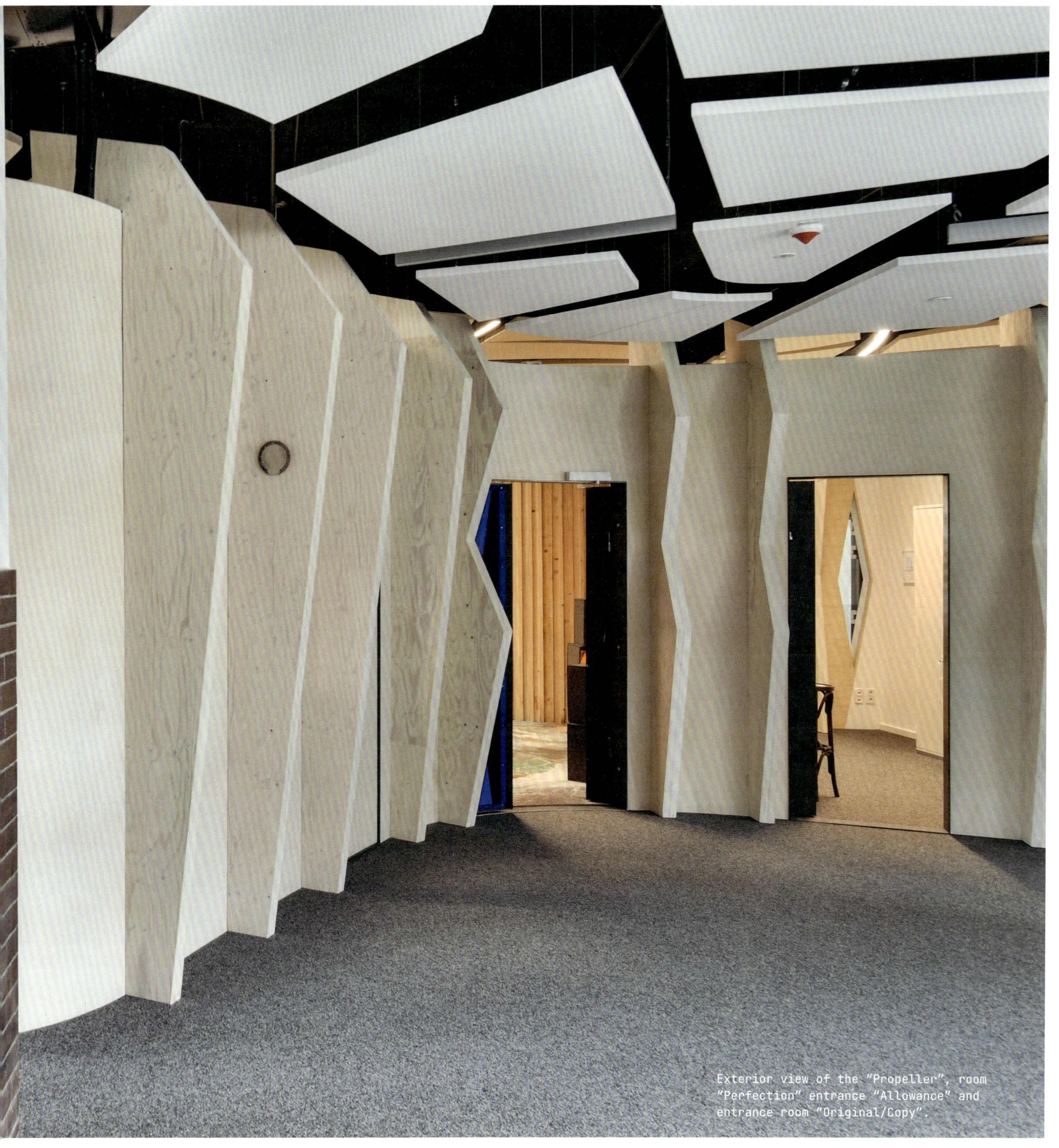

Exterior view of the "Propeller", room "Perfection" entrance "Allowance" and entrance room "Original/Copy".

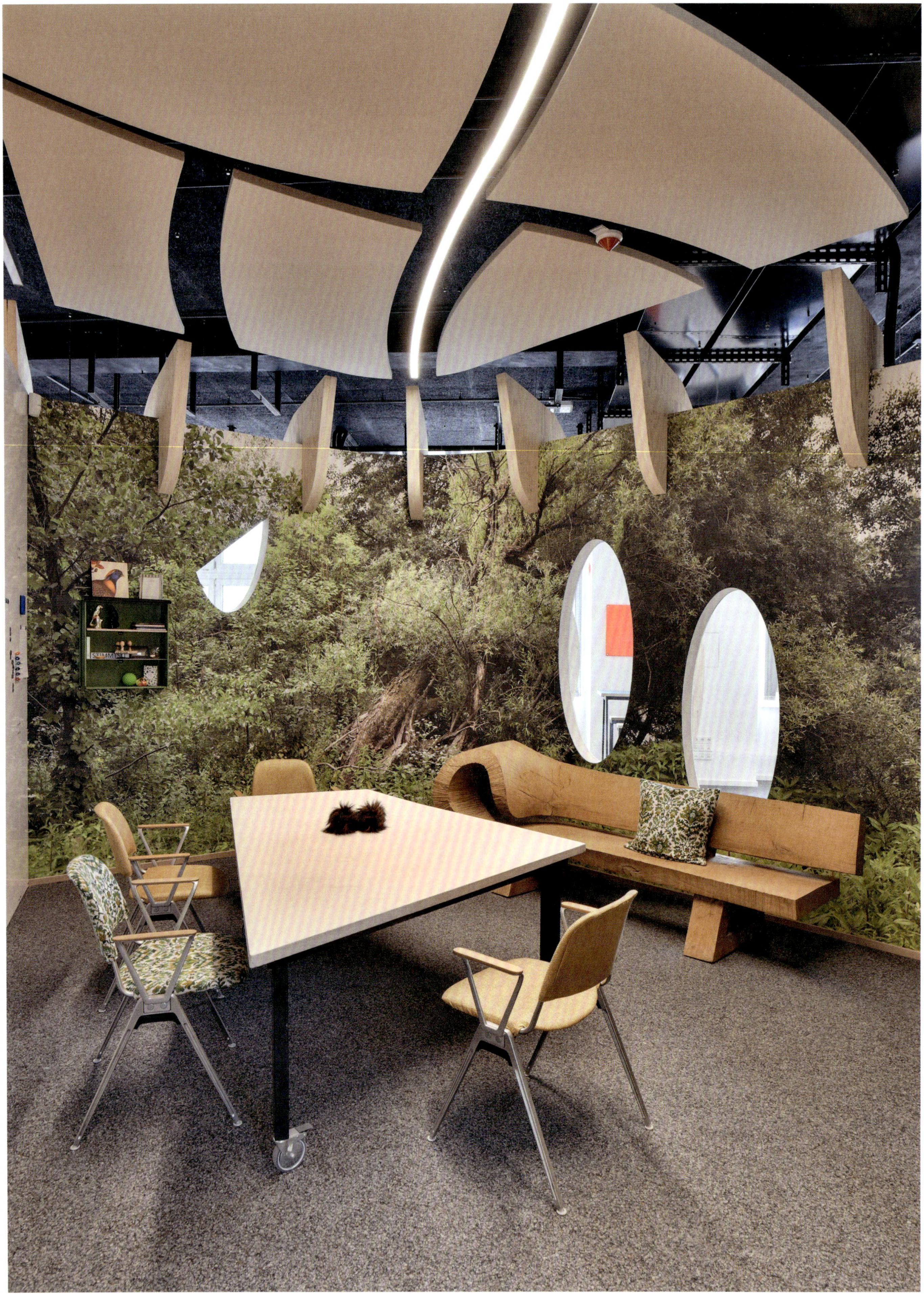

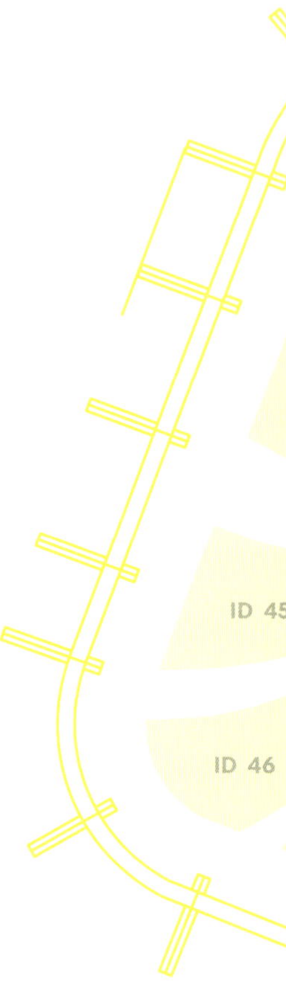

Interior view of the room "Trust"

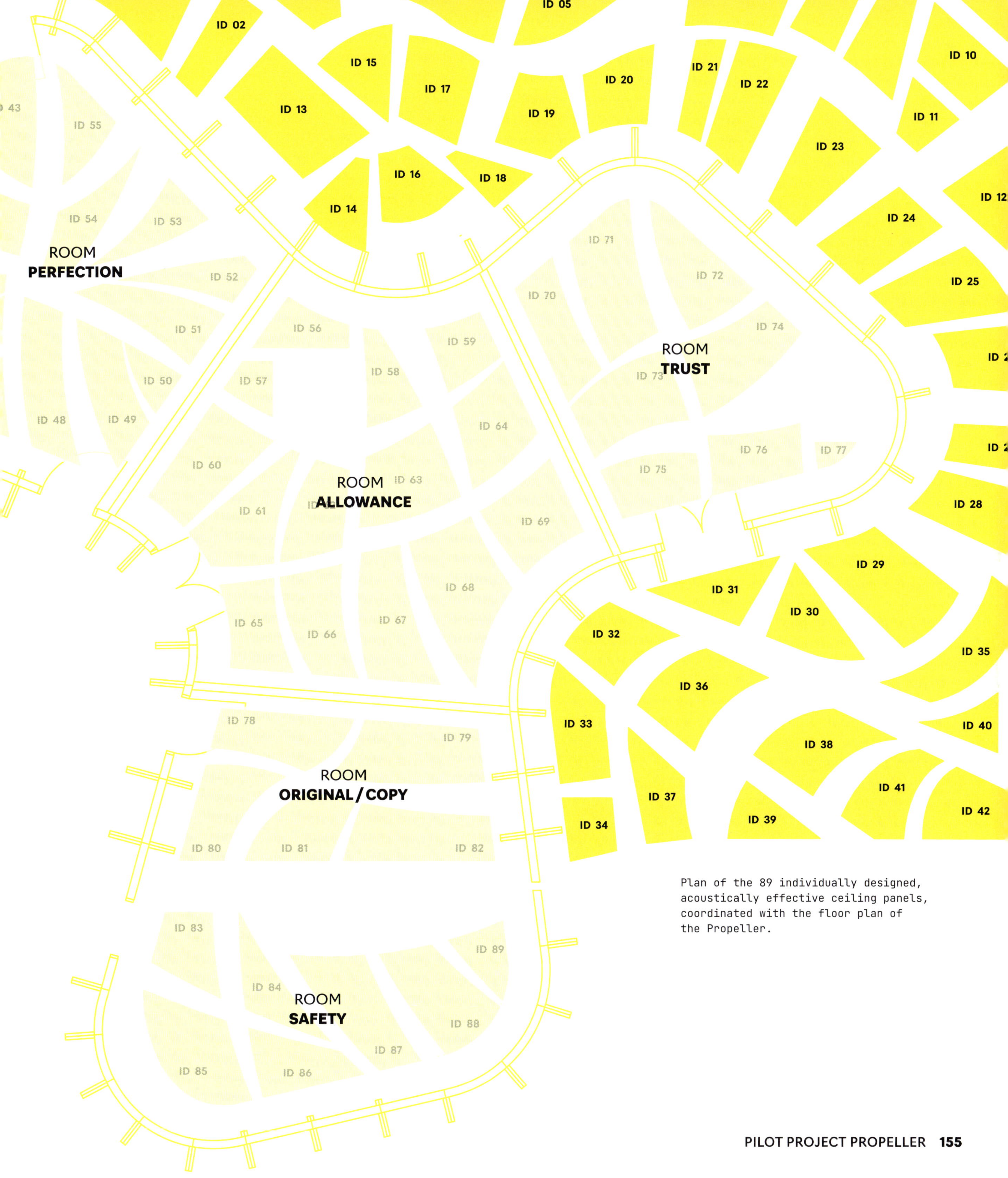

Plan of the 89 individually designed, acoustically effective ceiling panels, coordinated with the floor plan of the Propeller.

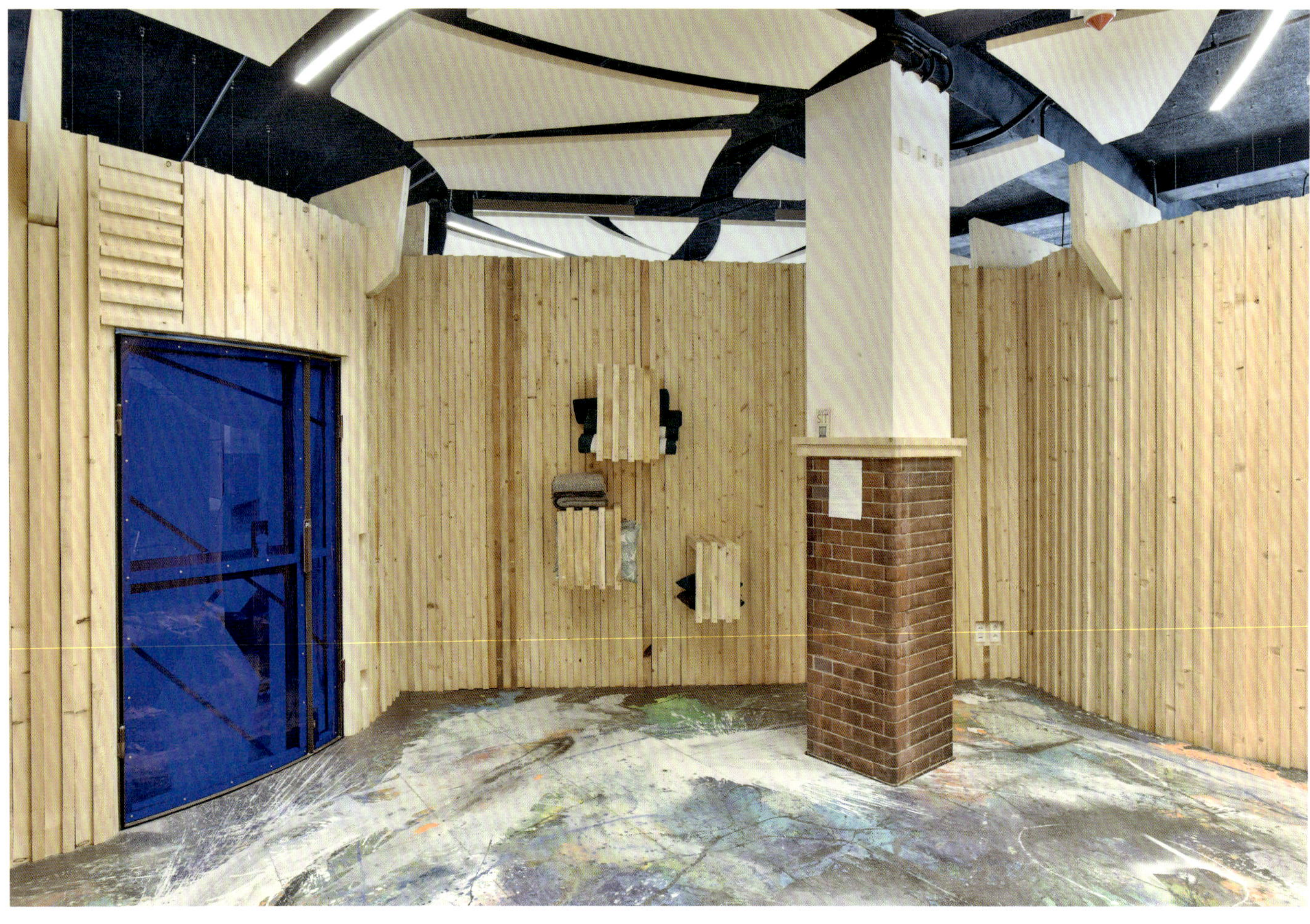

Interior view of the room “Allowance”.

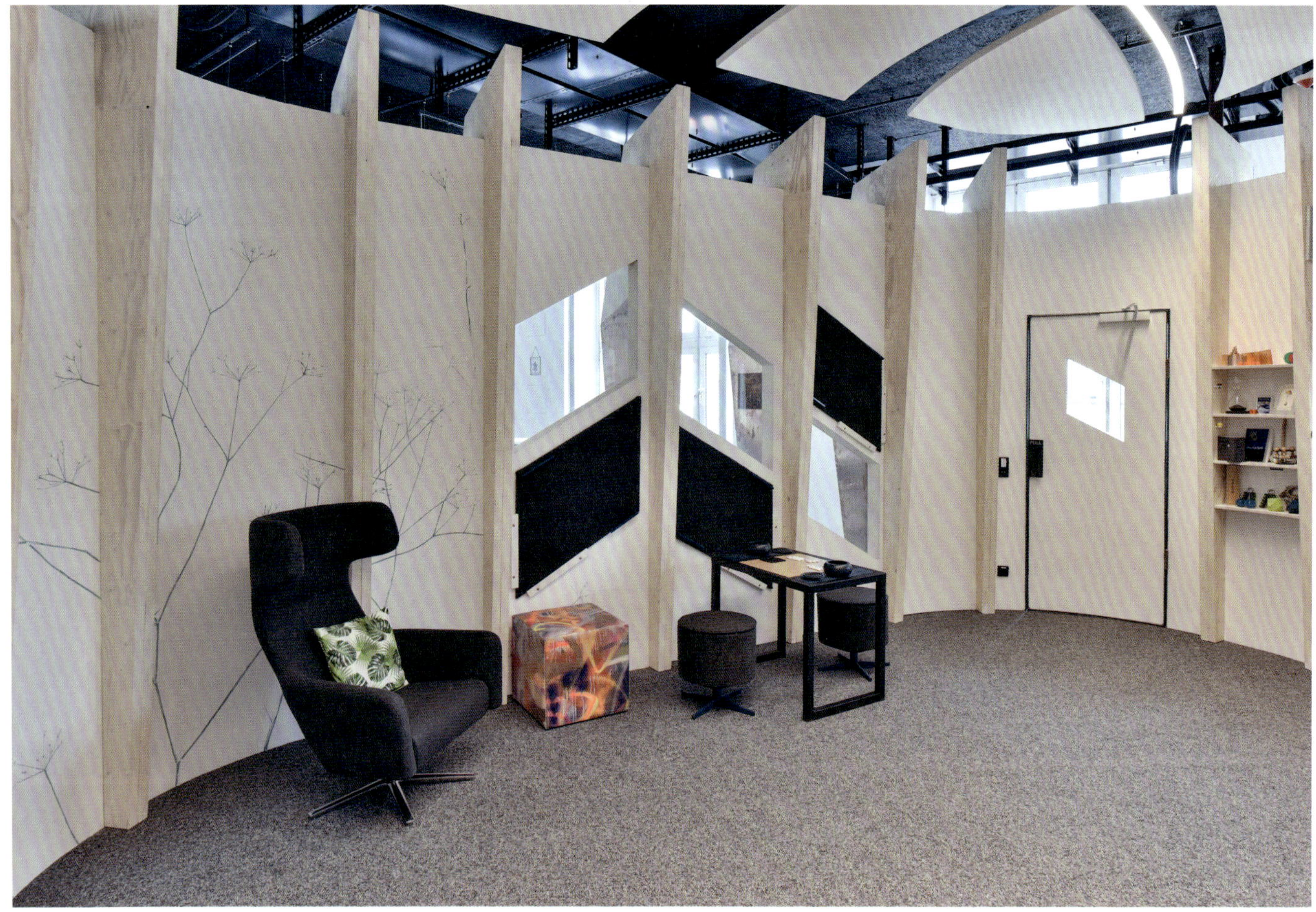

Interior view of the room “Perfection”.

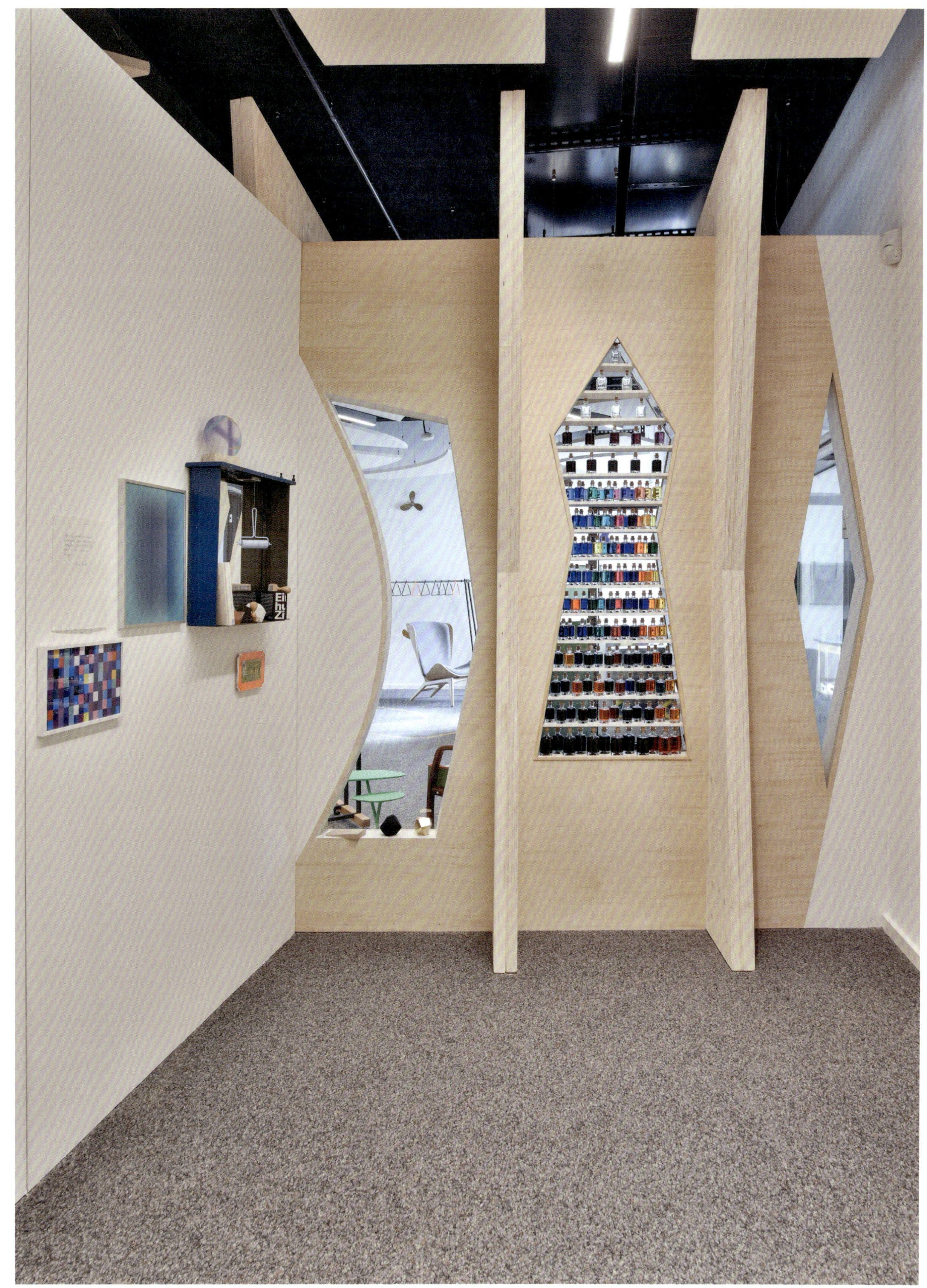

Interior view
of the room
"Original/Copy".

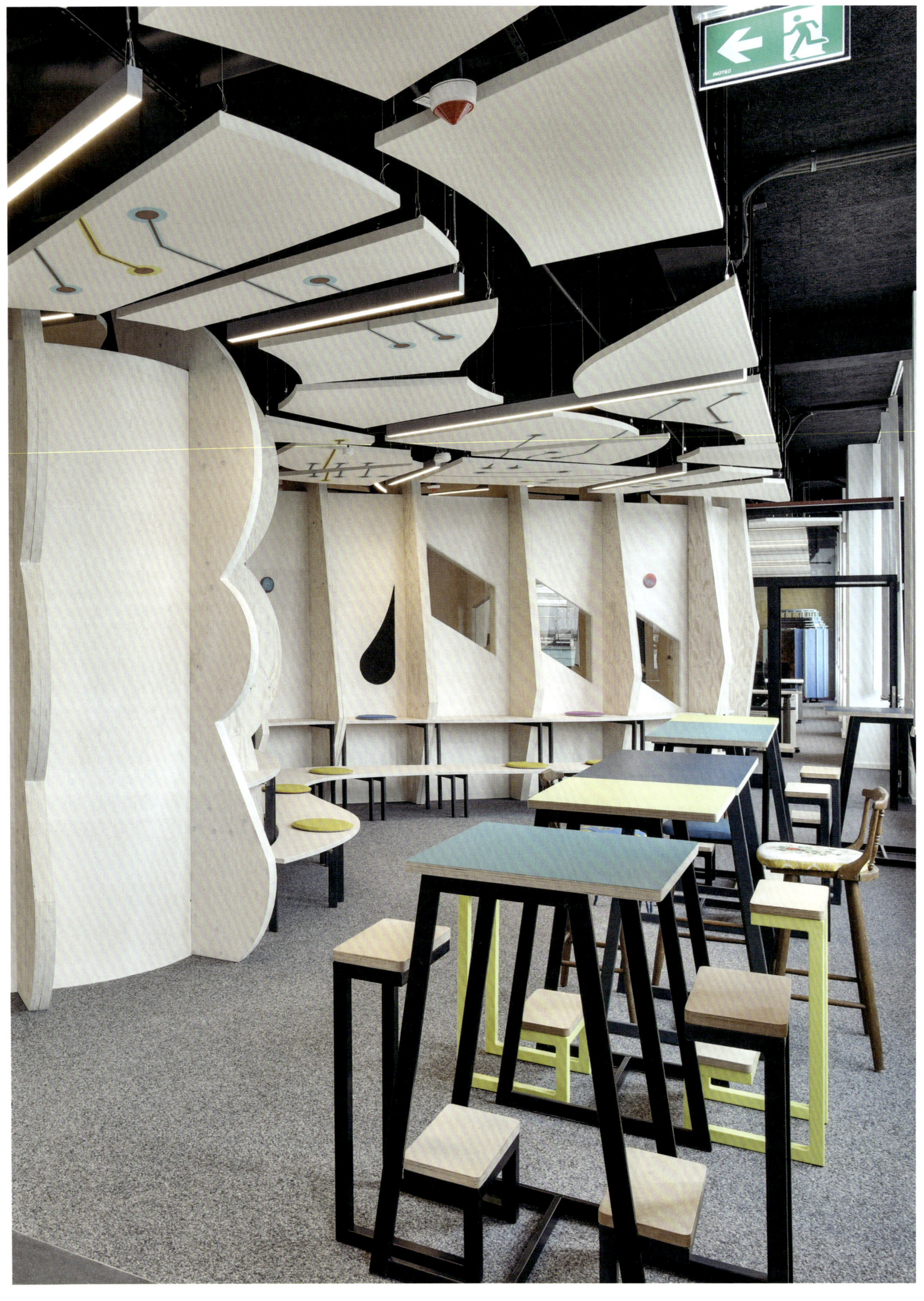

View tribune meetingpoint

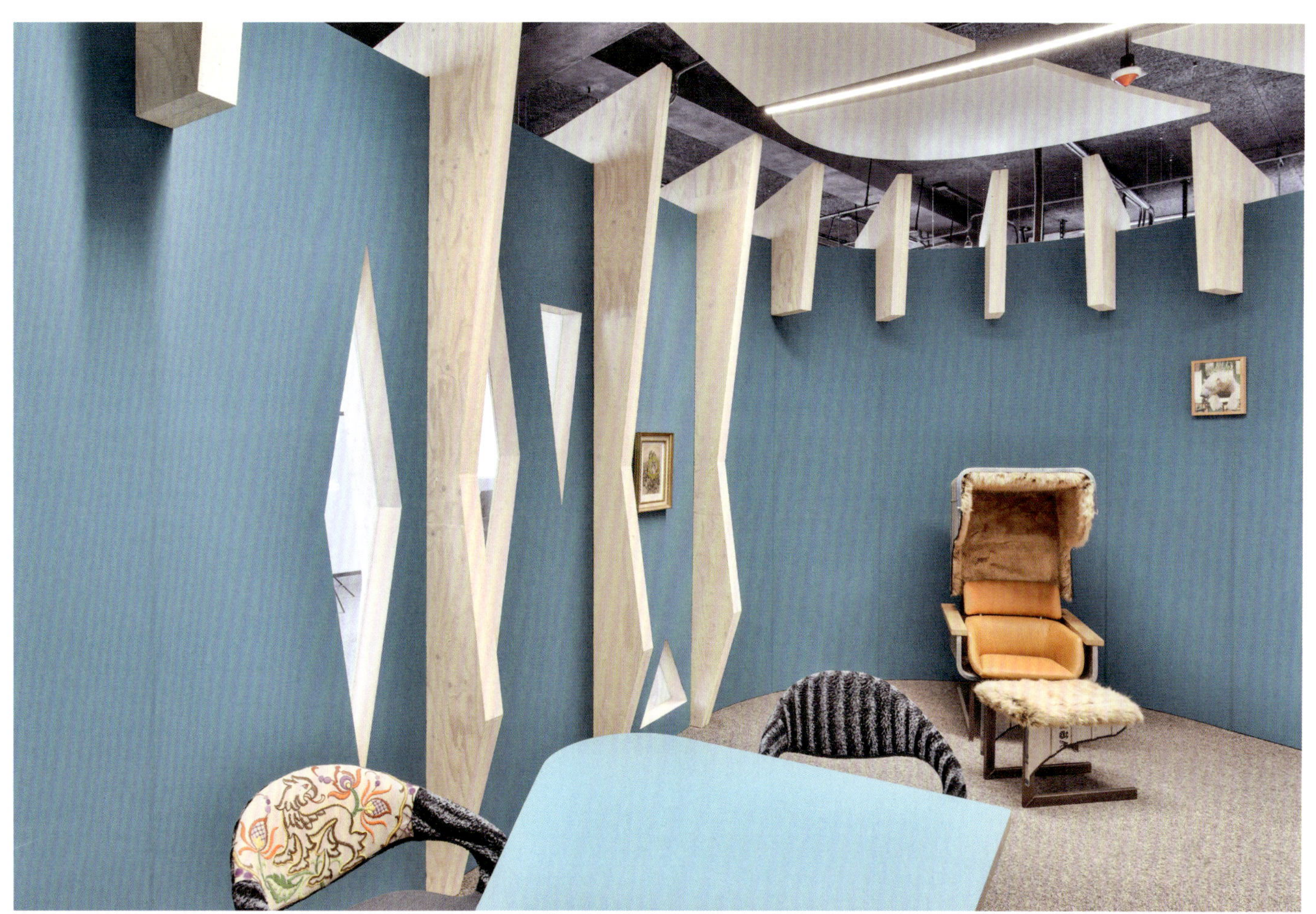

Interior view of
the room "Safety".

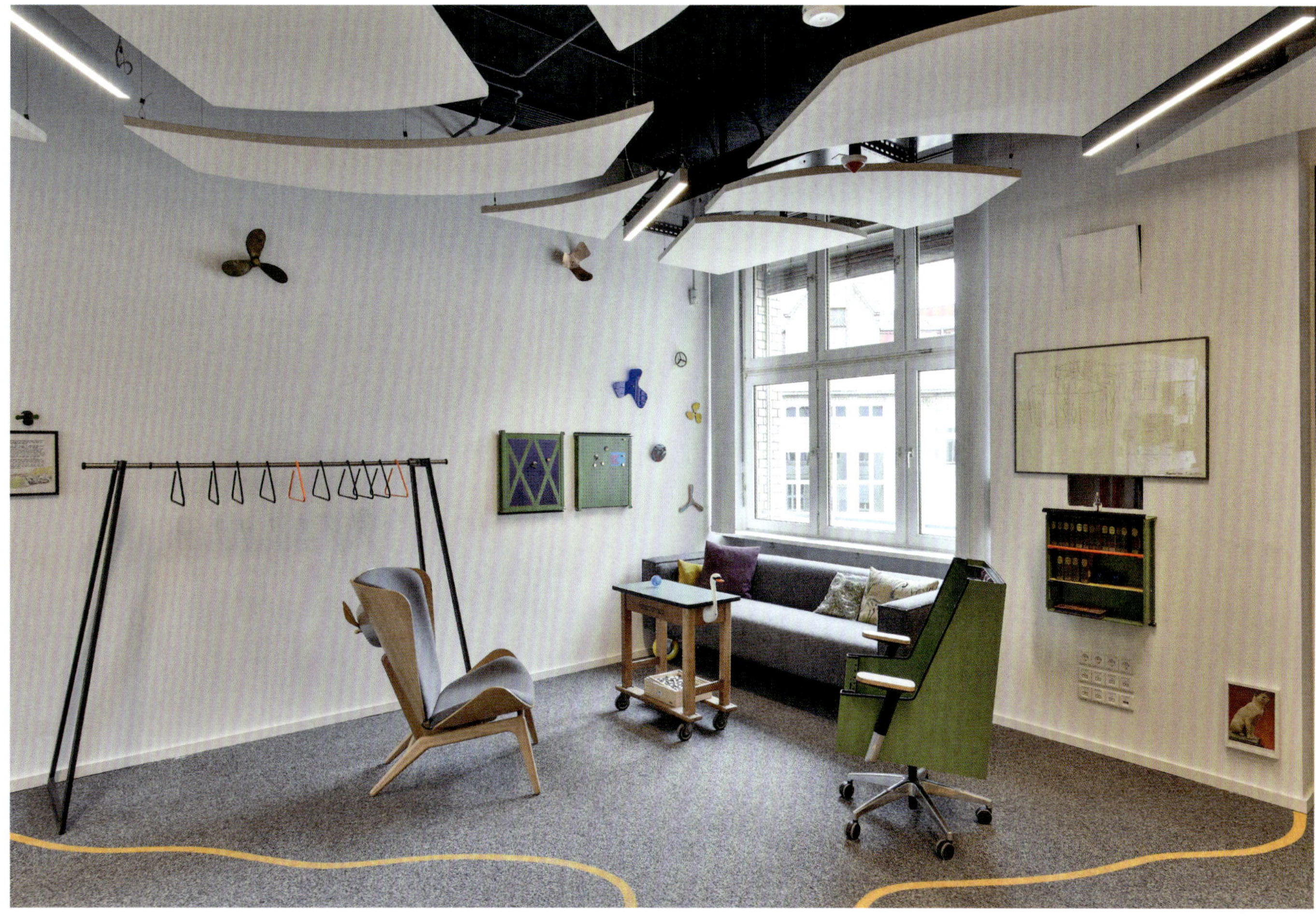

View
welcome area

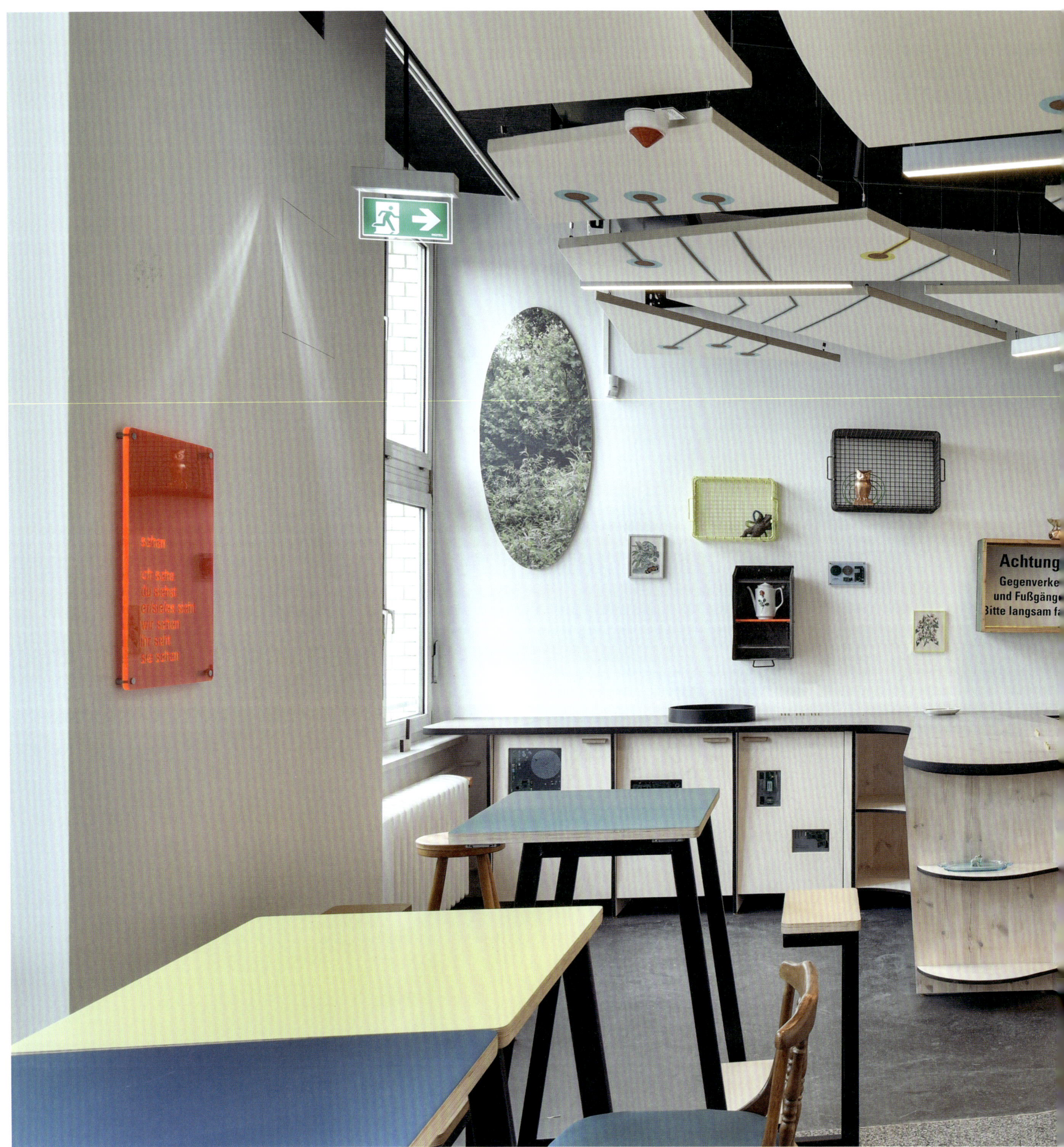
sehen
ich sehe
du siehst
er/sie/es sieht
wir sehen
ihr seht
sie sehen
Achtung

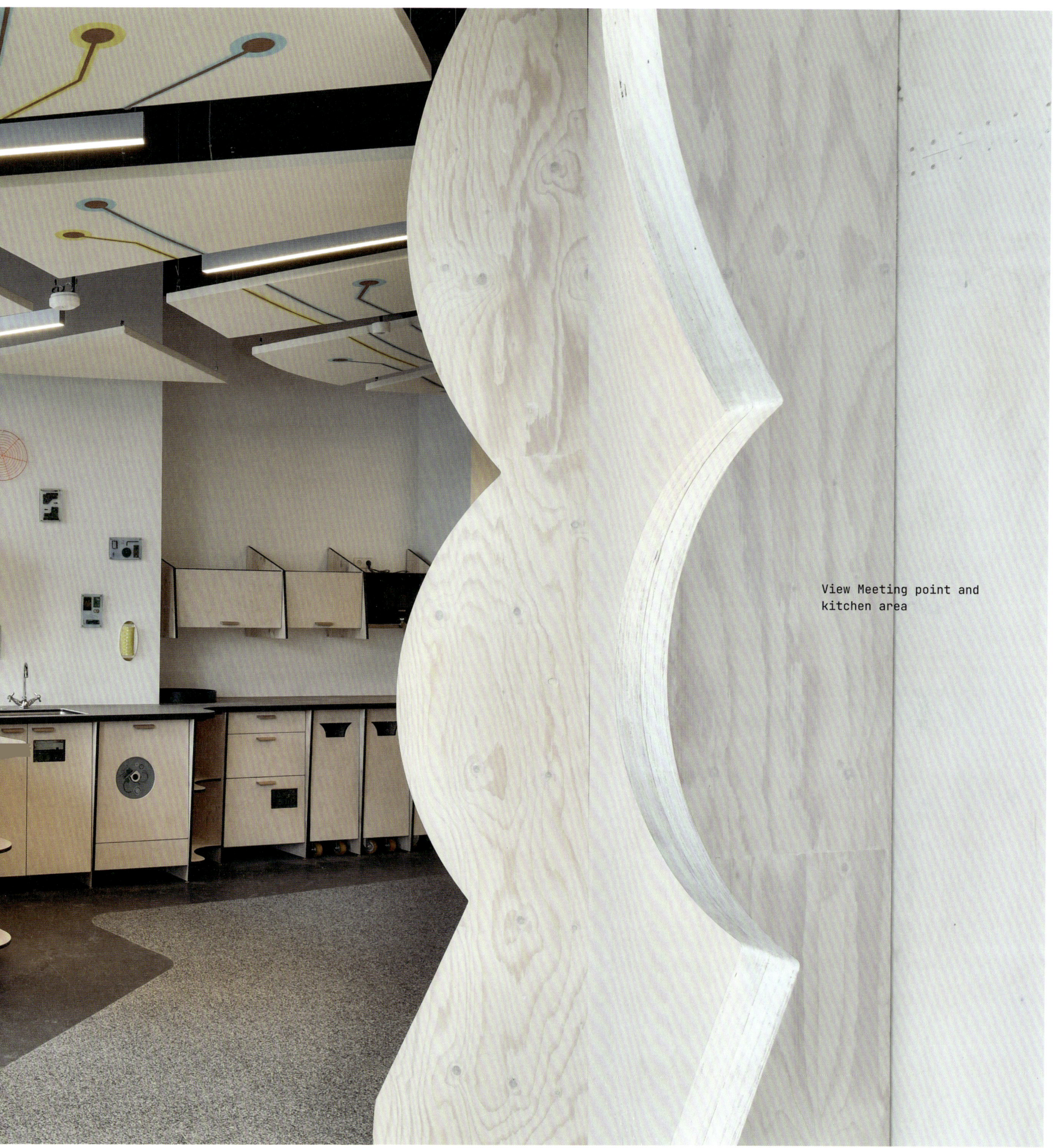

View Meeting point and kitchen area

GROW PLATFORM
A BOSCH COMPANY

Ludwigsburg 2017

The grow platform GmbH is a company of the Bosch Group. It is Bosch's internal incubator platform for start-ups and intrapreneurs. Currently, the grow platform portfolio includes more than 250 intrapreneurs worldwide. Companies such as triffix, Deepfield Connect, Remotion, My Scott, and Urbanmates, to name a few, have successfully emerged from the platform.

The relocation of the grow platform in 2017 to new, more spacious premises was the starting point for the collaboration with freeters.

Together we developed a variety of spatial concepts, usage scenarios, tools, furniture, and architectural interventions for the hall that covers over 4,000 square meters. At its core, we created five crystallization points, in the sense of five sculptural space-in-space solutions. These stand out in contrast to the usual office routine and the corresponding standard furniture and at the same time form specific anchor points, both visually and in terms of use. These anchor points are complemented, dynamically surrounded, and brought together by a spectrum of accents, furniture, and design approaches that are reflected, in particular, in the foyer and the several meeting rooms around the basement.

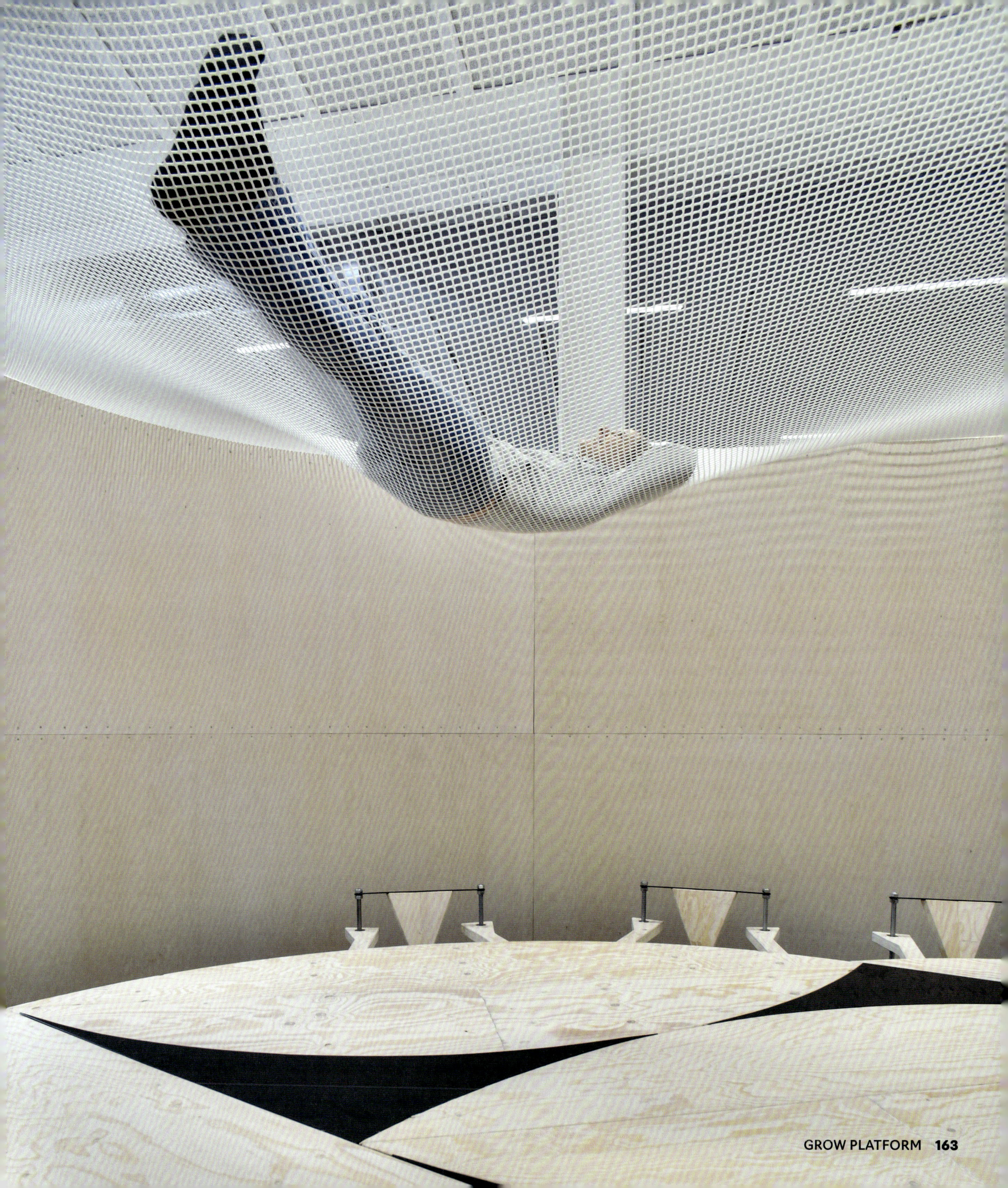

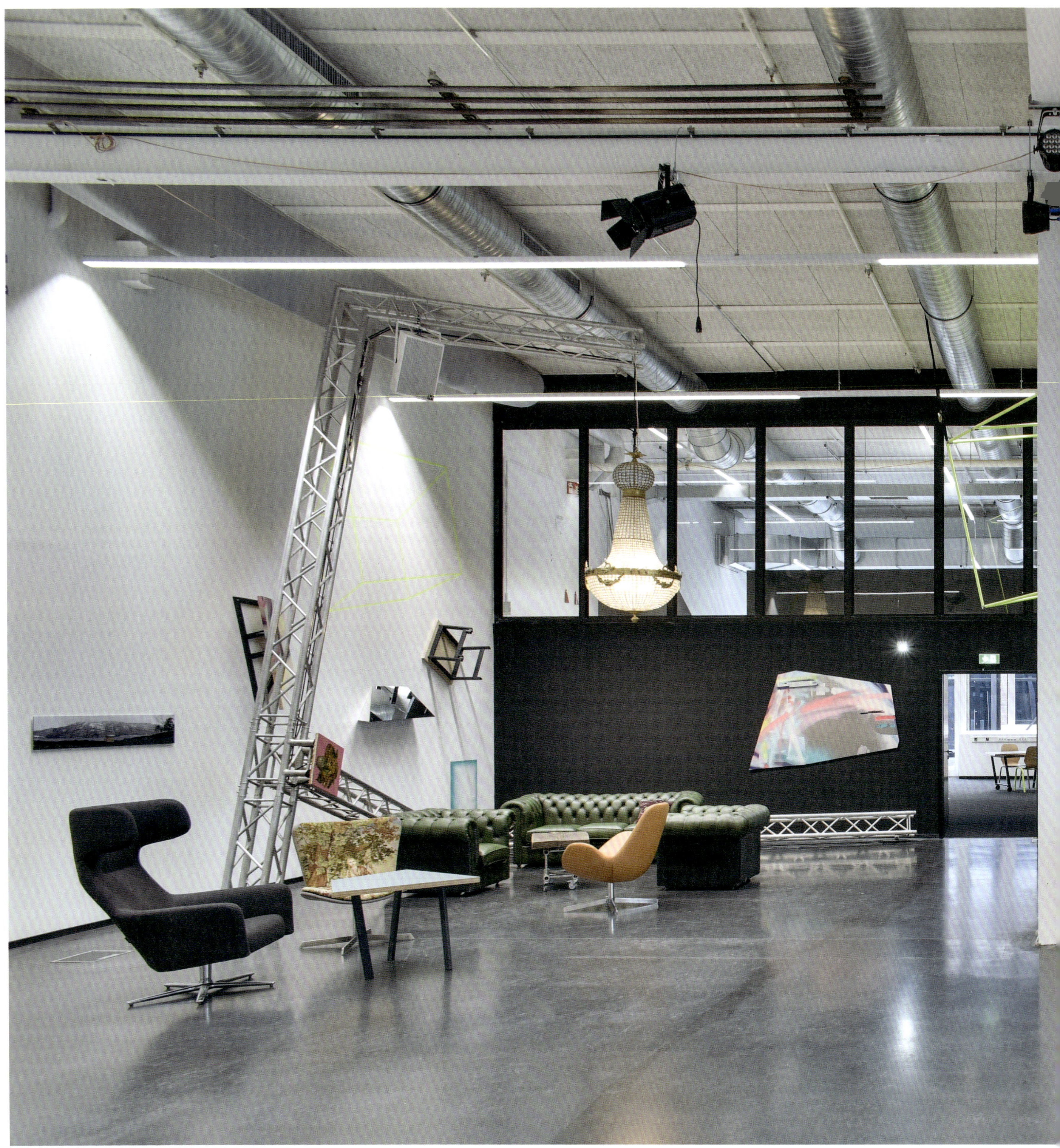

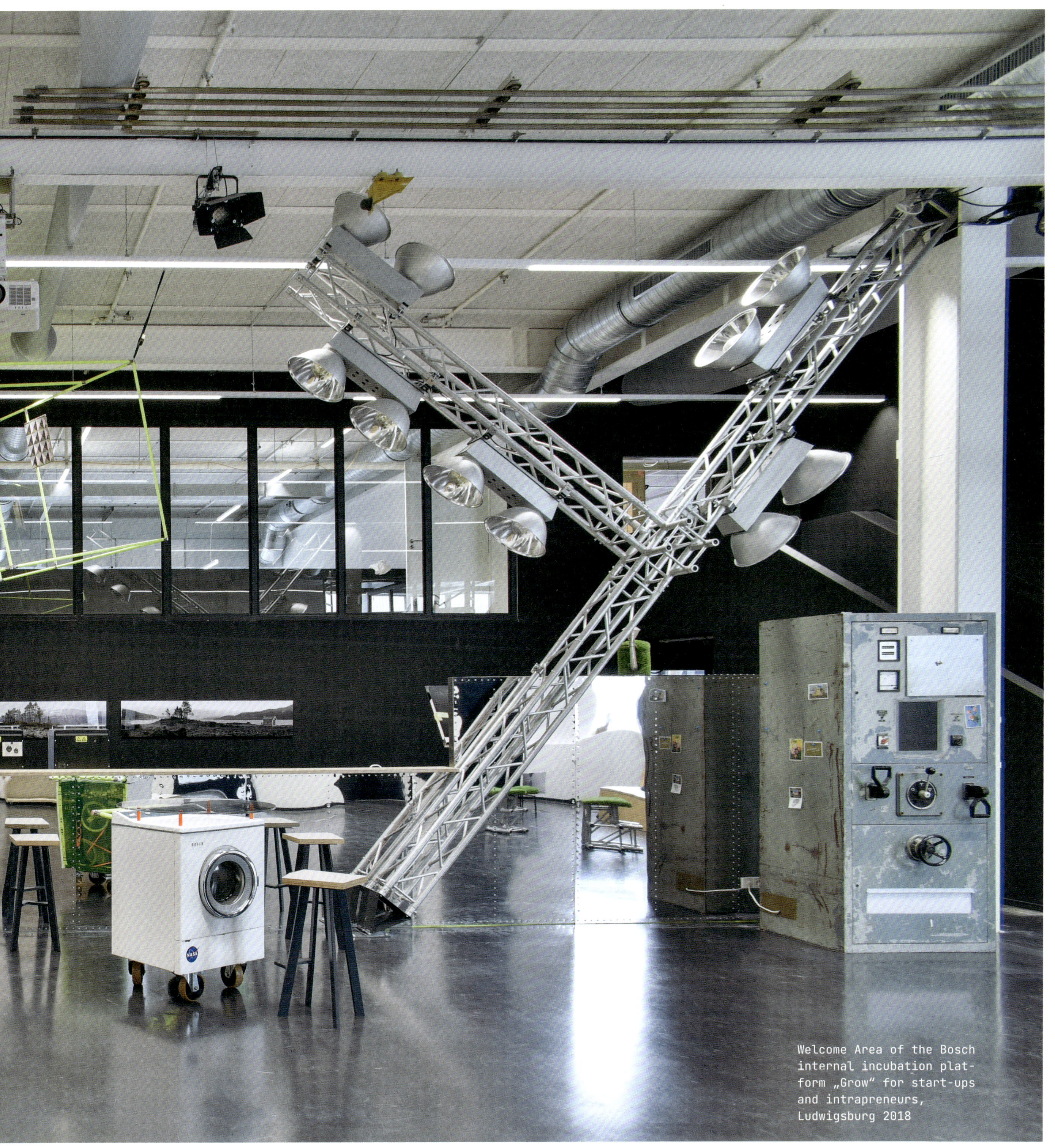

Welcome Area of the Bosch internal incubation platform „Grow“ for start-ups and intrapreneurs, Ludwigsburg 2018

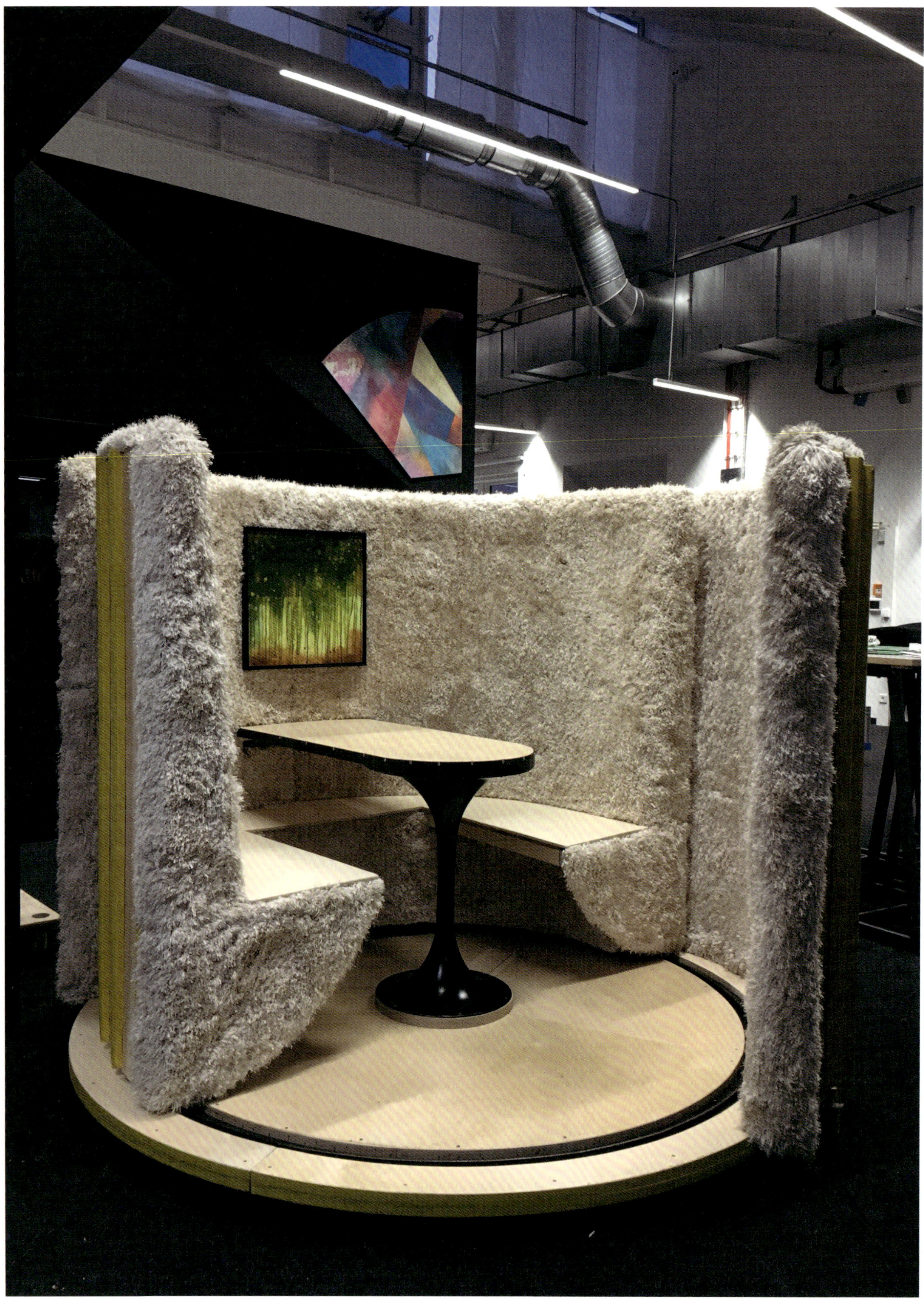

Interior view
1st floor, basement
and welcome area,
2018

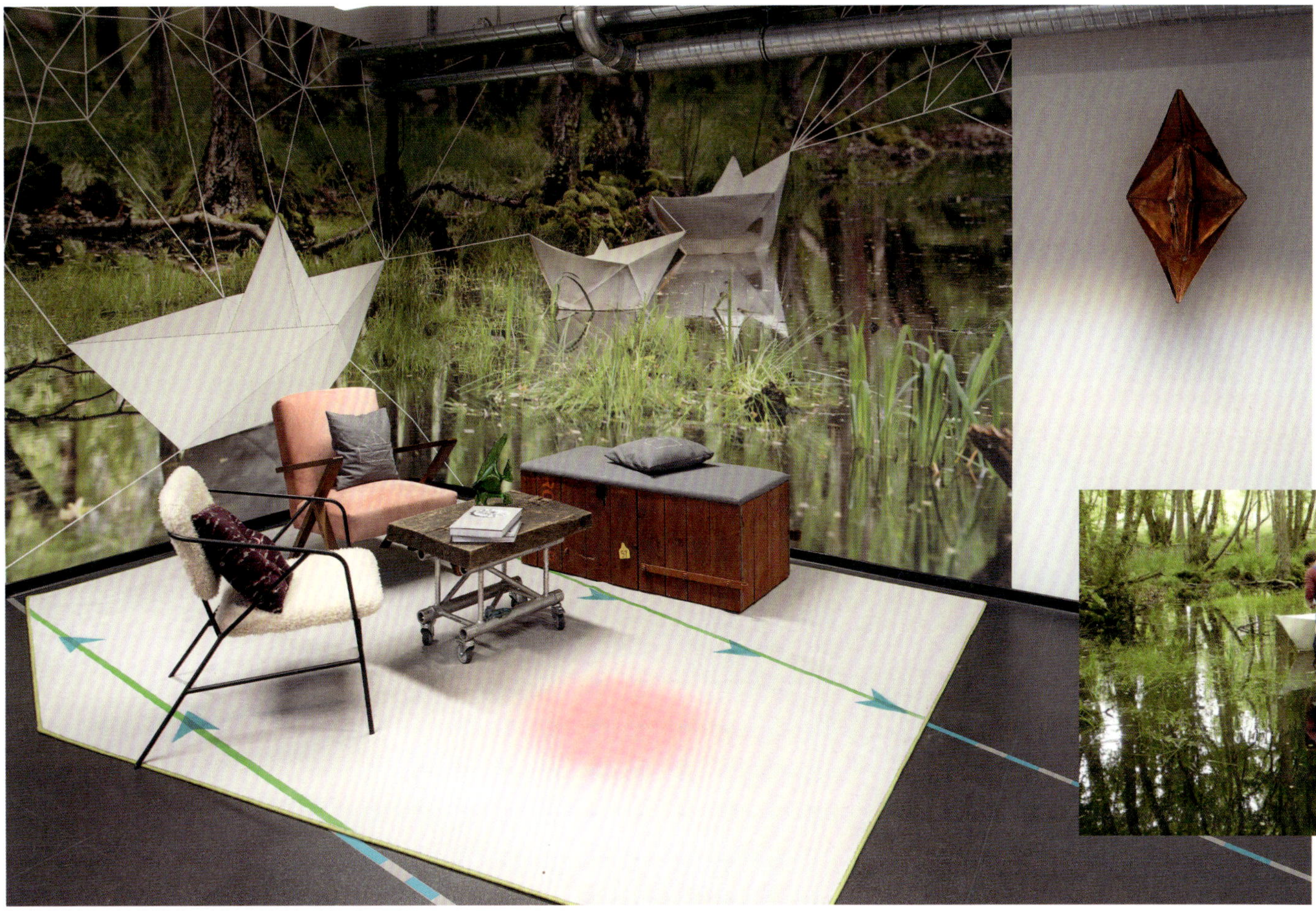

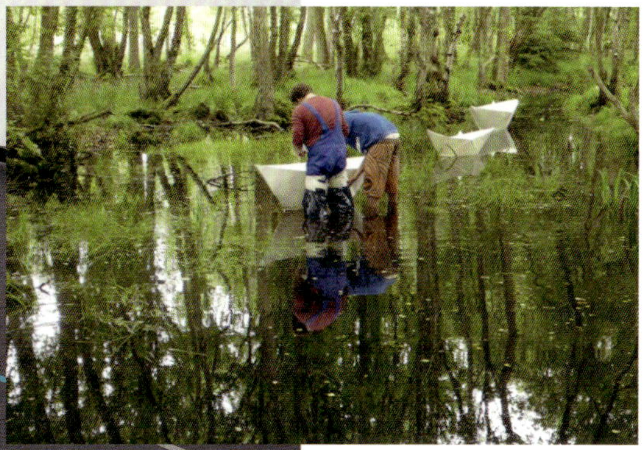

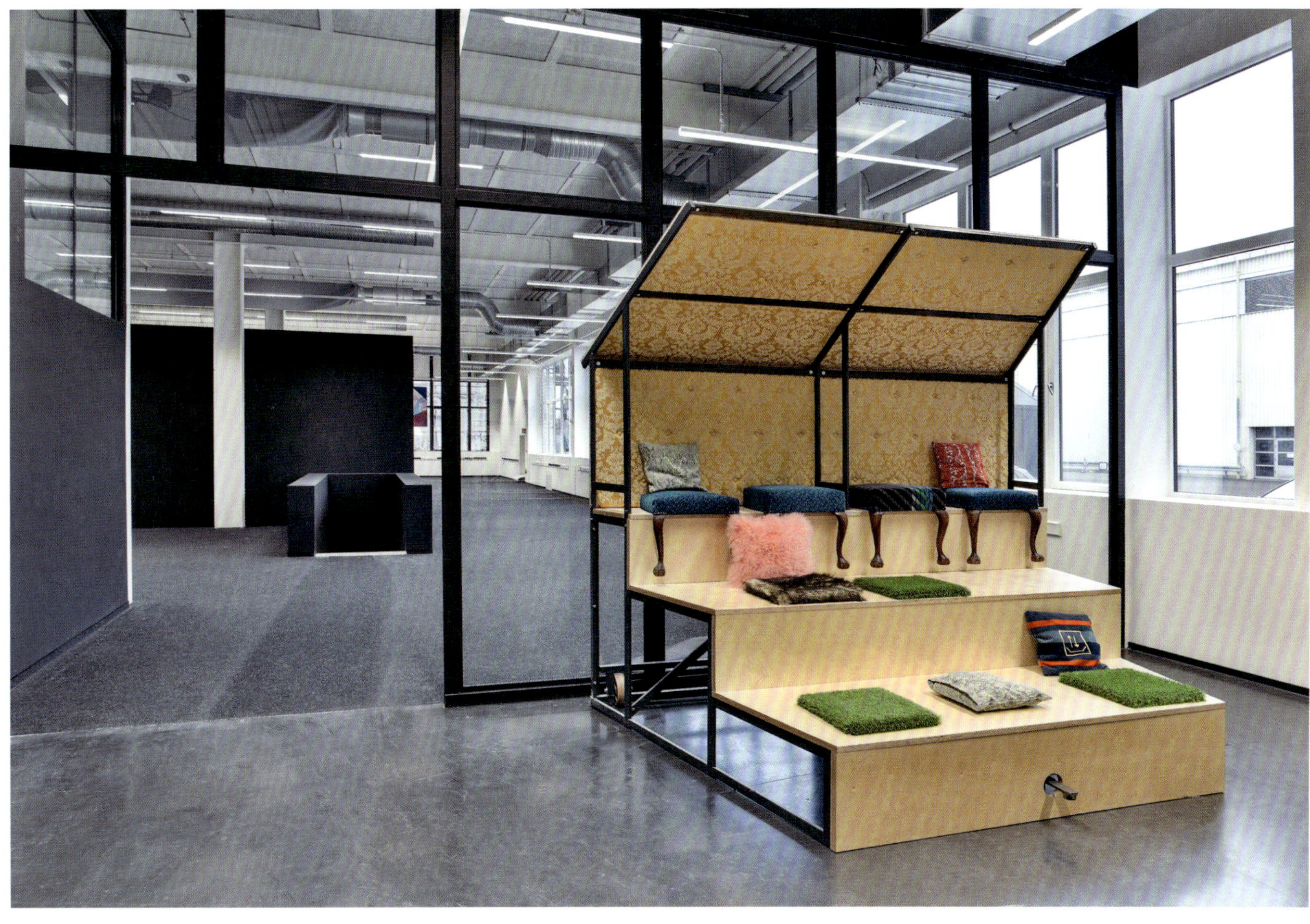

WHERE DO ARTISTS GET THEIR IDEAS

Interview with Johannes Hess,
Artist at freeters

Anyone who deals with growth or development, and particularly with man-made developments, will come across this question sooner or later: Where do these ideas, brainwaves, and strokes of genius come from? Or: Under what circumstances do I have good ideas and when not? Is there fertile soil, conducive circumstances, or even a recipe for this?

As a start-up campus for Robert Bosch GmbH, grow is an institution that is often confronted with these questions. After all, a start-up campus is the place where entrepreneurs and engineers develop ideas, which in the best case do not even exist on the market yet. But firstly, there need to be ideas.

So, where do these ideas come from? This is a question we artists also ask ourselves again and again. If there were an easy recipe for this, I would certainly share it. Or, one of my artist colleagues would have done so already.

From my point of view, there are two areas from which I as an artist can draw my ideas. One of them is the world around me. These are the impressions I have, my views and perceptions. They can be visual, acoustic, tactile, or any other kind of impression.

Jumping in cold water, the warmth of the sun, a mountain landscape ... or something quite small: the movements of an insect or a rare phenomenon that suddenly strikes me. In other words: simply everything that impresses or fascinates me from the outside world and stays stuck in my head.

The counterpart to this is the world within myself. The typical longings, wishes, and dreams a person has. But they can also be needs, like hunger, thirst, pain, or a fear of heights. The tingling in your stomach when you drive too fast over a bump, the desire to listen to music loudly or to exercise, to move. For me, it is often wishing to see a shape or color that I can't find in the world in the way I imagine it. But of course, these are also convictions, hopes, or even ideals. So, it's always interesting when I feel that there is something that I need to express or, in other words, something that I want to bring to life.

"It is eminently important not to want to understand too much too early."

Whenever something wants to make its way from the outside to the inside or from the inside to the outside, it becomes interesting to me. But here comes a key aspect. It is eminently important not to want to understand too much too early. I try not to understand too early why I have the need to express this or that, why I have the need to suddenly stop and listen to a completely trivial sound, or to deal with a certain book, be totally fascinated to observe an ant, or whatever it is. What is important is that I can do this without having to come up with an explanation as to why it's a good idea or where it might lead. Experience has taught me: we're generally much smarter than we think! When it comes to developing ideas, it's not the usual, well-known concepts that help me along. It's a question of common sense. I need to leave my safe surroundings behind if I want to move to another one. I shouldn't apply the old benchmarks when I want to set new ones. To a certain extent this means always thrusting myself into unknown territory. A bit of a paradox, but perhaps that's why it's the key factor here. From my point of view, without this point, there would be no developments at all. At least no man-made ones.

To sum it up, we could say that sensuality and passion can be considered wellsprings. And if we manage to dive into what we come up against there without drowning in intellect, we're sure to safely reach a place where, in my opinion, we can talk about inspiration. So inspiration is by no means something for which there is a simple recipe. It's not that you can just come up with a great idea whenever you want to.

But, and it's my personal wish to make this clear, it's not like there is a patent for inspiration either. Even artists are just ordinary folks. I know that it probably isn't something the art scene wants to hear, but anyone who's prepared to follow a couple of basic rules can show their inspiration to the world. You just need to be bold and follow the signs—they are everywhere! All the time!

SPACE
IGNITION SPARK

Johannes Hess and
Sebastian Keller, 2018

Anyone who has ever set out for new shores knows that it first has a lot to do with the unknown and unfamiliar. For the new areas to be opened up, the paths must first be found. This is not only the case physically – habits of thought also have to be broken in order to establish something new. Basically, this is an original artistic motif. This "spirit of departure" ignition spark tries to give expression to this "mood of departure", insofar as there is nowhere a vertical or horizontal surface or edge. Even the right angles we are so familiar with are searched for in vain. Each surface and each edge appears in a different way. Even the right angles we are so familiar with are searched for in vain. The formal recognition value of horizontal and vertical is nowhere given. Thus, one's own positioning or alignment must first be original. The oblique alignment of the walls, and in particular surfaces that cannot be clearly designated as walls or ceilings because they are located in an intermediate space, even provoke alignment with the user's own individual fixed point. A hold from the outside can only the clarity in which this principle of the "undefined space" is implemented. Almost crystalline, the different surfaces are clearly placed next to each other. The whole is underlined by the mirrored outer skin of the object. The reflection offers little clue of its own, it reflects the light and plays virtually as well as visually with its surrounding space. For me this space is essentially born of these sculptural or spatialartistic design principles.

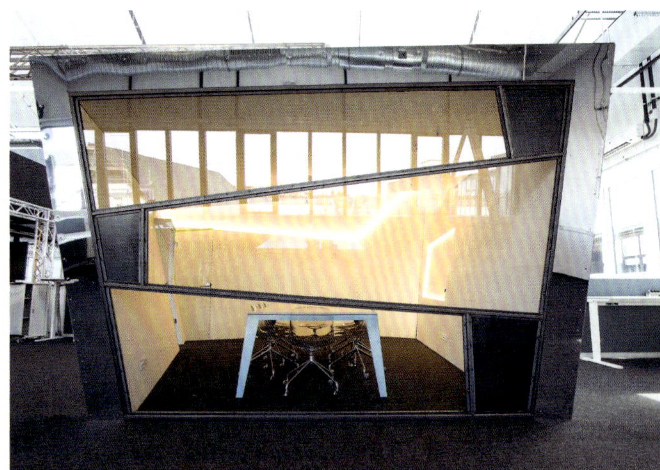

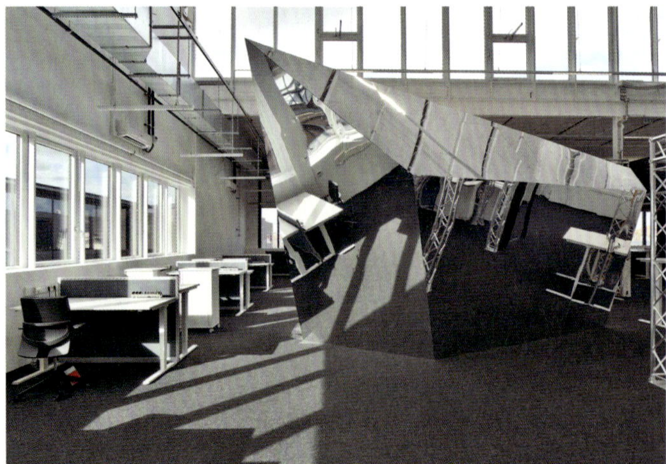

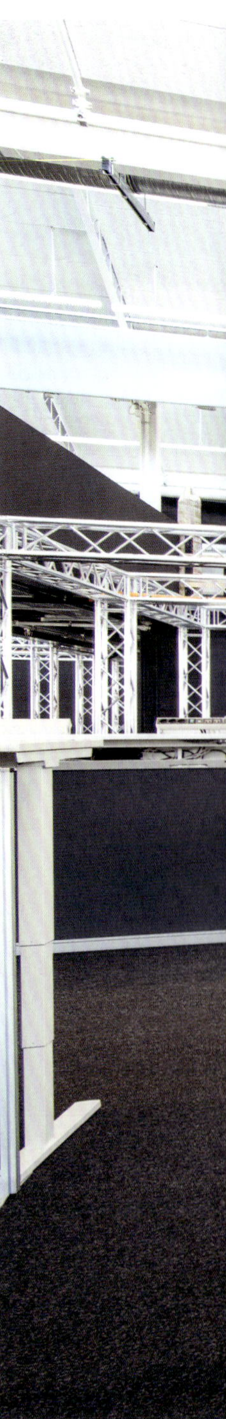

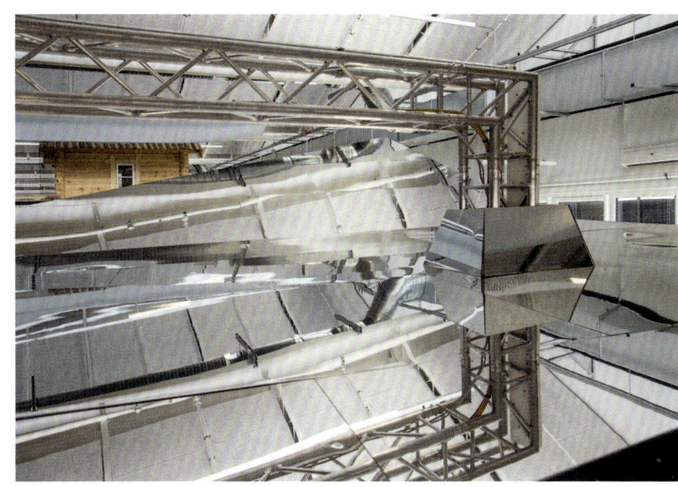

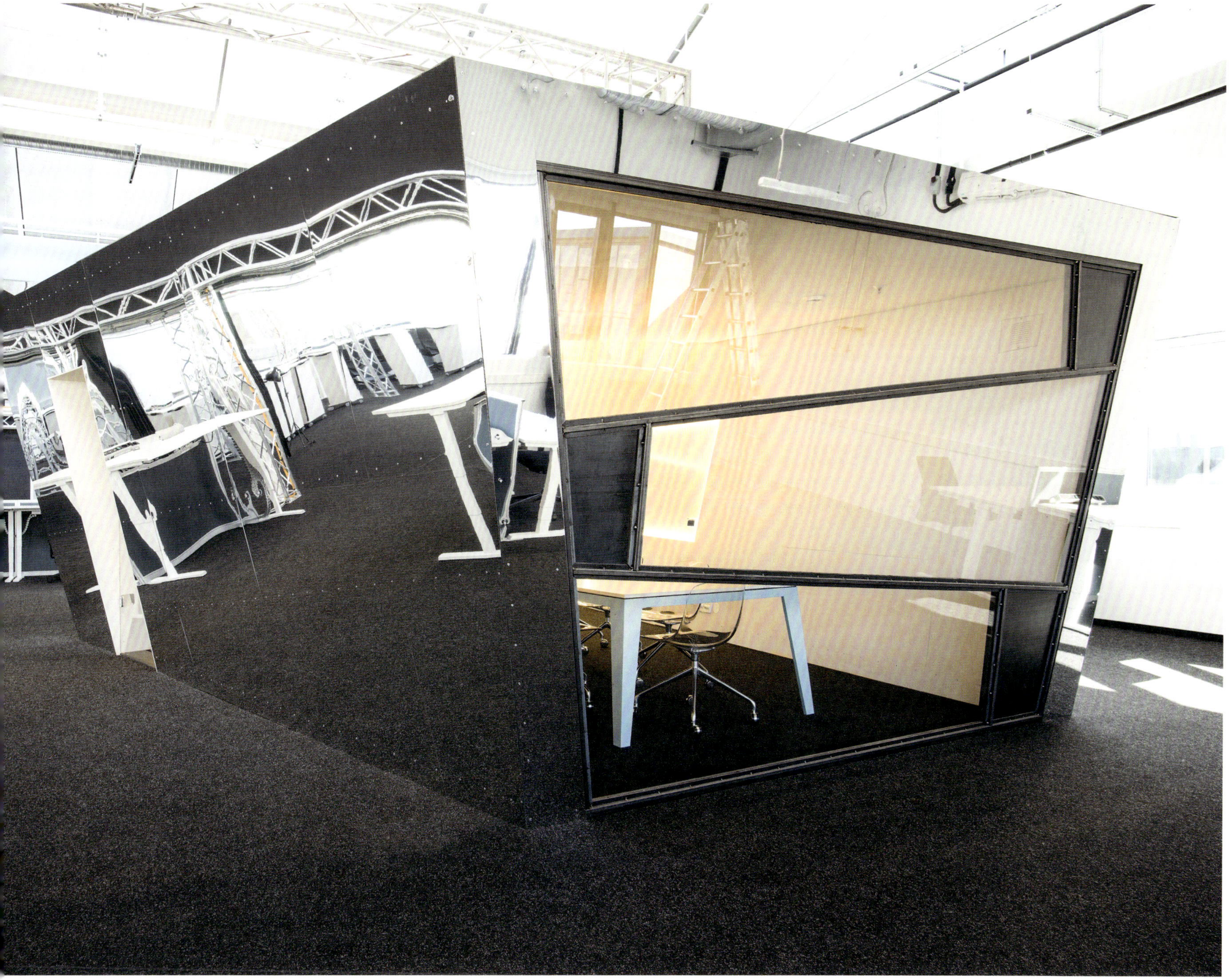

SPACE
INNER CIRCLE

Paul Jonas Petry, 2018

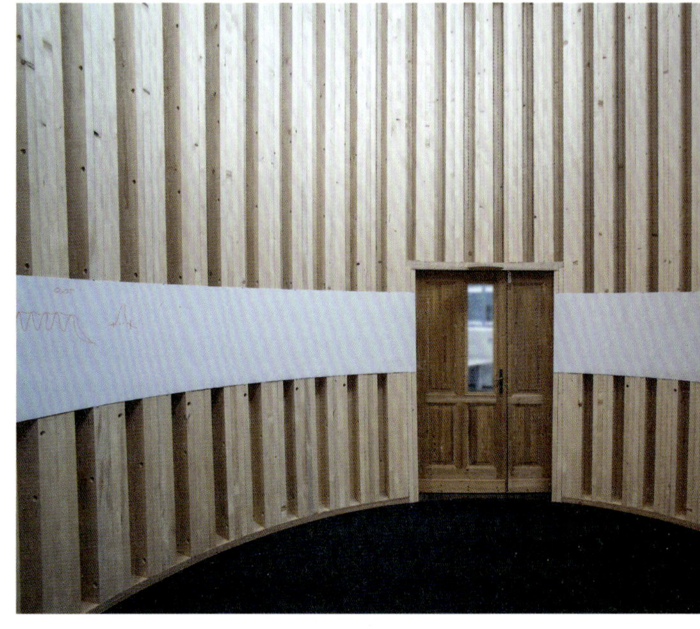

Motivically, two basic gestures form the basis of the design of the "Inner Circle".

Its environment, the fixtures, the building itself, the surrounding buildings are shaped in a bearing-like manner, and lying spaces characterize the image. Only the sloping roof elements break the orthogonal structure. On the other side of the content level, there is a strong visionary character: the work of the start-up companies. It rather describes the vertical gesture of form. The movements intersect with the floor space of the room.

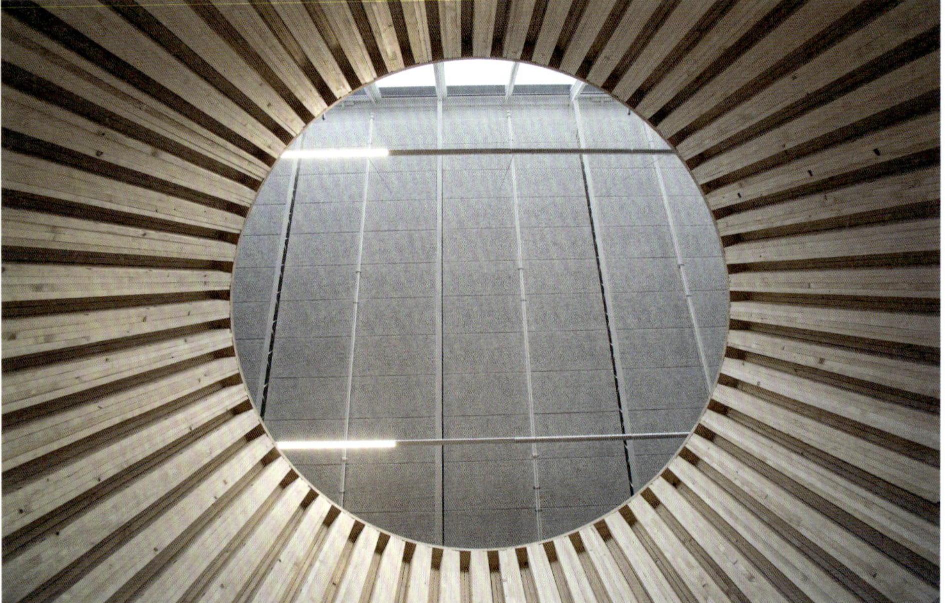

"It's about bringing visions from the mental world of ideas to the floor, bundling them and giving them form. From these two points of view I have developed the "Inner Circle": In contrast to the orthogonal, bearing structure of the enclosed space, the wooden body presents itself as a round skin that plays around the upright, a clear inside and outside, top and bottom emerges."

The "Inner Circle" consists of 336 upright building planks, each 480cm long. 112 of them are 25cm wide, 224 are 6cm wide, held by one multiplex ring each at the top and bottom. The individual elements are screwed together with approx. 3000 screws. The doors come from an old farmhouse in Bornheim / Rhineland, built about 1910.

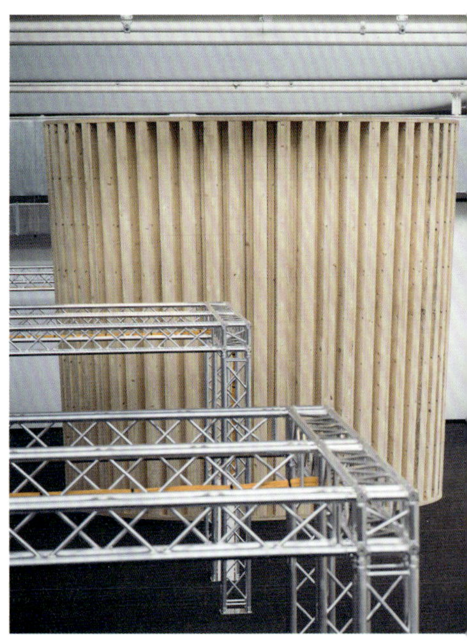

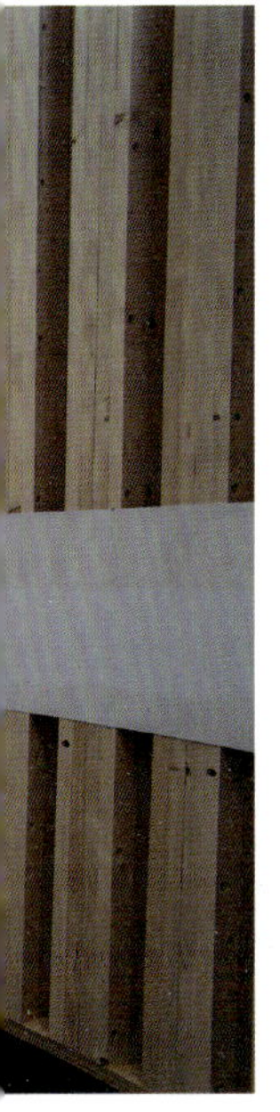

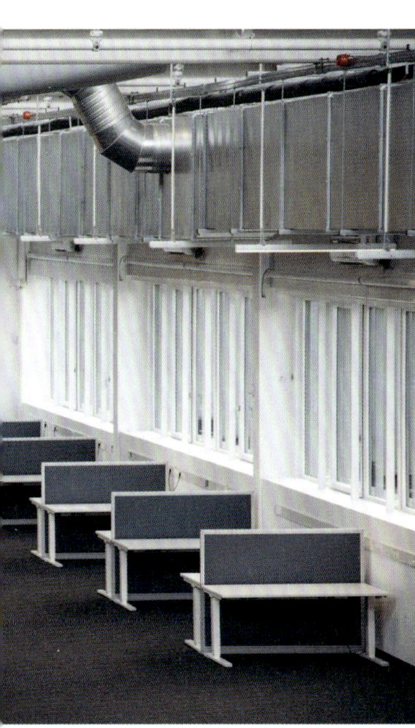

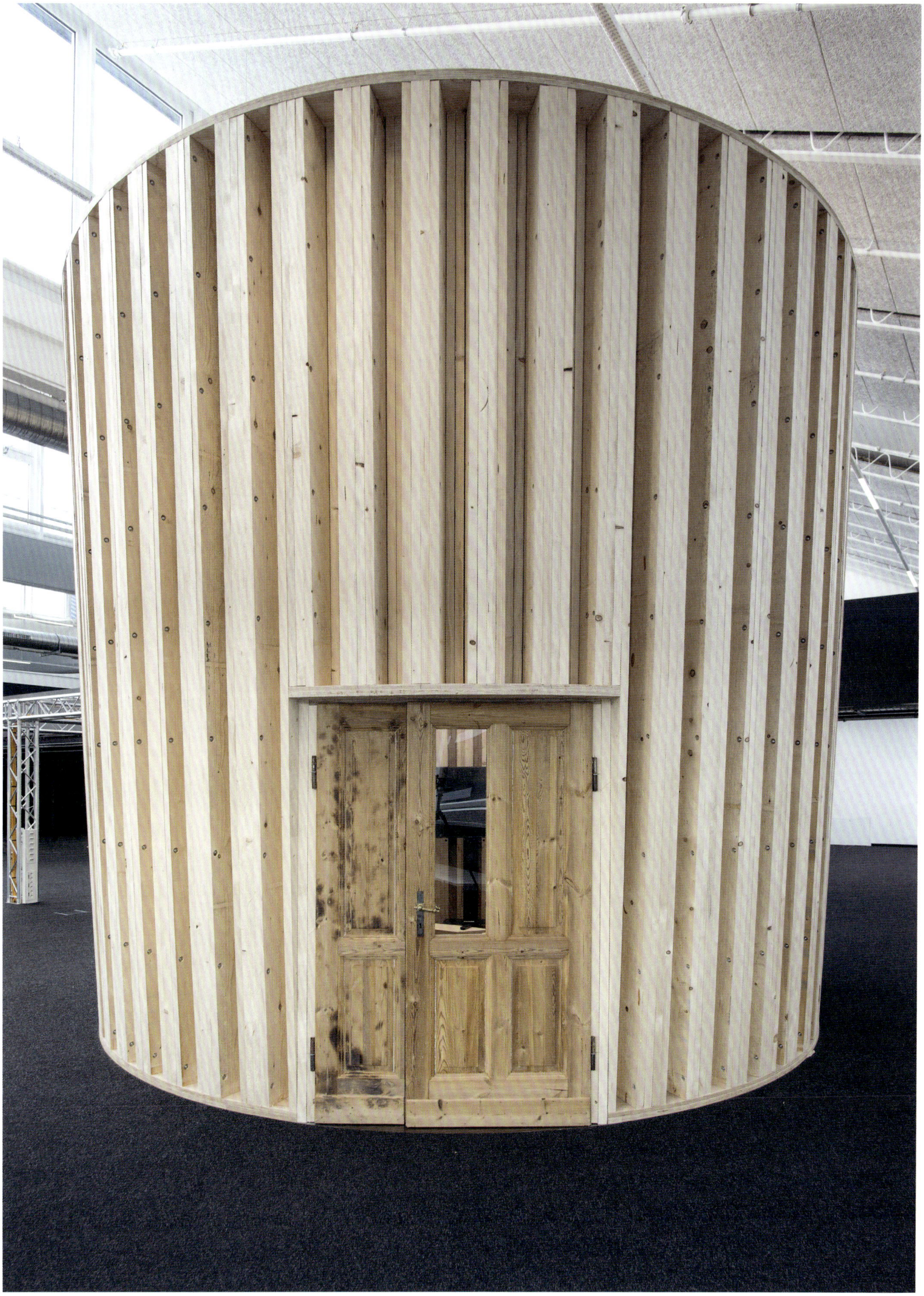

SPACE
THIS IS NOT A PIPE

Michael Sistig, 2018

The object, space or sculpture "This is not a Pipe" is inspired by the aesthetic observation of a half-pipe. The simple joining of two halves results in a whole, purely mathematically and logically. But because of the simplicity of the perspective rotation of the half-pipes and the joining of the riding surfaces, a space is created. The outer facade reflects and distorts the image of the sculpture's surroundings and thus becomes part of the sculpture. This means that it is not the real image that is part of the sculpture, but the perspective, mirrordistorted image. Here, the real image transitions into two-dimensionality. Similar to René Magritte's painting "Ceci n'est pas un Pipe" or "This is not a Pipe", he painted the pipe to demonstrate that the realistic image of an object is not itself identical with the object. You can't smoke or plug this pipe of Magritte's. In the same way, you can't ride the half-pipes. What is it?

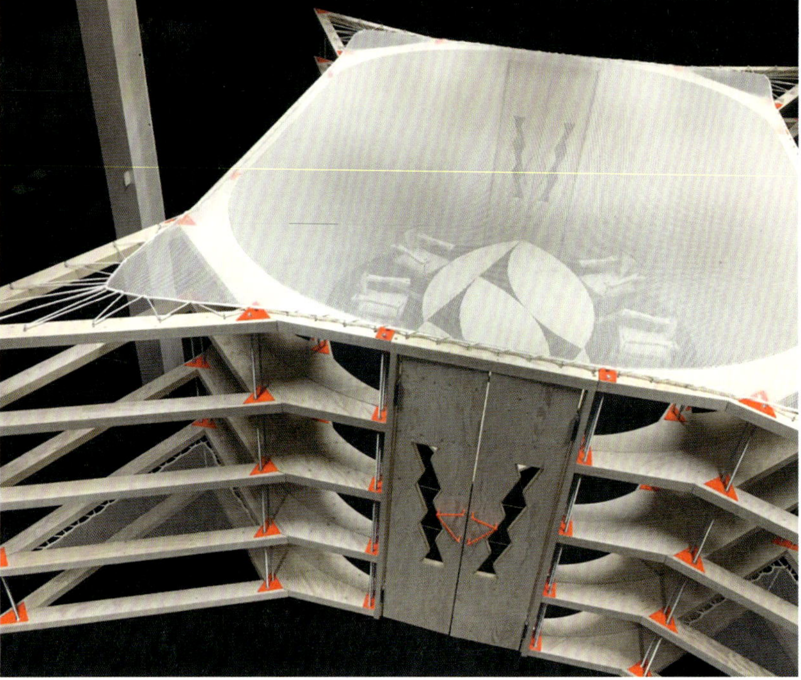

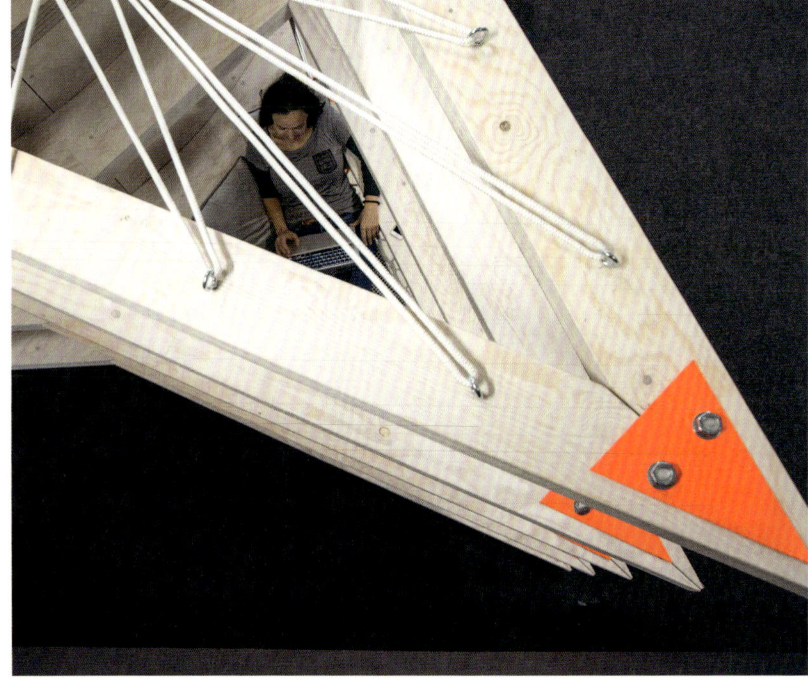

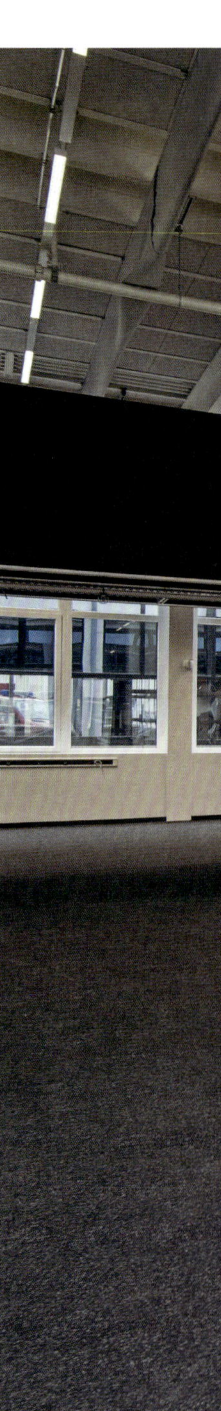

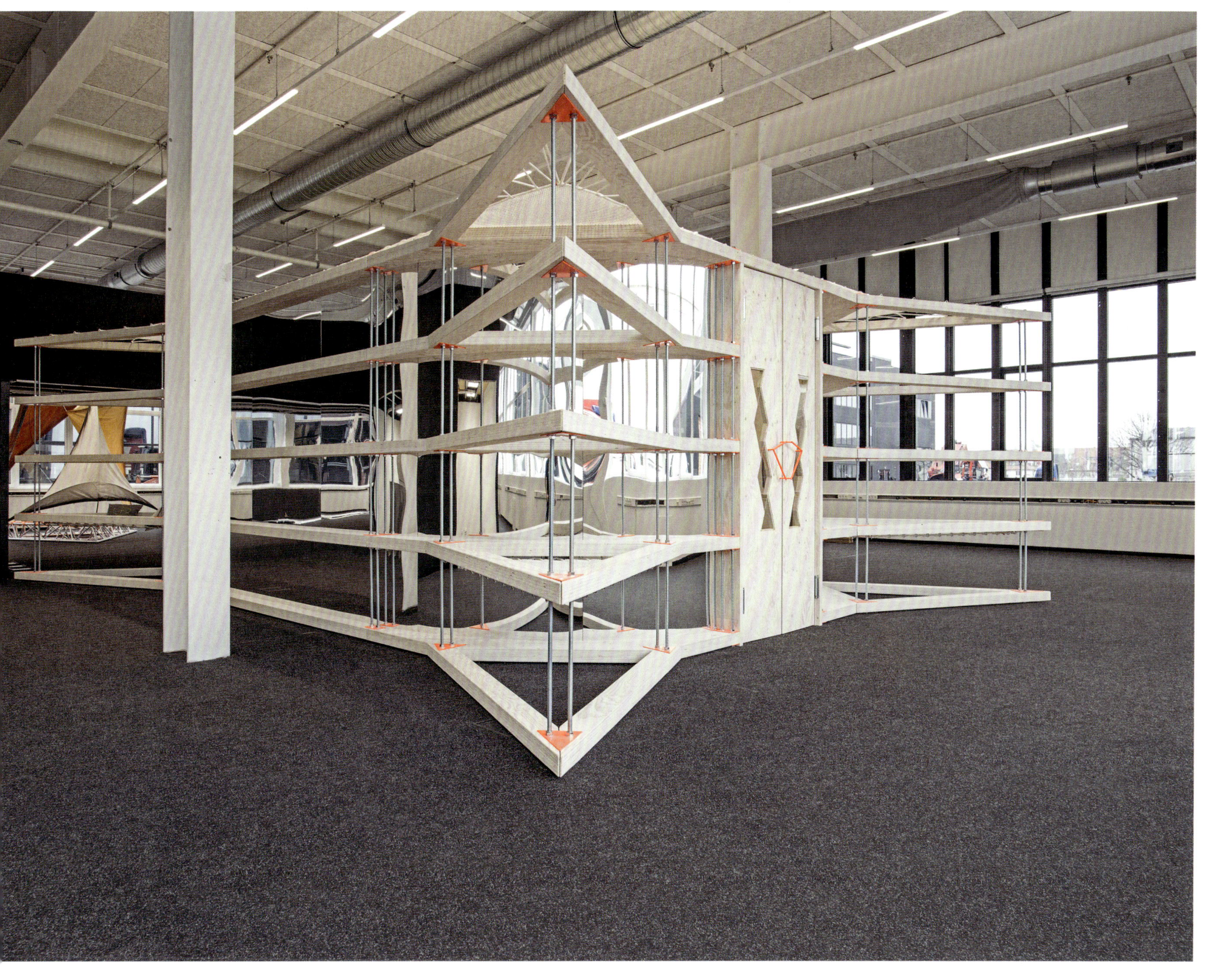

KIELER WELTRAUM

2016

Currently, controversies between traditional structures and the realities of social coexistence can be observed in many places. For example, policy measures bear no relation to the development of a completely new concept of culture, which we already live and experience in our everyday encounters with people from different nations.

The search for cultural security often takes place on the outside, instead of an "inner consolidation" of individual and cultural identity. An opportunity to break down boundaries and create something new out of existing structures can be experienced in engagement with artistic processes.

Since 2015, the Schusterkrug has offered shared accommodation for asylum seekers managed by the welfare organizations Arbeiterwohlfahrt Kiel and the German Red Cross Kiel. Up to 1,200 asylum seekers from conflict regions can live in the shared accommodation, which is located on a former federal armed forces site. In 2016, the Kiel Space project resulted in a small cosmos in the midst of the daily hustle and bustle of the Schusterkrug and the city of Kiel. Under the guidance of the artist collective Freeters, a team of about 200 helpers transformed an old aircraft hangar, creating a completely new cultural place and concept of community. Over a period of 10 days, the old hangar was developed into a place of gathering with coffee shops, a playground, a studio and workshop, a lounge, and a stage for larger events. Families, children, and especially young adults from the accommodation, as well as other residents of the city of Kiel, participated in various workshops in the construction of the cultural center. With the dynamics of a rocket launch, there was suddenly the sound of industrious saws and cordless screwdrivers, children's laughter, traditional Syrian music, and the dry and friendly North German greeting "Moinmoin." All around there were splashes of color and glitter, bicycle tires, an old trailer, and permeating it all, after ten days, the familiar smell of foreign spices and an outsized dimension of humanity, helpfulness, and warmth.

In everyday life, apart from charitable activities, there are few opportunities to create points of contact between refugees and other residents. Feeling threatened or mistrustful of strangers, on the one hand, encounters the dislocation and fear of the new on the other. The goal is to promote cultural diversity and overlap by creating together at the Schusterkrug. People who associate Kiel with a fixed place of residence meet people who have lost a connection to their home. The joint artistic work enables a collaboration that takes place outside of everyday structures and thus opens up a free space for something new. It is about creating a place together and sharing space in the broadest sense, which ultimately results in an opportunity for mutual understanding between those involved through artistic and aesthetic education.

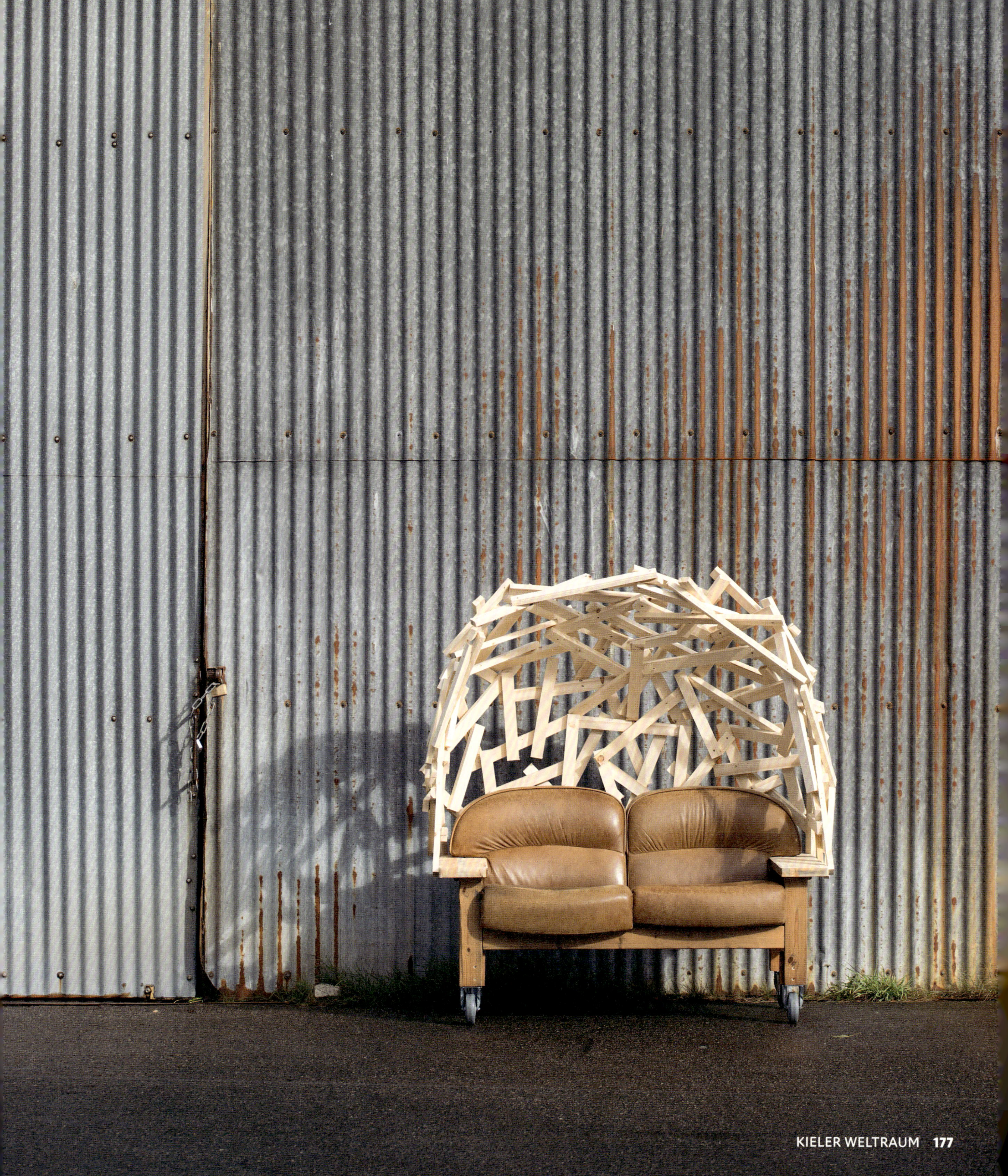

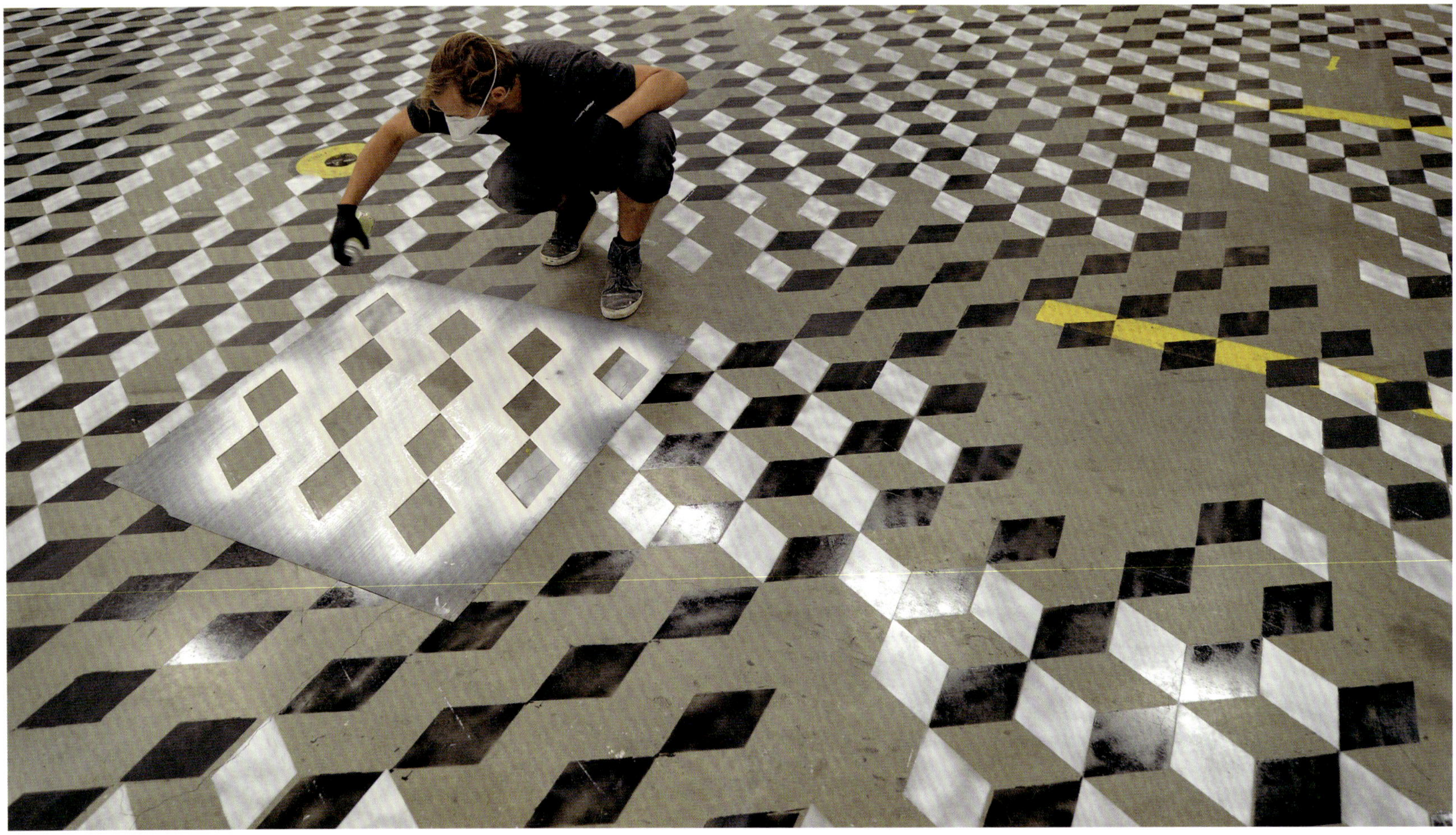

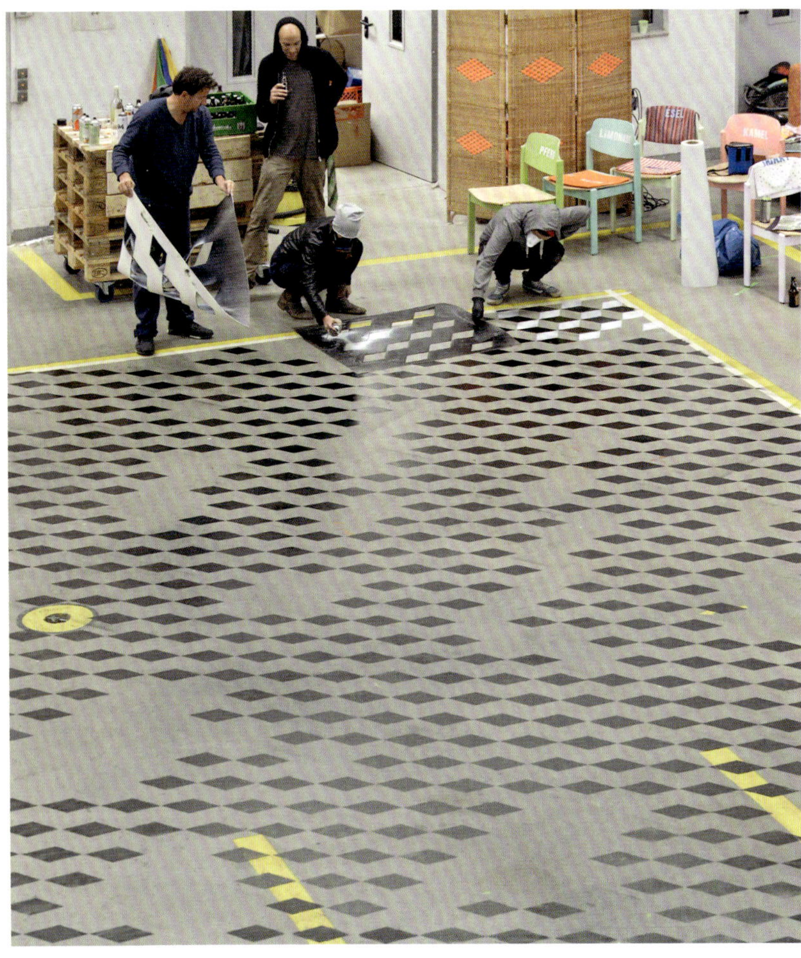

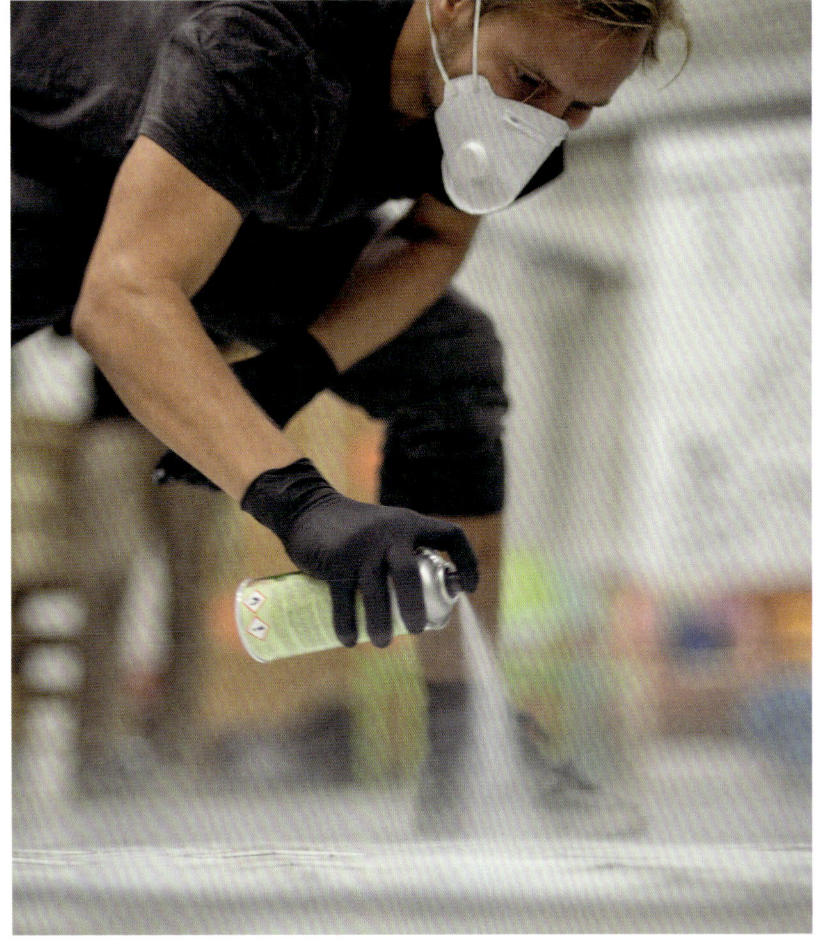

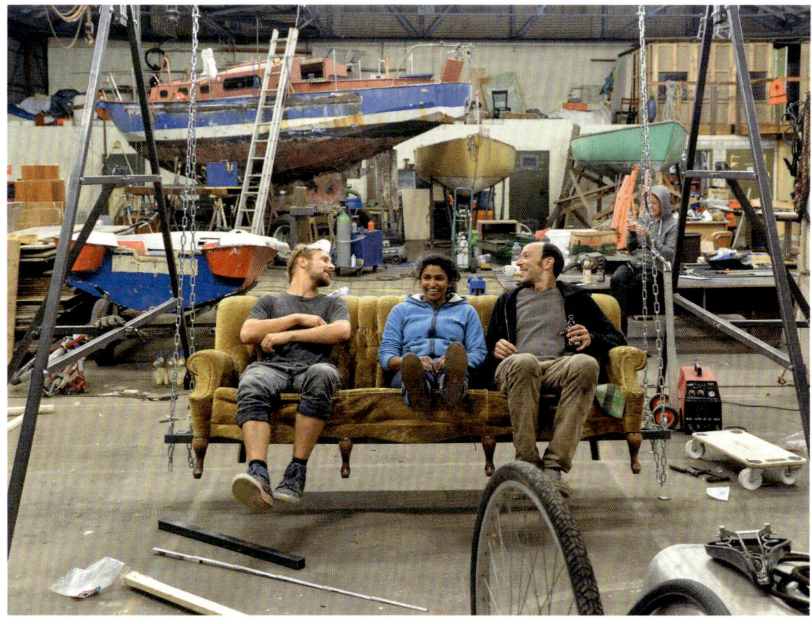
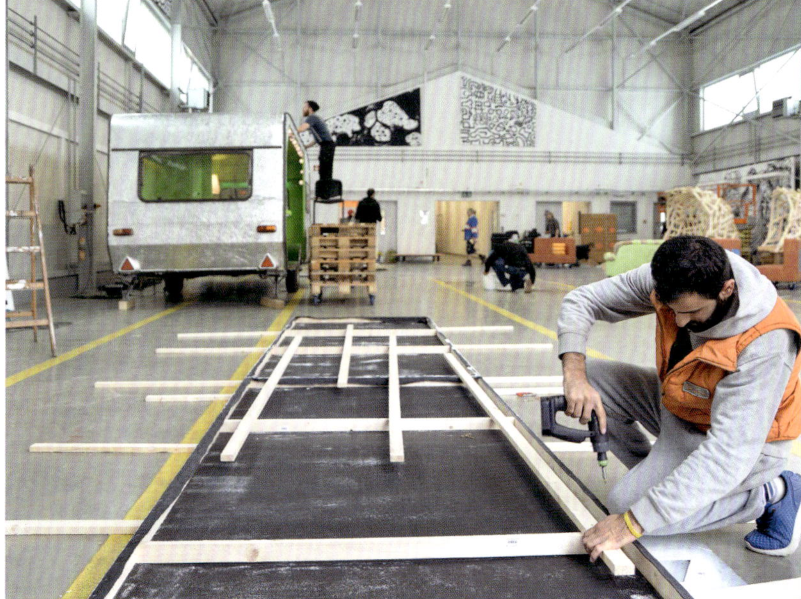
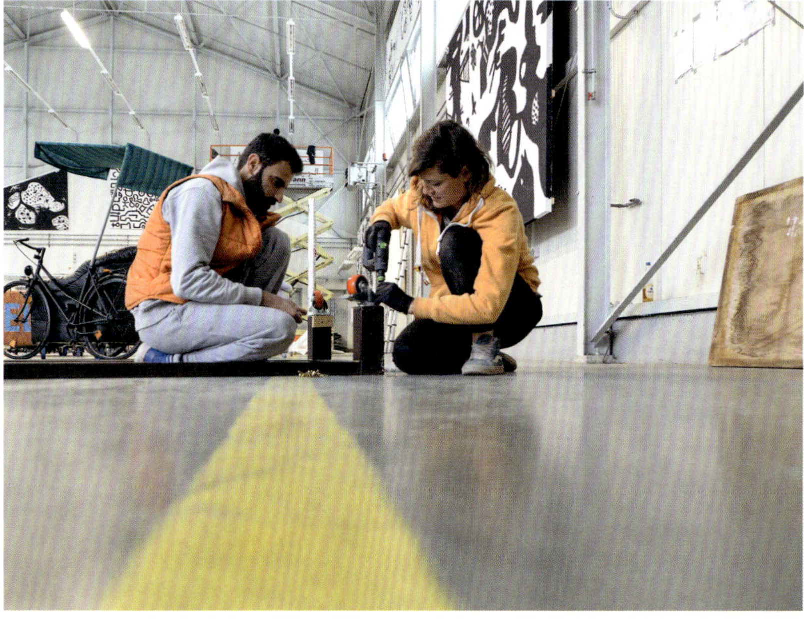
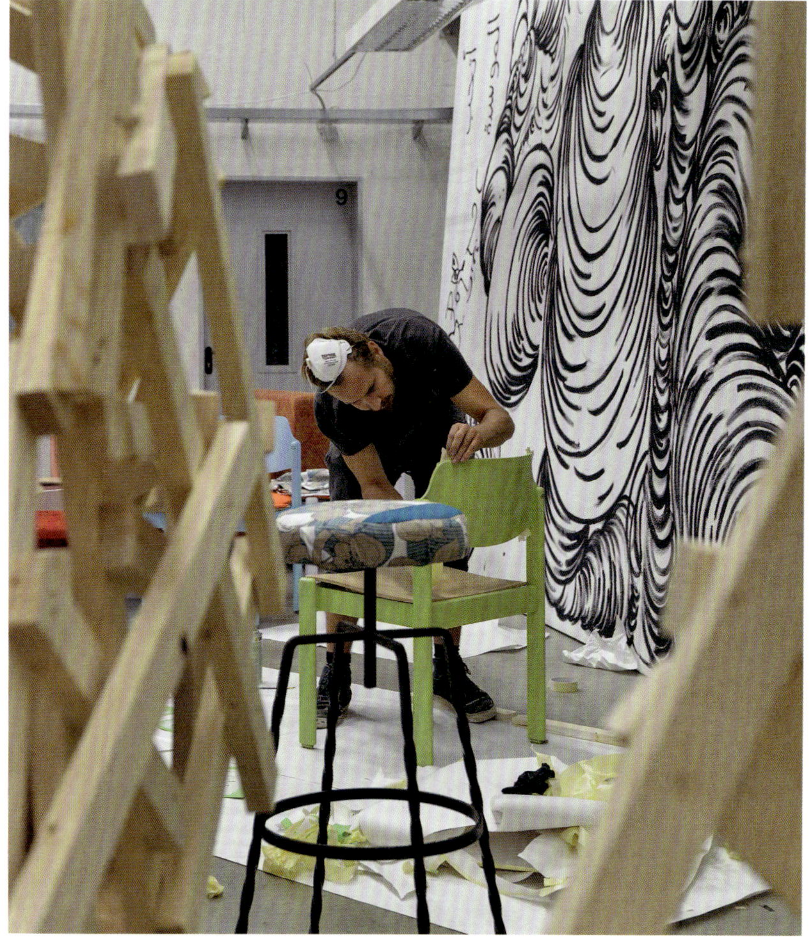
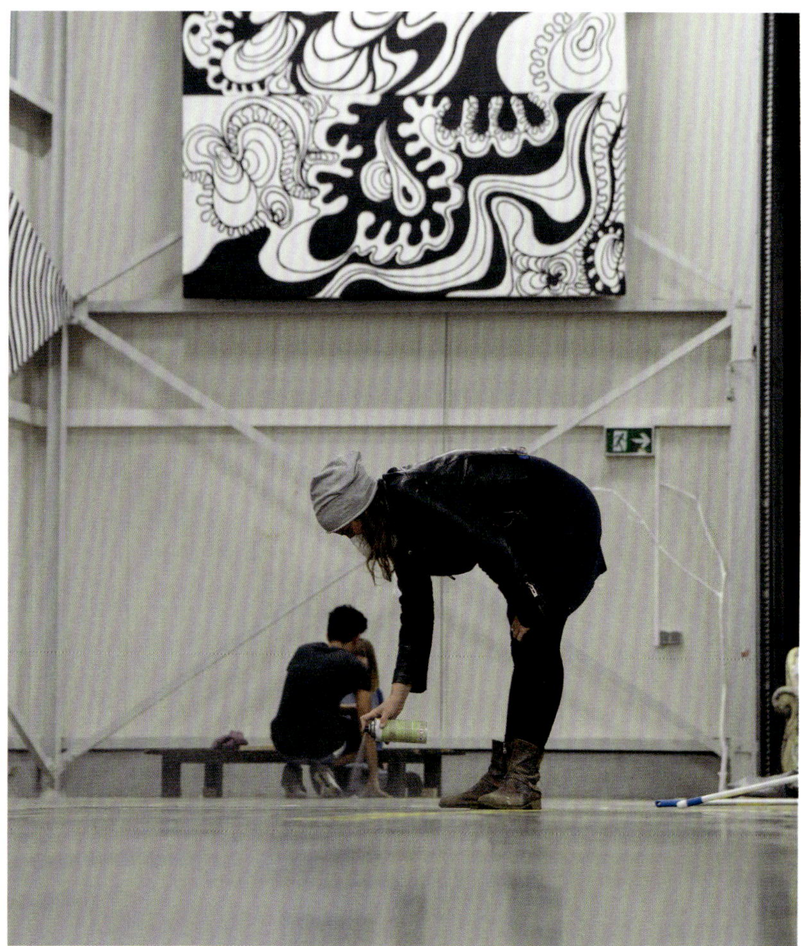

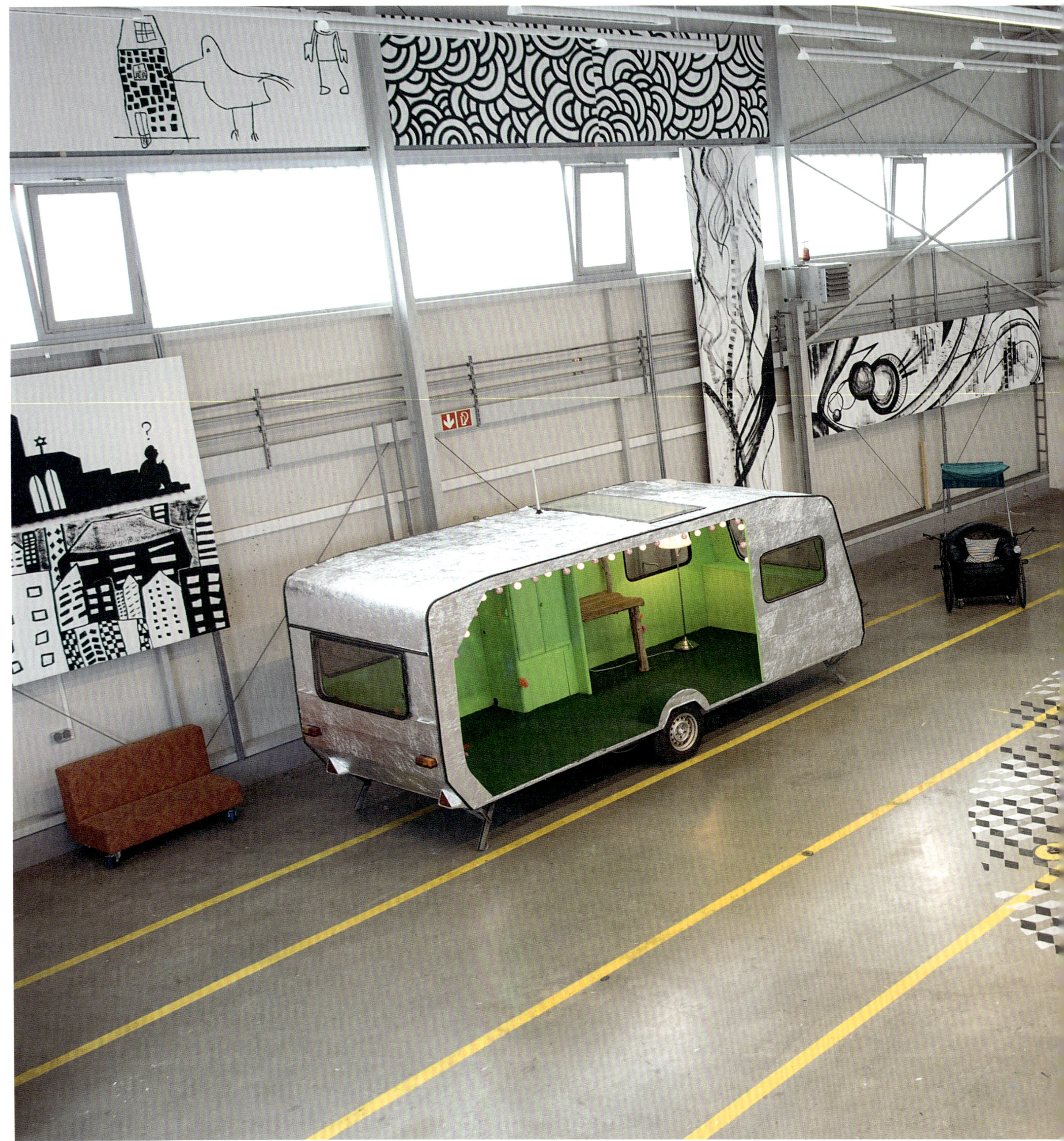

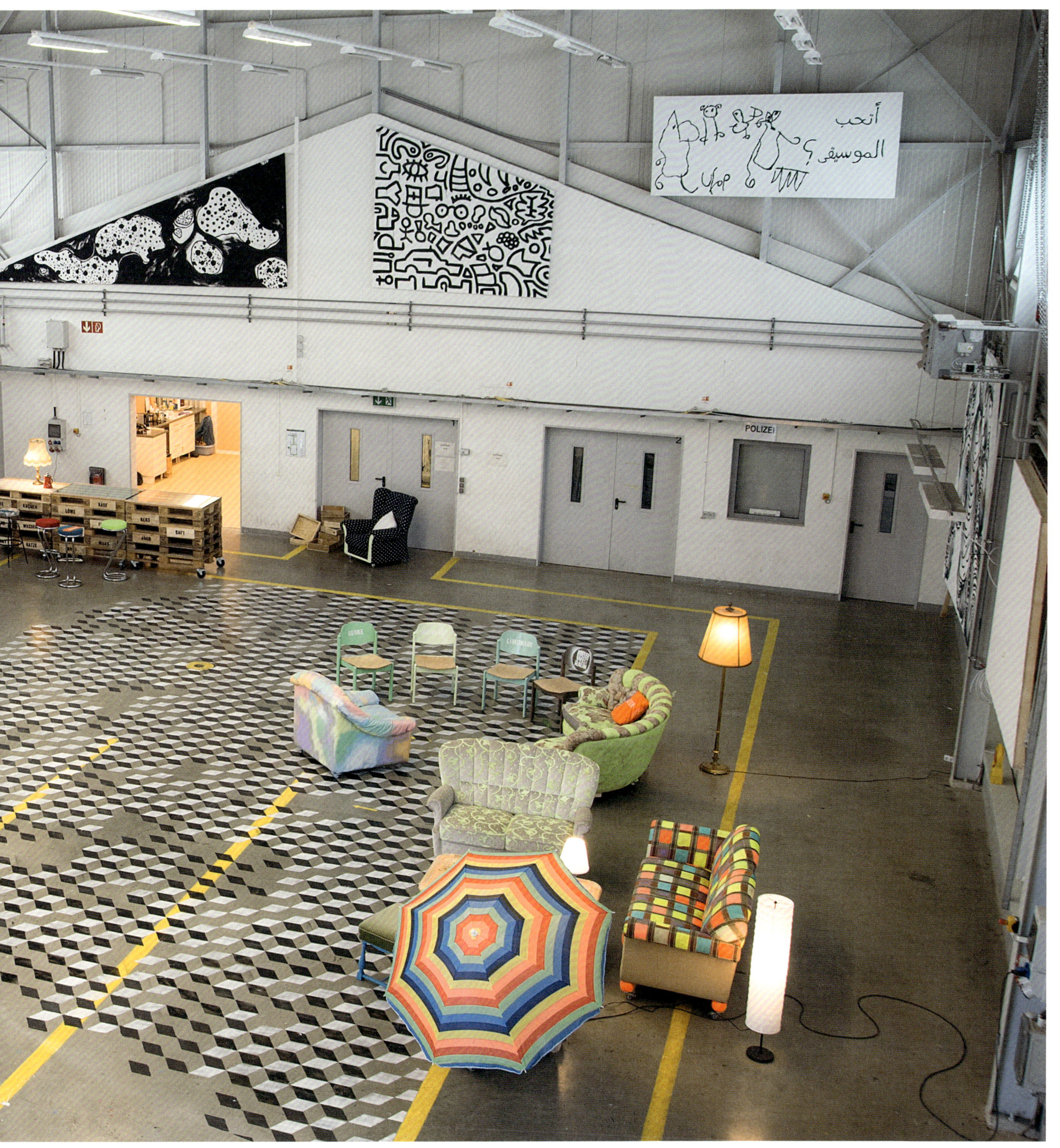
أتحب
الموسيقى؟
POLIZEI

ORGATEC COLOGNE TRADE FAIR

Visitors in 2018: 63,166
Most visited and most polarizing area: Plant 10.1

In the middle of Hall 10.1, from October 23 to 27, 2018, seven experiential scenarios invited visitors to throw virtually all previous ideas overboard and think in a completely new way about future-oriented forms of work and activity-based working. Orgatec, the consulting company detecon, the communications agency orange council and the artist collective Freeters collaborated to create Plant 10.1, a space that allows people to experience new, creative approaches to the working and living space in the office and shows artistic thinking processes, all in a spectacular, emotional, and also provocative way. Because now rigid organizations are dissolving, and flexible, agile structures are taking their place. This has a major impact on working environments, the design of the workplace, and the mindsets of all workforces. Innovation culture is the most important prerequisite for companies to successfully initiate transformation processes in the direction of "New Work" and "Artistic Intelligence Thinking," and thus be able to survive.

This approach should not simply be dismissed as an artistic gimmick that brings nothing of value to companies. The unusual joint venture of management consultancy and artist collective has long been advising and supporting the change management of companies with artistic spatial interventions, accompanying storytelling, and identity-creating inspiration.

The seven working environments presented were therefore oriented towards the needs of classic companies. Thus, the themes of Co-Working, presentation spaces, CreativeSpace, LivingRoom, and MiniHome were taken into account, as were spaces for creative refueling through sport and play (Playground) and spaces that help find new points of view (HochSitz).

Inspiration, intuition, imagination, improvisation, and interaction are important influencing factors for artistic thinking and thus for innovation.

Programmatically and creatively Plant 10.1 presented an emotional testing ground and a stage at the same time.

Thus it was shown in a completely new way how working environments and the people in them can become "innovative tools" to support change processes in companies. In many renovation concepts for office buildings today the focus is often exclusively on the functional, rational level of spaces: attention is paid to whether the chairs fit together, the occupational safety requirements are met, etc. The emotional, intuitive level is often neglected. The integration of cultural aspects into the working environment, for example, is important for the emotional bond of employees and leads to a stronger identification with the company.

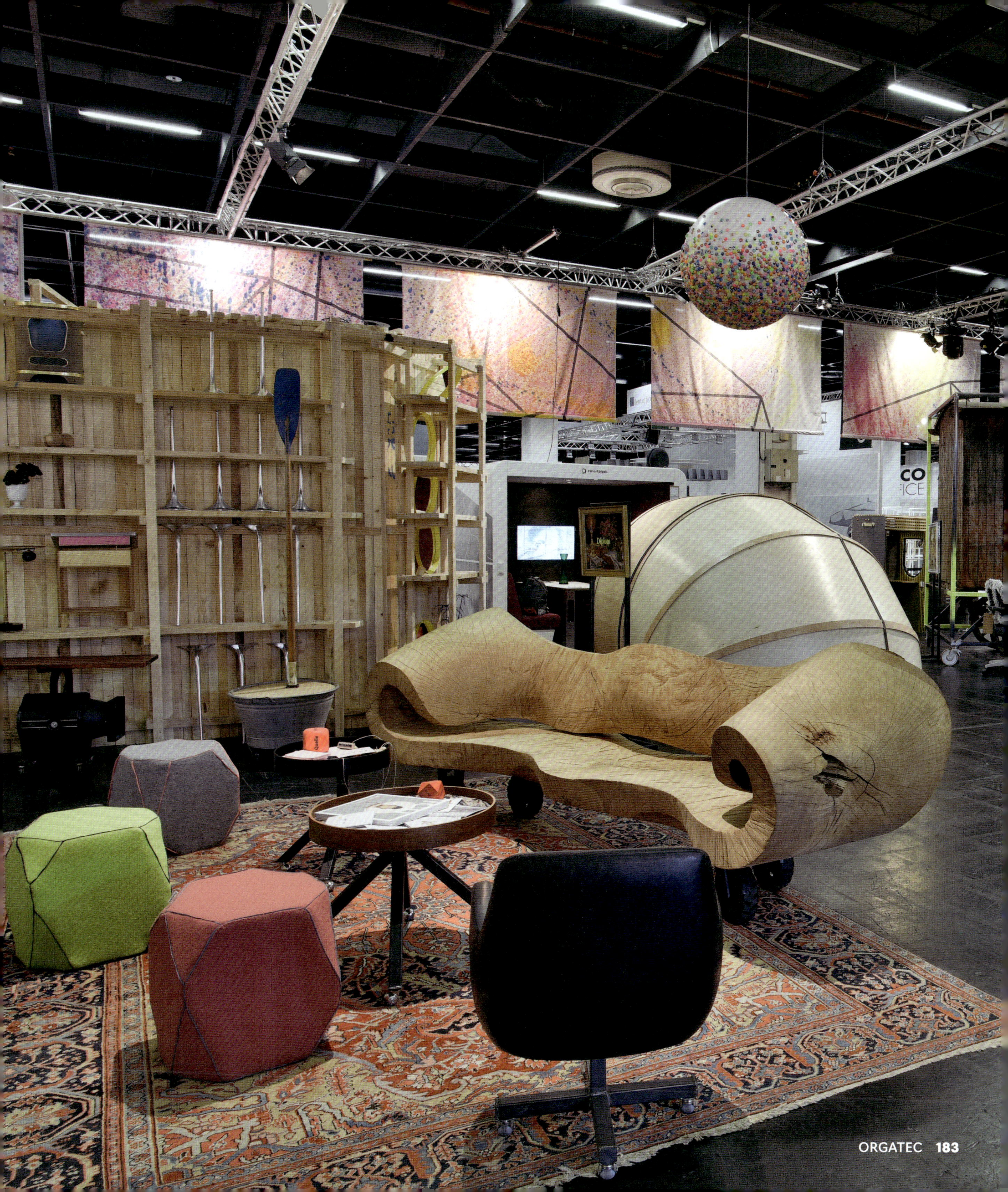

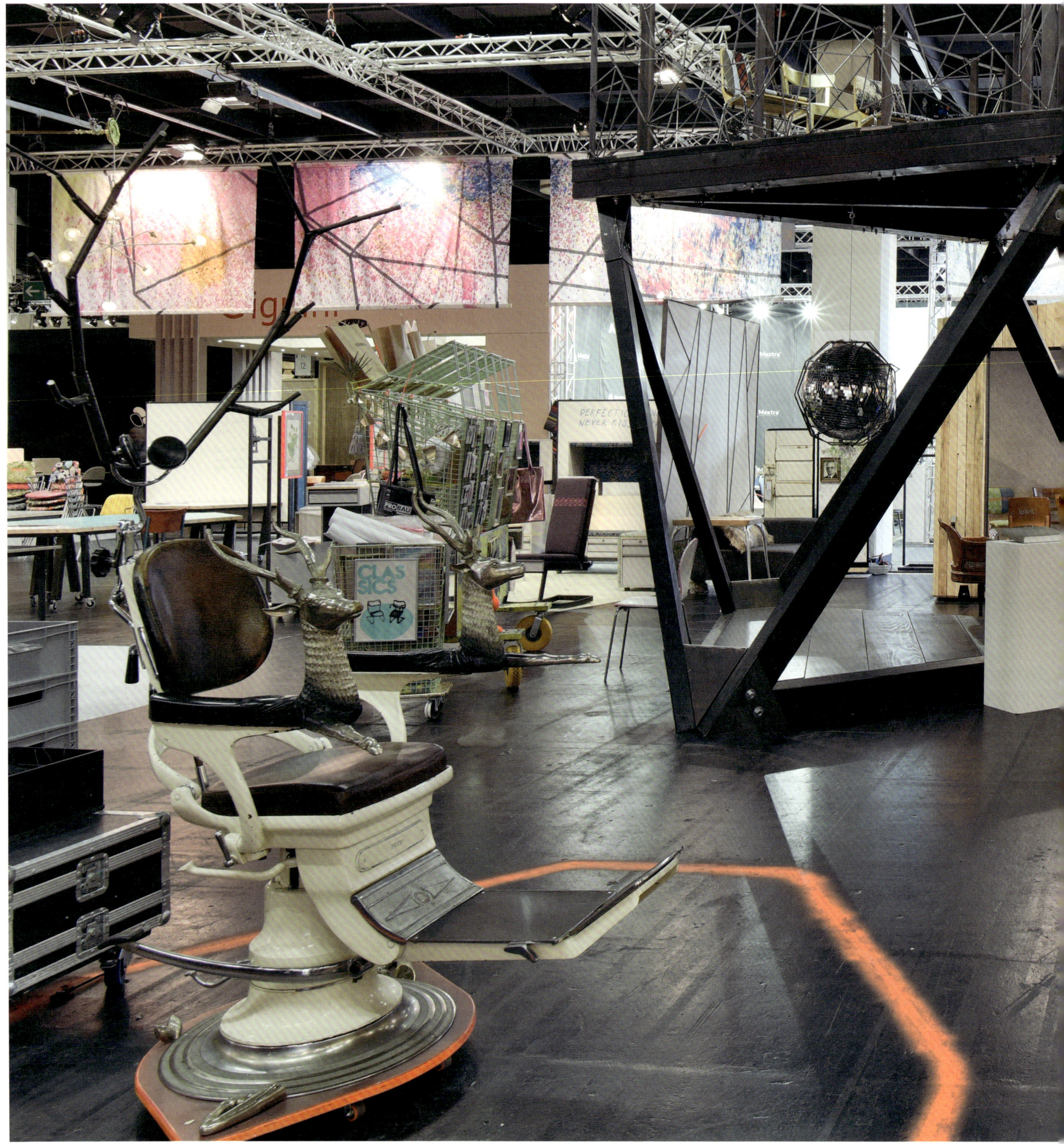
CLAS
SICS

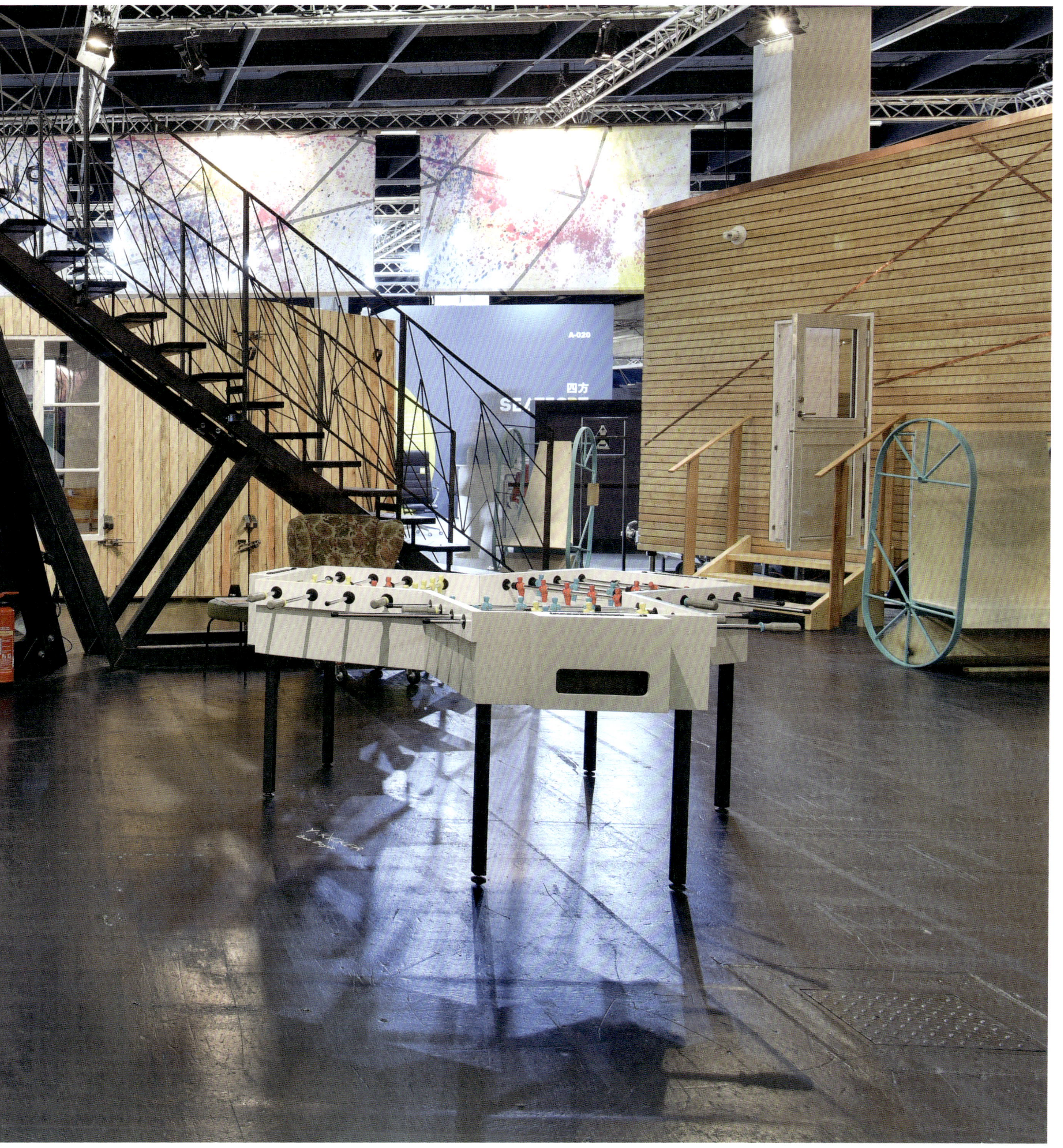
A-020
四方

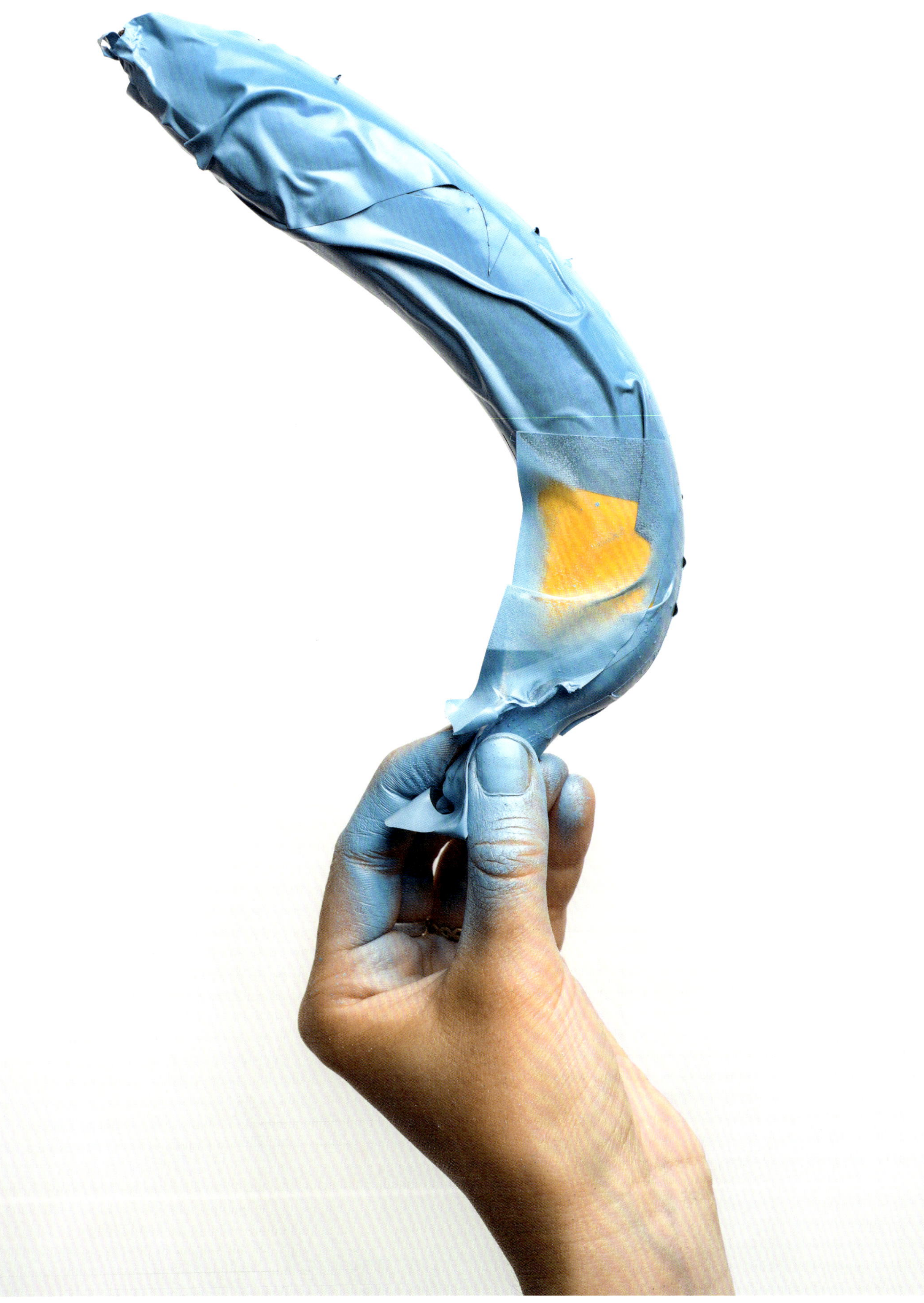

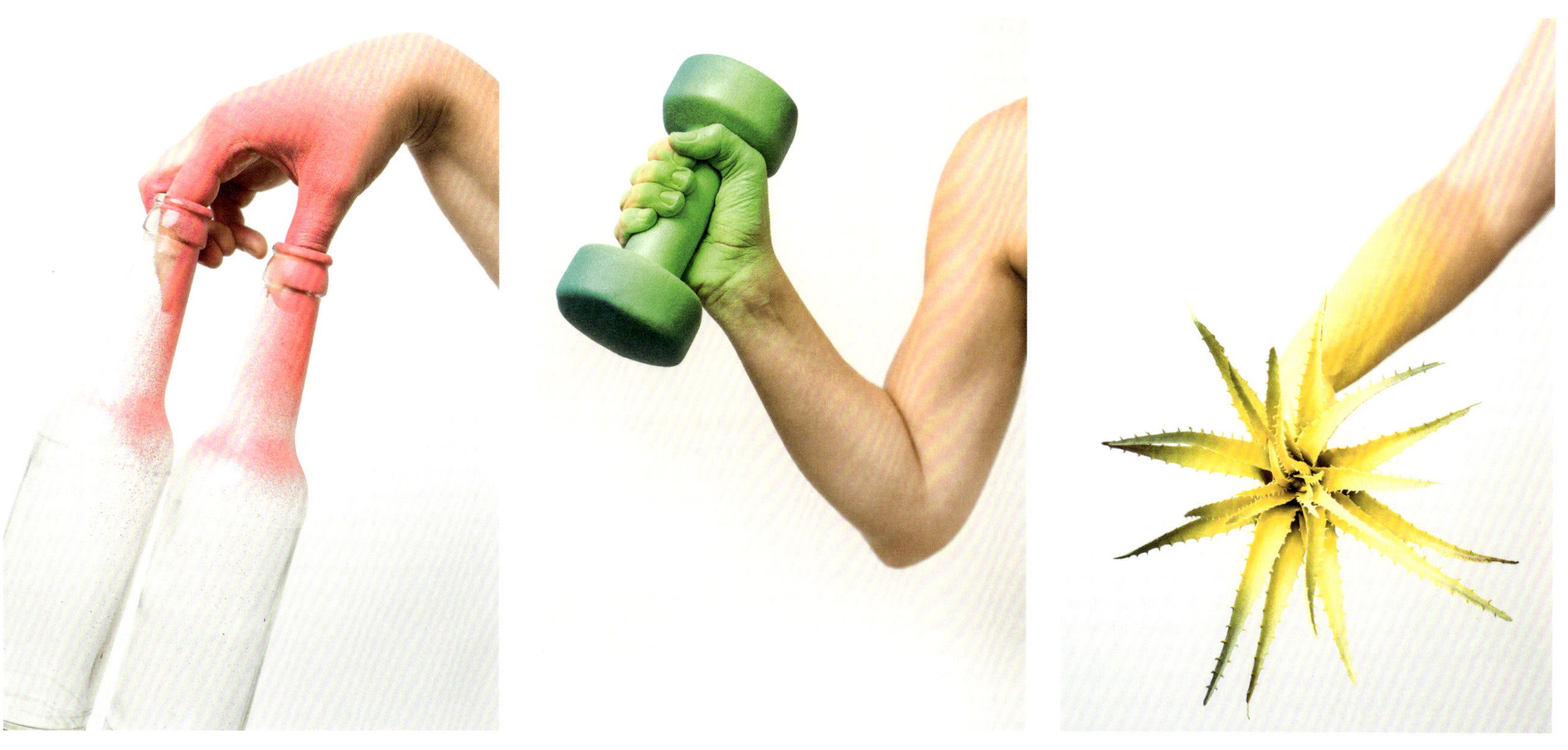

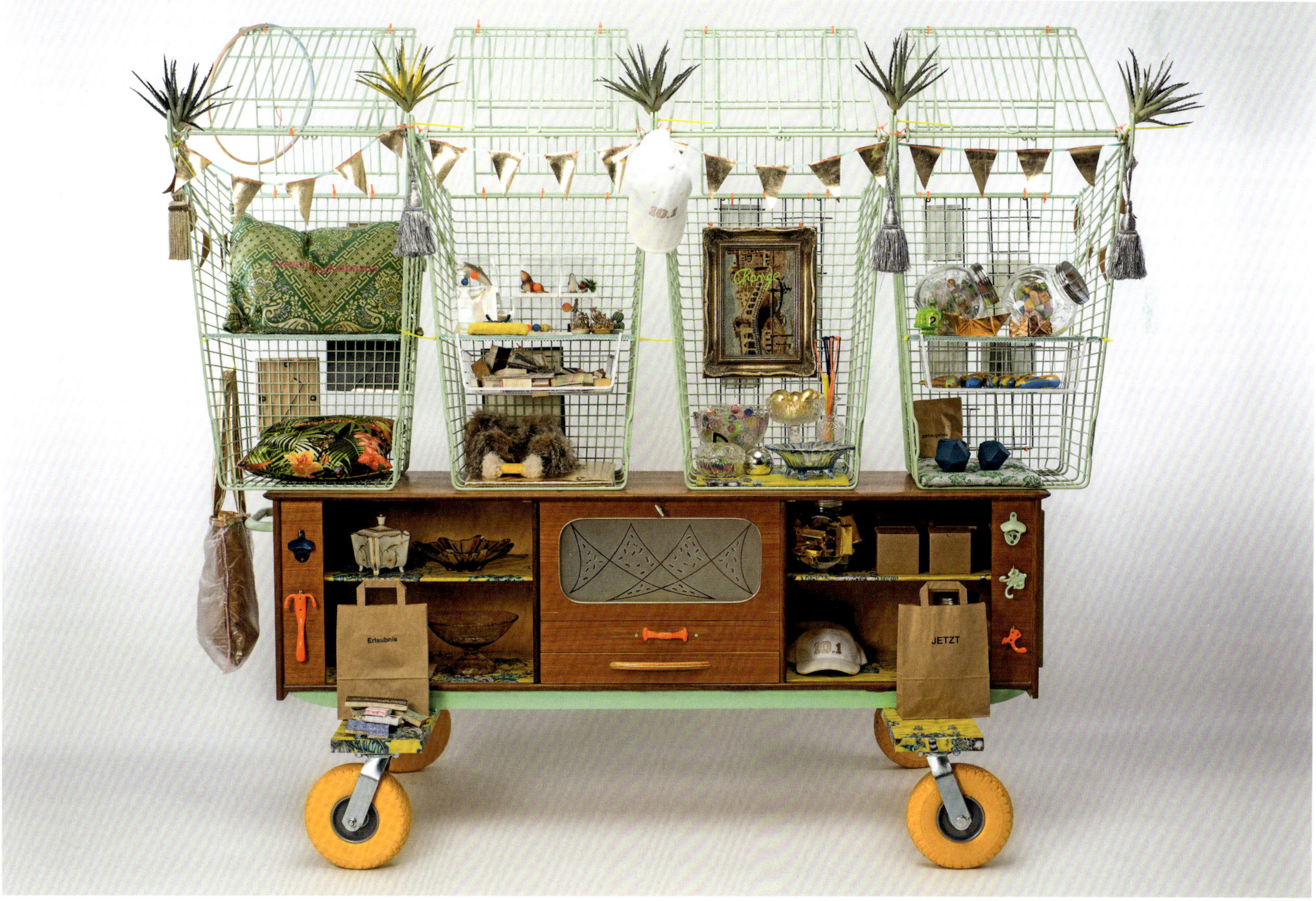

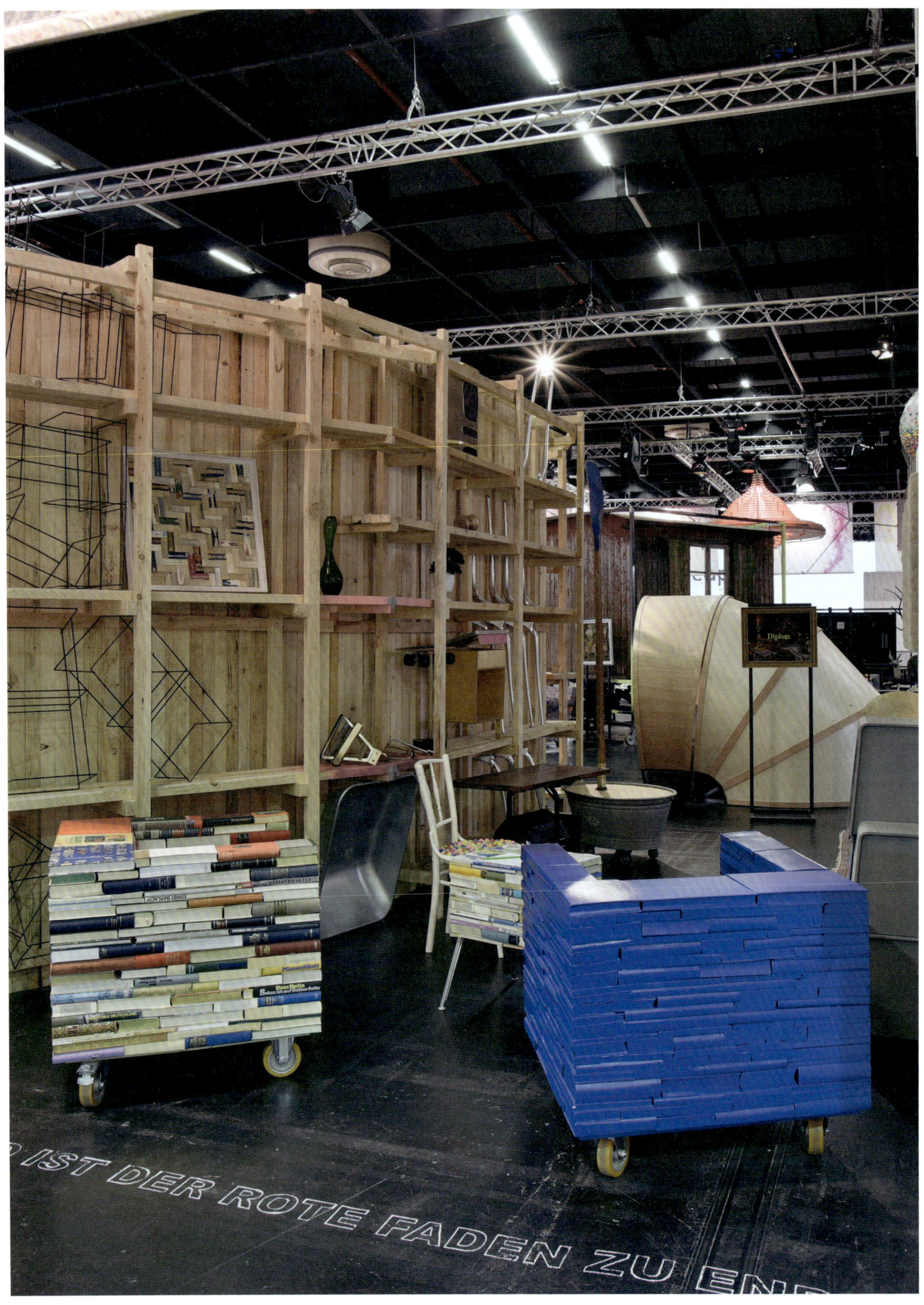
Diplom
IST DER ROTE FADEN ZU

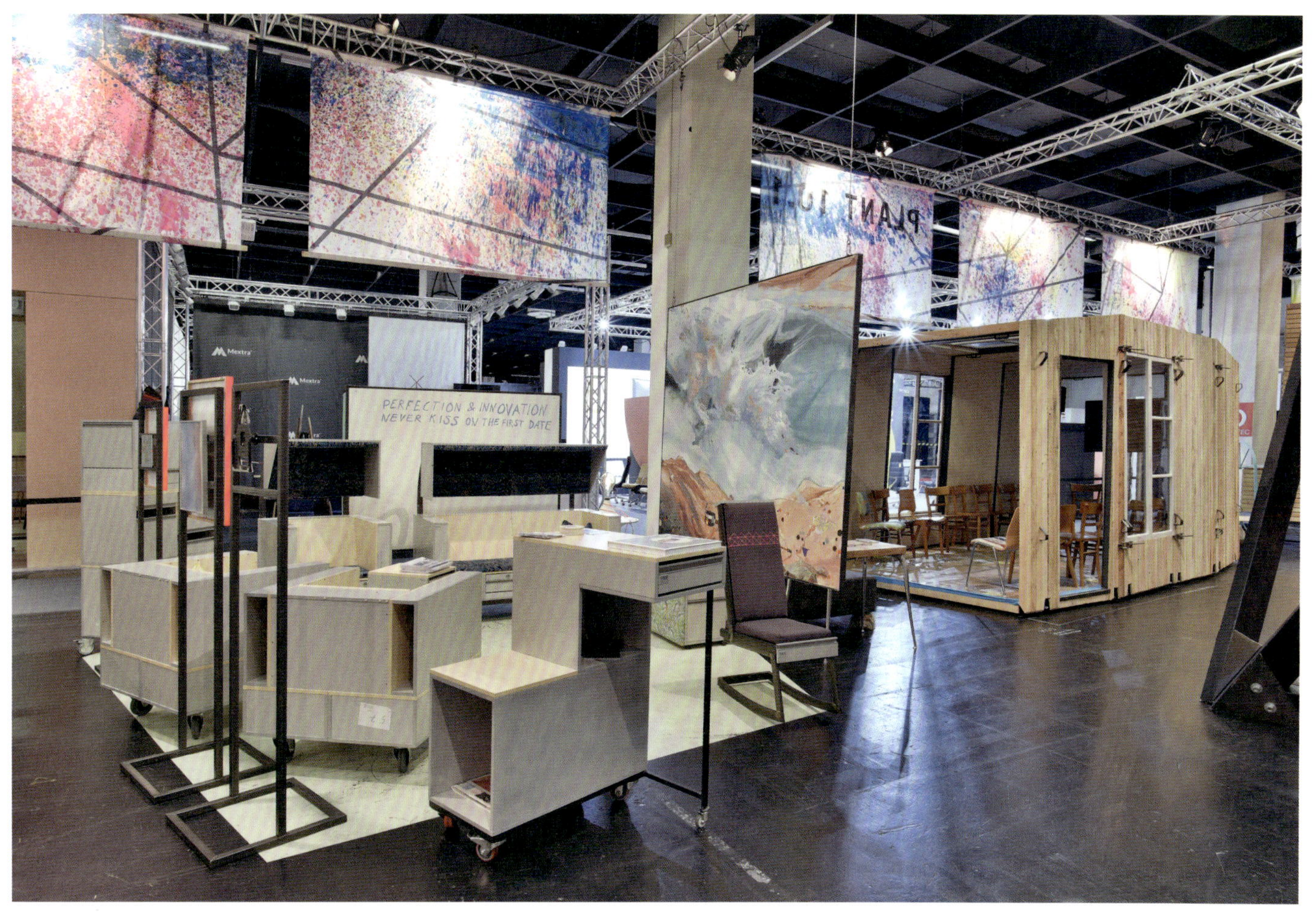
PERFECTION & INNOVATION
NEVER KISS ON THE FIRST DATE

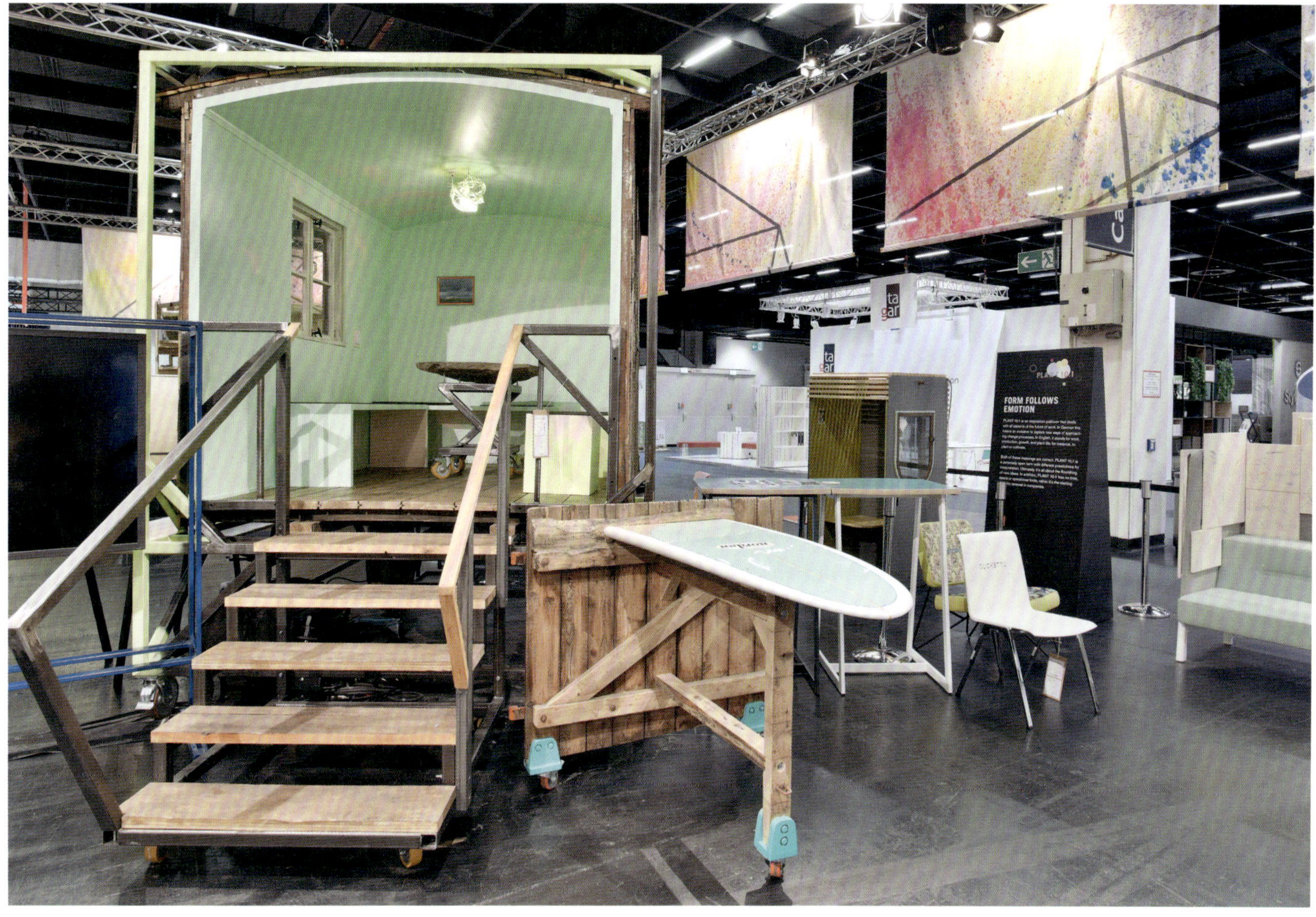
FORM FOLLOWS
EMOTION

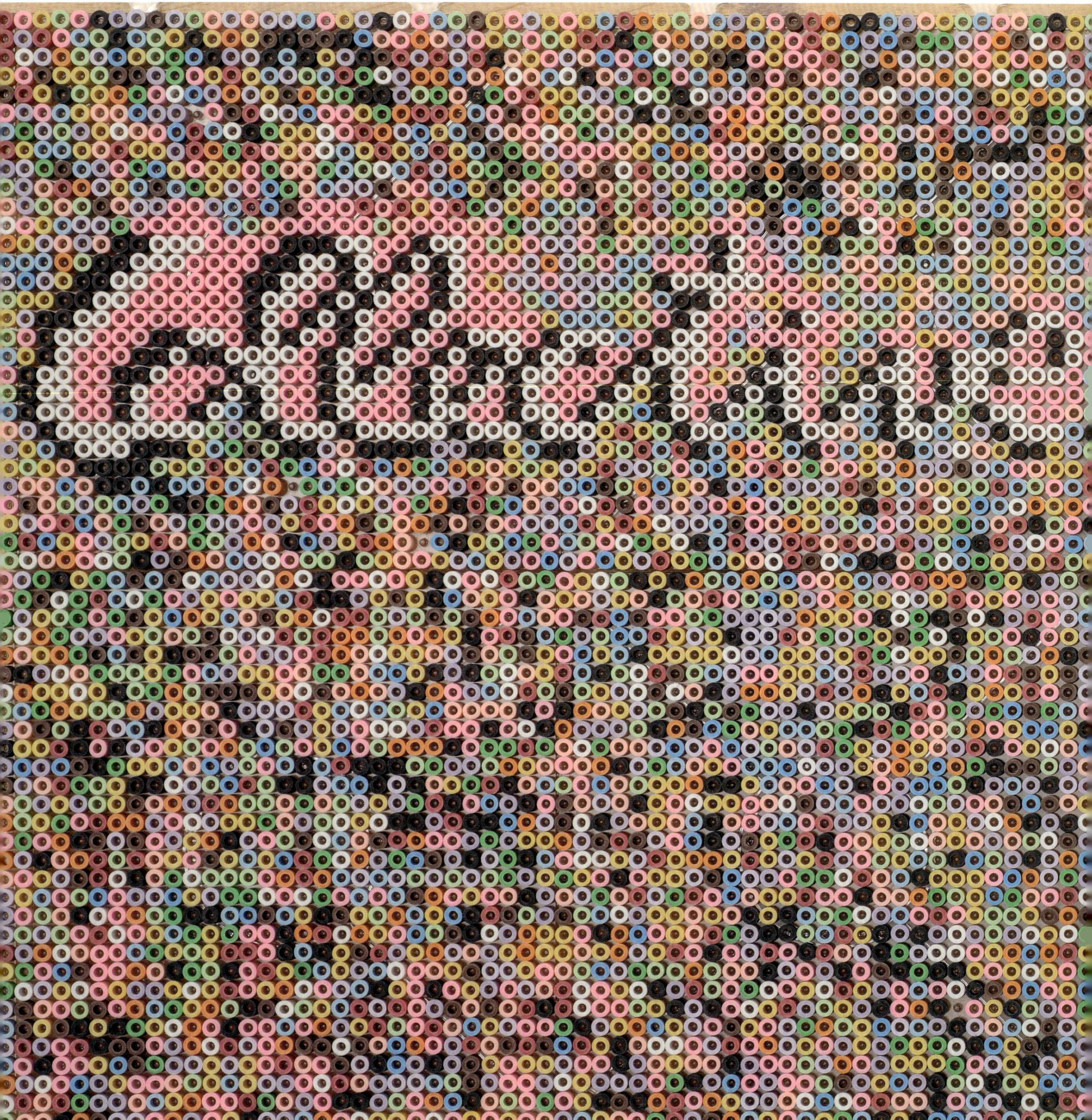

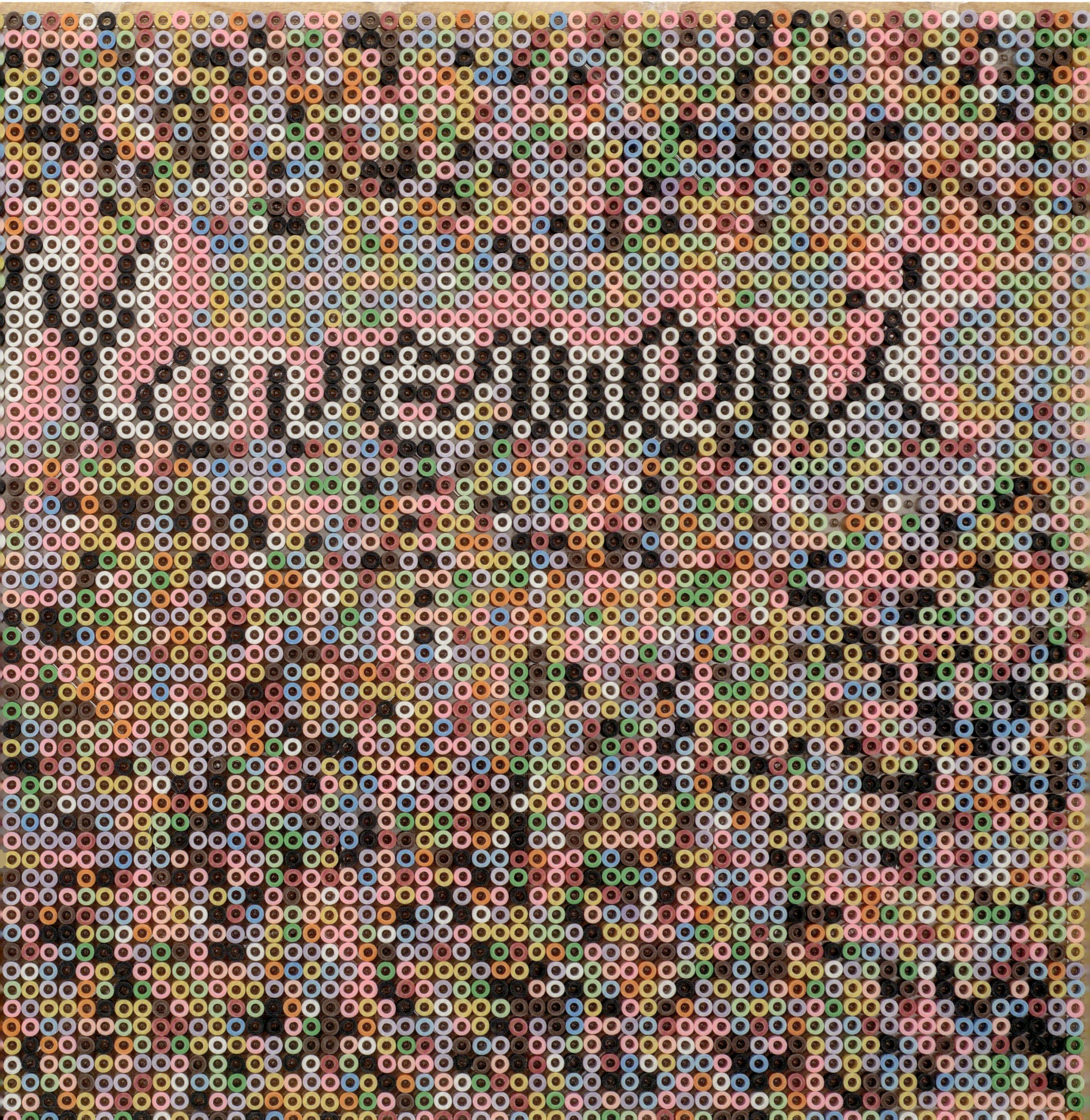

UNBEADABLE SPACE

UNBEADABLE SPACE is an interdisciplinary, participatory installation artwork in real as well as digital space. The approximately 30-square-meter Freeters showroom and individual pieces of furniture within it were completely covered with over seven million 100% biodegradable fusible beads. There were about 4,000 people who participated, placing and ironing beads in about 7,900 pegboards, i.e., all participating people received one or more 15 x 15 centimeter pegboards and the necessary 900 beads, and they conceived and created 7,900 pictures or mosaics.

In a time when almost all encounters and cultural works and productions were taking place in digital space, it was important to create a corresponding analog encounter: a work which appears digital through the pixel or voxel structure of the beads but was produced by hand and can also be experienced physically. In the times of the pandemic, the interdisciplinary community artwork functioned as a chance for various public institutions, artists, students, elderly people, companies, and for anyone interested to connect and come

together in joint creative work and to experience a feeling of community. It counteracts isolation, in that all participants feel and understand themselves as part of a larger whole and work to create something big together. The artist collective Freeters was part of an impressive, fascinating collective artwork. As initiator as well as coordinator and curator, Freeters was able to bring this work together, experience many friendly encounters on the way, and to gather the very beautiful experiences people had.

The first declared "herd aesthetics" of all time made it possible. We created a plastic, social sculpture through social, sculptural plastic. With the cooperation of and material donations by the plastic manufacturer NABBI Beads from Sweden and the craft supply manufacturer efco and the generous financial support of the Bonn art foundation artepreneur, we have been able to distribute all the necessary beads for the UNBEADABLE SPACE in the world.

Now it is time to check it out!

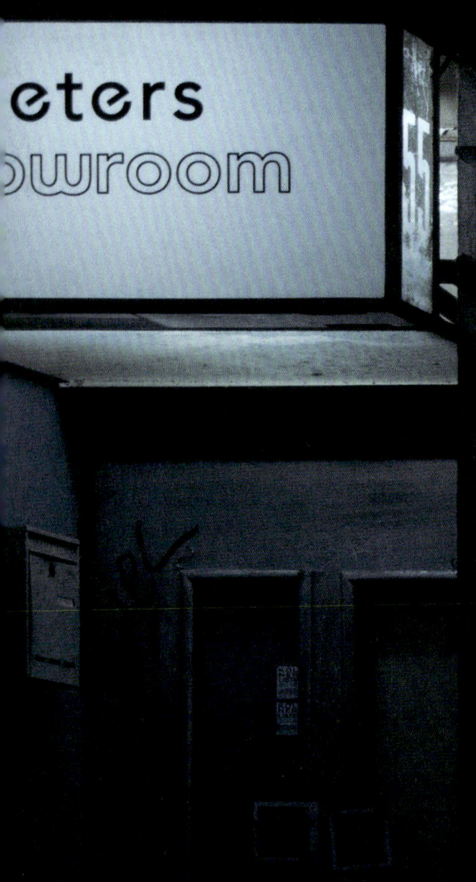
eters
owroom

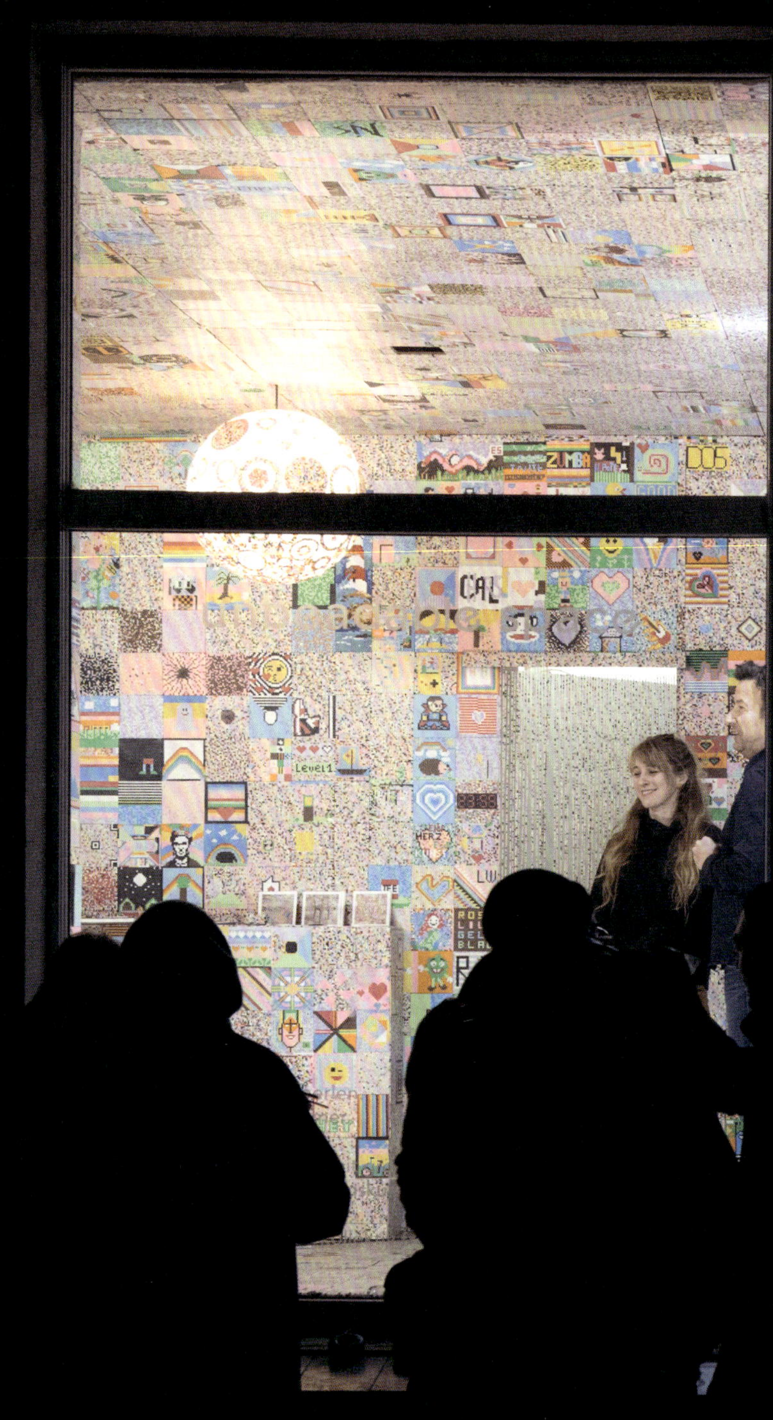

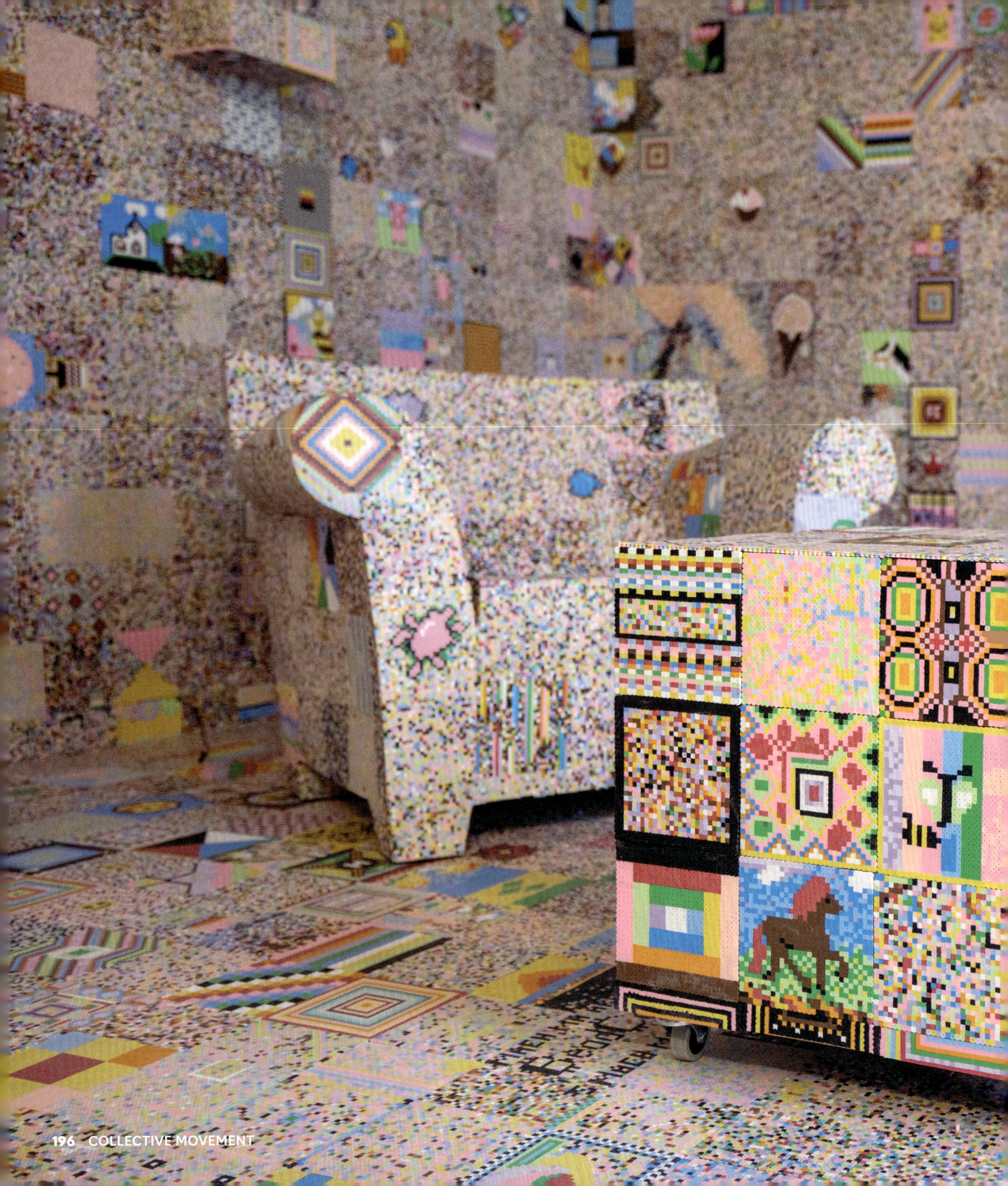

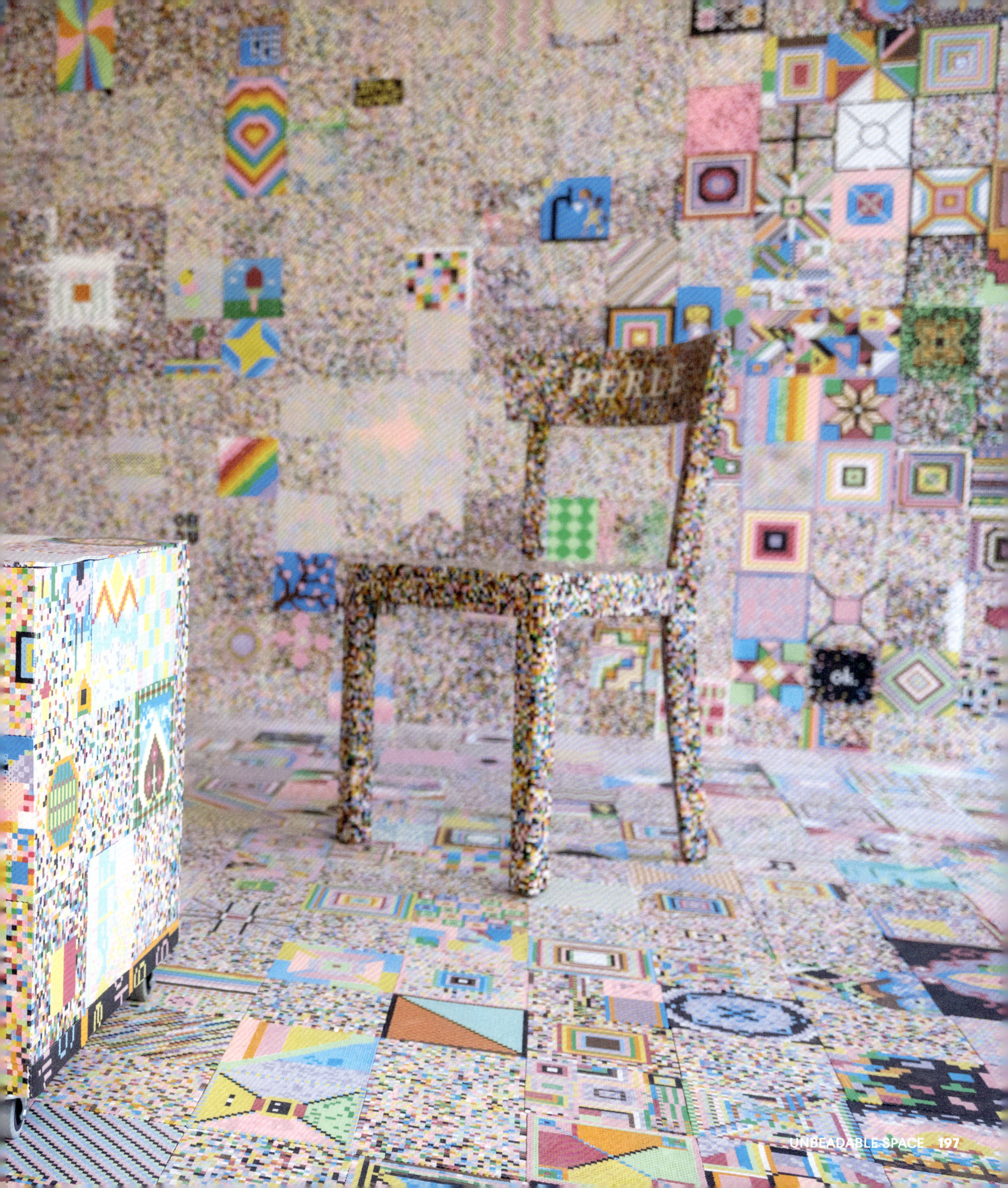
PERLE

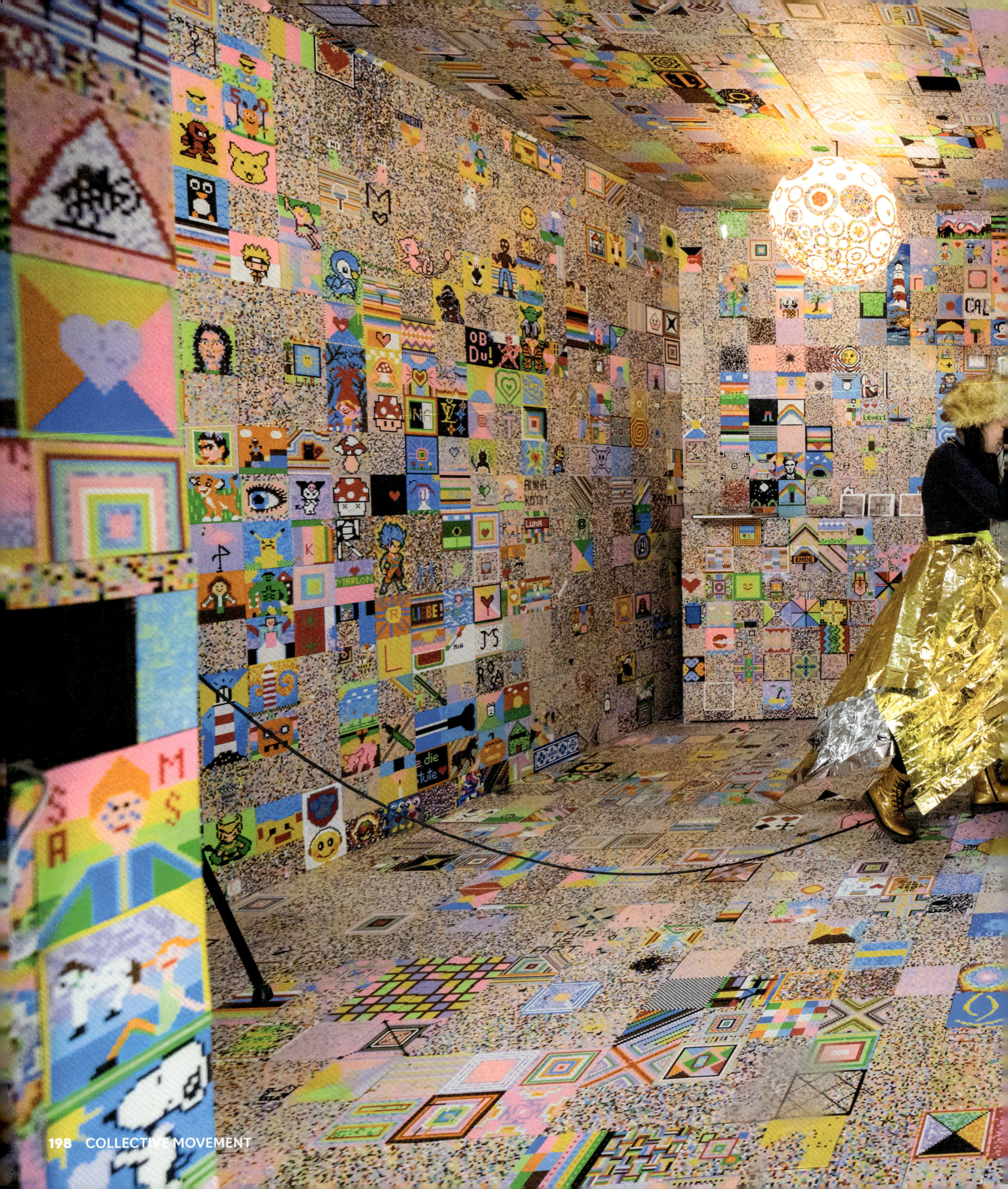

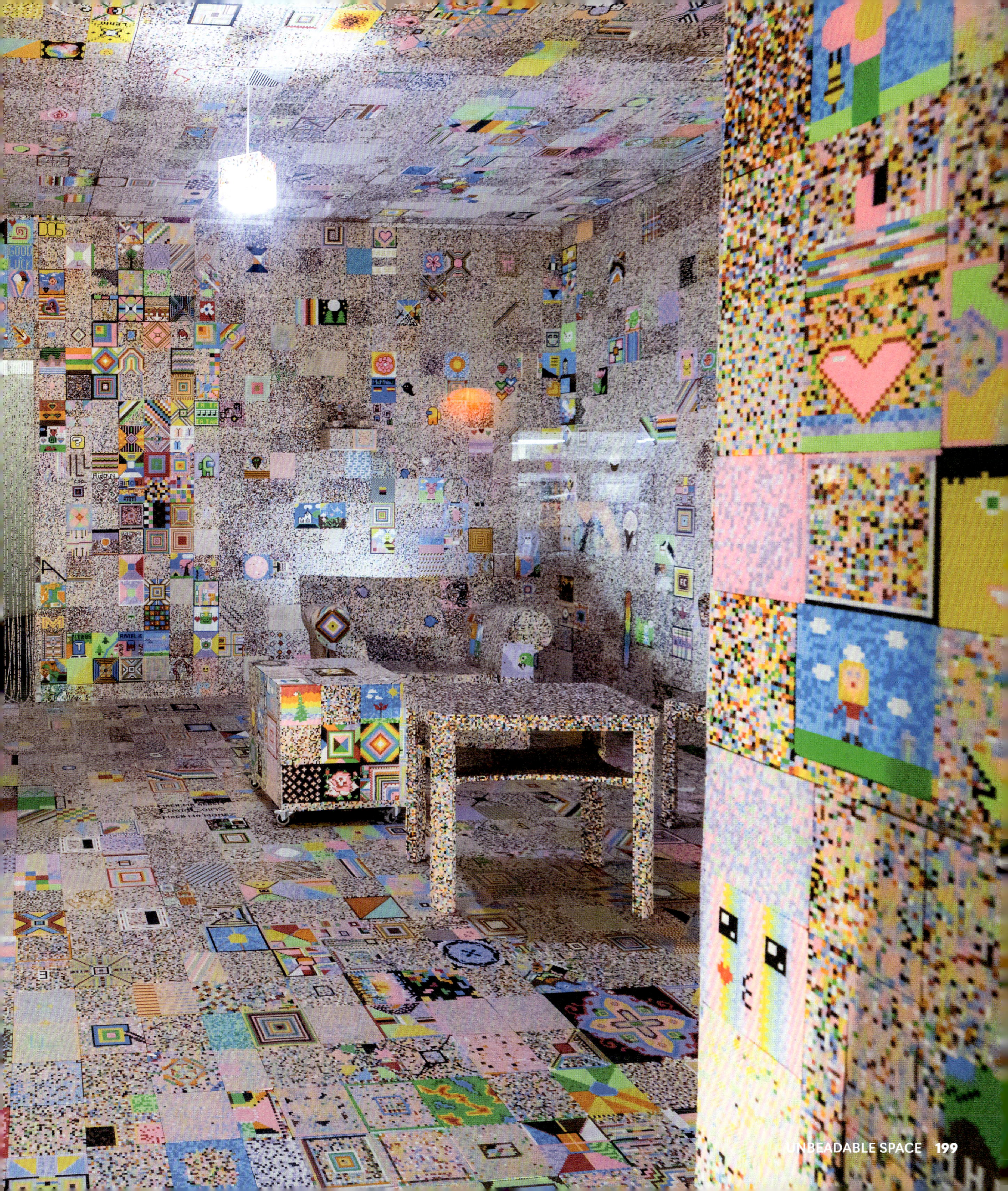

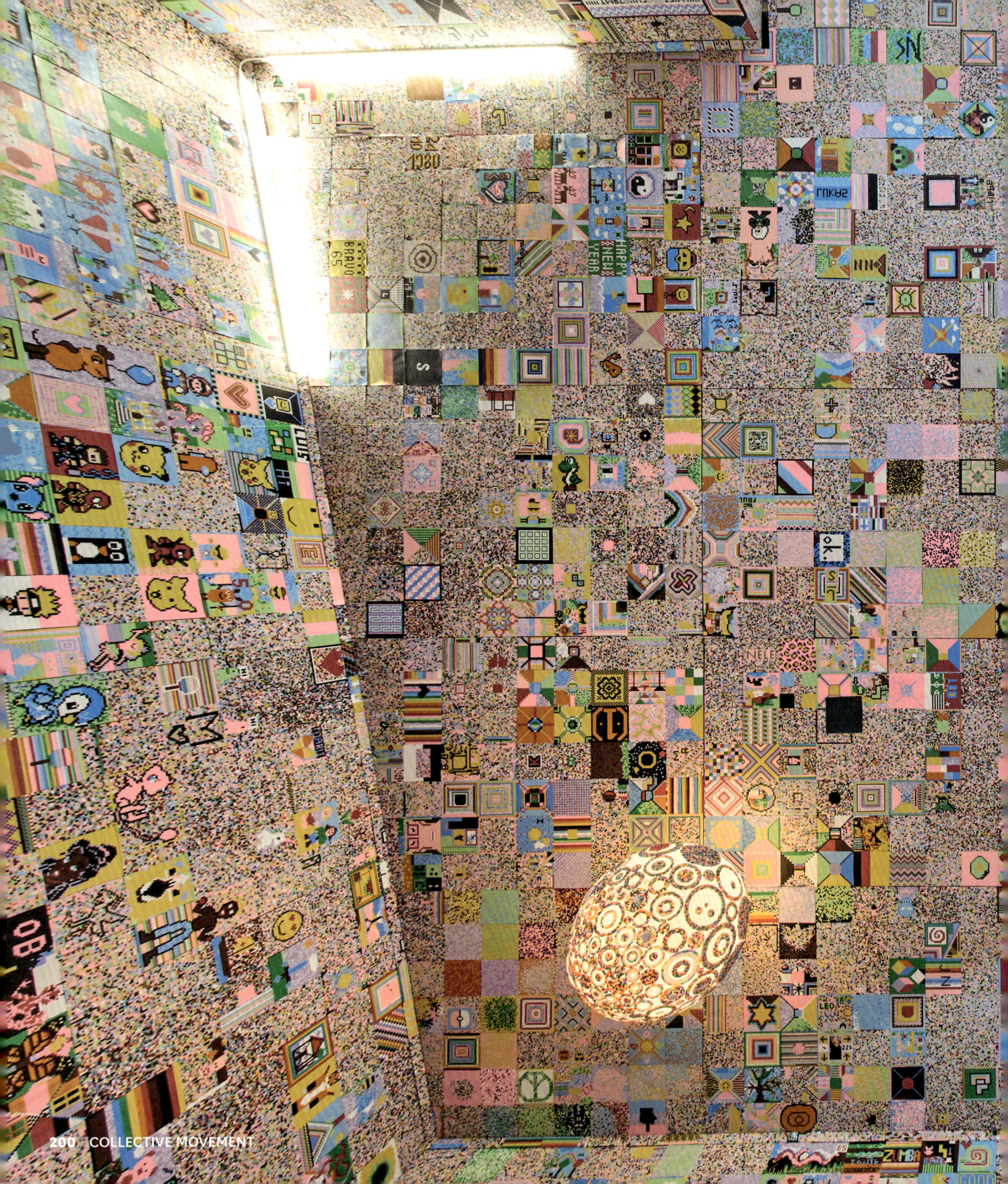

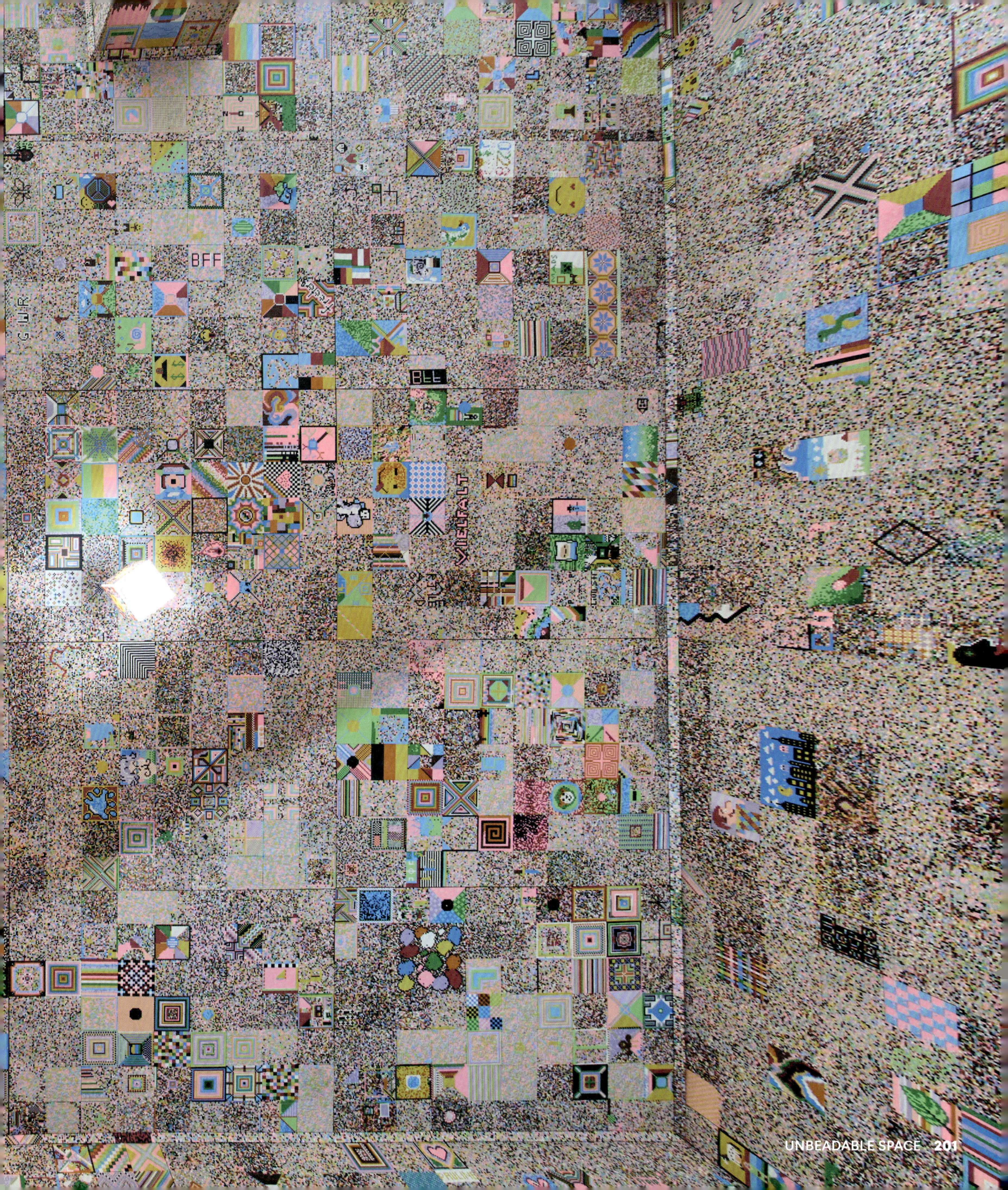
BFF
VIELFALT

MASS AND PATTERN

Thomas Lassner

TRISTESSE

If someone were commissioned to produce a film about the coronavirus pandemic that would convey the simultaneity of drama and tristesse in lockdown, it would almost certainly not be a box office hit. This is because the experience, probably shared by most people in this situation, was one of isolation and uncertainty. The isolation was necessary to prevent possible contagion, and the uncertainty stemmed from not knowing how the pandemic would progress, if mutations of the virus were possible, and if developing countermeasures would succeed. There is a bitter irony in the fact that the very global crisis that has the potential to shake the existing social orders first ensures that social institutions such as the state or the government take measures that reinforce the mechanisms of the current capitalist social order. While advocates of a neoliberal ideology like to praise globalization as an egalitarian mechanism that provides for a "growing together" of the earth's people, in fact, an advance of capitalist modes of production and socialization is accompanied by the opposite process. Competition and pressure to perform alienate people from one another; under the growth paradigm, society disintegrates into high achievers and superfluous people. In mass society, success always has the character of getting ahead.

"Since the principle of the capitalist production process does not originate purely in nature, it must burst the natural organisms which are means or resistances to it. Popular community and personality pass away when calculability is required; man alone, as a particle of mass, can climb smoothly up tables and operate machines."[1]

I'M A STAR, GET ME OUT OF HERE!

But the boundaries are fluid and those who were top performers yesterday may be written off tomorrow. Out of the mass of disposable individuals, certain ones seem to emerge again and again by chance, escaping arbitrariness because they "make a name for themselves." The "stars" of society function as figures the public projects upon, maintaining the hope for others that they can also make it someday.

The cultural industry has always had the function of diversion above all else. This is at the same time supported by the possibility of the audience identifying with the protagonists as a substitute, because these protagonists, in contrast, are able to cope with and solve conflicts that the audience perceives as painful. In this respect, this epochal crisis is not suitable as material for a blockbuster. For above all, the lack of options for action and the limitations on social interaction were the defining conditions for most people in the lockdown. No heroic story can unfold in such an environment.

ON SALE

What aesthetic experience is possible in mass society and mass culture? It was precisely in the lockdown that it became apparent that aesthetic experience is managed as a consumable commodity. Because art and culture have been revealed to be expendable in a state of emergency, it becomes apparent that they have a certain value, albeit small due to this expendability. The lack of distraction is an indication that aesthetic experience, if pleasing, is part of the now suspended normality. Are these the symptoms of a society of the spectacle?[2] It is obvious and has also been recognized some time ago that the sphere of aesthetic production, of artistic creation, is just as subject to the rules of capitalist value creation as all other spheres. But it goes even further.

1 **Siegfried Kracauer:** The Mass Ornament, Frankfurt am Main 2021, p.53

2 **cf. Guy Debord:** The Society of the Spectacle, Berlin 1996.

THE AESTHETICS OF THE MASSES

The masses themselves also develop their own aesthetic power. Think of the stands in a soccer stadium, where fans form a collective with an intoxicating archaic violence. But even less staged mass phenomena possess their own aesthetic form, which is always concretized and which, however, can usually only be recognized as such from the outside. Walking through a city, it could almost seem as if it consisted only of streets: facades, paths, squares, people, vehicles, and entrances. But viewed from above, it is striking that these public spaces only form something like streams of a larger overall pattern. These patterns occur on a small scale and on a large scale. Government always means managing these masses, although at the same time, as in the case of China, there is a need for increasingly sophisticated access to the mass particles. The masses remain, technology helps.

THE TECHNOLOGY OF MANAGEMENT

Digital encounters have in the past developed a special aesthetic quality. Whether leisure or work—in the lockdown, encounters were shifted to digital spaces, for good reason. The face, an essential point of sincere recognition from a philosophical point of view, became a digital mask. The immediacy of the other was thus shifted to the more or less correct representation of pixels. Even the display of the assigned portrait-like windows in the video conference, made possible by technology developed for this purpose, became a prefabricated arrangement of social interaction.

VANISHING POINT: BOREDOM

Leisure is a luxury. Even and especially in lockdown, the disproportion between occupation and leisure became apparent. While on the one hand the pressure of profitability was sold as happiness to work, on the other hand the monotony of private boredom, lacking the pleasures of public life, was experienced as despair. Caught between wage labor and the entertainment industry, the individual is merely one of many, no one special. This is countered by the need for self-realization, for the expression of specialness, which, however, is dependent on being able to bring home the bacon. Thus it comes about that wage labor in the present is in contrast to the Hegelian idea of labor. The latter conceived of that as a subjective form of reflection in the world. The subject who works recognizes himself in his work and thus gains self-consciousness. The subject in wage labor is kept from recognizing himself in the world through his own work by the occupation that secures his livelihood. It remains external to him and the world, alienated. At the same time, He is always haunted by the fear of being interchangeable, of not being special as an individual, but of being one of many. This is a mass phenomenon.

COLLECTIVE ORNAMENT

Of course, entry into the masses does not take place everywhere, but if it does, it feeds on the mechanisms described. In the leisurely occupation there is the possibility of reestablishing the relationship of recognition between subject and work. In communal work, disposability fades and the collective ornament becomes a work of art, because the masses make themselves a community.

GLOSSARY

A

acetone	problem solver
act	do it
activate	off to on
achievers	see roof batten / Dachlatte
Adapta	guitarist from “unterkomplex”
adaption	see Adapta
“Ach wie gut dass niemand weiss…”	filmclip by Feedback Films & Freeters
aesthetic experience	sensual habit of turning towards
aesthetic practice	see A. I. (artistic intelligence)
aesthetic production	sensuality on an assembly line the beautiful
A.I.	artistic intelligence
A.i.R.	artist in Residence
Alaner*in	someone associated with Alanus
Al Anus	person with a funny name
alienation	the dialectical movement of consciousness as a necessary transition to the opposite
ambidextry coaching	if you had a third hand you would use it too
ambiguity tolerance	pigeon-holing was yesterday
ambivalence	indistinguible concernig the thing
Anthro	Rudi
arbitrariness	pretending an X for a V
art	see Acetone
artful creation	see/combine art and create
artistic strategies	see coincidence, experiment, improvising, unintendend
art thinking	think about it
atom	indivisible
aura	original presence in time and space of a work of art

B

„BANANA!“	filmclip by Feedback Films & Freeters
band	unterkomplex
Bergfest	mountain party
Bosch grow	Bosch’s internal incubation platform for start-ups and intrapreneurs which have their origin within the Group
“Bring mal Herne”	“Could you kindly bring it to me?”
business	a type of long-term employment
Bügelperlenraum	see Unbeadable Space
Bügelperlentraum	dream made exclusively of ironing beads

C

calculability	intelligent sounding word for redictability
capitalist value creation	G-W…W’-G’
çatı çıtası	see Dachlatte
“Captain Appstore”	song from “unterkomplex”
chaos	without vacuum
Cloud Chamber	artistic concept by Freeters; particle detector; artist group (NL)
coincidence	identifiable by perception
collect	take everything that goes
collective	Freeters
collective ornament	see unbeadable space
confusion maker	the benefactor of confusion
connector / Verbinder	thing that connects without glue, Love
contemporary	neither yesterday nor tomorrow, consequently now
create	forbidden word but in the best sense it means head up, hand goes
creativity	forbidden word
creative Jamsession	a Paradoxon
crisis	the all-embracing surprise
crisis tendencies / Krisentendenzen	tending to encompass surprise
cube	a platonic body with 4 equal faces
culture	assimilated art, see yoghurt
cultural industrial	Netflix n’ Chill
curd	plural of milk

D

Dachlatte / roof batten	turkish: çatı çıtası, claim when something doesn’t work
decision maker	makes decisions, whether right or wrong
Denkstrategie	strategical brainwork
Denkraum	phsycal: brain, abstract: art
Detecon	Management and technology consulting company
“DieDie”	Song from “unterkomplex”, the others
difference	the gap between art and culture
digital discovery	the attempt to rediscover digital space as a real existing space for action
disposable	interchangeable
dissonance	discord between resonance and renaissance, see resonace
distraction	mental salt in the sauce of consciousness
“Double Fucker Roller Skater”	Song from “unterkomplex”
Dreibeiner / three-legged	thing with three legs
“Du bisset”	simply the best

E

ecosystem scouting	an inventory of the immediate environment of organizational units
efco	Manufacturer and distributor of handcraft products
egalitarianism	thesis of the fundamental equality of perso
Einbeiner / one-legged	thing with one leg
„El Segundissimo“	Exhibition of Freeters in 2018 at ESMoA

emotional evaluation ... new documentation and evaluation formats, elude conventional procedures or provide new insights
encounters ... opposite so close that it touches
ephemeral ... volatile, see Acetone
error culture ... cultivation of "shit happens"
ESMoA ... El Segundo art laboratory
essential ... see need
explorer ... one of the four aesthetic stereotypes of Freeters
experiment ... it requires courage, curiosity, observation, conclusion, repetition, patience, love
expression ... a cafè please [sic!]
E105 ... a company that brings the goal of a culture of innovation closer to reality

F

"Fach C 2" ... filmclip by Feedback Films & Freeters
Fairy dust ... traces of Freeters
"Fake News" ... song from "unterkomplex", true lies
fear ...
Feedback Films ... Cologne based Film Studio
female choices ... no longer a man's business
FFF ... Freeters For Future
Firma ... see Magic Ground
"Free" ... song from "unterkomplex"
Freeters ... artist collective or portmanteau of the English word "free" and the German word "Arbeiter" ("labourer")
Freeters Showroom ... Art Gallery
funny products ... Fun, fun, fun!
Fünfbeiner / fife-legged ... thing with five legs

G

gardener ... one of the four aesthetic stereotypes of Freeters
genaugenau ... absolutely aggree
globalisation ... growing together and unifying
glossary ... utmost effort of the term
grabegabel ... digging fork and problem solver for the gardener
growth paradigm ... higher, faster, further; see paradigm
guerilla Installation ... direct integration of individual productions into the reality of life and connection of spontaneous and planned elements

H

HaHahAhAhAhHA! ... answer to all questions
Handlungsstrategie ... ACTION STRATEGY !
Halle / hall ... largest area and playground @ Magic Ground
Help! ... song of the Beatles and book of the Freeters
Herdenästehtisierung ... herd aestheticization
heroic story ... egg – larva – cocoon – butterfly
humor ... see HaHahAhAHAHA!

I

identify ... this there!
identity - not identity ... Hegels core
improvising ... provoke unintended coincidences
indistinguishability ... indistinguishability concernig the reception
ingenious genius ... see Mozart or van gogh's ear
Inspiration Trigger Tool ... the tool leads to serious and lasting insights and inspirations
irritation ... inspiring state of mind
isolation ... atomic state without mass

J

JaJa ... appreciative resignation
job shadowing ... accompanying expedition of employees; uncover the existing operational reality; experience the subjective view of used cases / workflows beyond mission statements

K

Kantenöl ... problem solver like acetone but much more effective and fragrant
Kaizen ... consistent innovation management, from Japanese, Kai = change, transformation; Zen = for the better
calculability ... intelligent sounding word for predictability
Keinbeiner / no-legged ... thing with no leg
Kitsch ... forbidden plaesure

L

leisure ... not sleep, not work; see Muße
LOLLIPOP ... funny product for linguistic education measures
loss of relevance ... non mi tangere
love ... LIEBE
Luftmutter ... nut screw made of air
"Luftschlößer müssen verdichtet werden!" ... "Castles in the air must be compressed!"
luxury ... pleisure

M

madness ... dubious state of mind, district of Cologne
Marvin ... a friend whose name you constantly forget
Magic Ground ... best place to be
matching ... for example, pot and lid

mass .... a bunch of atoms, without individuality
mass phenomenon .... it seems that the whole is no more than the sum of its parts
mass society .... society of atoms
mass particle .... see atom
"Meanwhile" .... filmclip by Feedback Films & Freeters
meeting Point .... for example in Italy the "Piazza" or a the bar
Mett-Eagle .... drumer from "unterkomplex"
magician .... one of the four aesthetic stereotypes of Freeters
mind mapping .... creation of a vision landscape; through mental work to sausage, inside-out processing
Mini Cloudchamber .... present for "Ruangrupa" shipped to Indonesia
modeling .... creation of a spatial sensory basis for the decision of further process steps
monotony .... one colour tone
mutation .... increase in diversity through spontaneous change
Muße .... not to be confused with mousse, see curd
mystery shopping .... experience journey; takes on a customer perspective that is as unbiased as possible

N

NABBI .... Manufacturer of biodegradable iron beads, partner and supporter of the "unbeadable space"
necessity .... indispensable
need .... absolutely necessary
"Nikolatte" .... filmclip by Feedback Films & Freeters

O

"OB DU" .... question of questions / Song from „unterkomplex"
occupation .... hijacked by action
OPEN .... annual art event at Magic Ground
OPPOS .... Nickname of "OPPOSITION STUDIOS", Bonn based Film Studio
ORANGE COUNCIL .... communication office that accompanies change processes

P

Pallettenfett .... probably a palette made of fat
panoramic thinker .... thinking with the knee, thinking with Google Earth in your head
paradigm .... modus operandi
participation .... just make it together
pattern .... repetitio sine qua non
PAUSEFILM .... Bonn based documentary Film Studio founded by Aljoscha Pause
Perlen-Peter .... Eloquent and visionary entrepreneur
Perlensommer / "Pearl Summer" .... period between May and September 2021
Perl'nsteinzimmer .... another term for the unbeadable space, neologism from the word "Bernsteinzimmer" / Amber Room
Piff Paff .... music style of the band unterkomplex; onomatopoeic for a rifle or pistol shot
Pille Palle .... something insignificant, trivial
pixel .... see mass
player .... one of the four aesthetic stereotypes of Freeters
positive documentation .... The media is the massage
power of pictures .... declination of pictorial worlds / overall visual experiences beyond the fixed and moving image
practice .... opposite of theory
precise .... specify what is already clear
Primärreiz .... pain or primary stimulus
process .... everything that happens
Prof. Freeters .... multiple person
projection figures .... in projection, the figure is the canvas of hope
propeller .... room in room concept, a dancing dervish
prototype .... Almost finished and yet completed

Q

quality .... insufficiently achievable through diversity
quantity .... not synonymous with diversity; see Mass

R

Raumgeber .... mobile multifunctional room divider who separates space and opens up new
rapid prototyping .... core approach of every conception; real experience and perceptible pre-production; transition from fiction to realisation in order to create a comprehensible meaningful conception
rebirth dead horses .... Transformer
recipient .... Vessel
regular table .... trunk table = drunk at the trunk, see trivial chatter
resonance .... sounds similar to renaissance
"Rio Reise" .... filmclip by Feedback Films & Freeters
rischtije Künstler / "true Artist" .... person who carves beautiful writing in tombstones
Ritzenwasser, die Essenz .... funny Product for internal applications
roof batten / Dachlatte .... turkish: çatı çıtası, claim when something doesn't work
Ruangrupa .... artist collective from Indonesia
"Rumkugeln" .... filmclip by Feedback Films & Freeters

S

safety officer .... guinea pig made of styrofoam and fauxfur, also a Person without ability and too much power
Salon .... irregular meeting at the Magic Ground with friends, unknowns and business partners, garnished with good food and conversation
salvation .... hope in art
Schnappel .... thing that holds everything together, problem solver

see what's coming ... Vision
self-realisation ... absence of art
serious Play ... contradictory behavior
Signet Ring ... 3d printed Ring for "unique" people
Sissi Top ... frontal lobes from "unterkomplex"
sleep ... not work, not leisure
"Smooth" ... filmclip by Feedback Films & Freeters
social sculpture ... You will meet him at the stations
society ... to blame for everything
soziales Plastik ... "social plastic"; neologism of "social sculpture" (Beuys)
spaces are Interfaces ... concretising experience; space is not only purely physical, rather it contains a psychological dimension
speed curation ... rapid merging of the most diverse partial productions into a meaningful whole
spötziell ... particularly aestheticized
"Stardust" ... exhibition of Freeters in 2019 at ESMoA
state of exception ... often occurs in appearance with crisis
state of mind ... constitution of thinking
stock ... Freeters treasure mine
story Building ... attempt of a first fiction, which is suitable both as a coherent narration to be the starting point of a progressive development, but also as "breadcrumbs" to create crystallization points for a game that is constantly being recreated
strategy ... the belief in being able to plan goal-oriented and in advance
Superheroes ... in the real sense of the word artists
sustainibility rules ... the Gestalt transformation of objects into new functionalities in order to support the cyclical consideration of life realities and reflects today's productions
S.Y.L.A. ... Support Your Local Art
S.Y.L.A.H.Q / S.Y.L.A.NTENHEIM ... art gallery that allows unconditional exhibitions to everyone; german neologism of the word "Asylantenheim" (asylum seekers' home) english: SupportYour Local Art Head Quarter
S.Y.L.A.PPLICATION ... application form of S.Y.L.A.H.Q.

T

team building ... social sculpture
theory ... opposite of practice
thinking ... brainwork
"Touché" ... filmclip by Feedback Films & Freeters
Transformer ... rebirth
treasure hunt ... a search in the positive for "emotional reverses" that can be liftedand, in the negative for "black holes" that suck energy and should be trasformed
tristesse ... absence of surprise
trivial chatter ... as the saying goes
true Artis / "rischtije Künstler" ... person who carves beautiful writing in tombstones

U

umfallt ... thing that fell over, unable to stand
unbeadable space ... gallery made of iron beads
"Unbegrenztes Halteverbot" ... filmclip by Feedback Films & Freeters
uncertaintly ... imminent danger; vagueness
unintendend ... welcome in the best case
unterkomplex ... name of the most undercomplex music band

V

vacuum ... without chaos
value ... irregular unit of measurement, dispensable
vanishing point: boredom ... the exact point where abundance becomes superfluity
Verbinder / connector ... thing that connects without glue, Love
Vielecker ... thing with many corners, commonly called polygon
Vierbeiner / four-legged ... thing with four legs
vision ... latin visio for "sight, appearance"
vision operator ... probably an artist or another kind of freak

W

madness ... dubious state of mind, district of Cologne
Wandaktivierung / "to activite a wall" ... epic wall
Winkelding ... inspirational tool for throwing, playpolon
words move mountains ... clarification of the power of words beyond the supposedly neutral-objective use of words
work ... not sleep, not leisure
Wunderkammer ... see Cloudchamber
Würfelding ... inspiration throwing tool

X

X ist mit ohne scharf ... X is sharp with without

Y

Y-Kicker ... funny product, three field table football
yoghurt ... singular of curd

Z

Z ... not russian at all
"Zamma Zumma" ... filmclip by Feedback Films & Freeters
Zufallsverteidiger / random defender ... lucky defender, see coincidence
Zweibeiner ... thing with two legs

5

"5G war gestern" ... filmclip by Feedback Films & Freeters

IMPRINT

EDITOR
Freeters e.G.

EDITORIAL STAFF
Pasquale Demeco, Michael Sistig

CONCEPT
Freeters e.G. | www.freeters.de
Philipp Rose | www.gisbert.koeln

DESIGN
Philipp Rose | www.gisbert.koeln

TYPEFACE
Navigo, JetBrains Mono

TEXTS
Pasquale Demeco, Cornelia Funke, Sandra Freygarten, Johannes Hess, Thomas Lassner, Silke Mattern-Specht, Miriam Nolte, Melusine Reimers, Michael Sistig, Amely Spötzl, Dr. Bernhard Zünkeler, Ulrich Zünkeler

TRANSLATIONS
Dr. Bernhard Zünkeler

COPY EDITING
Thea Miklowski

PHOTO CREDITS & PHOTOGRAPHY
Bernd Zöllner | www.fotografie-zoellner.de
Patrick Gawandtka | www.patrickgawandtka.de
Mark Knight | www.fivetoninephotography.com
Jo Hempel | www.johempel.com
Freeters e.G. | www.freeters.de
El Segundo Museum of Art | www.esmoa.org

COVER & BACK COVER
"Help!", fuse beads, 50x29cm,
Pasquale Demeco & Silke Mattern-Specht

freeters

PRODUCTION MANAGEMENT
DCV

PRINTING AND BINDING
Westermann Druck, Braunschweig

DISTRIBUTION AND MARKETING
DCV
sales@dcv-books.com

ISBN 978-3-96912-097-2
Printed in Germany

PUBLISHED BY
DCV
www.dcv-books.com

DCV

ARTIST COLLECTIVE FREETERS
Florian Benet, Ben Beyer, Sebastian Chorus, Pasquale Demeco, Sandra Freygarten, Johanna Hendel, Johannes Hess, Rafael-Maria Hildebrandt, Sebastian Keller, Silke Mattern-Specht, Miriam Nolte, Frowin Schweer, Michael Sistig, Amely Spötzl, Bernhard Zünkeler

SPECIAL SUPPORT
Maya Moll

INTERDISCIPLINARY FREETERS
Rita Baus, Ingrid Blessing, Roman Thomas

ARTISTS, PEOPLE AND FRIENDS WHO HAVE CONTRIBUTED TO THE PROJECTS IN THIS BOOK
Nina Adams, Thea Altmann, Johannes Baum, Yamila Bernd, David Beyer, Lavanya Boesten, Brunhild Bordeaux-Groult, Barbara Böhm, Holly Crawford, Olaf Didszun, Dagmar Ecken, Robert Elfgen, Hannah Gernhäuser, Rafael Ginbar, Peter Guse, Dirk Hansmeier, Maria Hughes, Julian Janke, Nikolas Jürgens, Cosima Kaye, Charlotte Klausener, Thieß Krause-Sparmann, Kelsey Lee-Offield, Nils Machel, Sandra Machel, Konrad Magin, Nicole Maloney, Laura Maßmann, Tonia Meyer, Ludger Molitor, Birte Moyé, Stefan Nowak-Beckmann, Julien Parsonneau, Aljoscha Pause, Caspar Pauli, Paul Jonas Petry, Daniel Raabe, James Reid, art collective ruangrupa, Barbara Schiller, Robert Schramm, Martin Schüßler, Jan Moritz Stahl, Brian Sweeney, Eva Sweeney, Taka Kagitomi, Lukas Thein, Eugenia Torre, Marc Wagner, Claudia Weiser, Bernd Zöllner

COLLABORATIONS
Detecon, EFCO, ESMoA, E105, Feedback Films, NABBI, Opposition Studios, ORANGE COUNCIL, PAUSEFILM, Stiftung artepreneur, S.Y.L.A.NTENHEIM, UNTERKOMPLEX